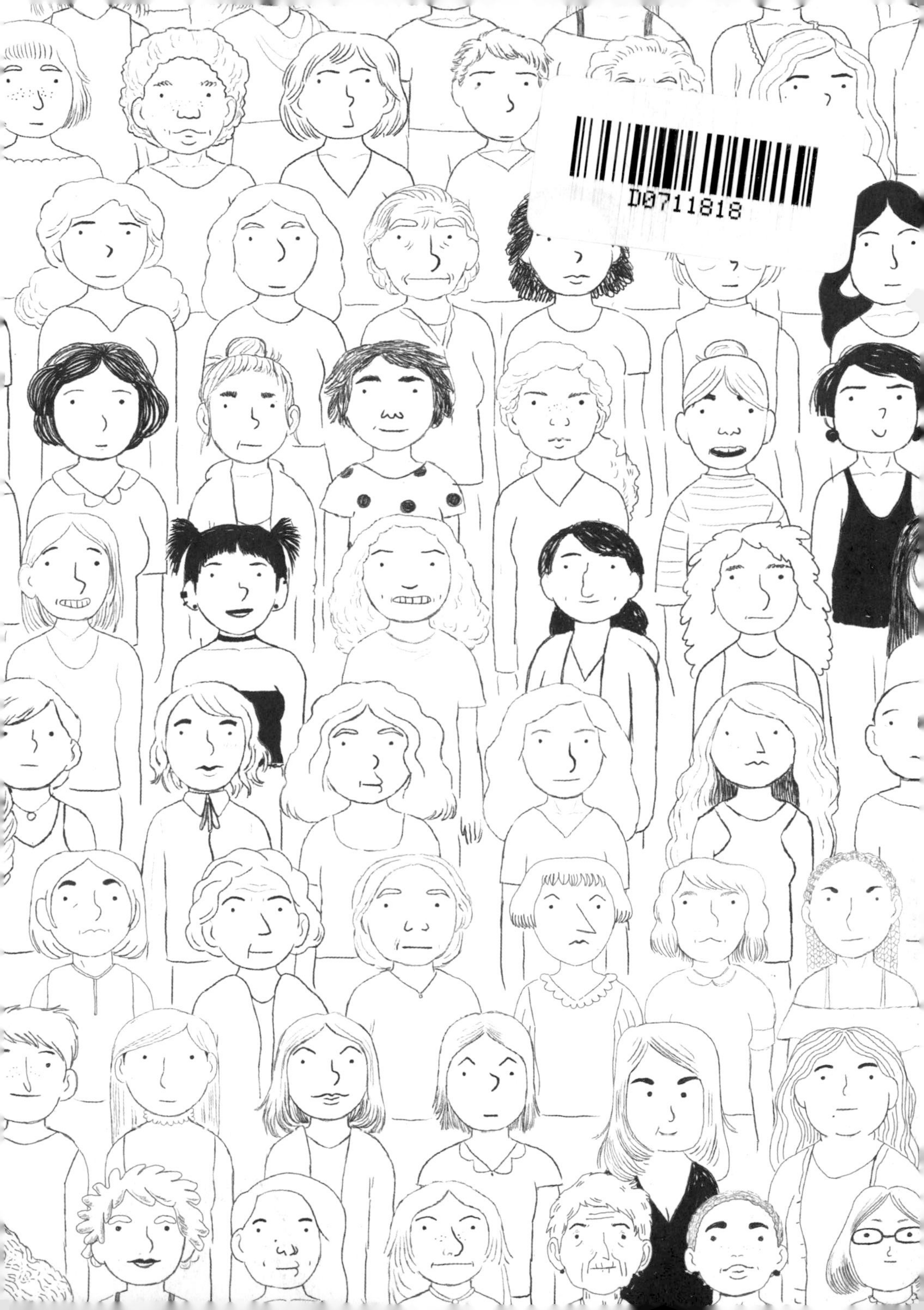

THEY WERE A PUBLISHING
COMPANY
IN THE OLD WORLD...
when men were still around

DRAWN
AND
QUARTERLY

drawnandquarterly.com
aminderdhaliwal.com

978-1-77046-335-6
First edition: September 2018
Printed in China
0 9 8 7 6 5 4 3 2 1

Cataloguing data available from Library and Archives Canada.

Published in the USA by Drawn & Quarterly, a client publisher of Farrar, Straus and Giroux. Orders: 888.330.8477 | Published in Canada by Drawn & Quarterly, a client publisher of Raincoast Books. Orders: 800.663.5714 | Published in the United Kingdom by Drawn & Quarterly, a client publisher of Publishers Group UK. Orders: info@pguk.co.uk

Canada ❦ Drawn & Quarterly acknowledges the support of the Government of Canada and the Canada Council for the Arts for our publishing program.

Thank You
Nikolas Ilic, Kenneth Hung, Megan Dong, Maha Tabikh,
Miranda Tacchia, Amber Robinson, Mayumi Nose, and
all the supporters along the way.

Thank you to my mom and all the amazing
women in my world.

WOMAN WORLD

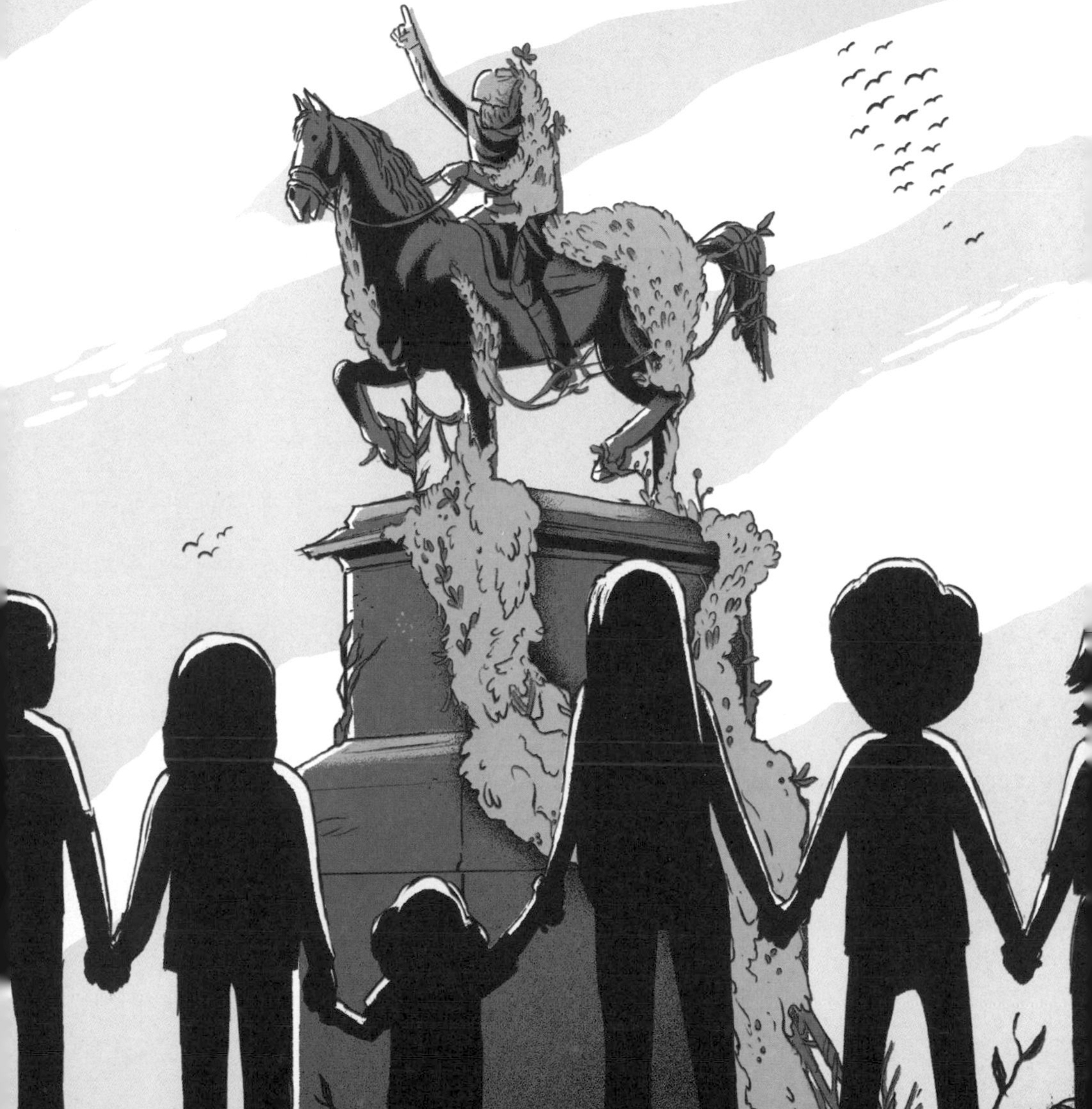

AMINDER DHALIWAL

COLOR BY NIKOLAS ILIC

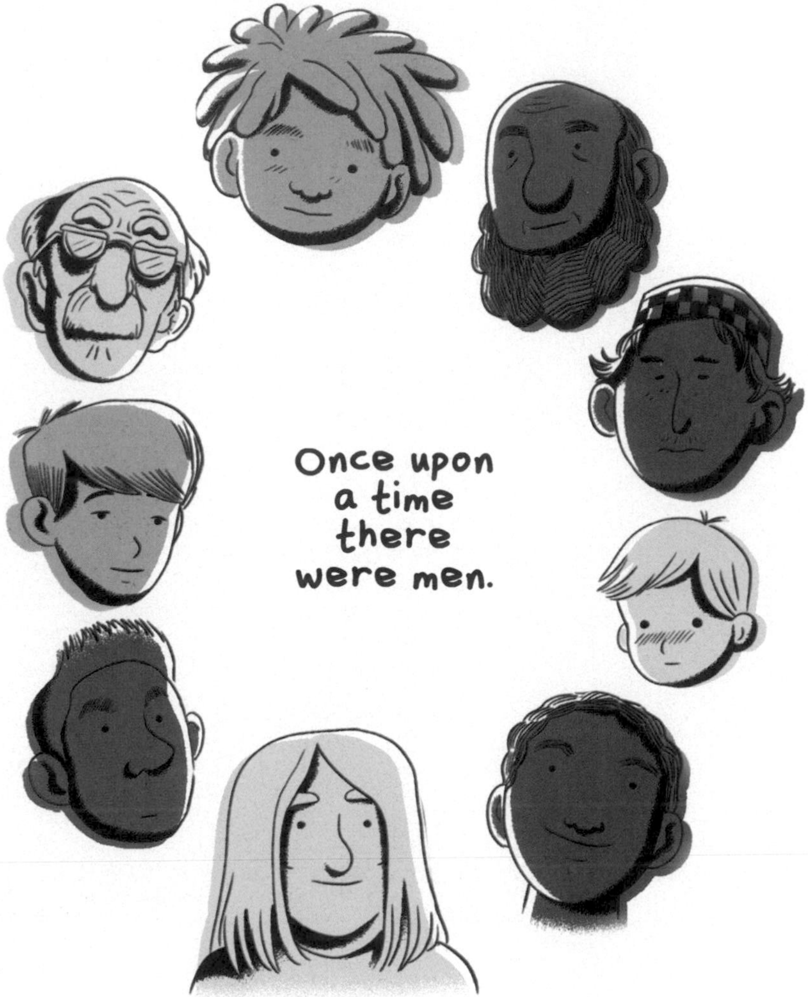
Once upon a time there were men.

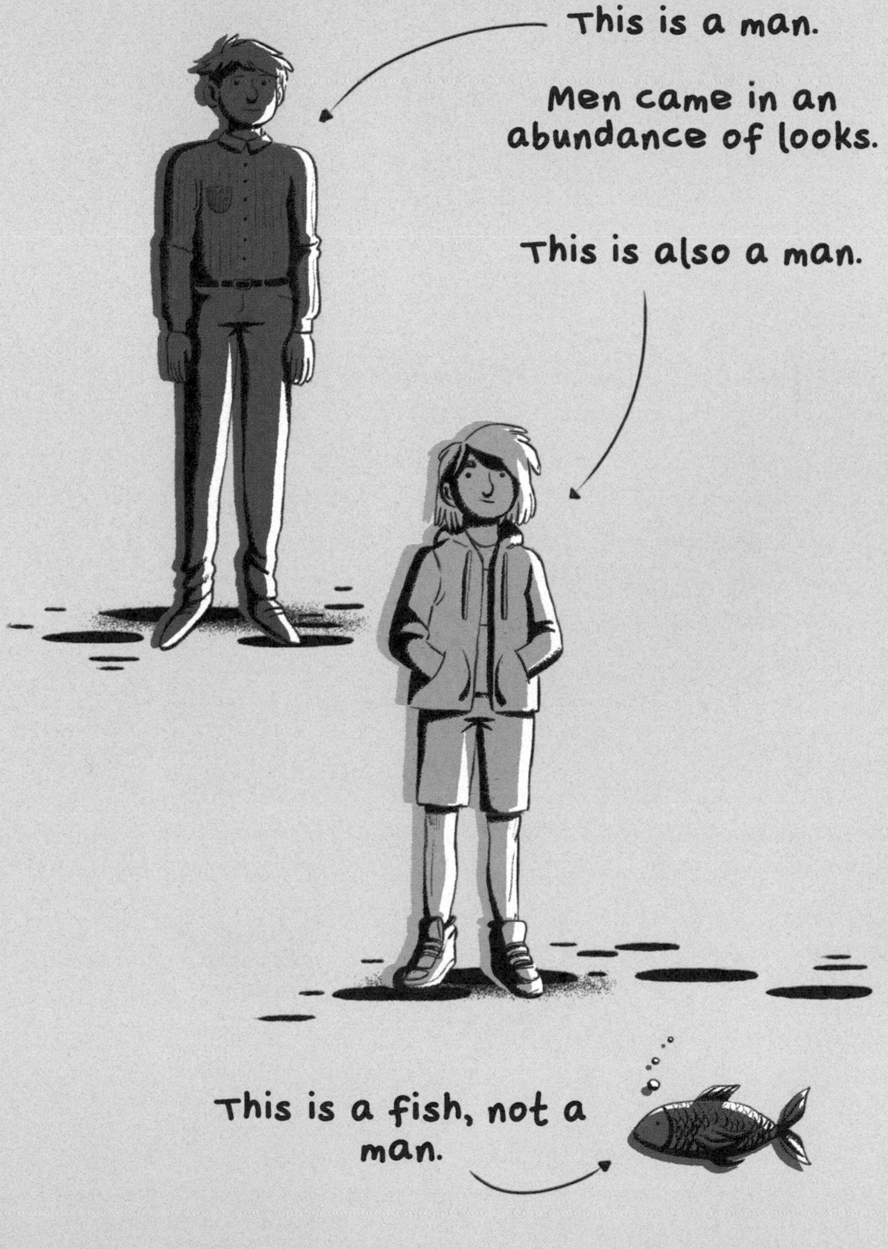
This is a man.
Men came in an abundance of looks.
This is also a man.
This is a fish, not a man.

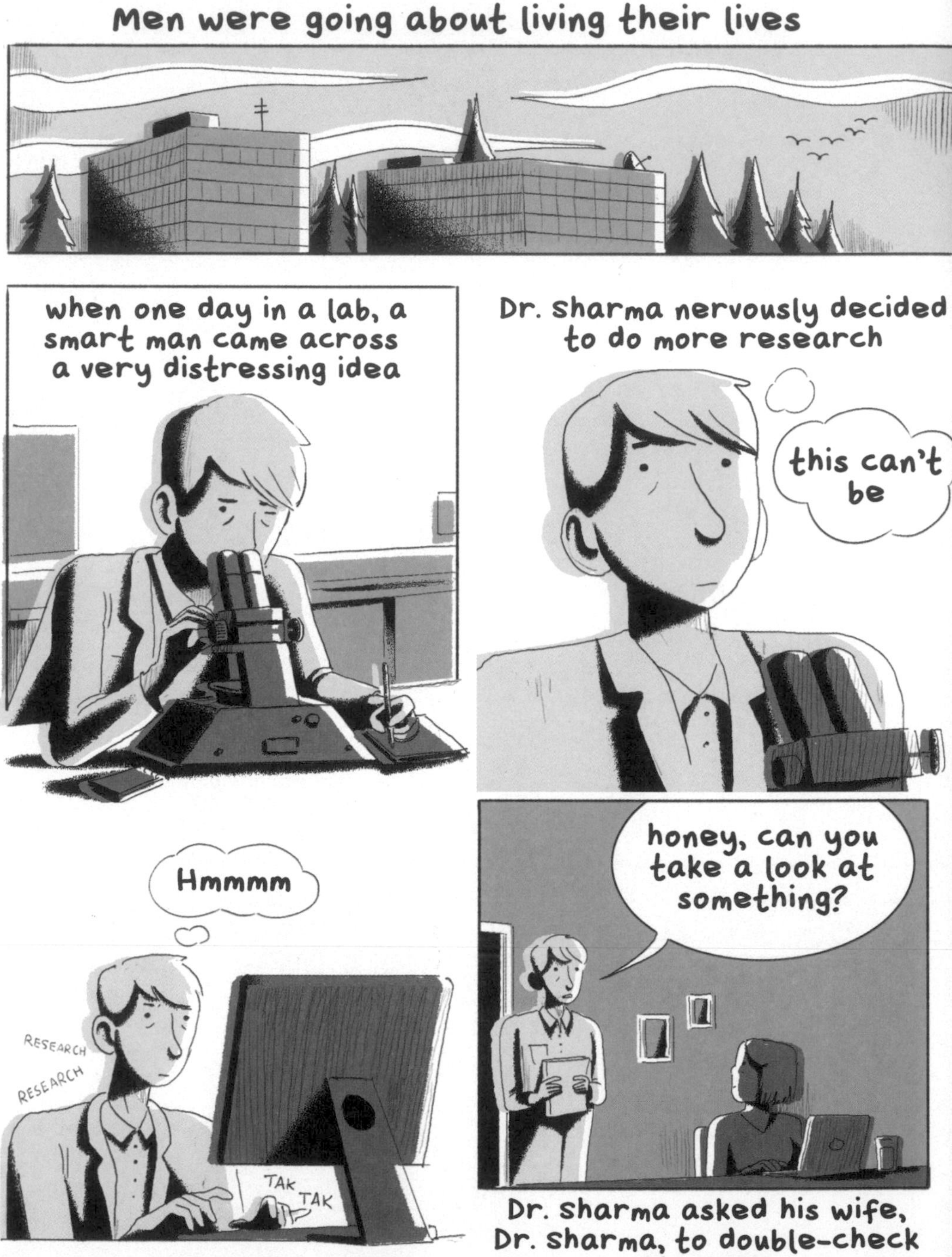
Men were going about living their lives
when one day in a lab, a smart man came across a very distressing idea
Dr. sharma nervously decided to do more research
this can't be
Hmmmm
RESEARCH
RESEARCH
TAK
TAK
honey, can you take a look at something?
Dr. sharma asked his wife, Dr. sharma, to double-check his work

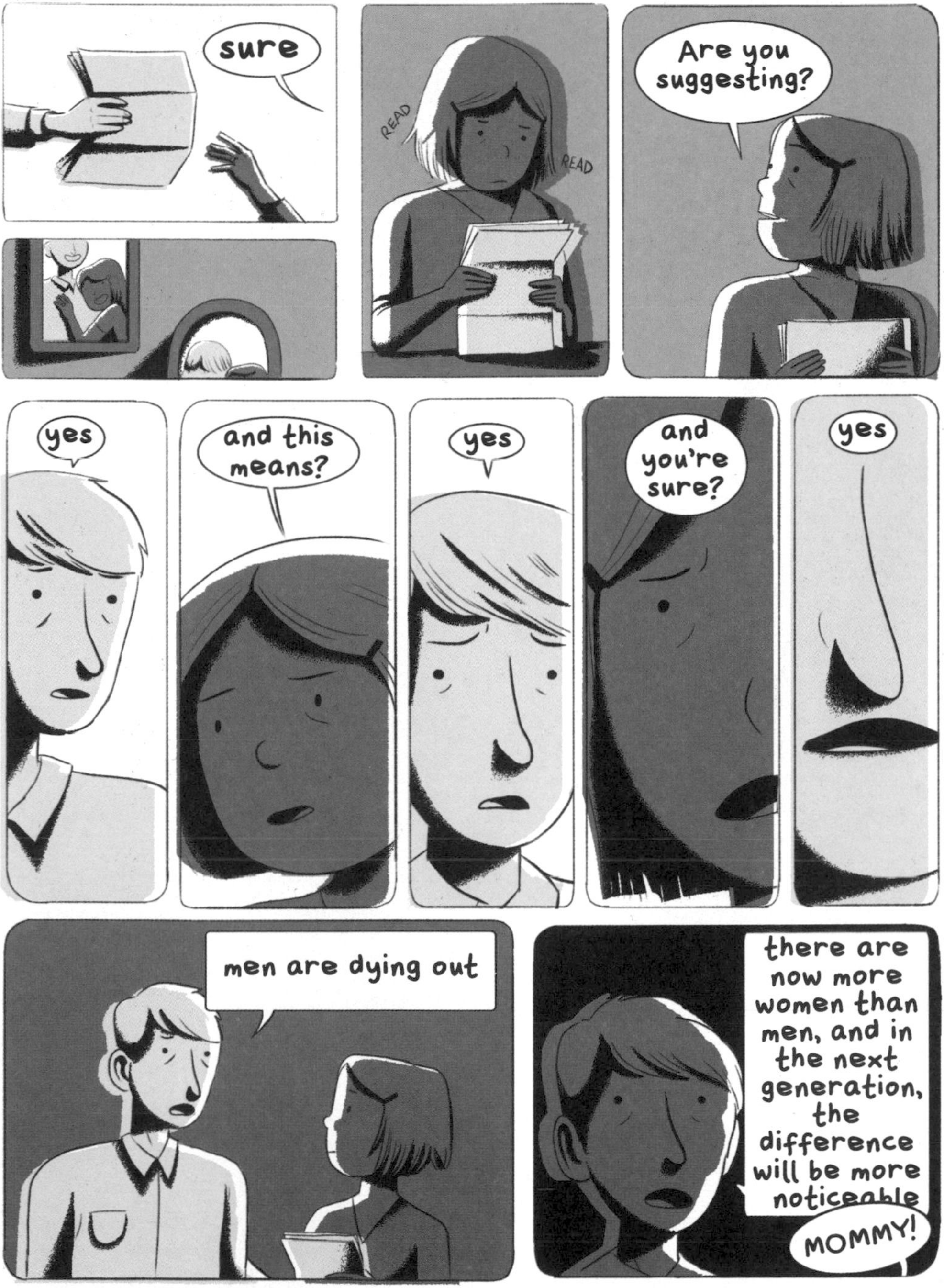
sure
READ
READ
Are you suggesting?
yes
and this means?
yes
and you're sure?
yes
men are dying out
there are now more women than men, and in the next generation, the difference will be more noticeable
MOMMY!

mommy!!!
not now, sweetie. you'll wake up your sister
...the generation after that, there may be no men at all.

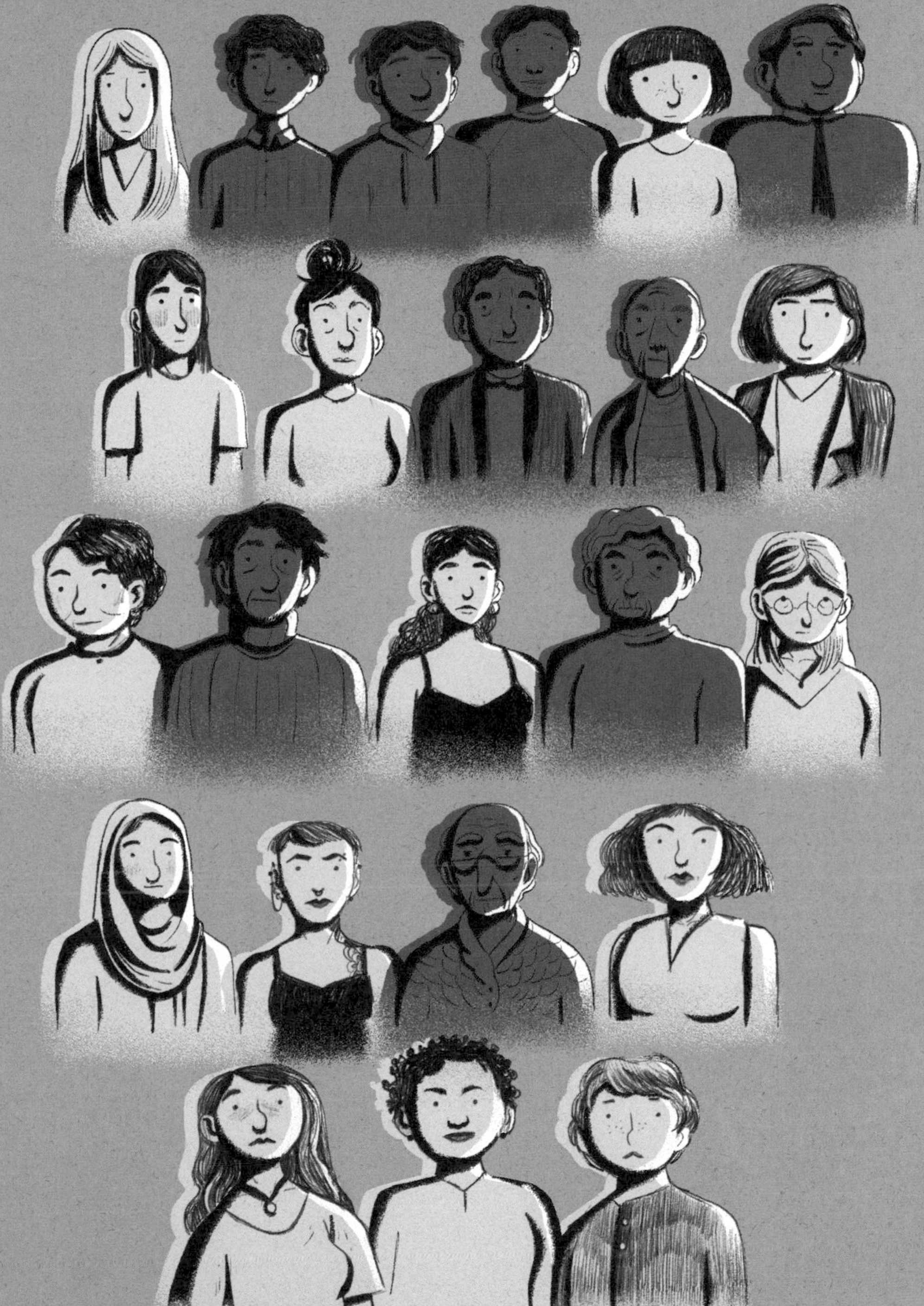

And although the scientific community agreed with Dr. sharma's findings, there seemed to be no effect.

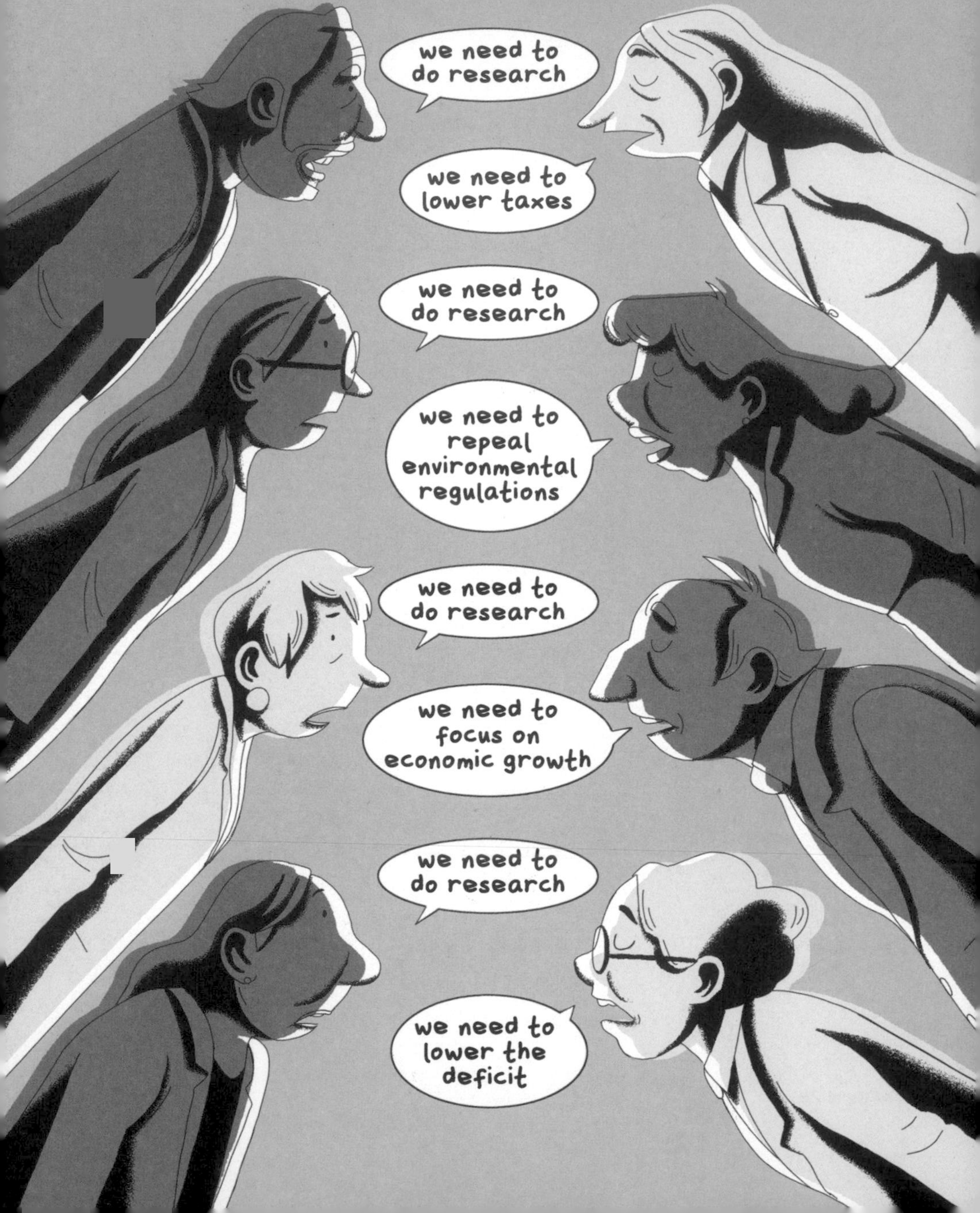
we need to do research
we need to lower taxes
we need to do research
we need to repeal environmental regulations
we need to do research
we need to focus on economic growth
we need to do research
we need to lower the deficit

no one would listen
do you think men are really disappearing?
pffft... it's all anecdotal evidence

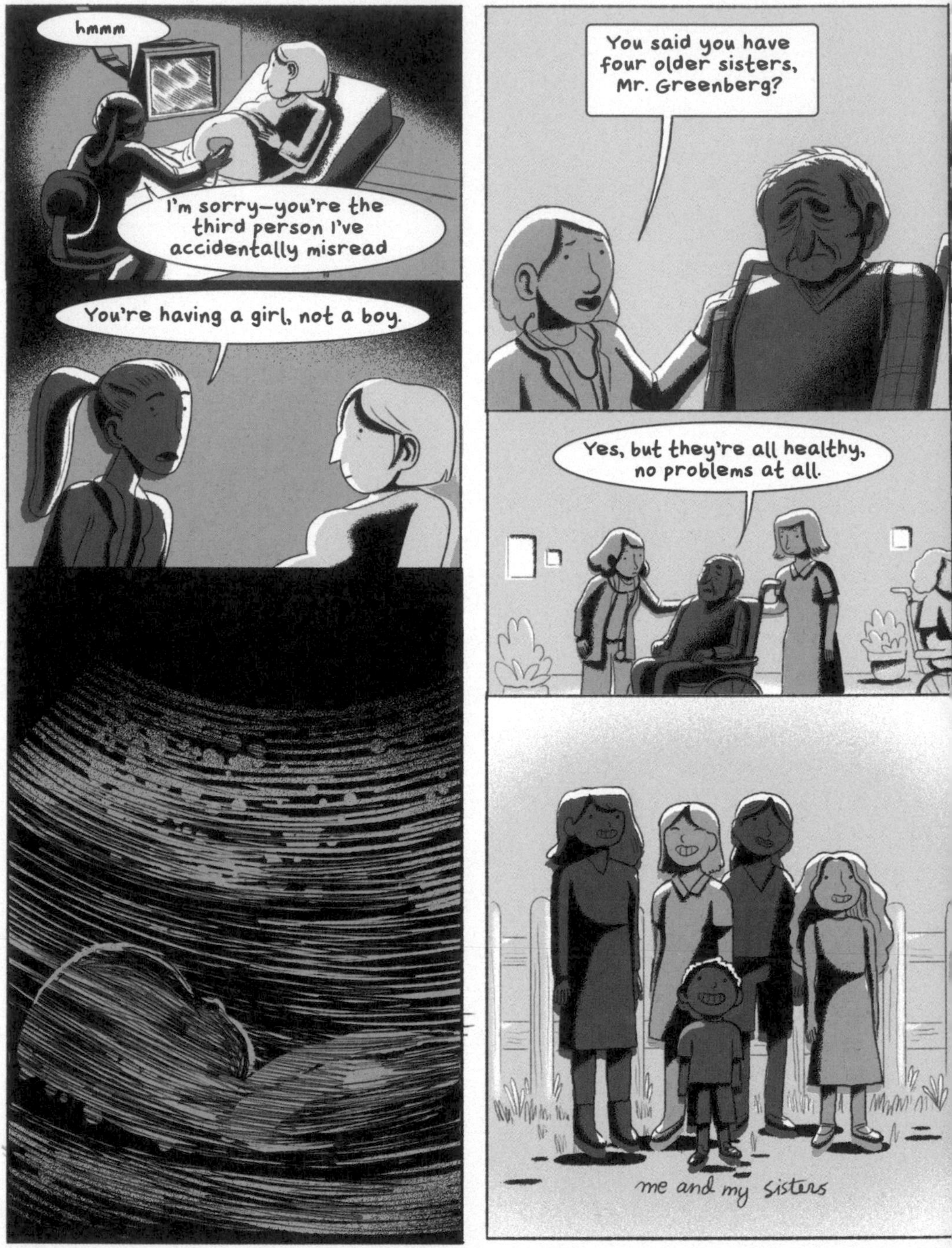
hmmm
I'm sorry—you're the third person I've accidentally misread
You're having a girl, not a boy.
You said you have four older sisters, Mr. Greenberg?
Yes, but they're all healthy, no problems at all.
me and my sisters

NEWS

interesting News story!

IT'S A MAN'S WORLD?

A historic day, the summit is attended by all female leaders

a maternity ward in Franklin has become the first ward ever to have an entire week of all girls

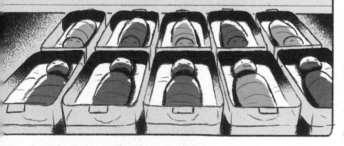

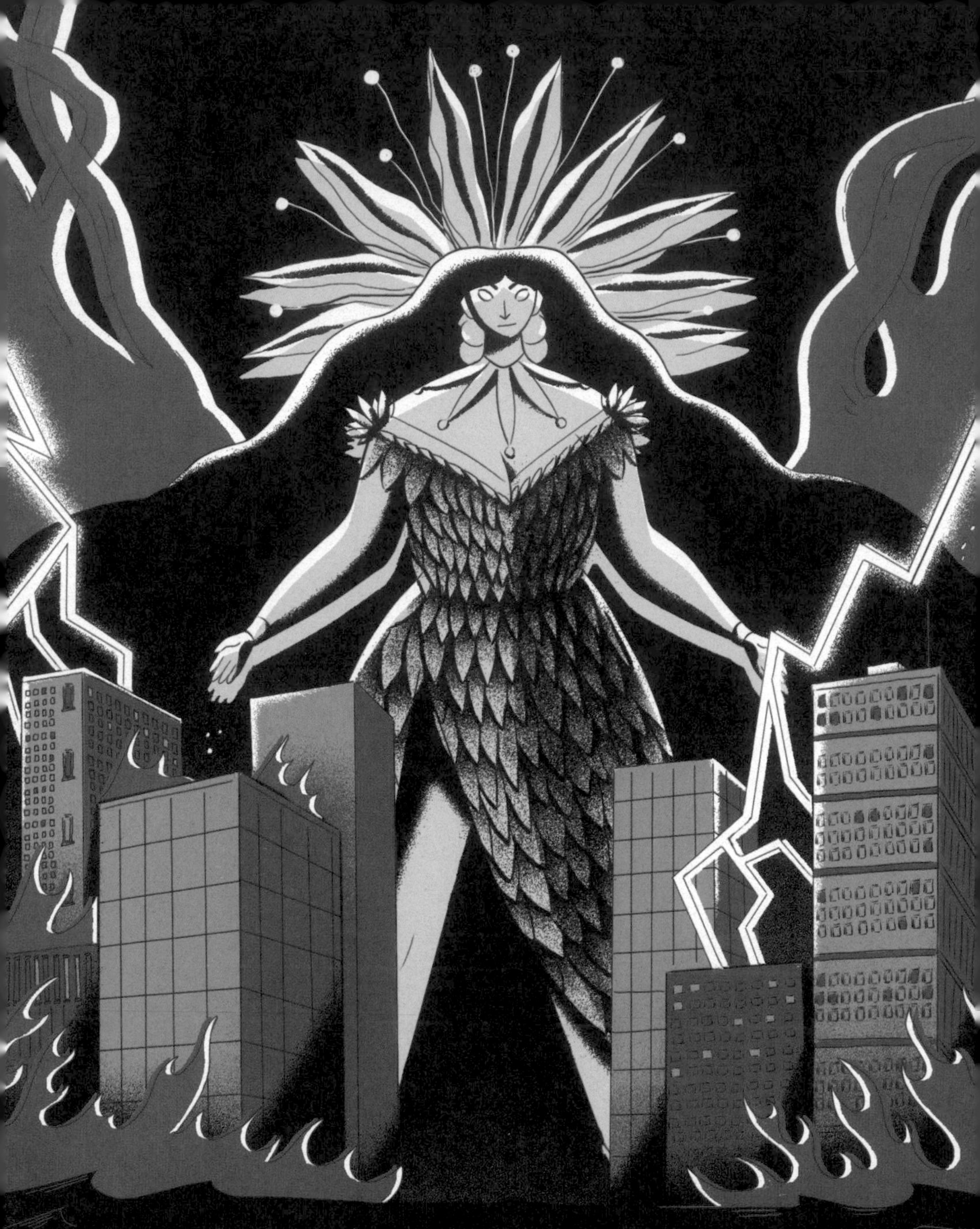

The world was further distracted by a series of natural disasters. It was as though mother nature

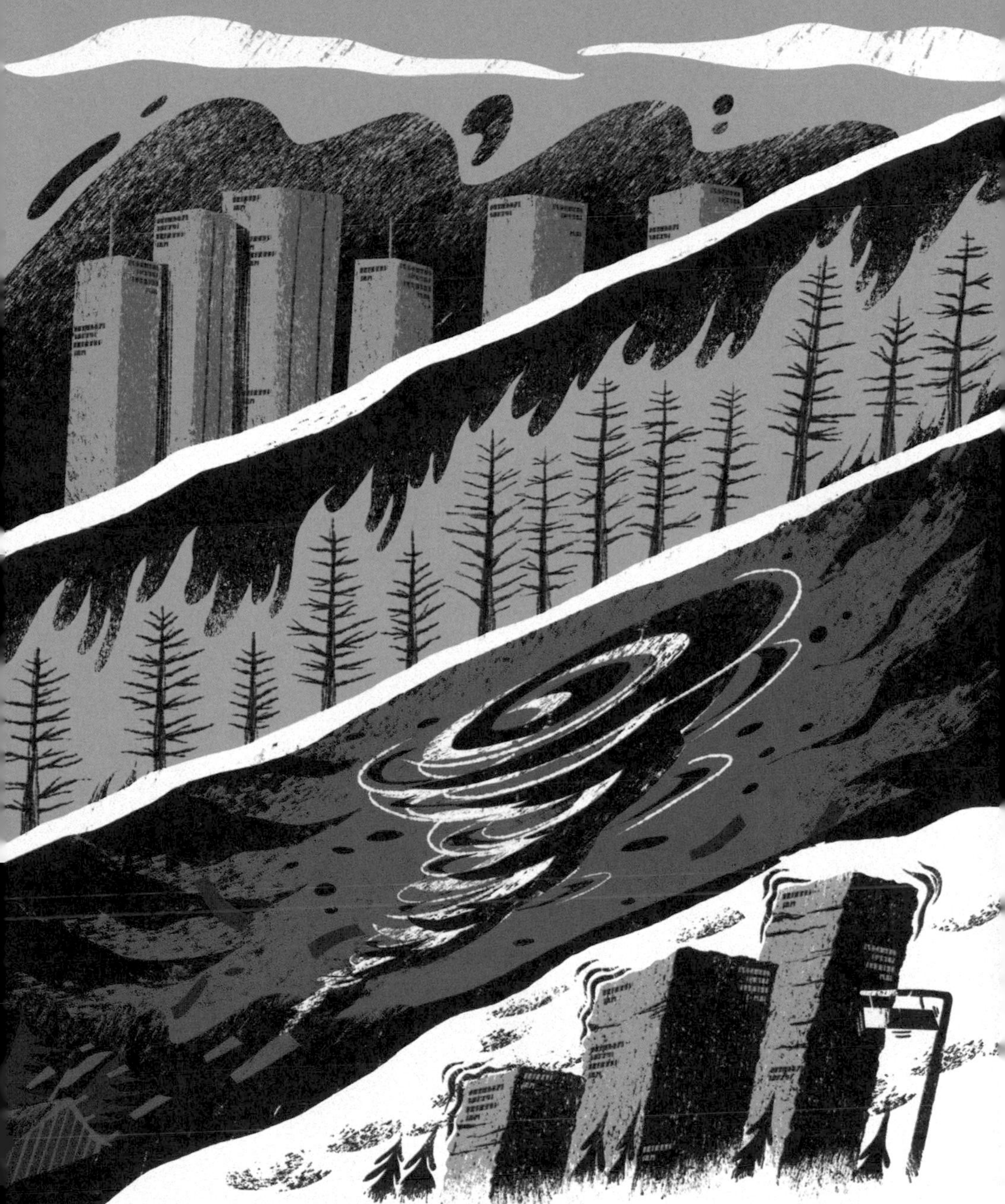

had craftily picked the most
inconvenient time to show her strength.
Civilization was torn to shreds.

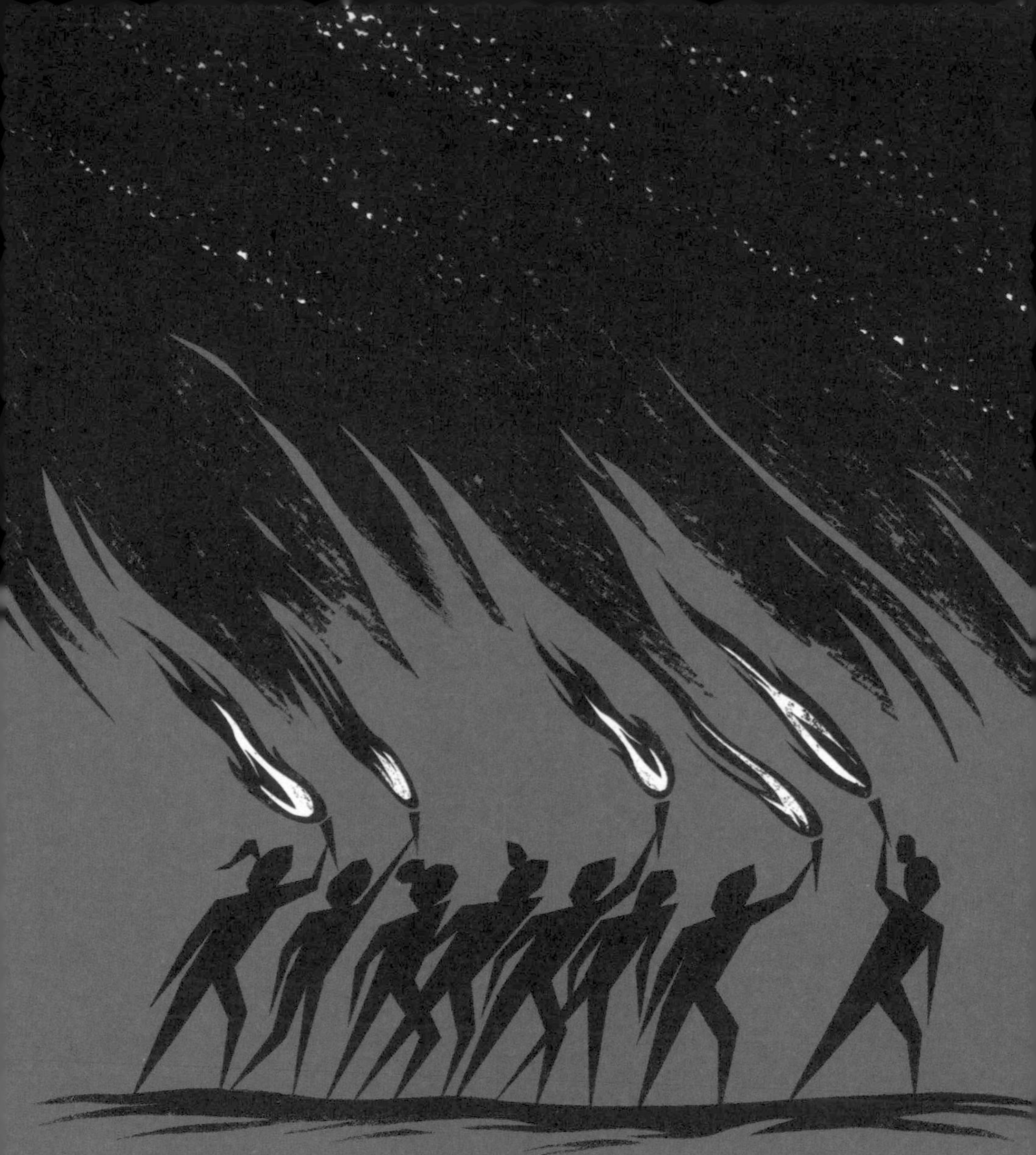

The world spiralled into chaos. There were riots, the market crashed, war declared.

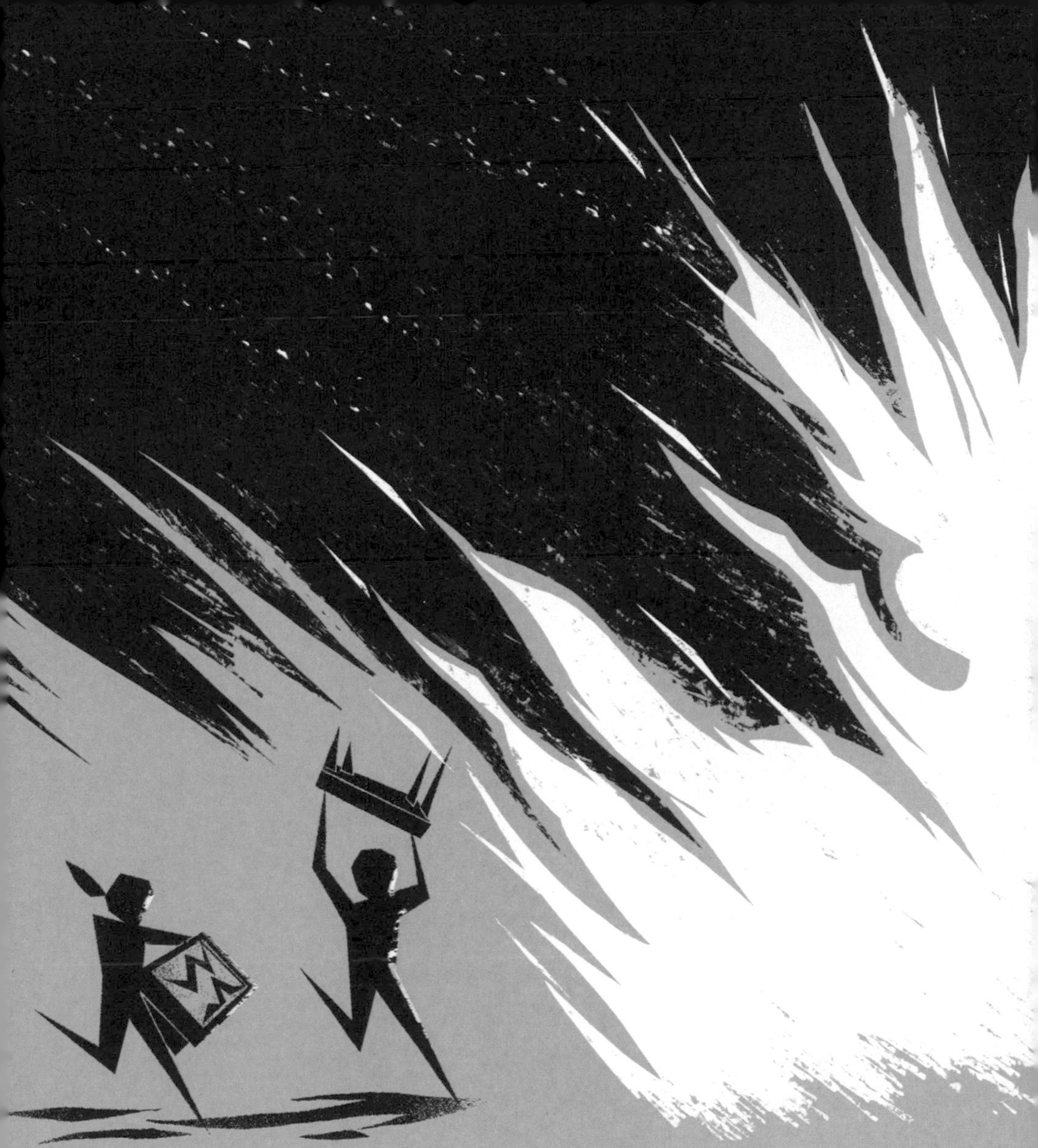

who possibly had time to listen to a doctor
and his theory about men?

Older, grayer, and having survived a very strange decade, Dr. Sharma, in fear of the future of humanity, decided to focus on female-only pregnancy.

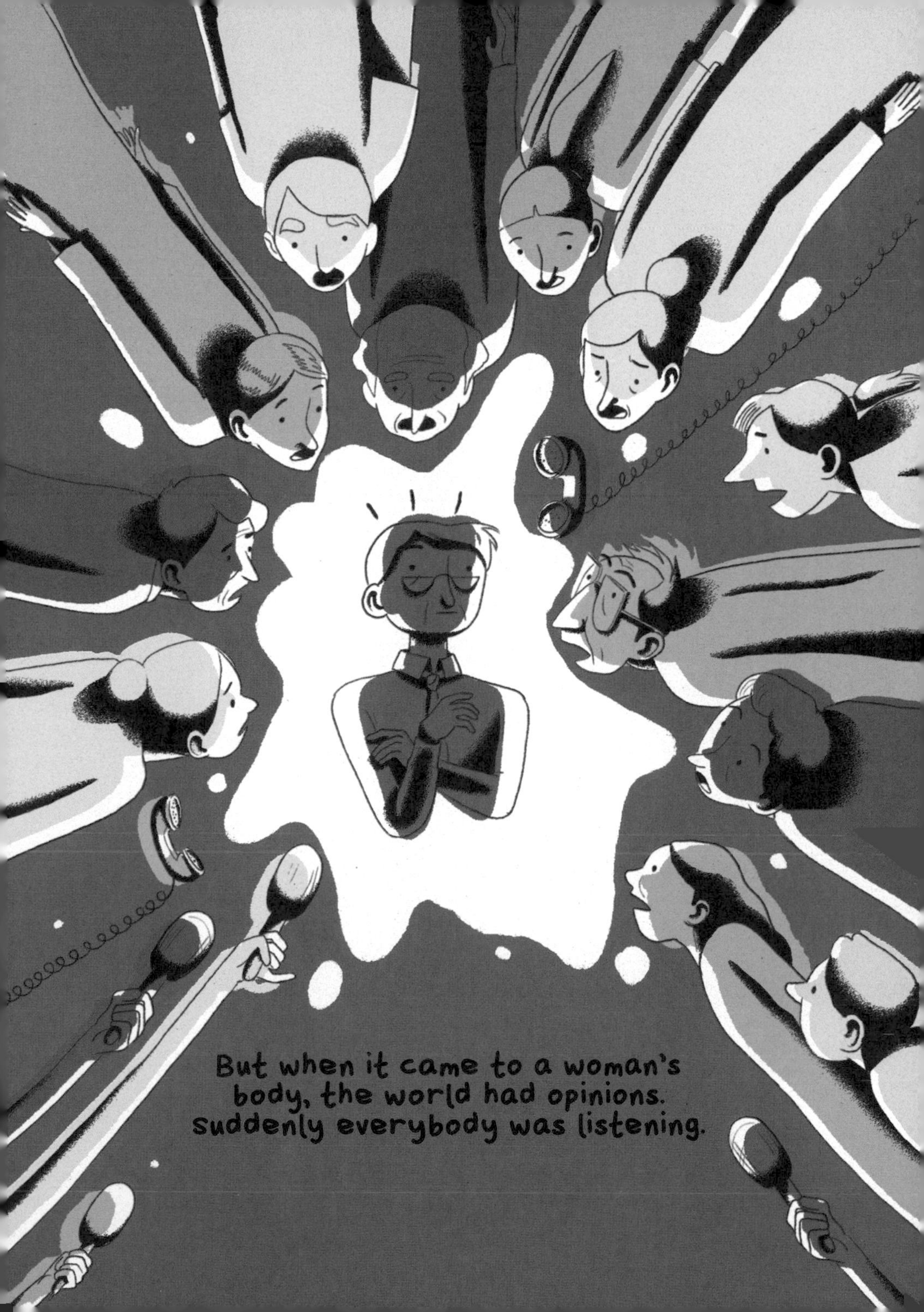
But when it came to a woman's body, the world had opinions. Suddenly everybody was listening.

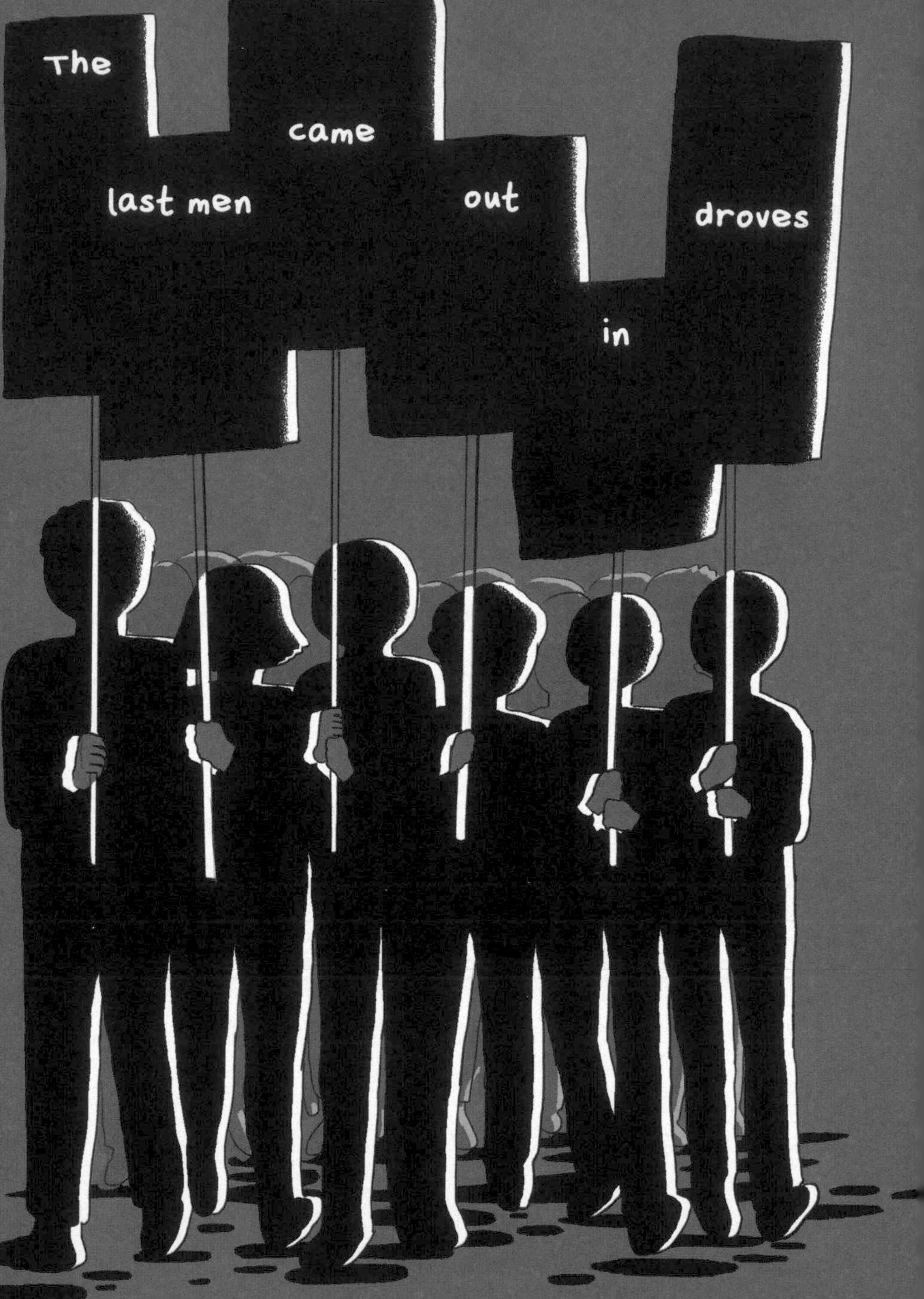
The
came
last men
out
droves
in

countless men went

MISSING

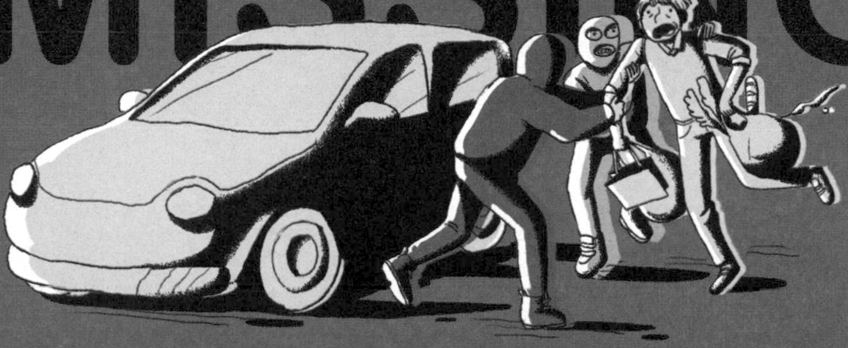

and a black market for the buying and selling of men and male ejaculate began...

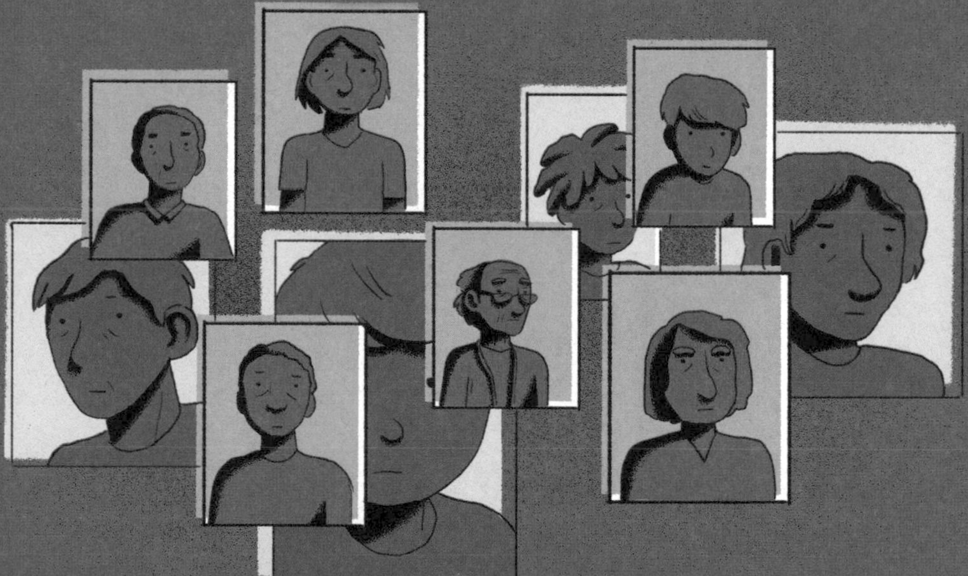

Dr. sharma was never able to finish his work

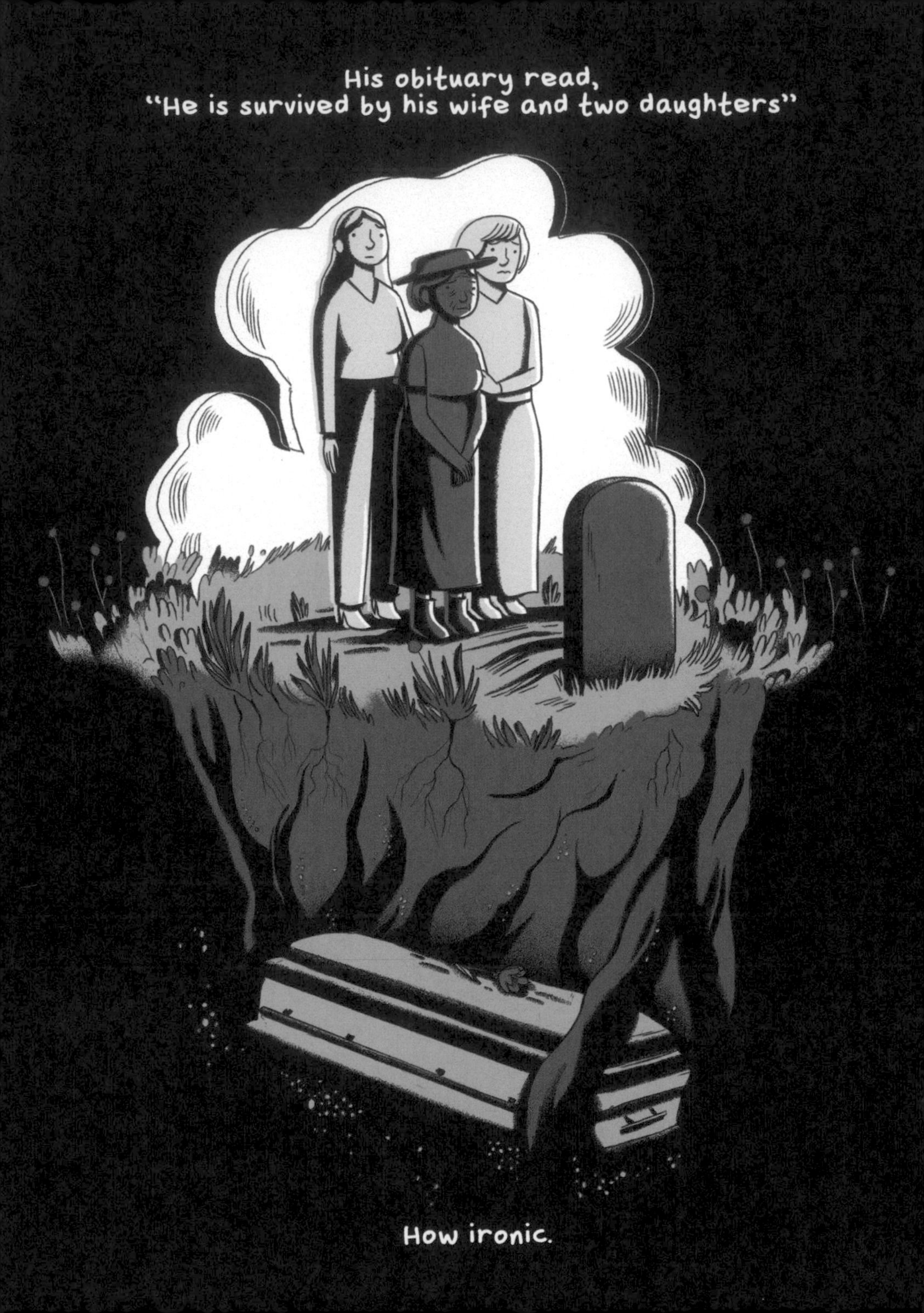
His obituary read,
"He is survived by his wife and two daughters"
How ironic.

once upon
a time
there were

no

men

Now, years later, this is the story
of a village in this new world.

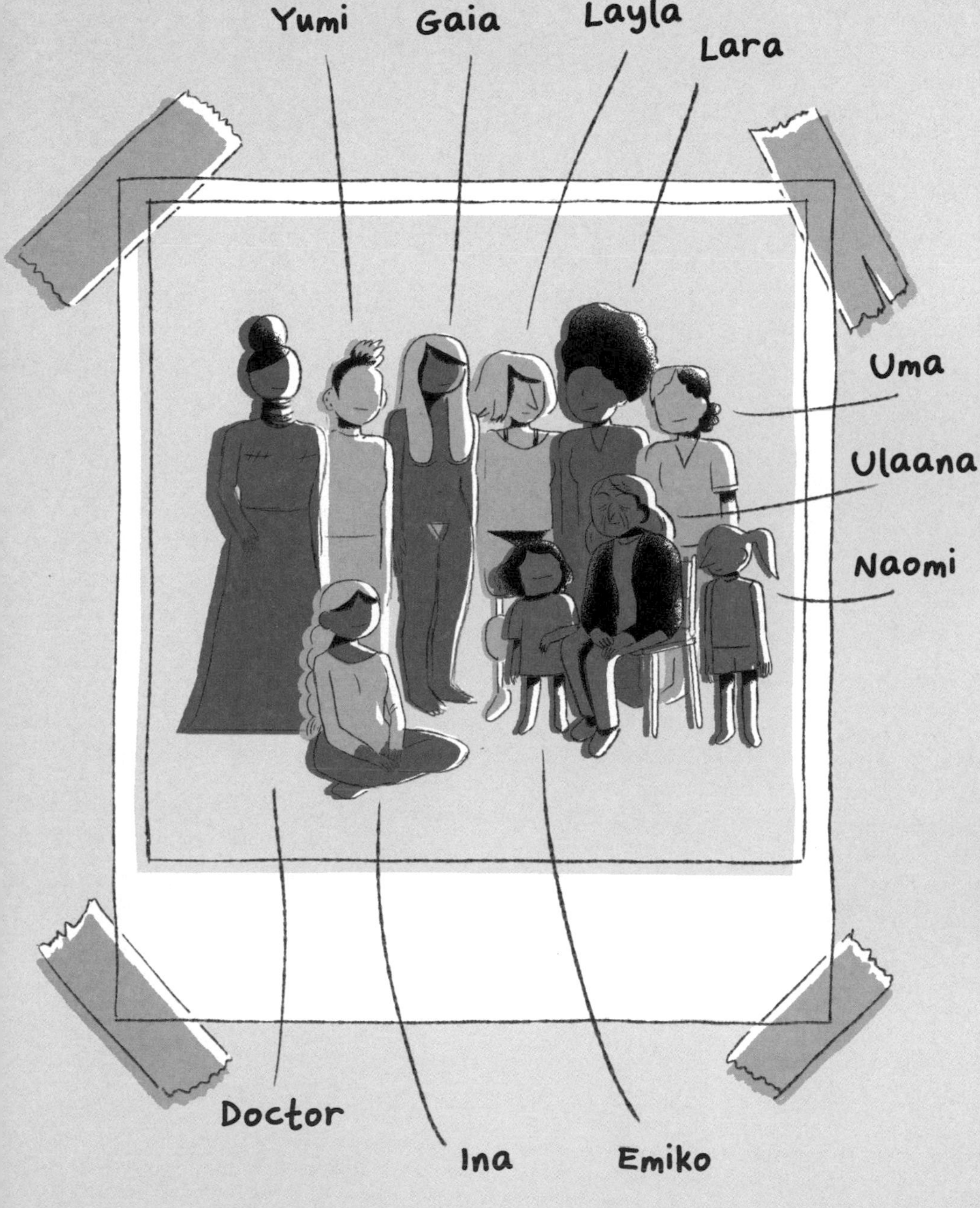
Yumi
Gaia
Layla
Lara
Uma
Ulaana
Naomi
Doctor
Ina
Emiko

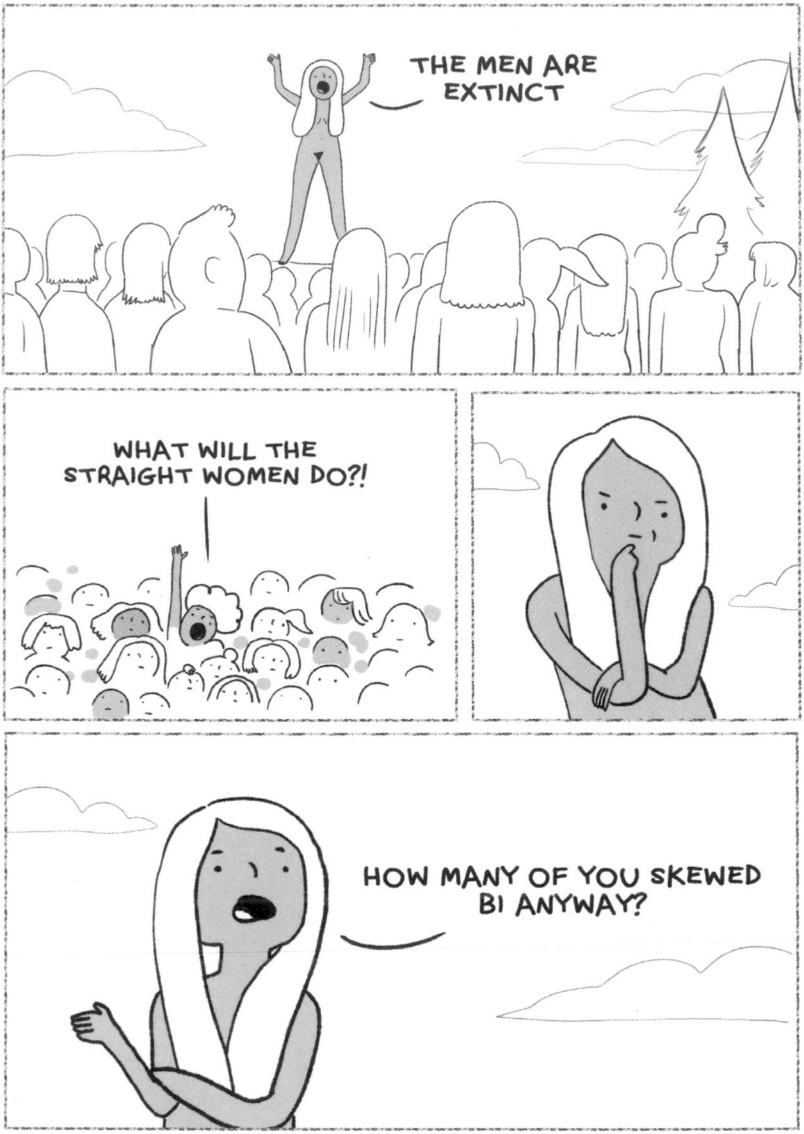
THE MEN ARE EXTINCT
WHAT WILL THE STRAIGHT WOMEN DO?!
HOW MANY OF YOU SKEWED BI ANYWAY?

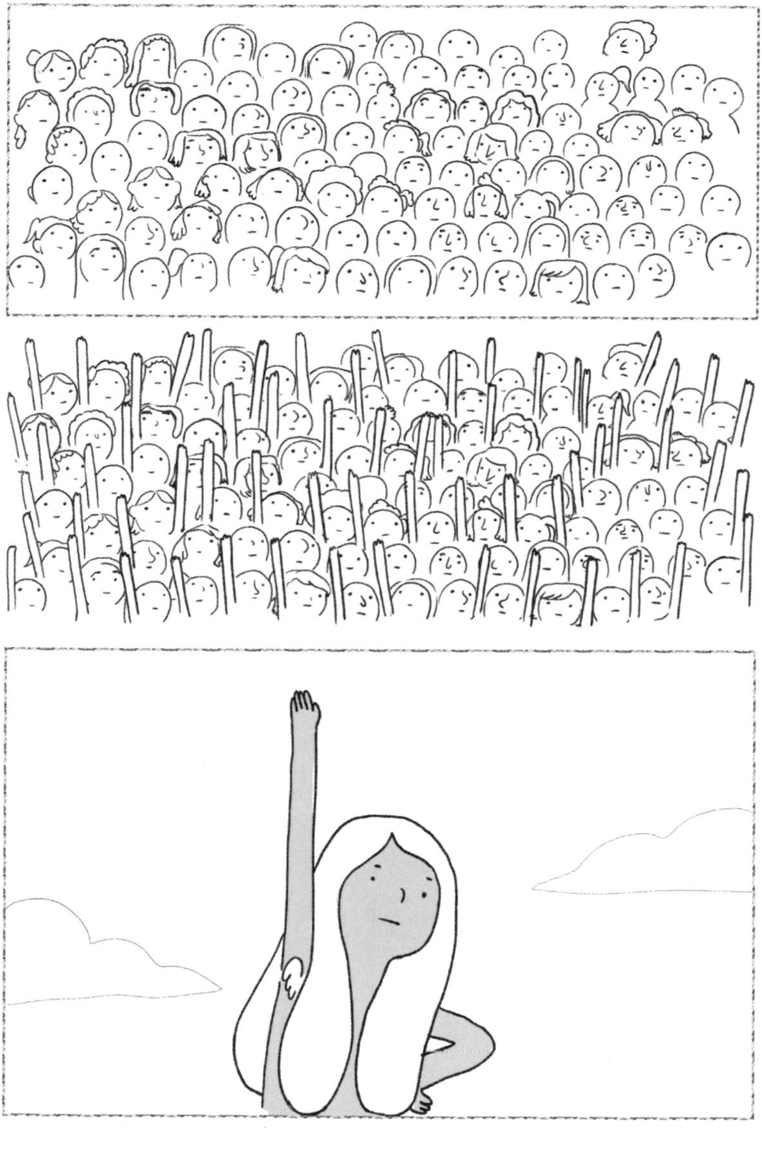

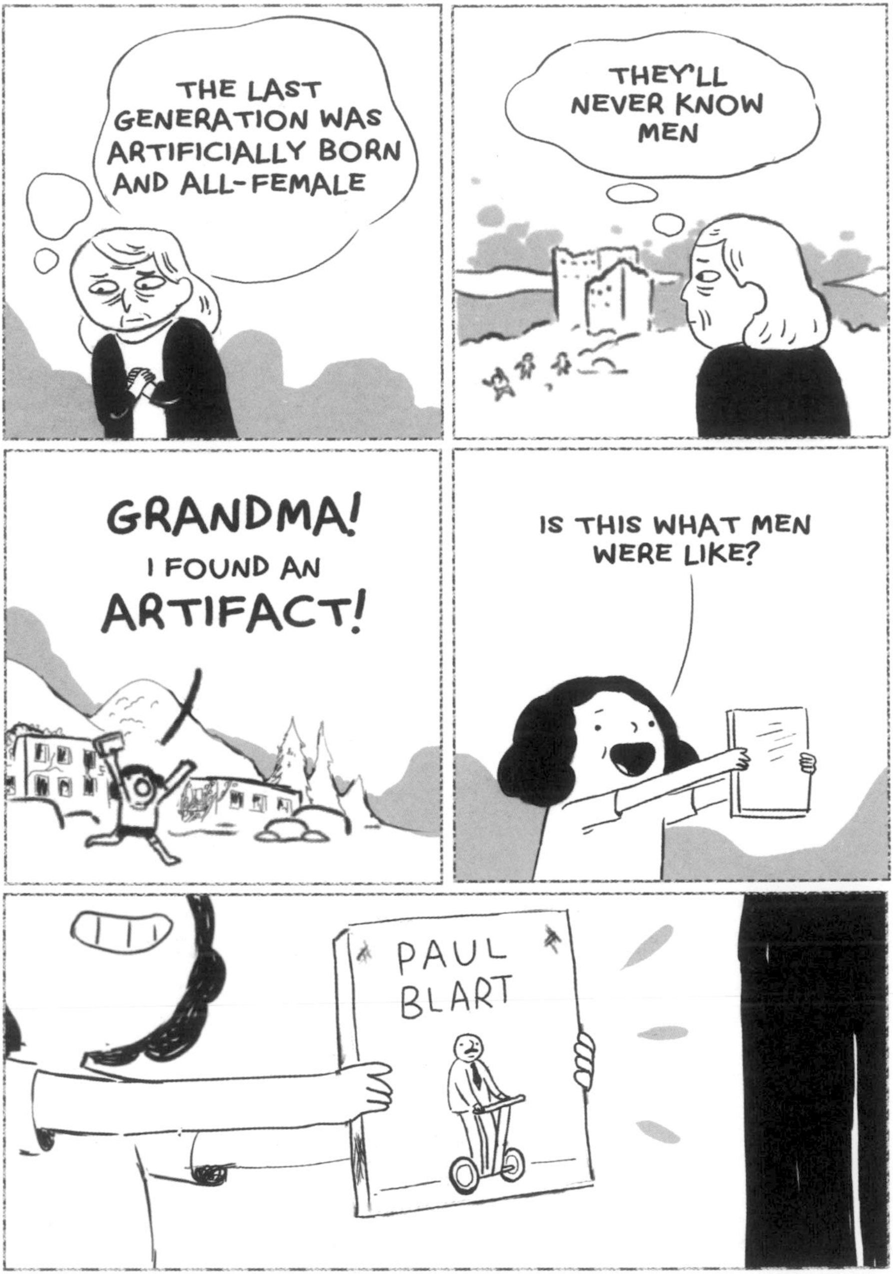
THE LAST GENERATION WAS ARTIFICIALLY BORN AND ALL-FEMALE
THEY'LL NEVER KNOW MEN
GRANDMA! I FOUND AN ARTIFACT!
IS THIS WHAT MEN WERE LIKE?
PAUL BLART

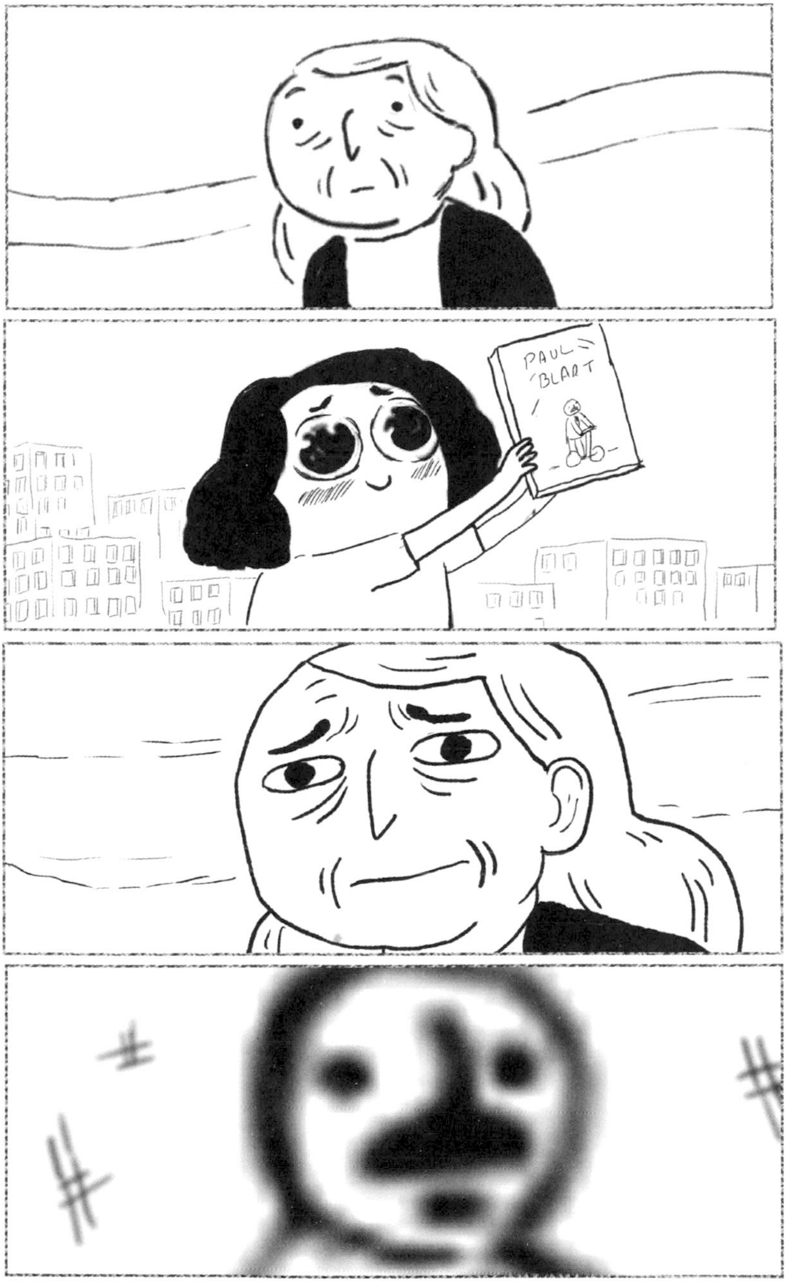
PAUL BLART

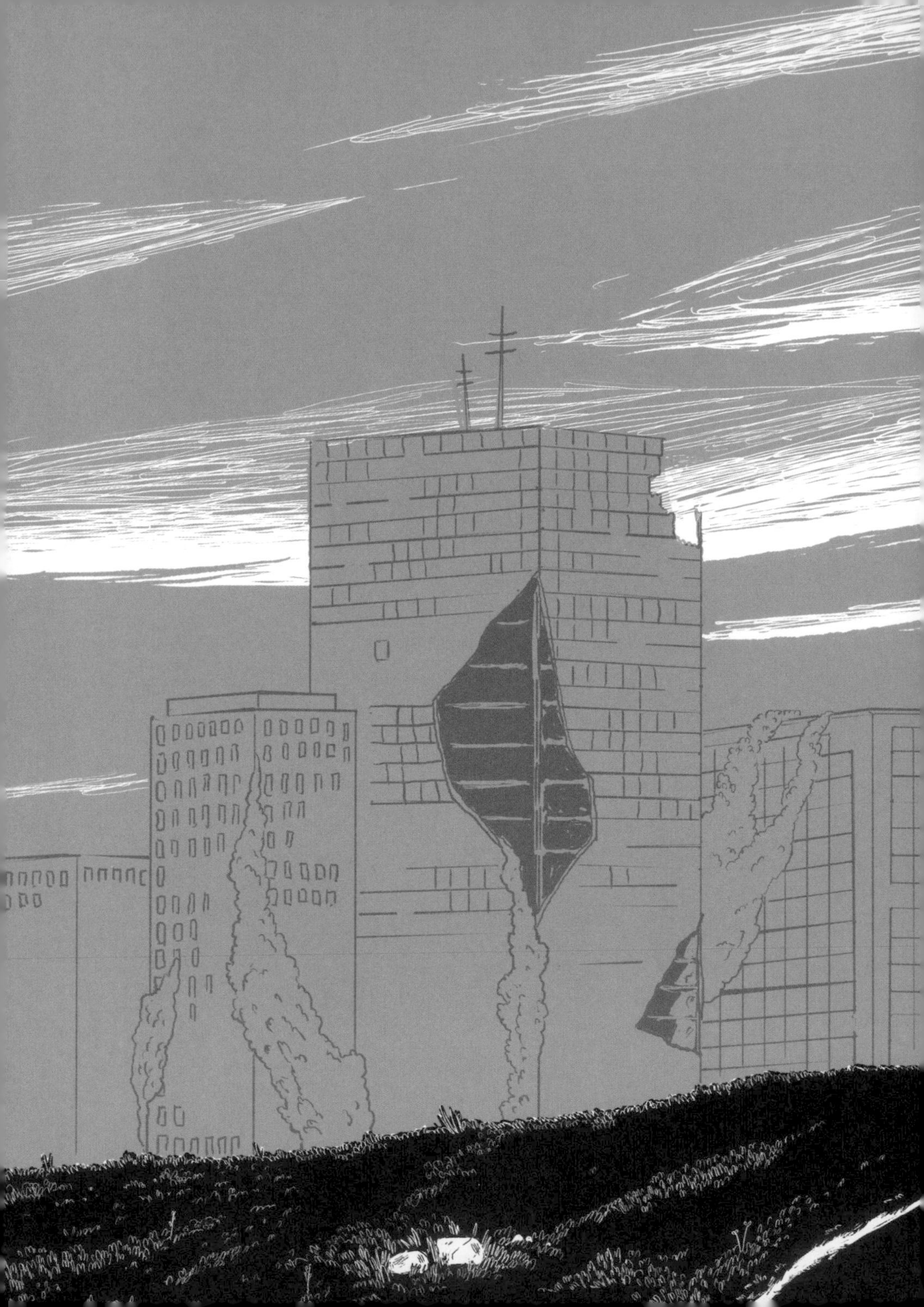

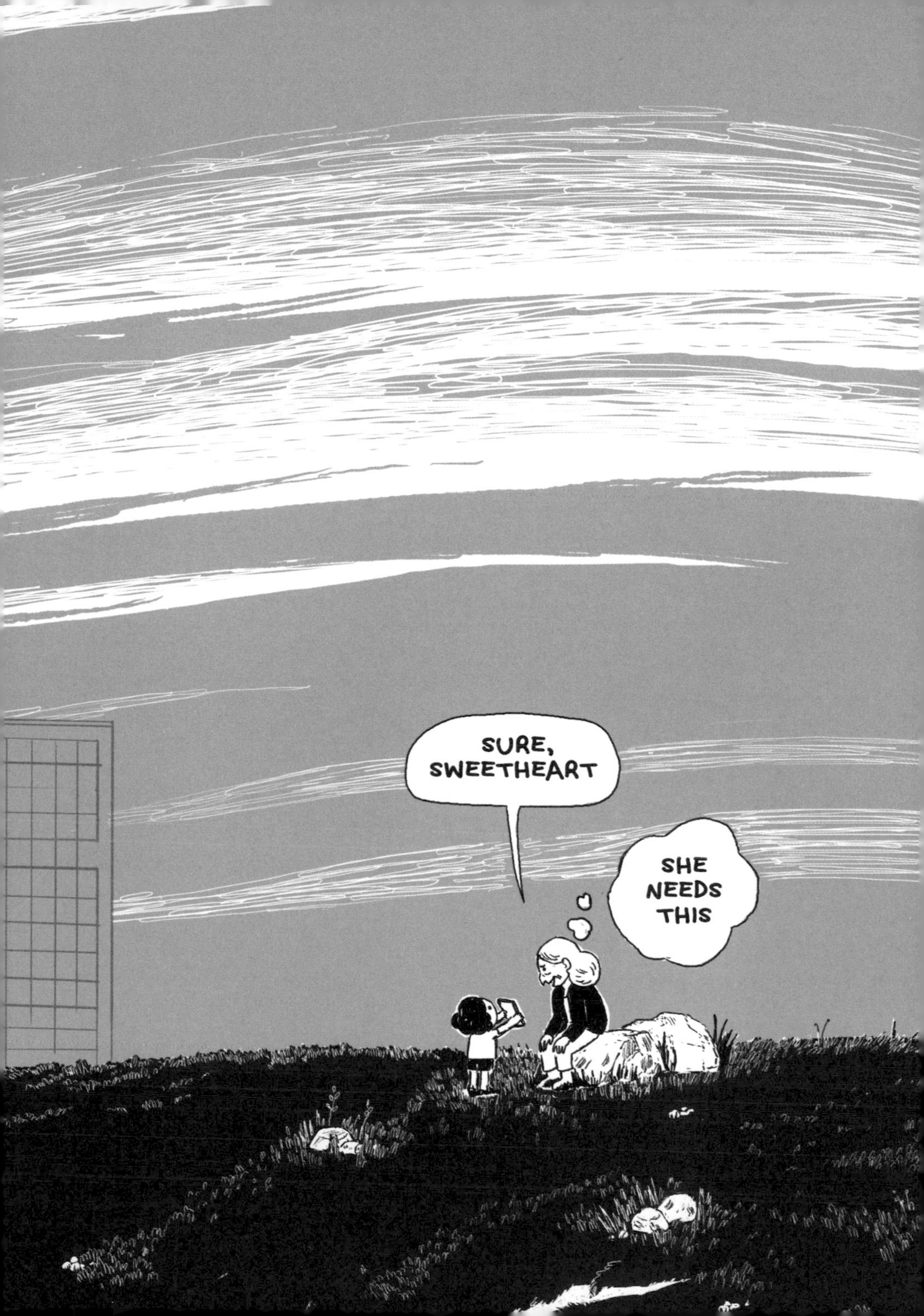
SURE, SWEETHEART
SHE NEEDS THIS

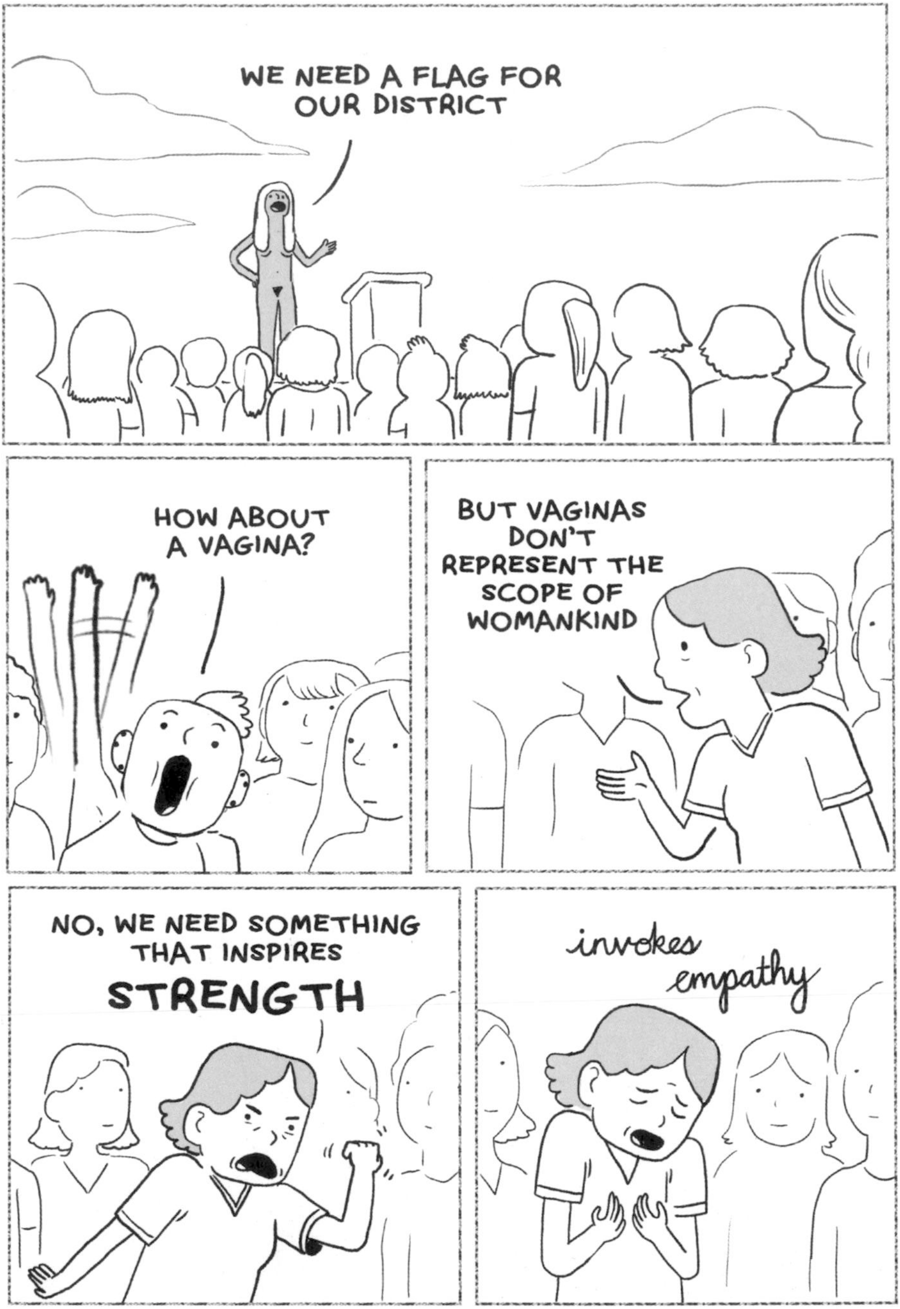
WE NEED A FLAG FOR OUR DISTRICT
HOW ABOUT A VAGINA?
BUT VAGINAS DON'T REPRESENT THE SCOPE OF WOMANKIND
NO, WE NEED SOMETHING THAT INSPIRES STRENGTH
invokes empathy

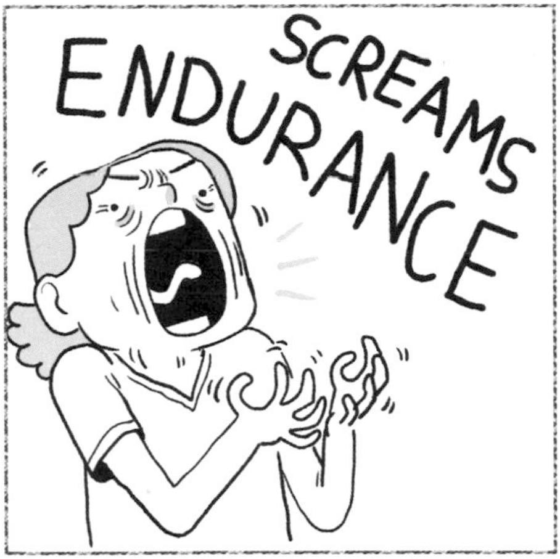
SCREAMS
ENDURANCE

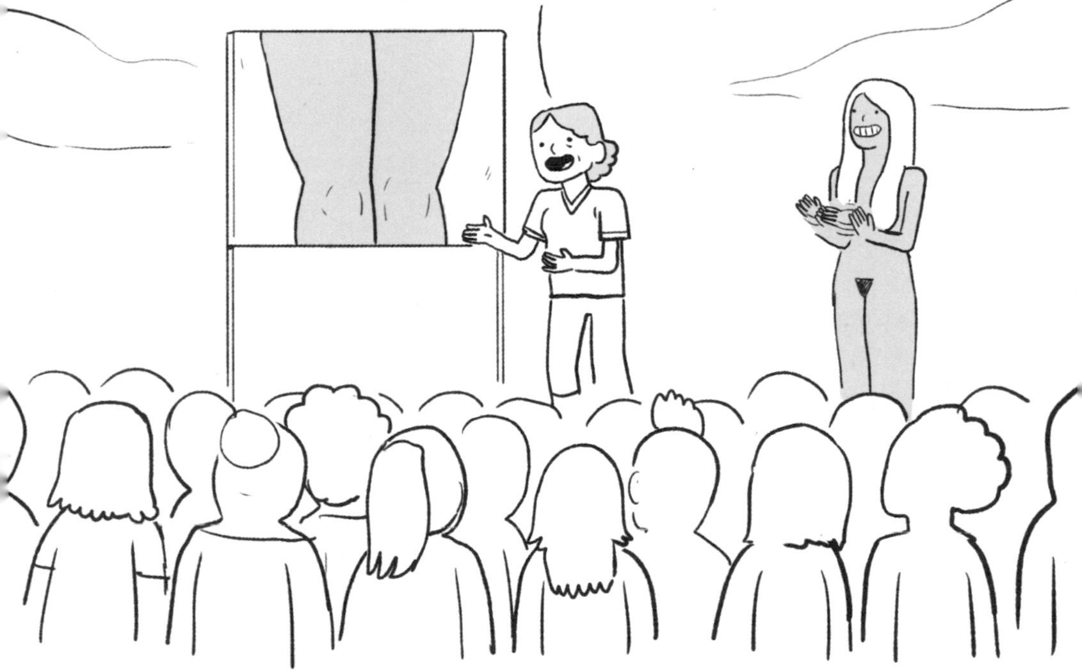
I CALL IT BEYONCE'S THIGHS

SOMETIMES I FEEL
LIKE I CAN
TRANSCEND TIME

TRAVEL BACK
GENERATIONS

AND TALK TO MY
MALE ANCESTORS

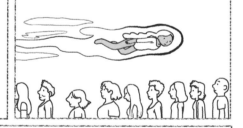

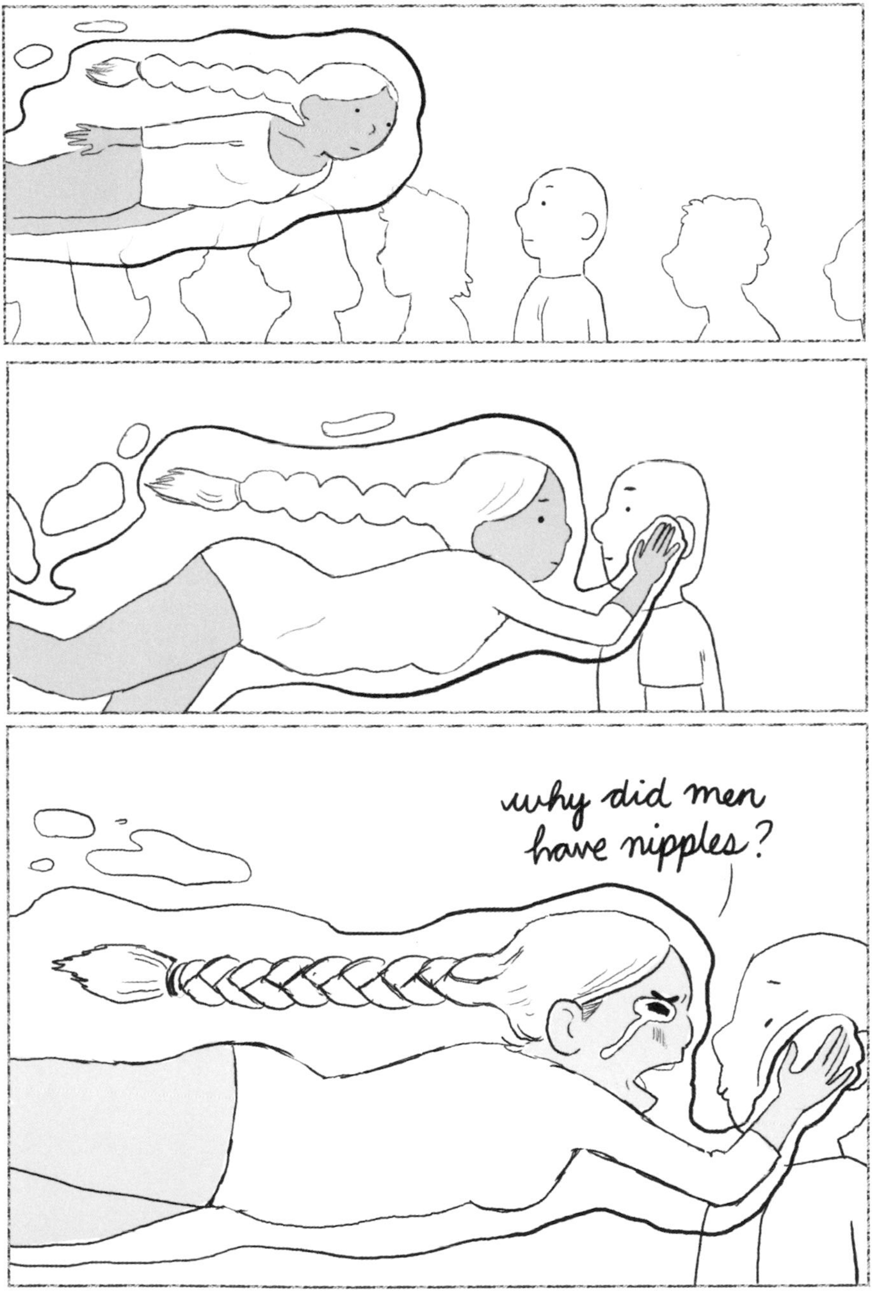
why did men
have nipples?

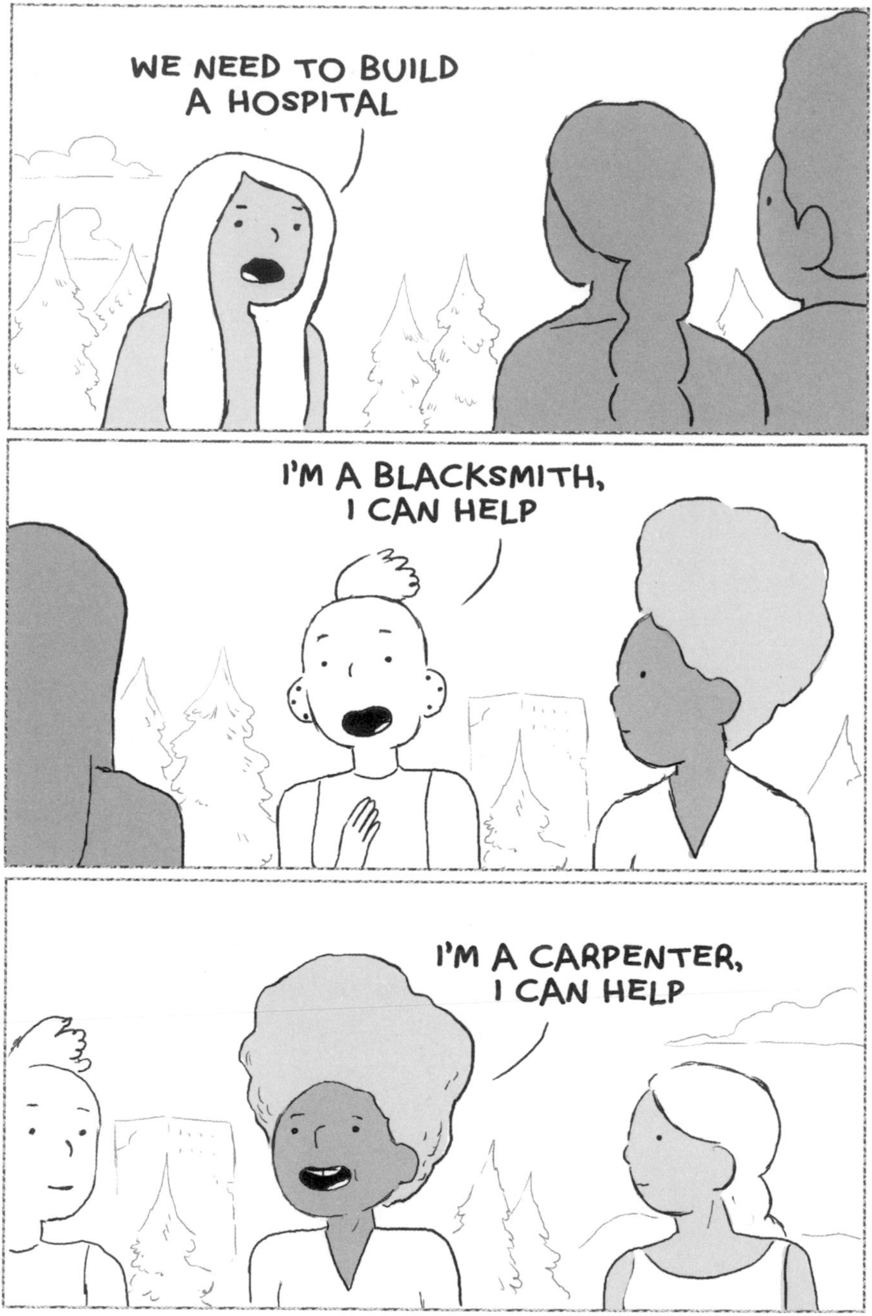
WE NEED TO BUILD A HOSPITAL
I'M A BLACKSMITH, I CAN HELP
I'M A CARPENTER, I CAN HELP

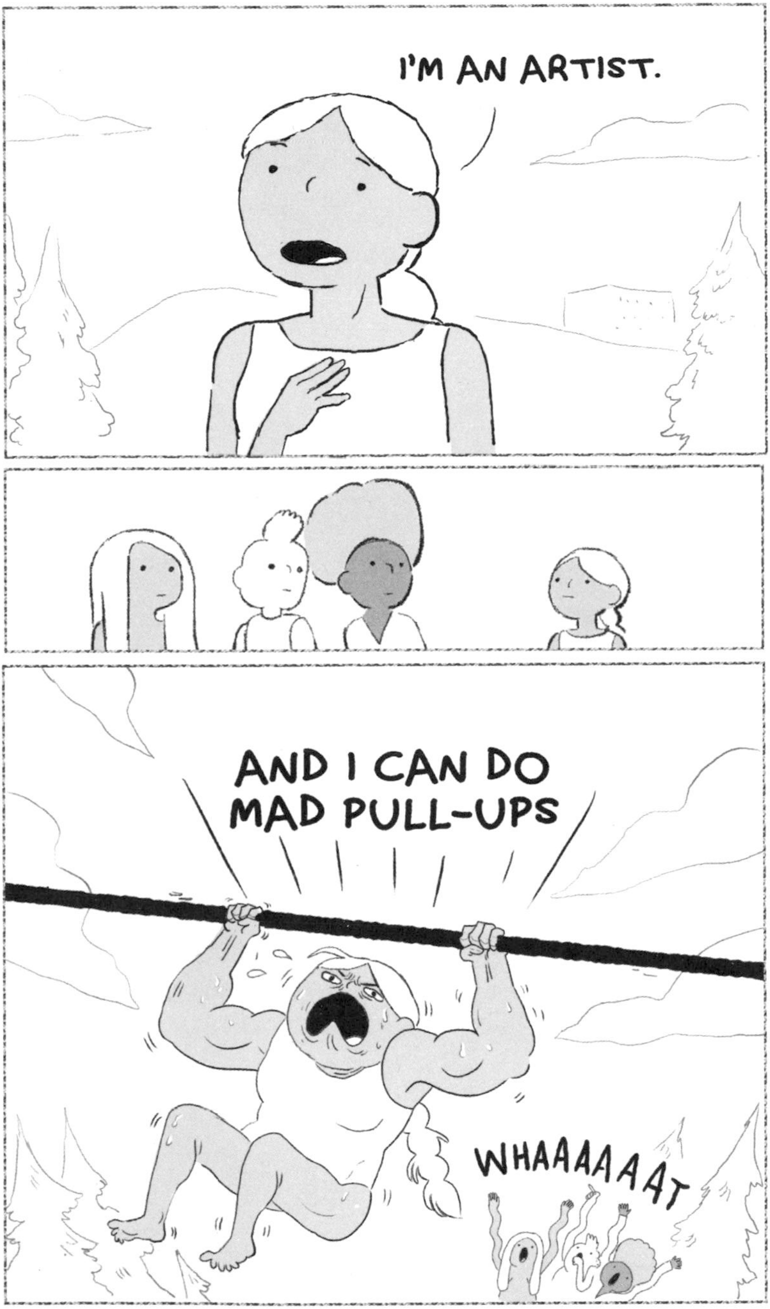
I'M AN ARTIST.
AND I CAN DO MAD PULL-UPS
WHAAAAAAT

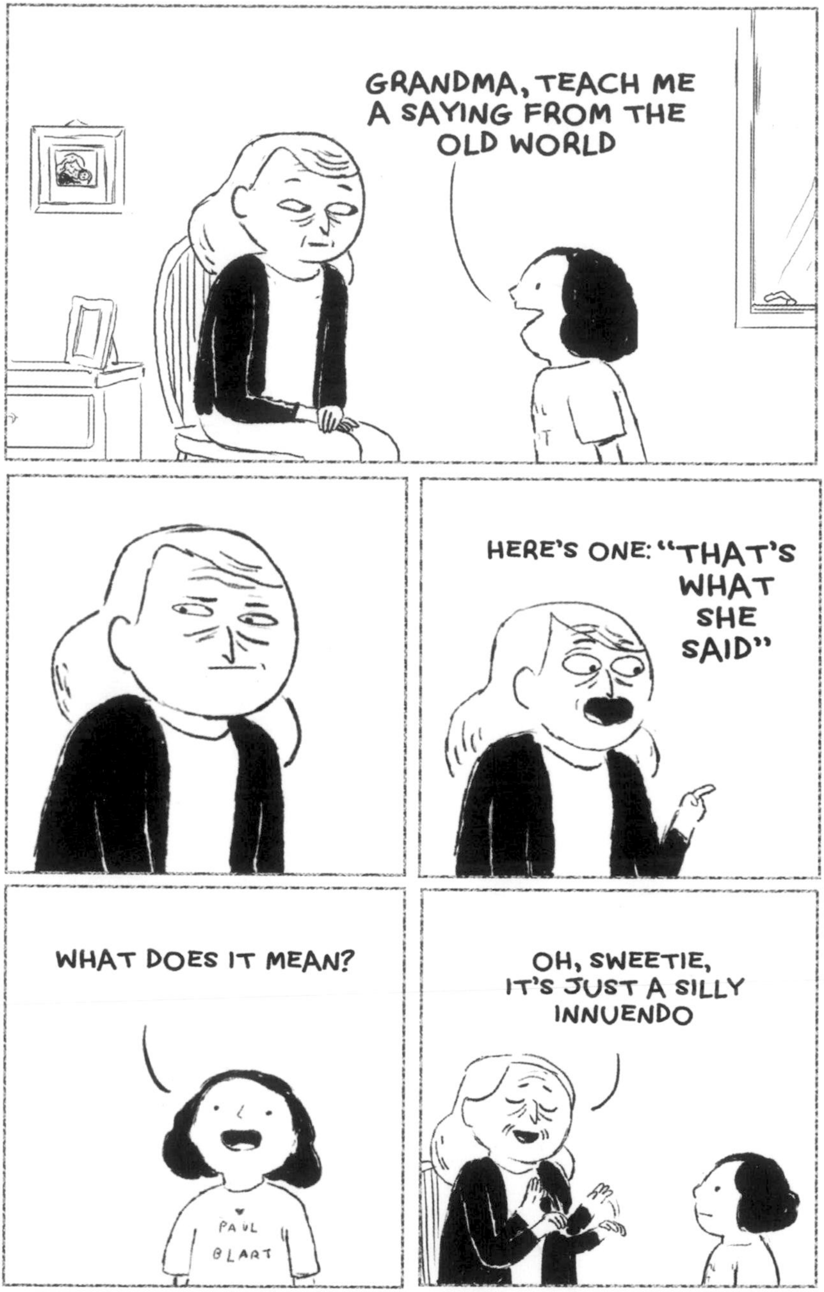
GRANDMA, TEACH ME A SAYING FROM THE OLD WORLD
HERE'S ONE: "THAT'S WHAT SHE SAID"
WHAT DOES IT MEAN?
PAUL BLART
OH, SWEETIE, IT'S JUST A SILLY INNUENDO

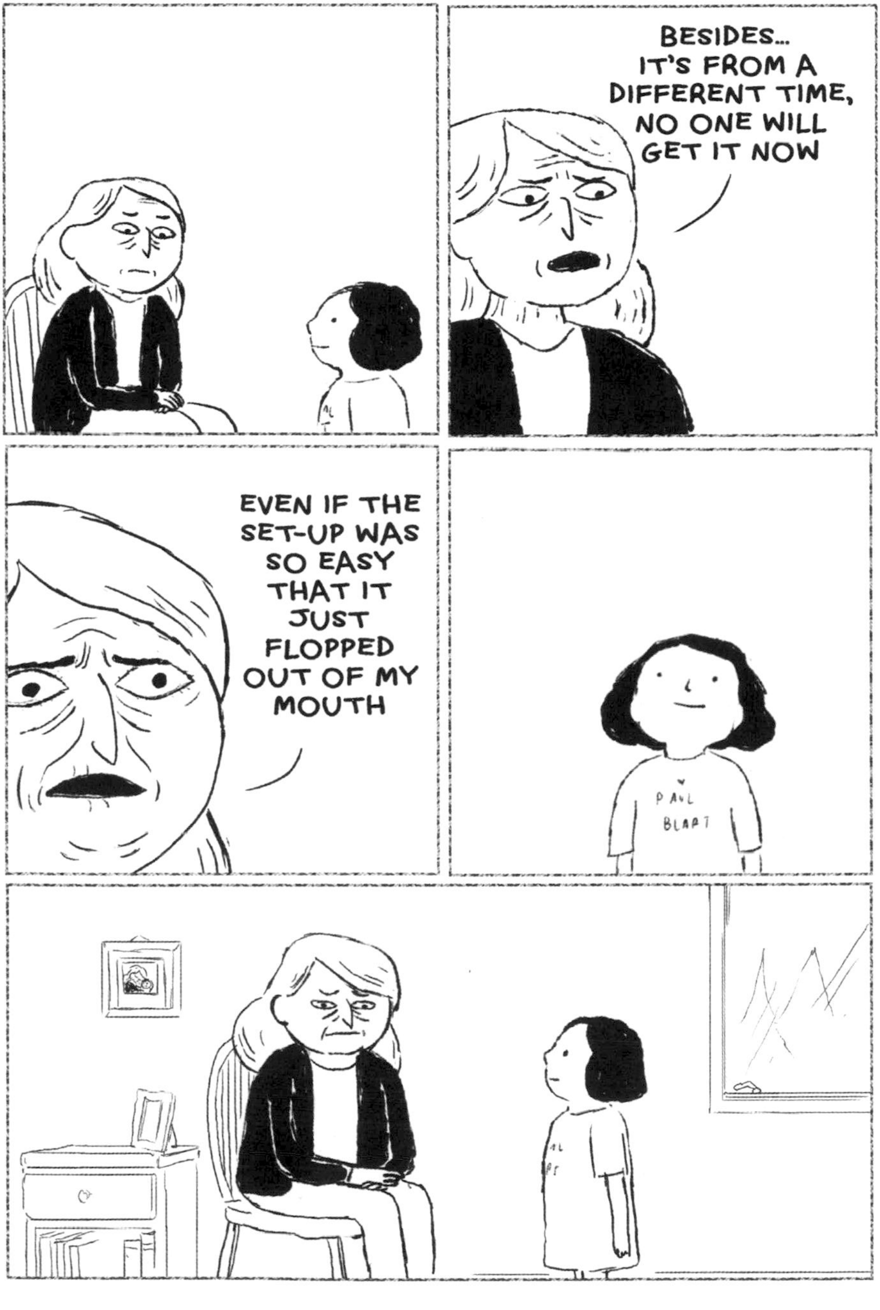
BESIDES... IT'S FROM A DIFFERENT TIME, NO ONE WILL GET IT NOW
EVEN IF THE SET-UP WAS SO EASY THAT IT JUST FLOPPED OUT OF MY MOUTH

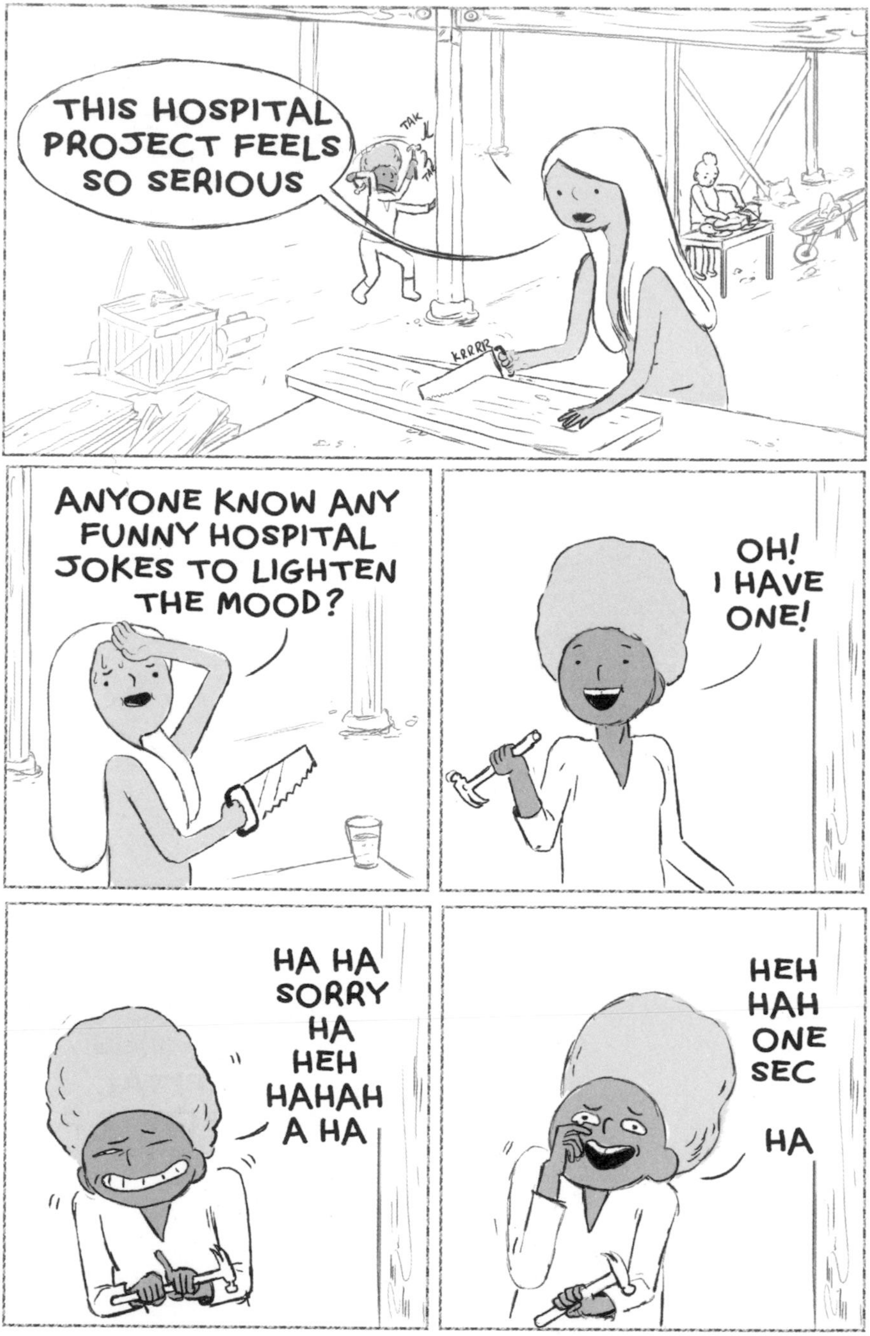
THIS HOSPITAL PROJECT FEELS SO SERIOUS
TAK
TAK
KRRRR
ANYONE KNOW ANY FUNNY HOSPITAL JOKES TO LIGHTEN THE MOOD?
OH! I HAVE ONE!
HA HA SORRY HA HEH HAHAH A HA
HEH HAH ONE SEC
HA

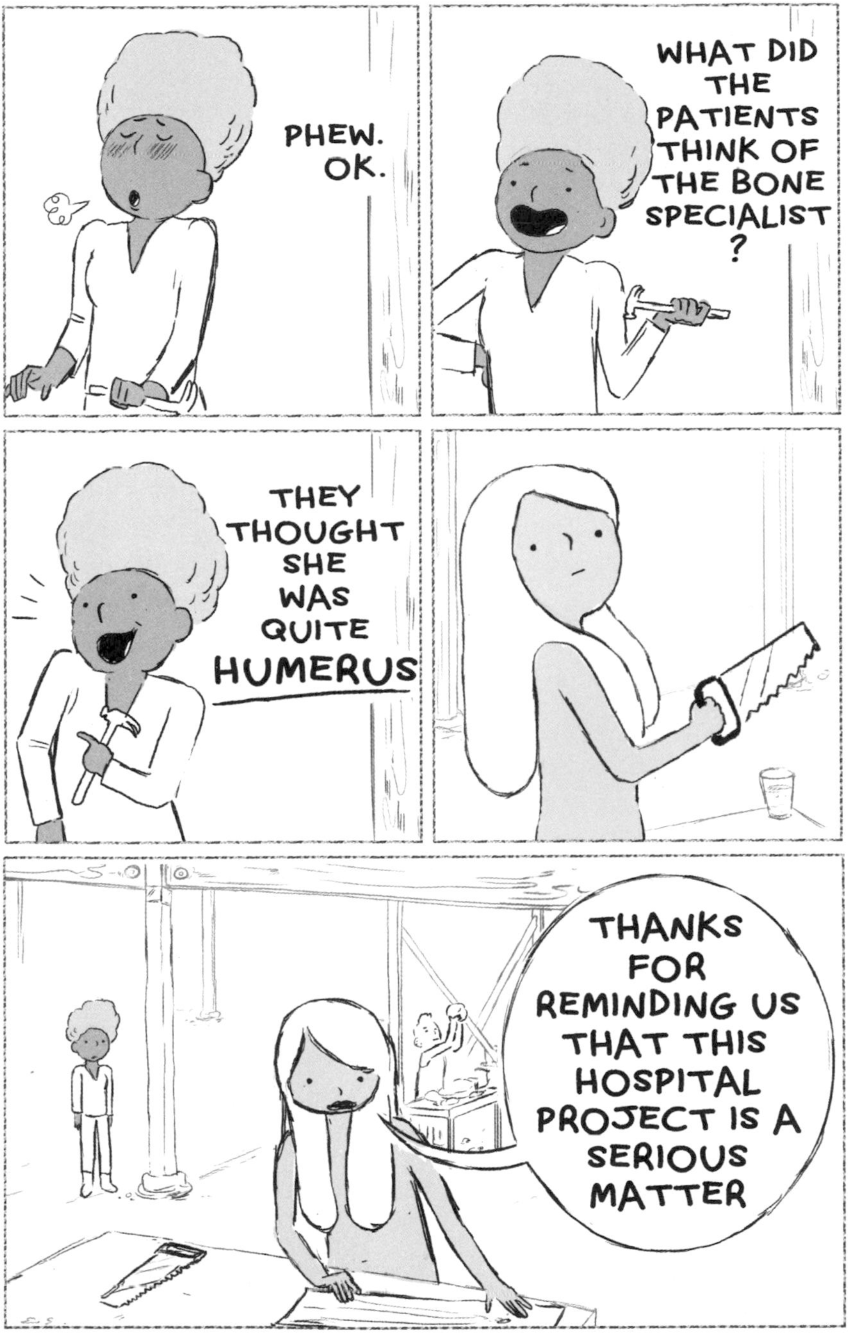
PHEW. OK.
WHAT DID THE PATIENTS THINK OF THE BONE SPECIALIST?
THEY THOUGHT SHE WAS QUITE HUMERUS
THANKS FOR REMINDING US THAT THIS HOSPITAL PROJECT IS A SERIOUS MATTER

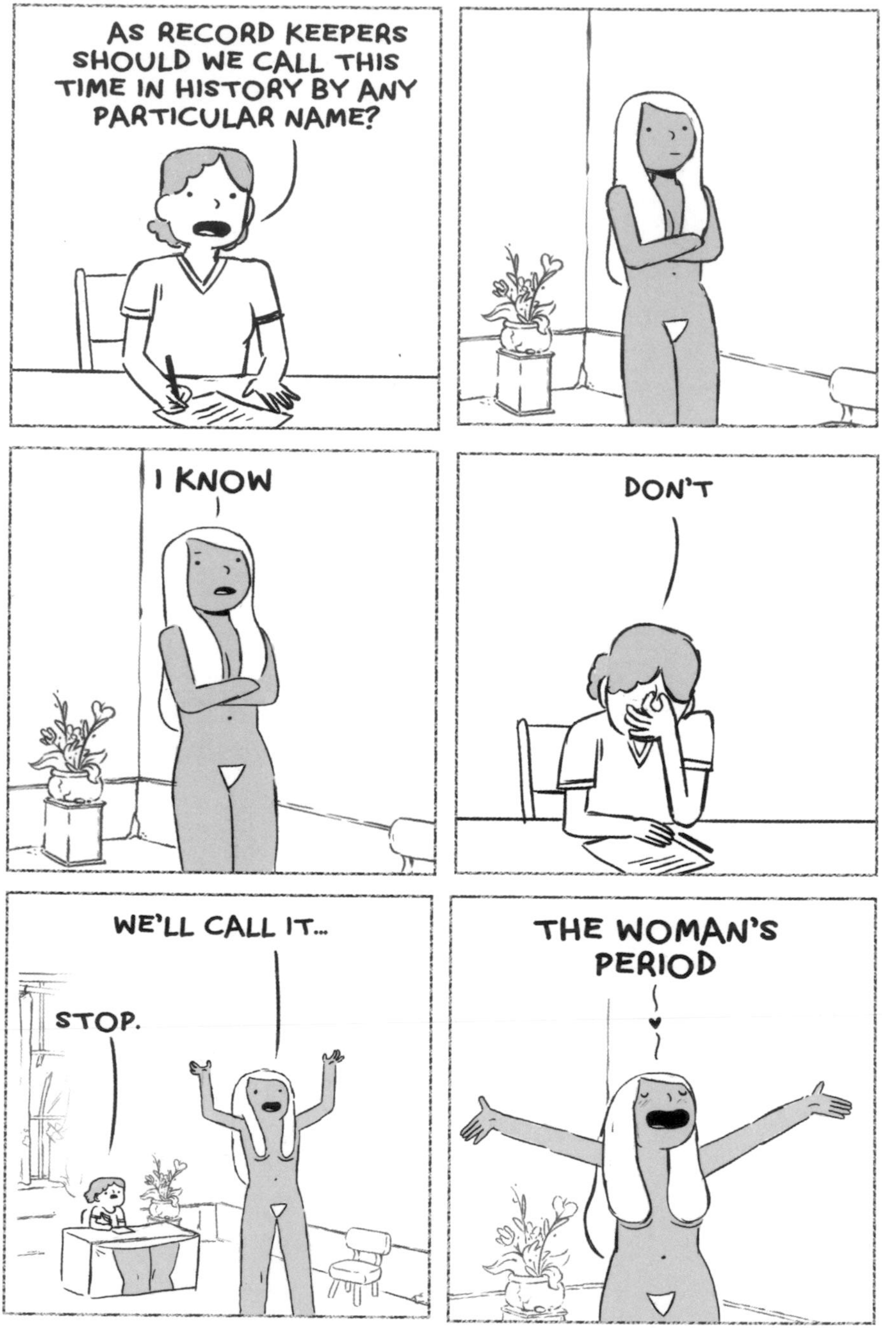
AS RECORD KEEPERS SHOULD WE CALL THIS TIME IN HISTORY BY ANY PARTICULAR NAME?
I KNOW
DON'T
WE'LL CALL IT...
STOP.
THE WOMAN'S PERIOD

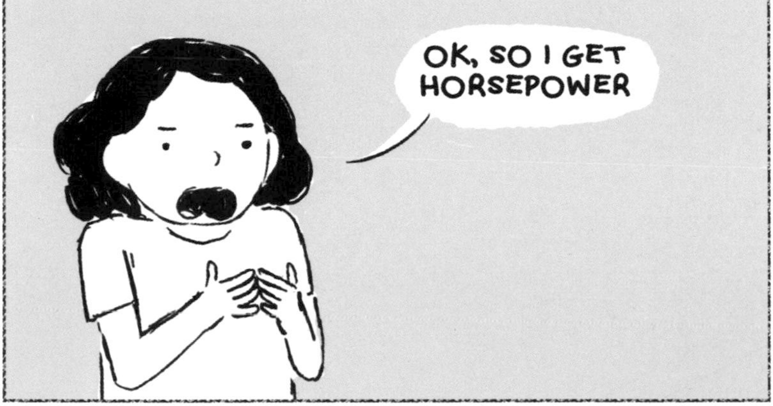
OK, SO I GET HORSEPOWER

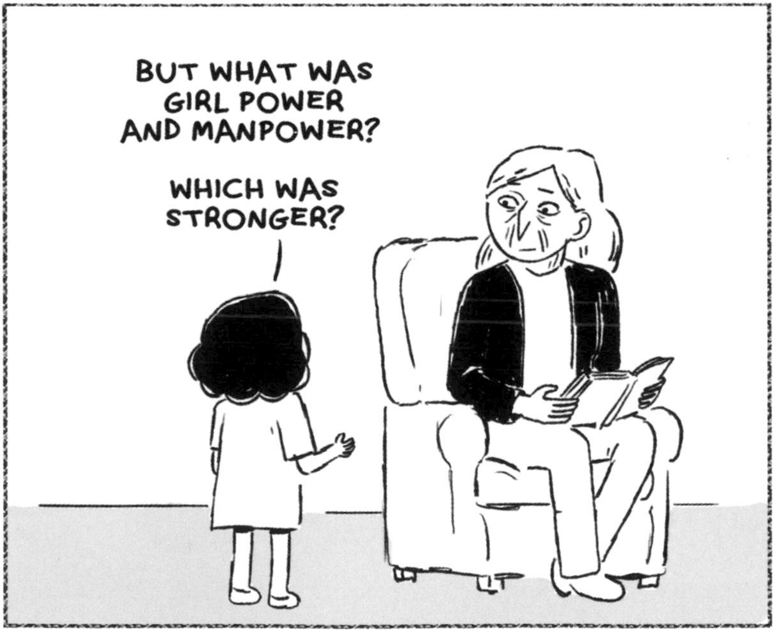
BUT WHAT WAS GIRL POWER AND MANPOWER?
WHICH WAS STRONGER?

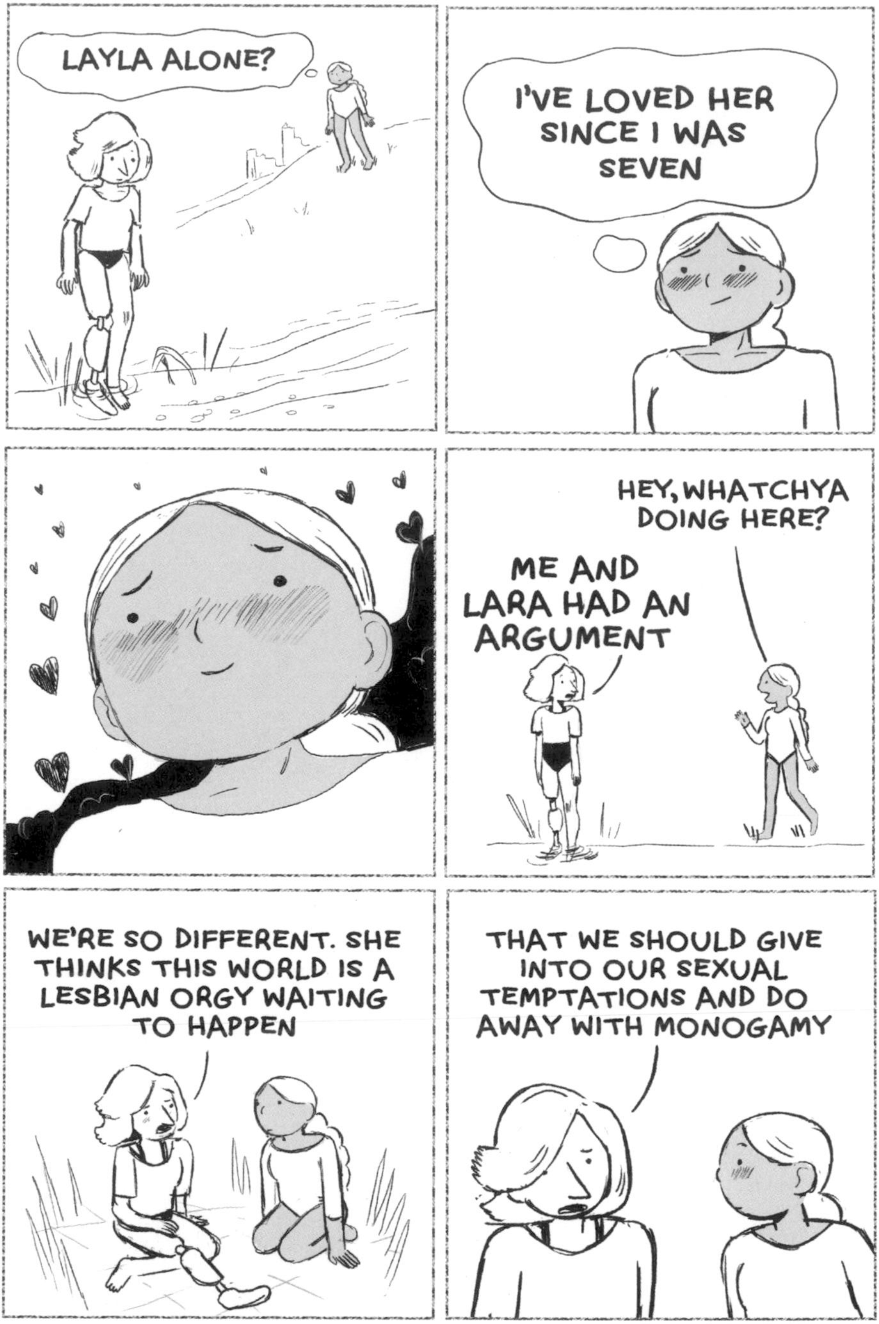
LAYLA ALONE?
I'VE LOVED HER SINCE I WAS SEVEN
HEY, WHATCHYA DOING HERE?
ME AND LARA HAD AN ARGUMENT
WE'RE SO DIFFERENT. SHE THINKS THIS WORLD IS A LESBIAN ORGY WAITING TO HAPPEN
THAT WE SHOULD GIVE INTO OUR SEXUAL TEMPTATIONS AND DO AWAY WITH MONOGAMY

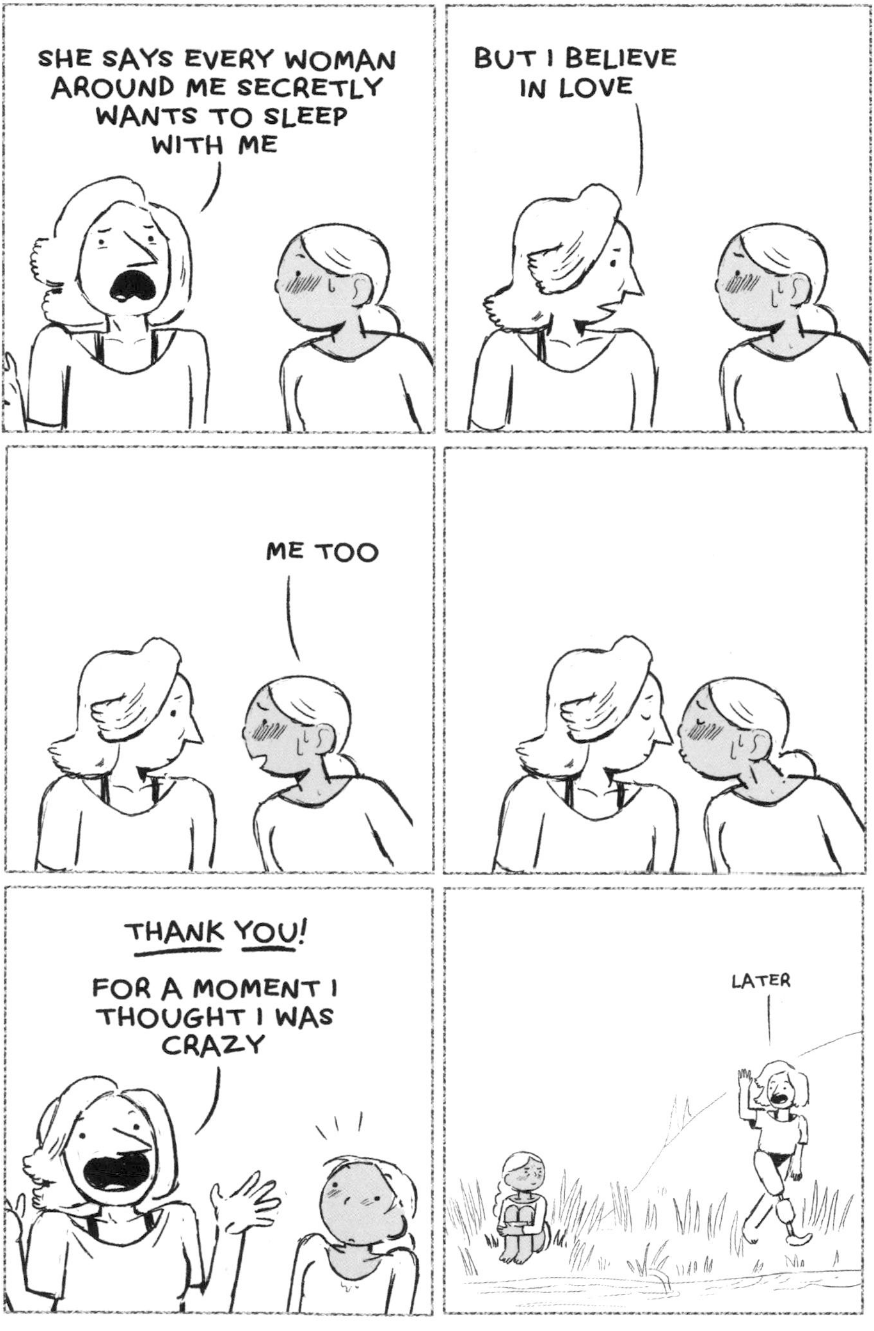
SHE SAYS EVERY WOMAN AROUND ME SECRETLY WANTS TO SLEEP WITH ME
BUT I BELIEVE IN LOVE
ME TOO
THANK YOU!
FOR A MOMENT I THOUGHT I WAS CRAZY
LATER

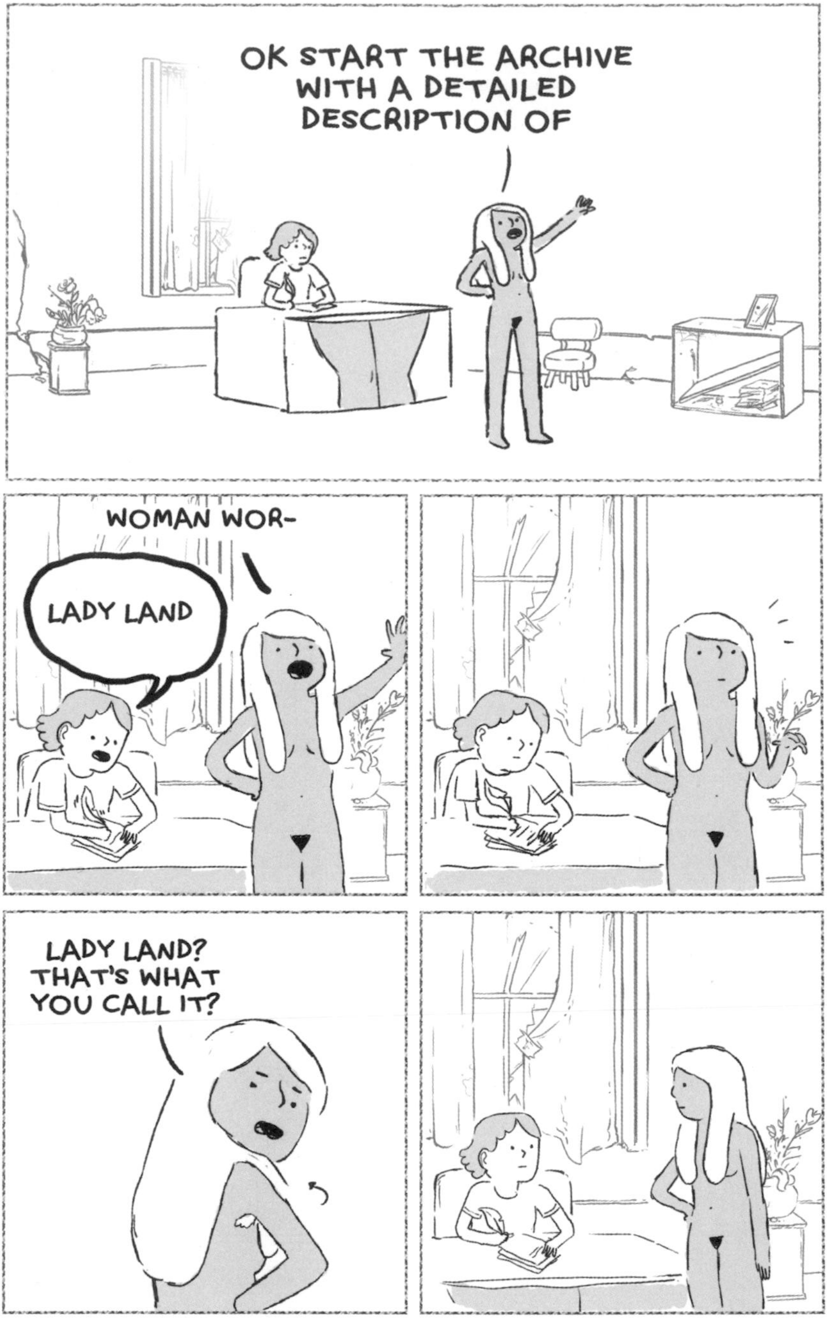
OK START THE ARCHIVE WITH A DETAILED DESCRIPTION OF
WOMAN WOR-
LADY LAND
LADY LAND? THAT'S WHAT YOU CALL IT?

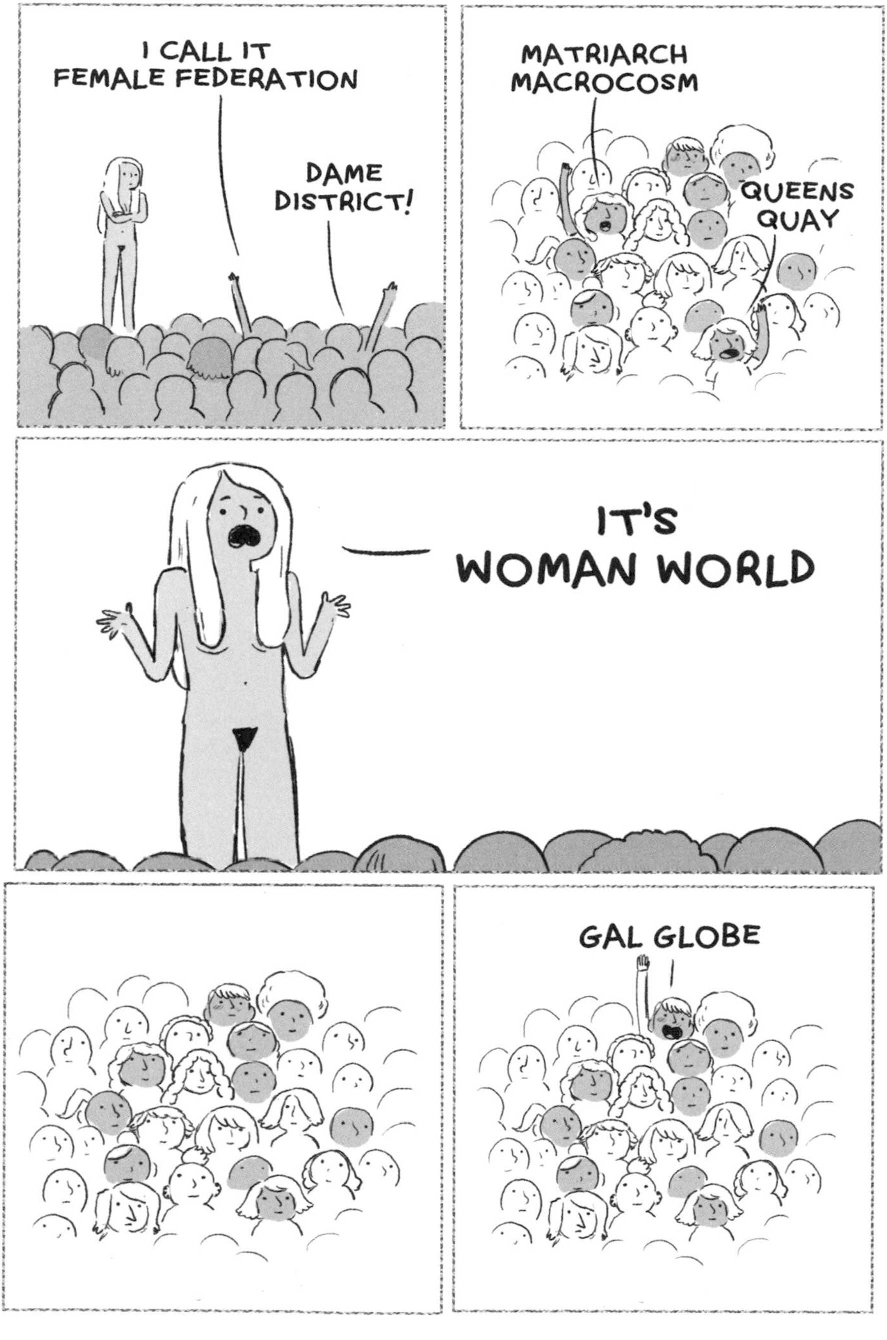
I CALL IT FEMALE FEDERATION
DAME DISTRICT!
MATRIARCH MACROCOSM
QUEENS QUAY
IT'S WOMAN WORLD
GAL GLOBE

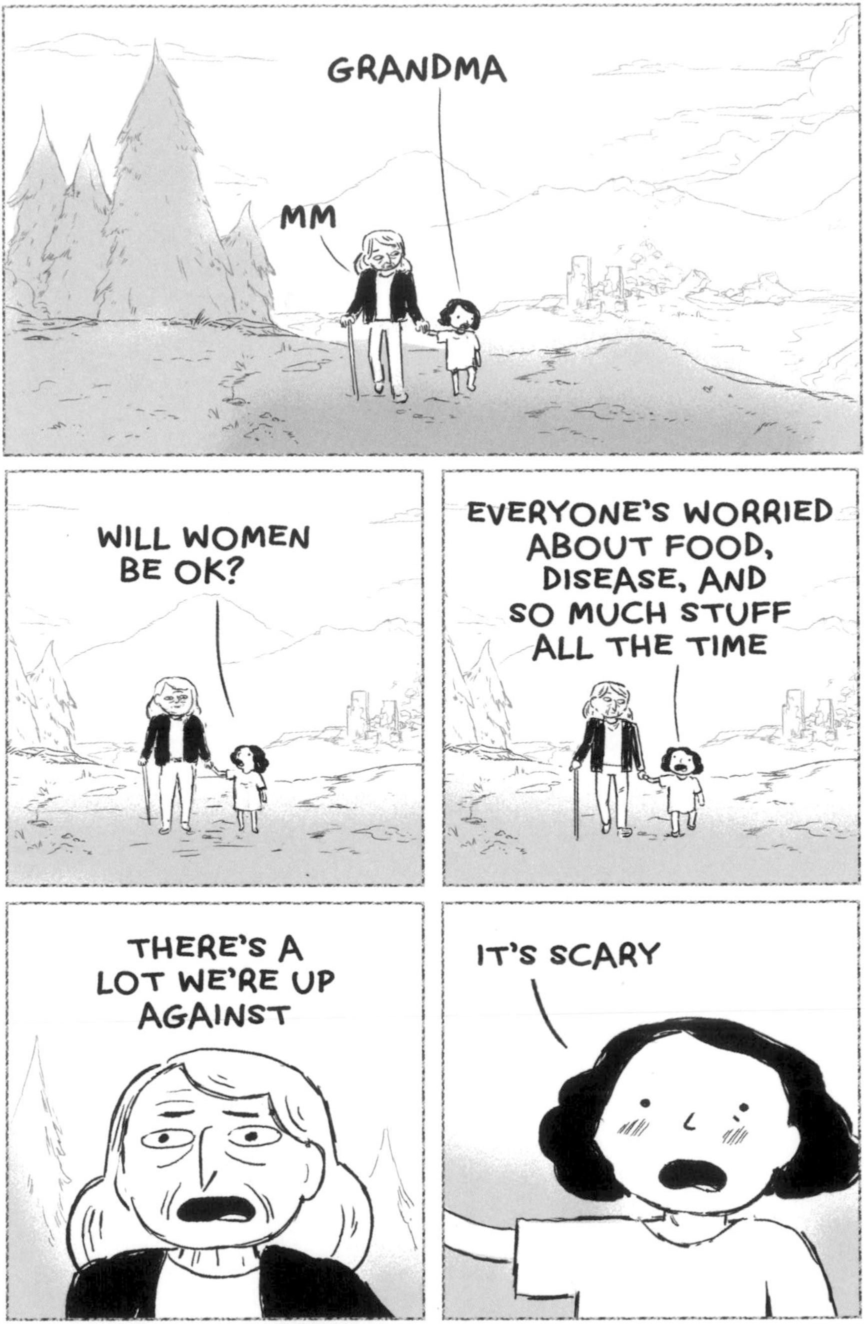
GRANDMA
MM
WILL WOMEN BE OK?
EVERYONE'S WORRIED ABOUT FOOD, DISEASE, AND SO MUCH STUFF ALL THE TIME
THERE'S A LOT WE'RE UP AGAINST
IT'S SCARY

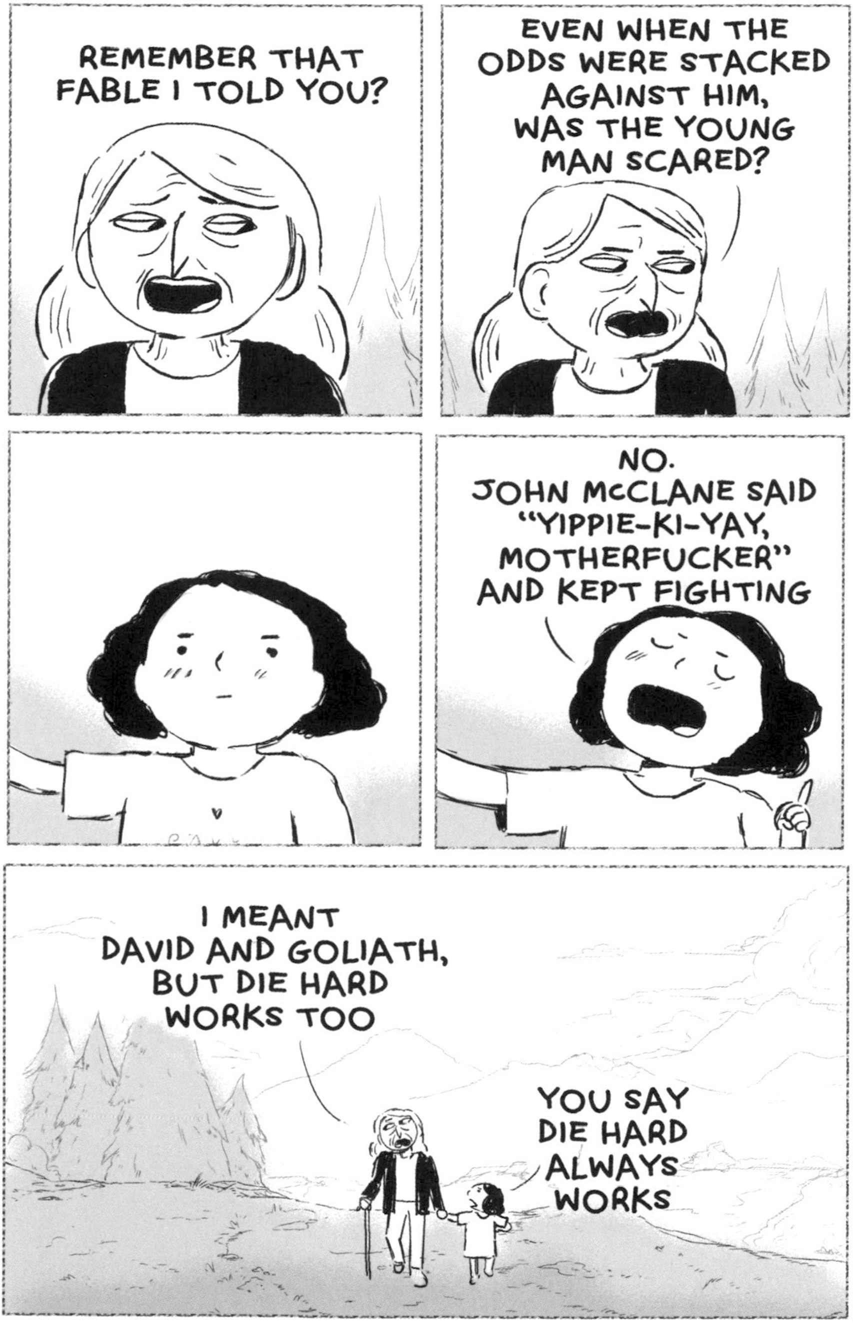
REMEMBER THAT FABLE I TOLD YOU?
EVEN WHEN THE ODDS WERE STACKED AGAINST HIM, WAS THE YOUNG MAN SCARED?
NO. JOHN McCLANE SAID "YIPPIE-KI-YAY, MOTHERFUCKER" AND KEPT FIGHTING
I MEANT DAVID AND GOLIATH, BUT DIE HARD WORKS TOO
YOU SAY DIE HARD ALWAYS WORKS

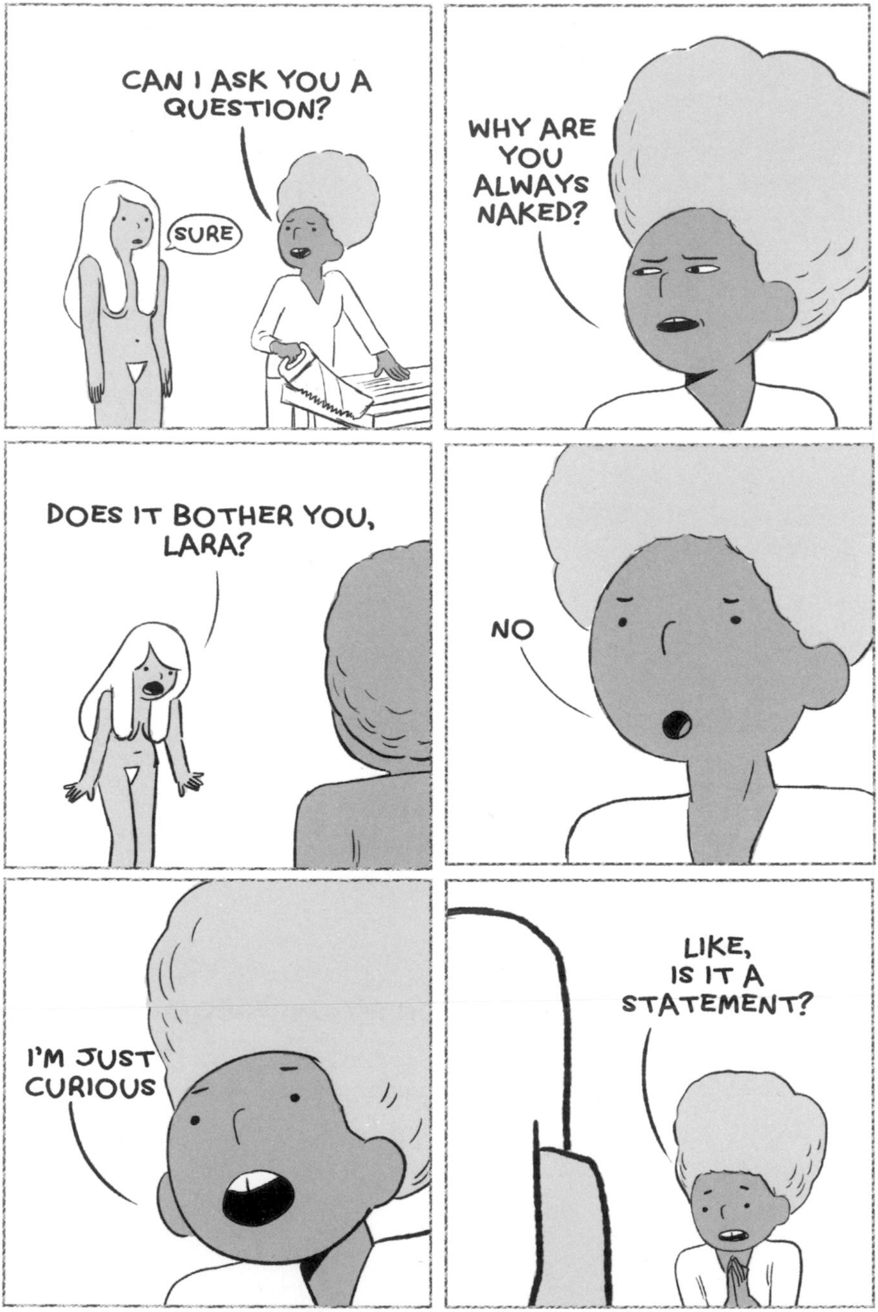
CAN I ASK YOU A QUESTION?
SURE
WHY ARE YOU ALWAYS NAKED?
DOES IT BOTHER YOU, LARA?
NO
I'M JUST CURIOUS
LIKE, IS IT A STATEMENT?

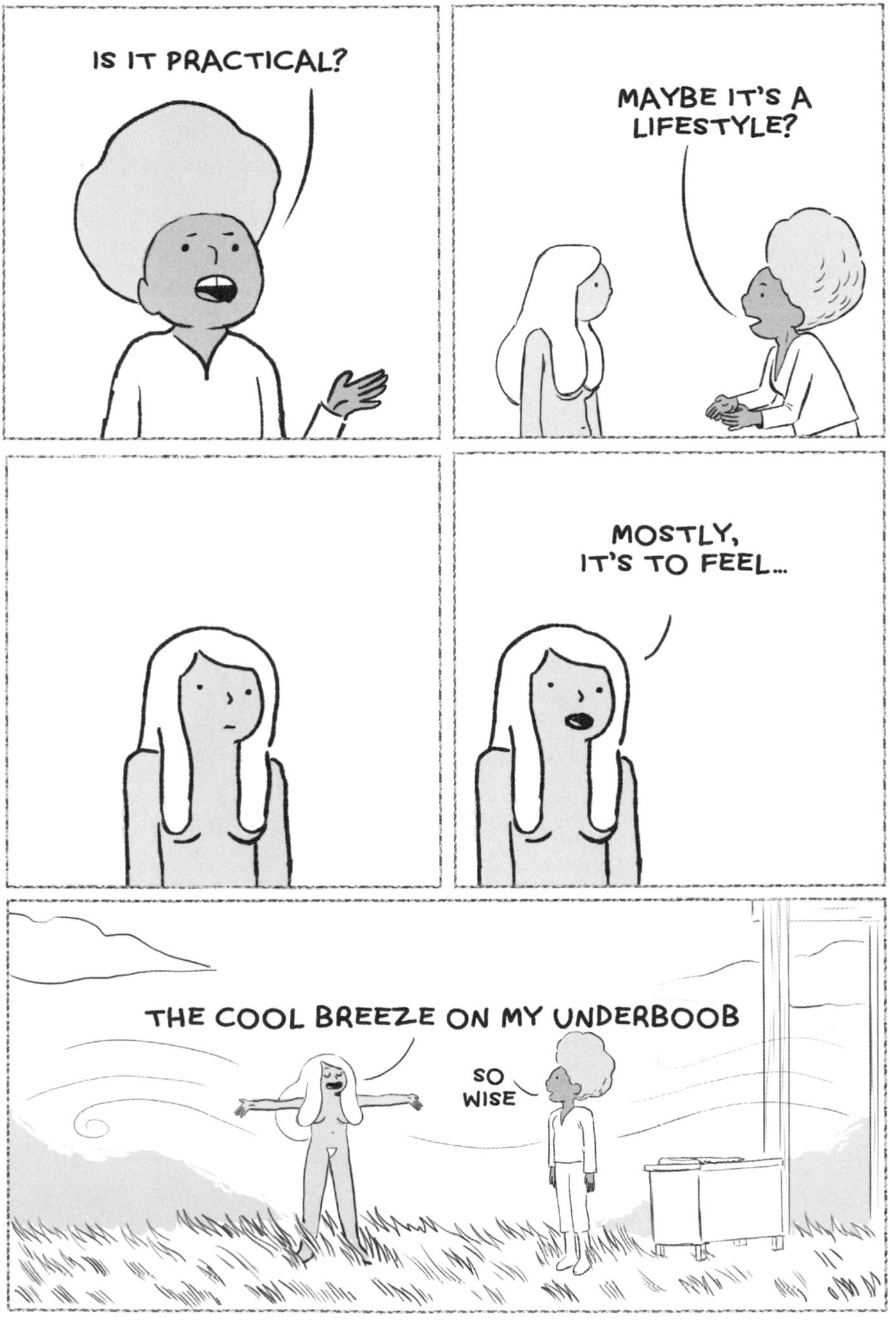
IS IT PRACTICAL?
MAYBE IT'S A LIFESTYLE?
MOSTLY, IT'S TO FEEL...
THE COOL BREEZE ON MY UNDERBOOB
SO WISE

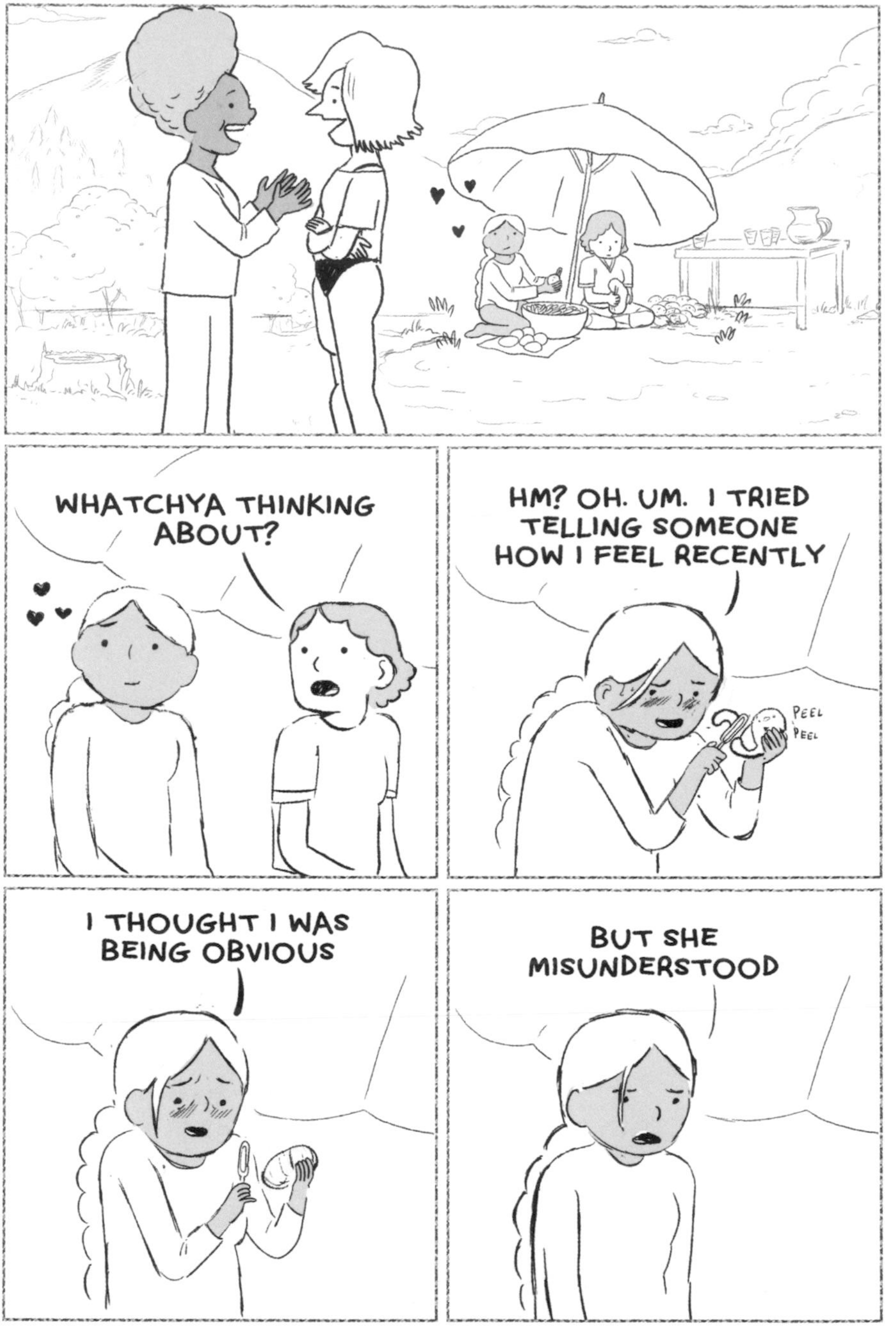
WHATCHYA THINKING ABOUT?
HM? OH. UM. I TRIED TELLING SOMEONE HOW I FEEL RECENTLY
PEEL PEEL
I THOUGHT I WAS BEING OBVIOUS
BUT SHE MISUNDERSTOOD

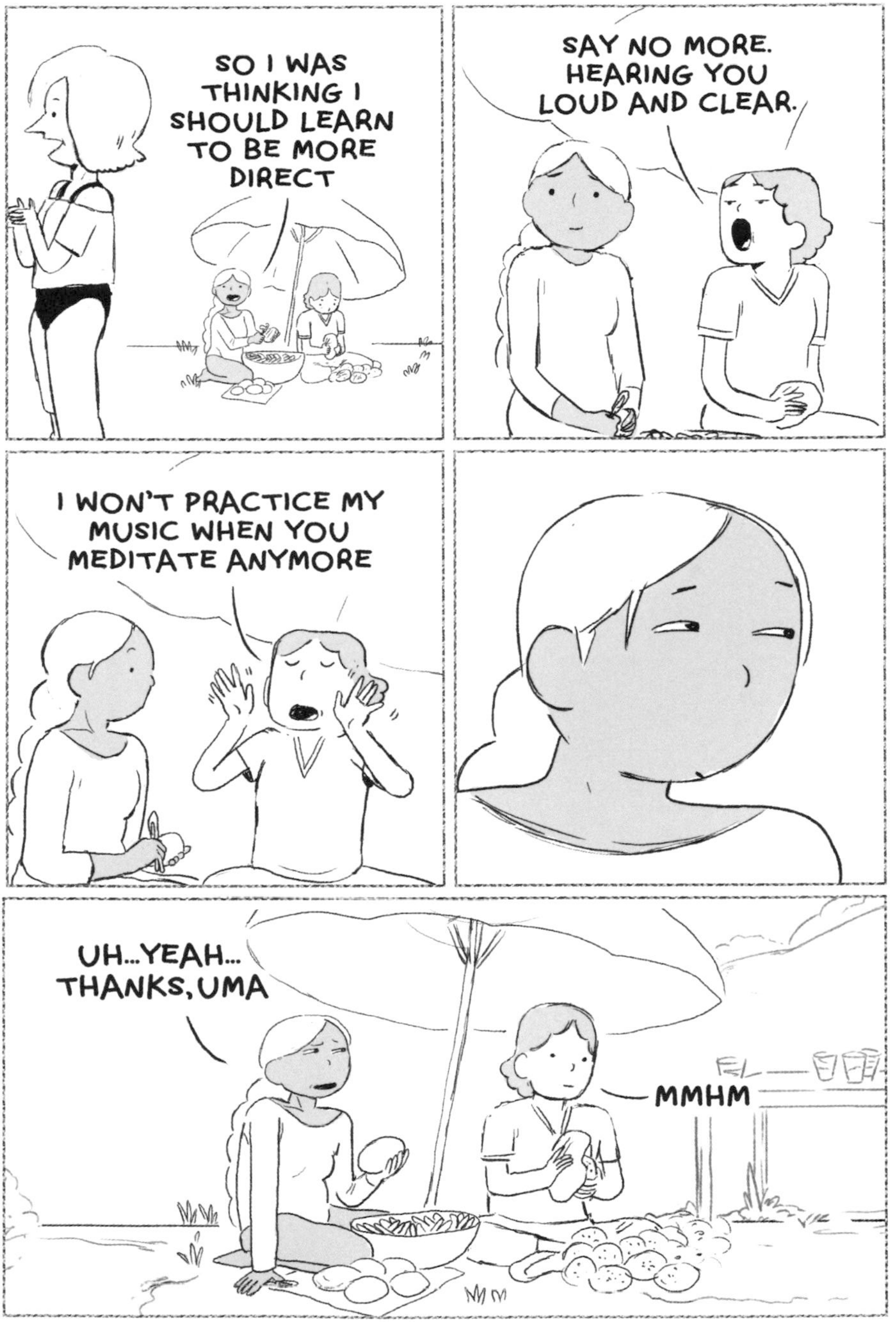
SO I WAS THINKING I SHOULD LEARN TO BE MORE DIRECT
SAY NO MORE. HEARING YOU LOUD AND CLEAR.
I WON'T PRACTICE MY MUSIC WHEN YOU MEDITATE ANYMORE
UH...YEAH... THANKS, UMA
MMHM

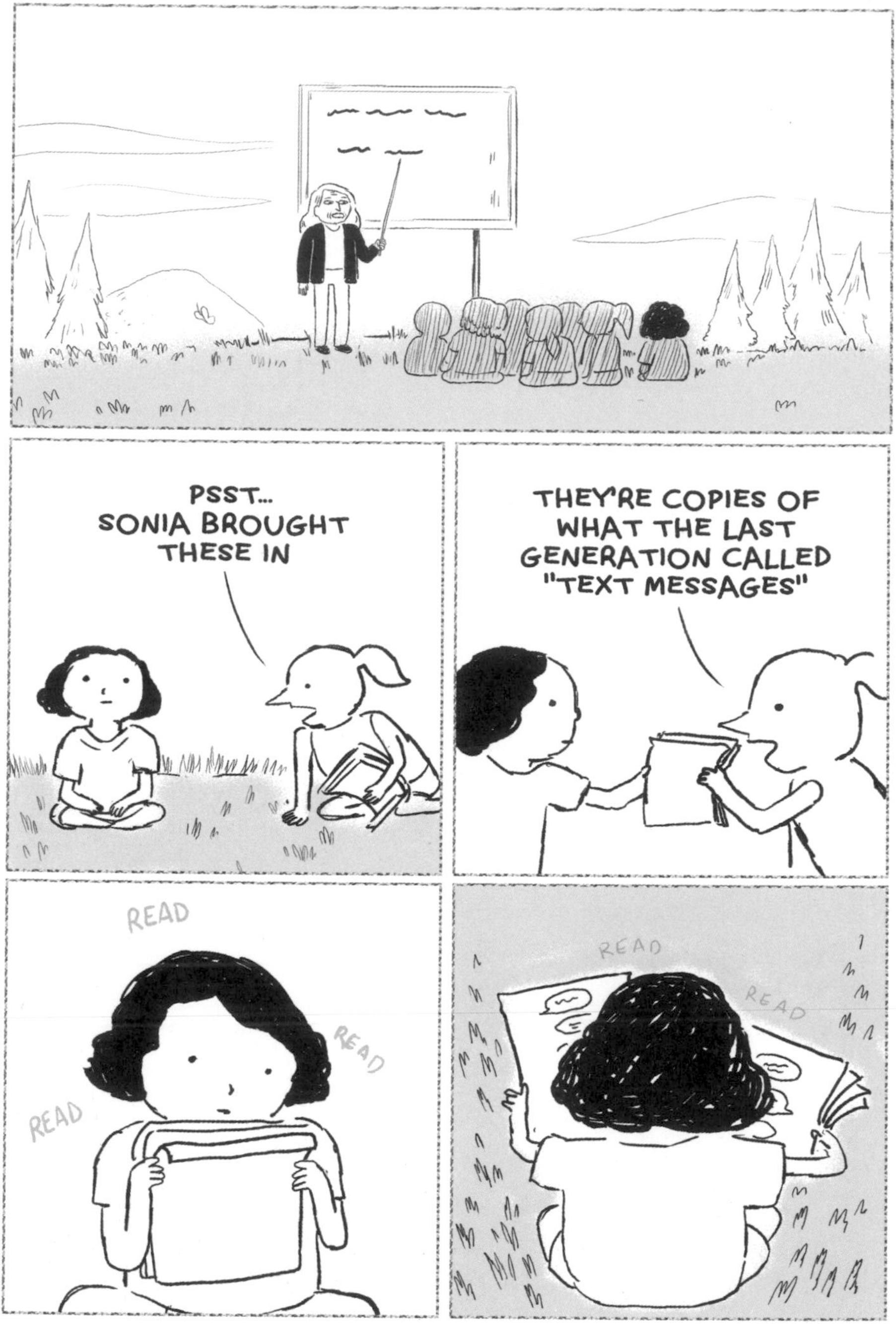
PSST... SONIA BROUGHT THESE IN
THEY'RE COPIES OF WHAT THE LAST GENERATION CALLED "TEXT MESSAGES"
READ
READ
READ
READ
READ

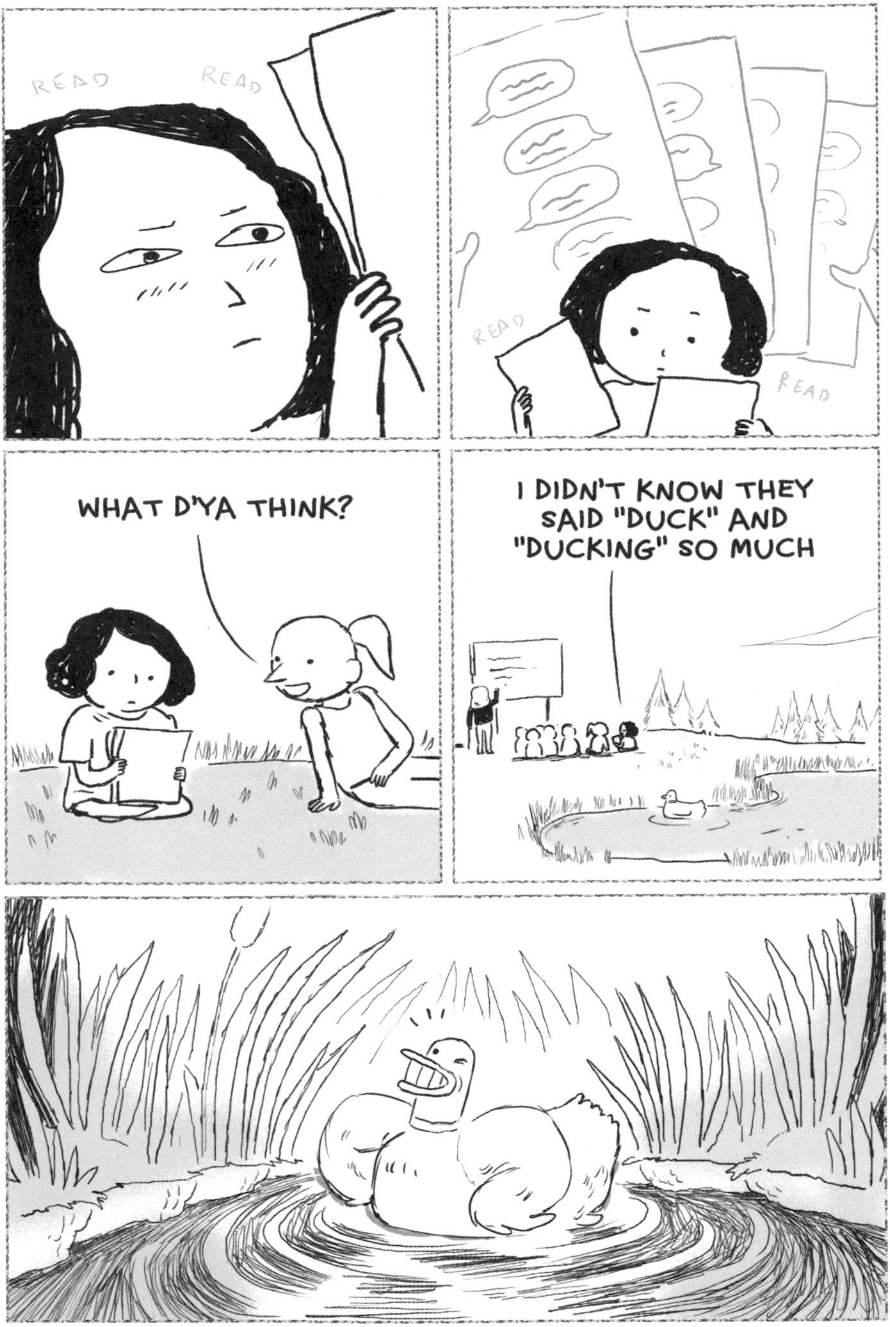
READ
READ
READ
READ
WHAT D'YA THINK?
I DIDN'T KNOW THEY SAID "DUCK" AND "DUCKING" SO MUCH

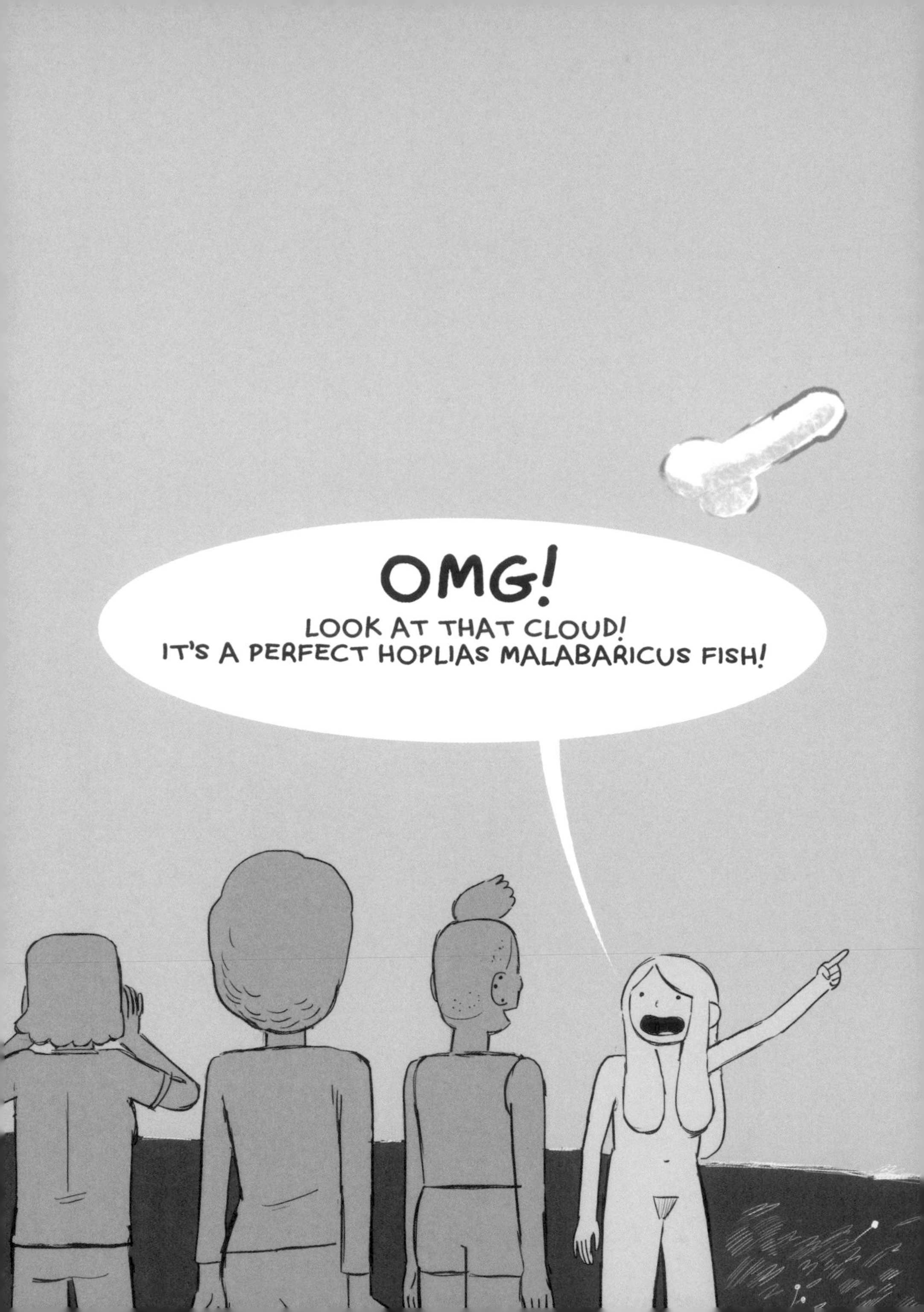
OMG!
LOOK AT THAT CLOUD!
IT'S A PERFECT HOPLIAS MALABARICUS FISH!

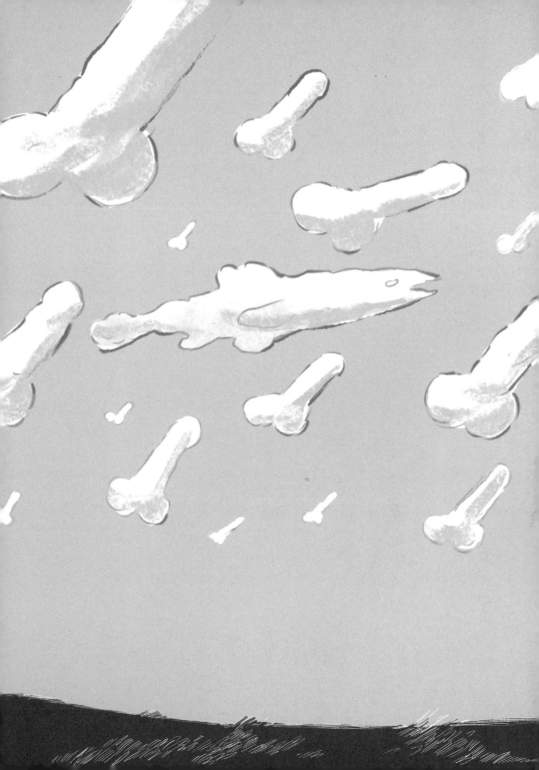

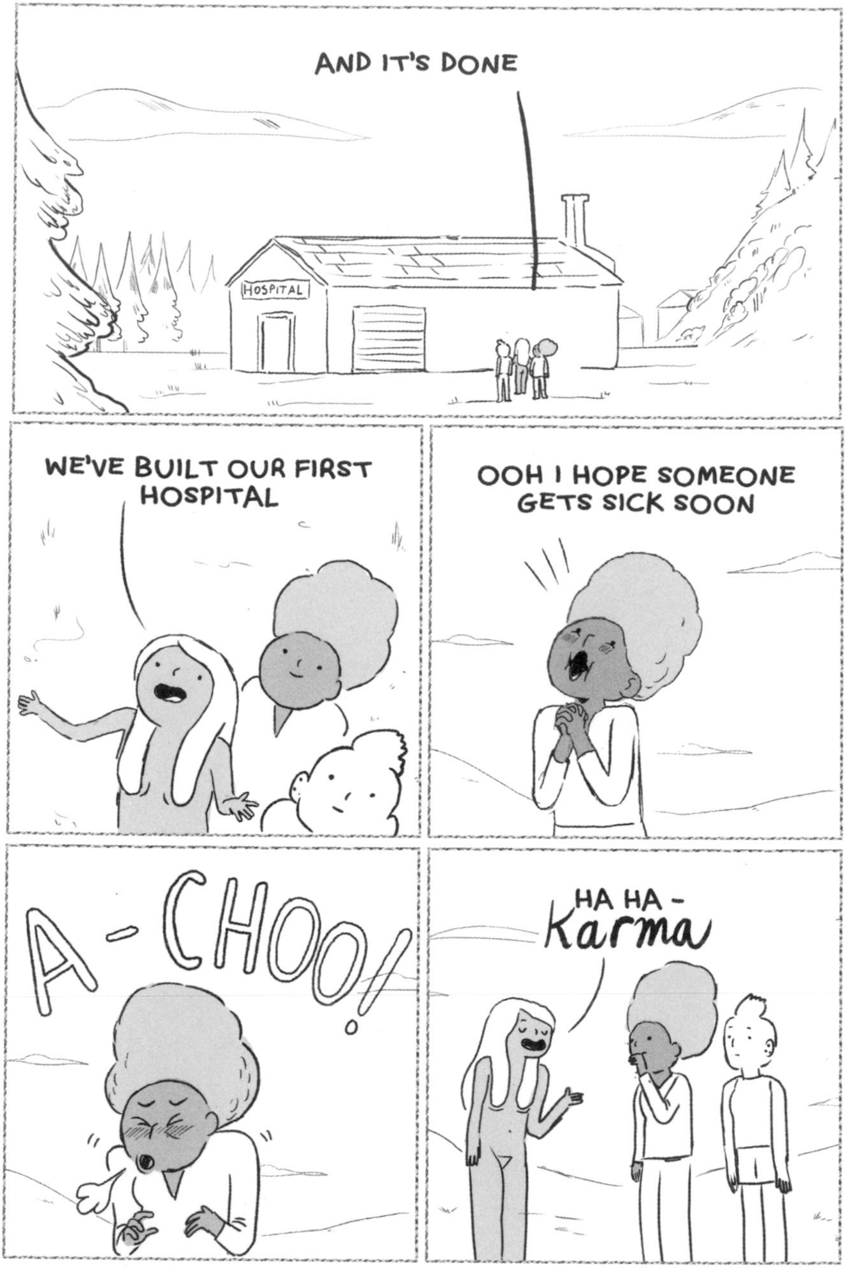
AND IT'S DONE
HOSPITAL
WE'VE BUILT OUR FIRST HOSPITAL
OOH I HOPE SOMEONE GETS SICK SOON
A-CHOO!
HA HA - Karma

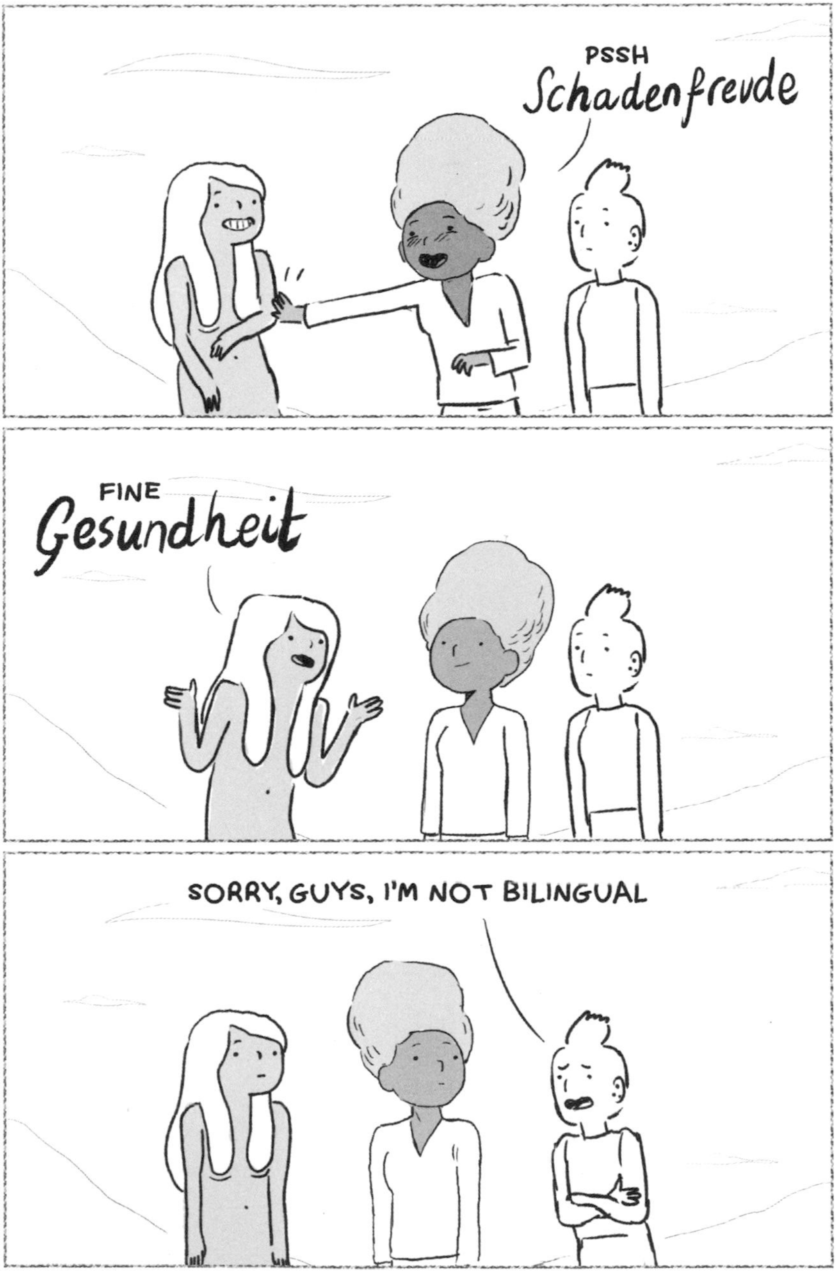
PSSH
Schadenfreude
FINE
Gesundheit
SORRY, GUYS, I'M NOT BILINGUAL

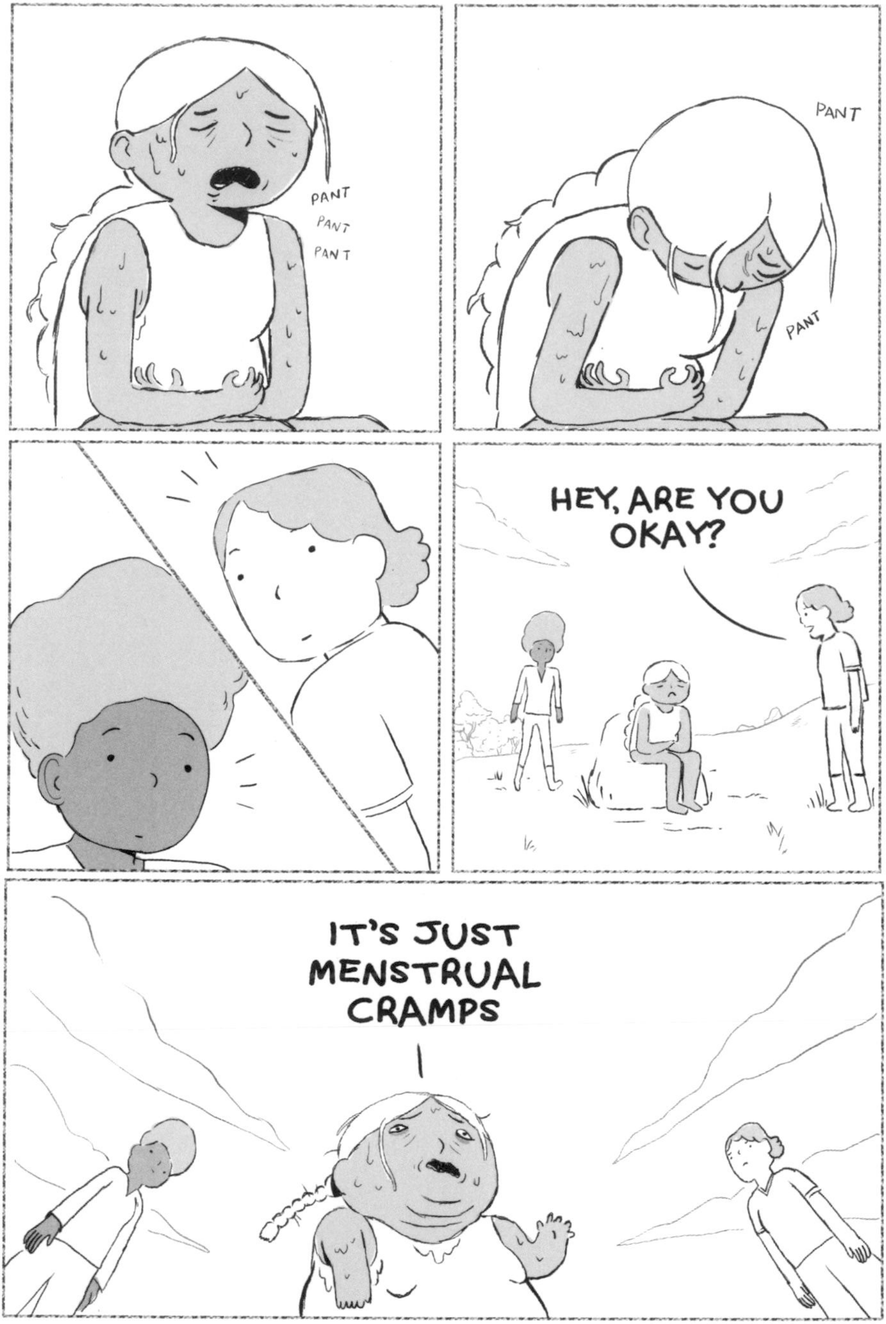
PANT
PANT
PANT
PANT
PANT
HEY, ARE YOU OKAY?
IT'S JUST MENSTRUAL CRAMPS

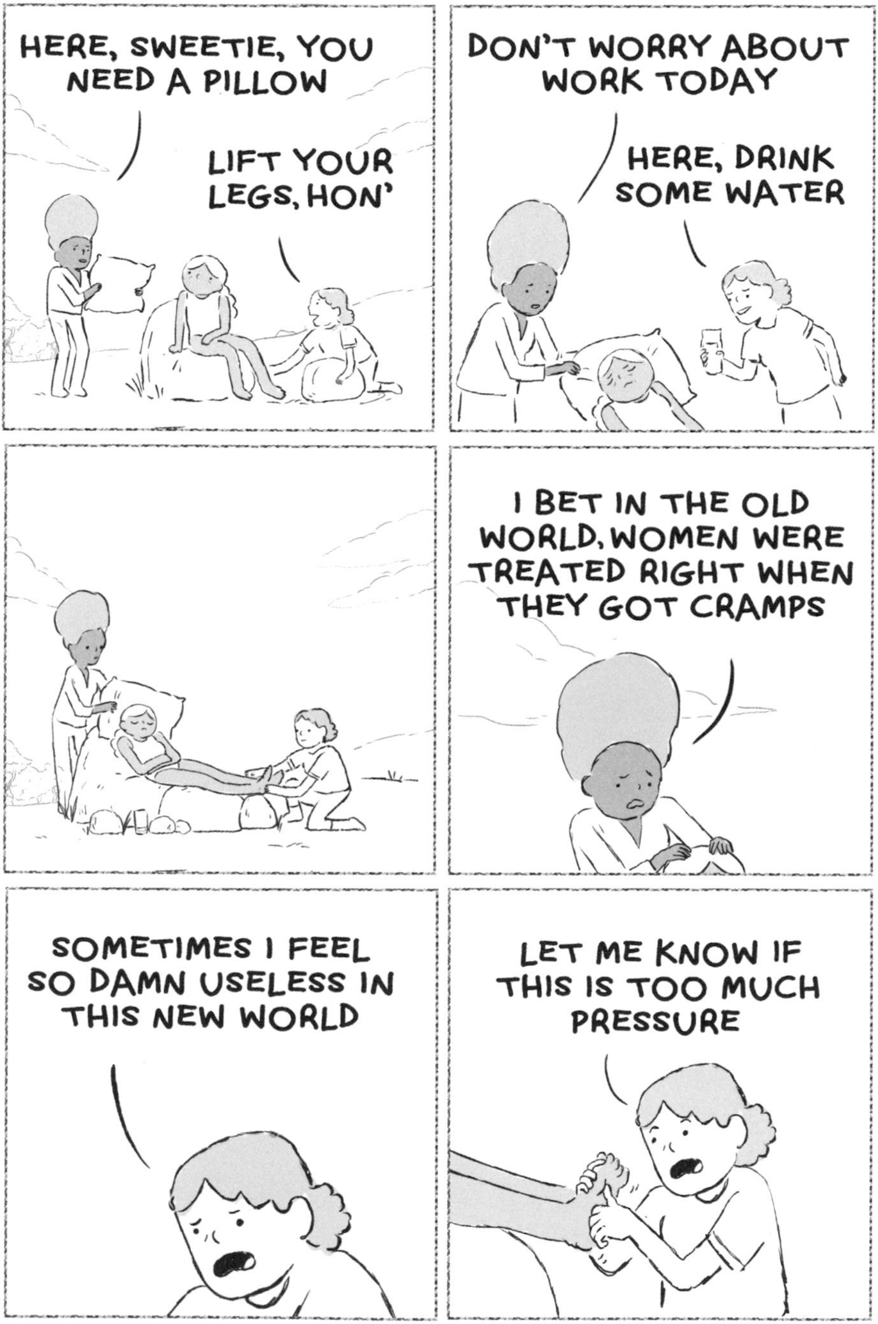
HERE, SWEETIE, YOU NEED A PILLOW
LIFT YOUR LEGS, HON'
DON'T WORRY ABOUT WORK TODAY
HERE, DRINK SOME WATER
I BET IN THE OLD WORLD, WOMEN WERE TREATED RIGHT WHEN THEY GOT CRAMPS
SOMETIMES I FEEL SO DAMN USELESS IN THIS NEW WORLD
LET ME KNOW IF THIS IS TOO MUCH PRESSURE

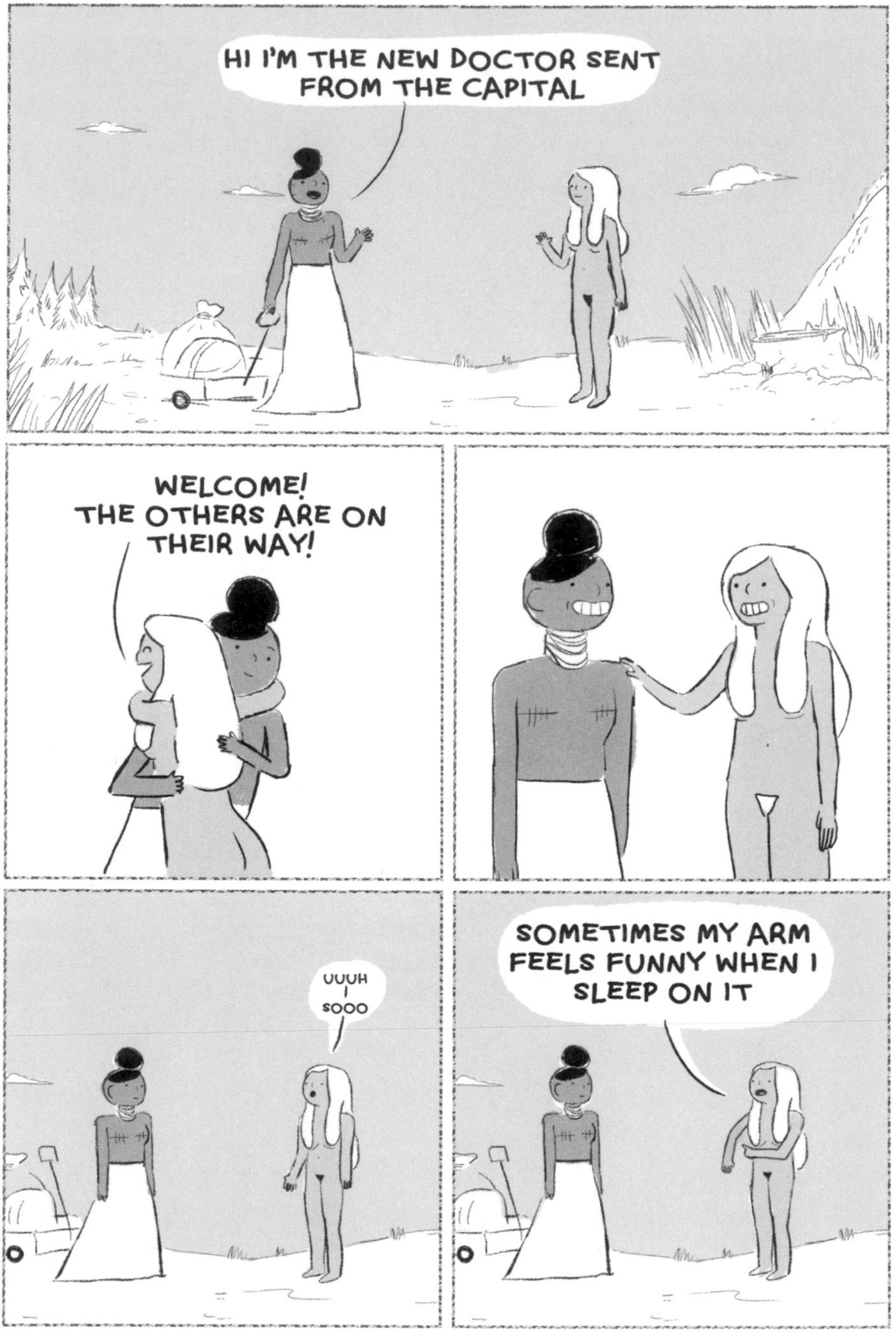
HI I'M THE NEW DOCTOR SENT FROM THE CAPITAL
WELCOME! THE OTHERS ARE ON THEIR WAY!
UUUH I SOOO
SOMETIMES MY ARM FEELS FUNNY WHEN I SLEEP ON IT

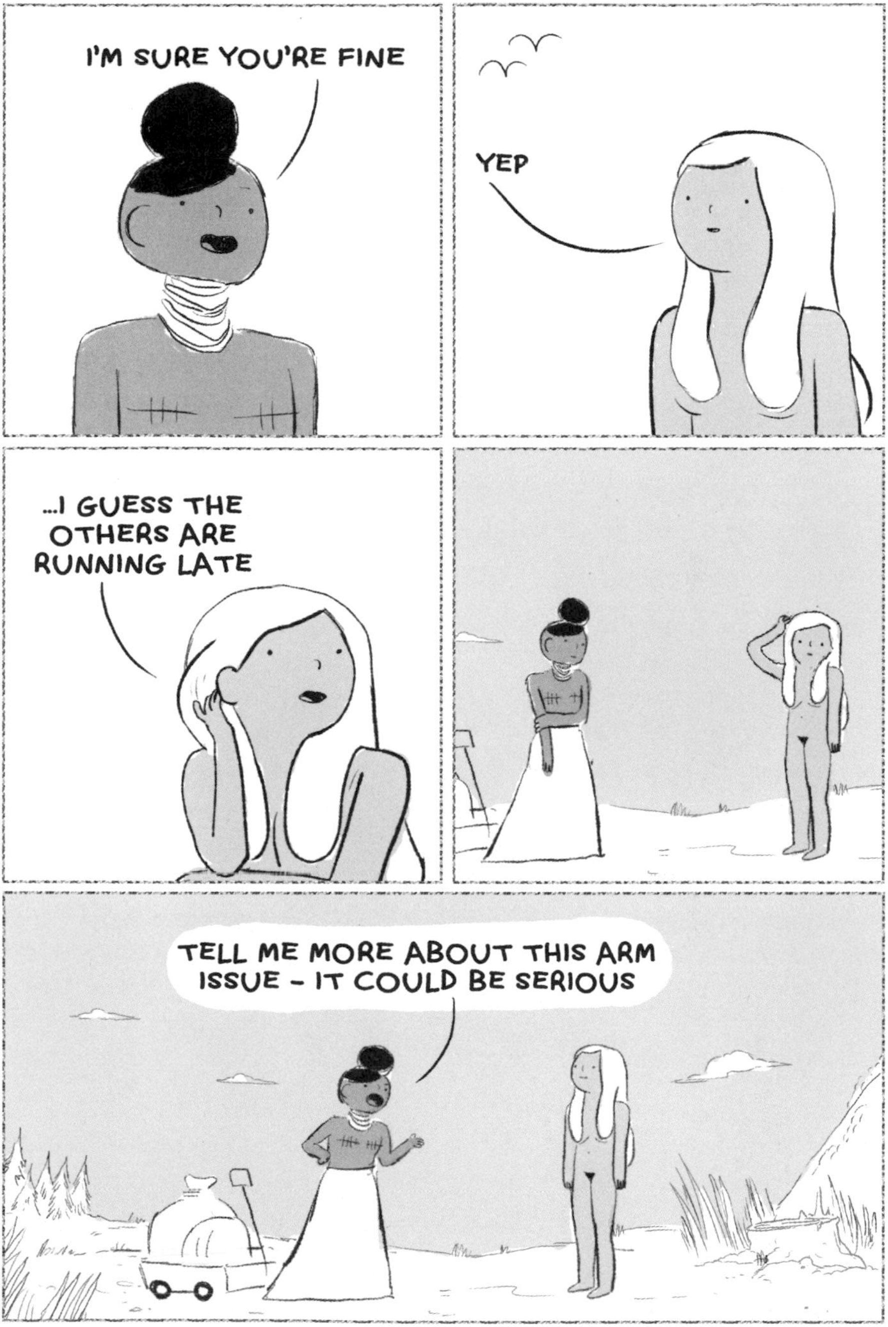
I'M SURE YOU'RE FINE
YEP
...I GUESS THE OTHERS ARE RUNNING LATE
TELL ME MORE ABOUT THIS ARM ISSUE - IT COULD BE SERIOUS

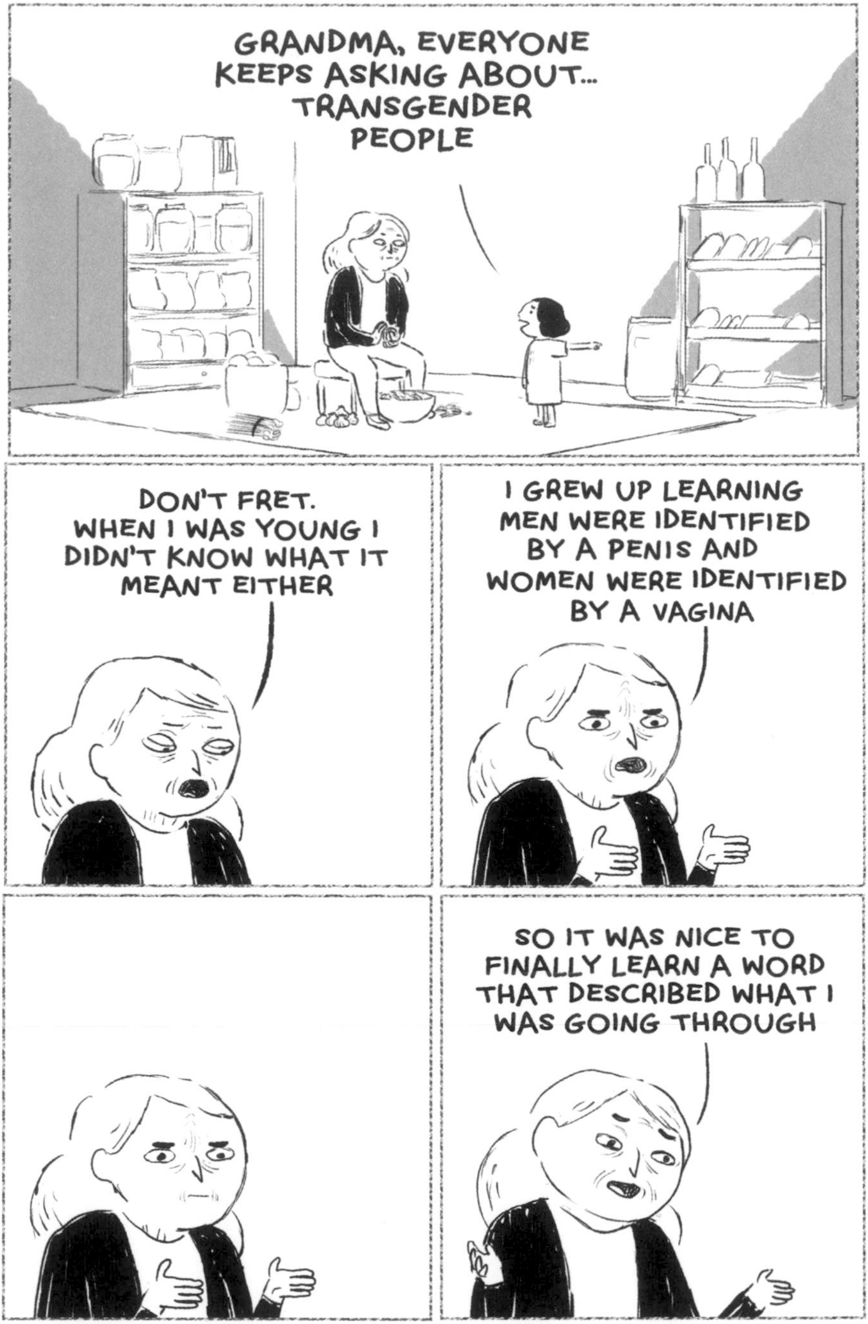
GRANDMA, EVERYONE KEEPS ASKING ABOUT... TRANSGENDER PEOPLE
DON'T FRET. WHEN I WAS YOUNG I DIDN'T KNOW WHAT IT MEANT EITHER
I GREW UP LEARNING MEN WERE IDENTIFIED BY A PENIS AND WOMEN WERE IDENTIFIED BY A VAGINA
SO IT WAS NICE TO FINALLY LEARN A WORD THAT DESCRIBED WHAT I WAS GOING THROUGH

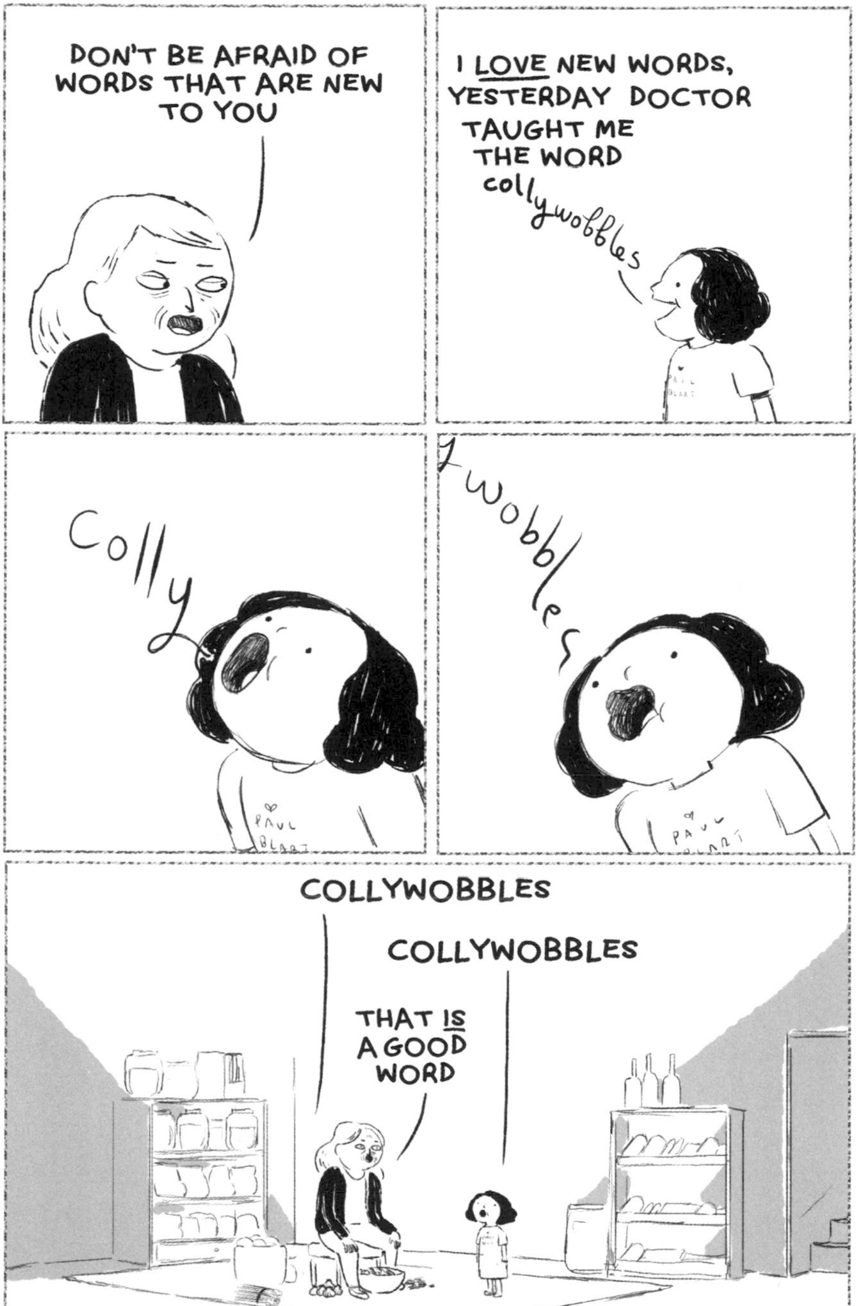
DON'T BE AFRAID OF WORDS THAT ARE NEW TO YOU
I LOVE NEW WORDS, YESTERDAY DOCTOR TAUGHT ME THE WORD collywobbles
Colly
wobbles
COLLYWOBBLES
COLLYWOBBLES
THAT IS A GOOD WORD

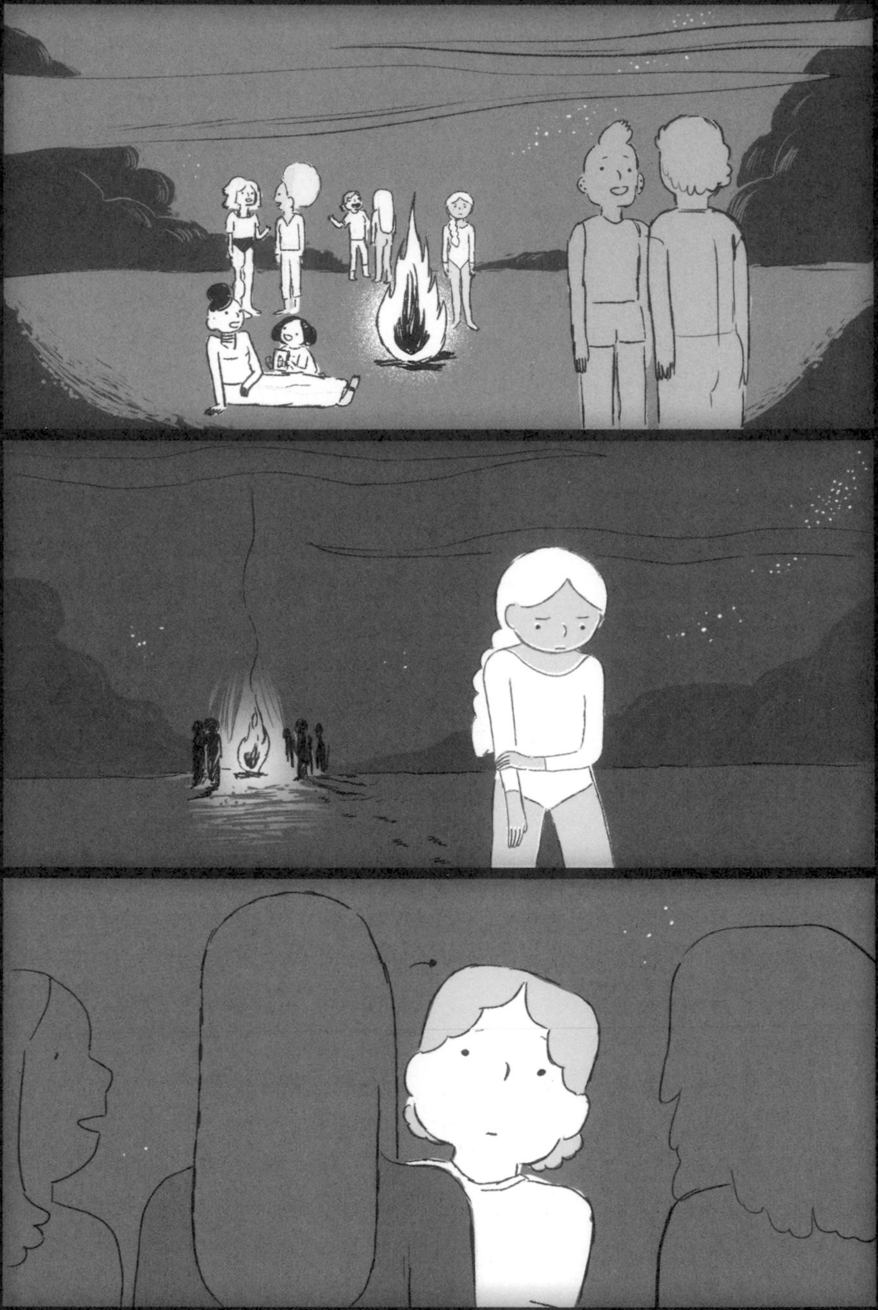

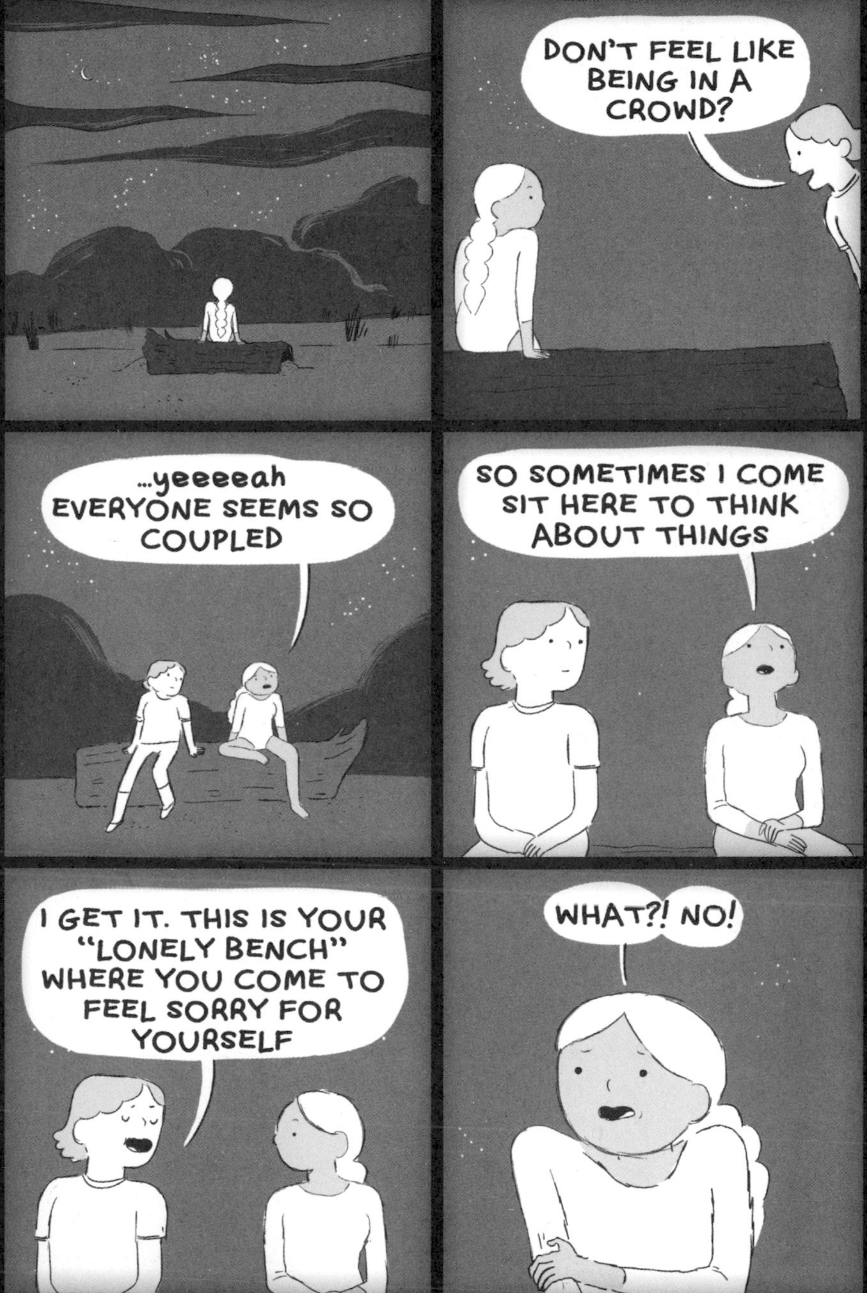
DON'T FEEL LIKE BEING IN A CROWD?
...yeeeeah EVERYONE SEEMS SO COUPLED
SO SOMETIMES I COME SIT HERE TO THINK ABOUT THINGS
I GET IT. THIS IS YOUR "LONELY BENCH" WHERE YOU COME TO FEEL SORRY FOR YOURSELF
WHAT?! NO!

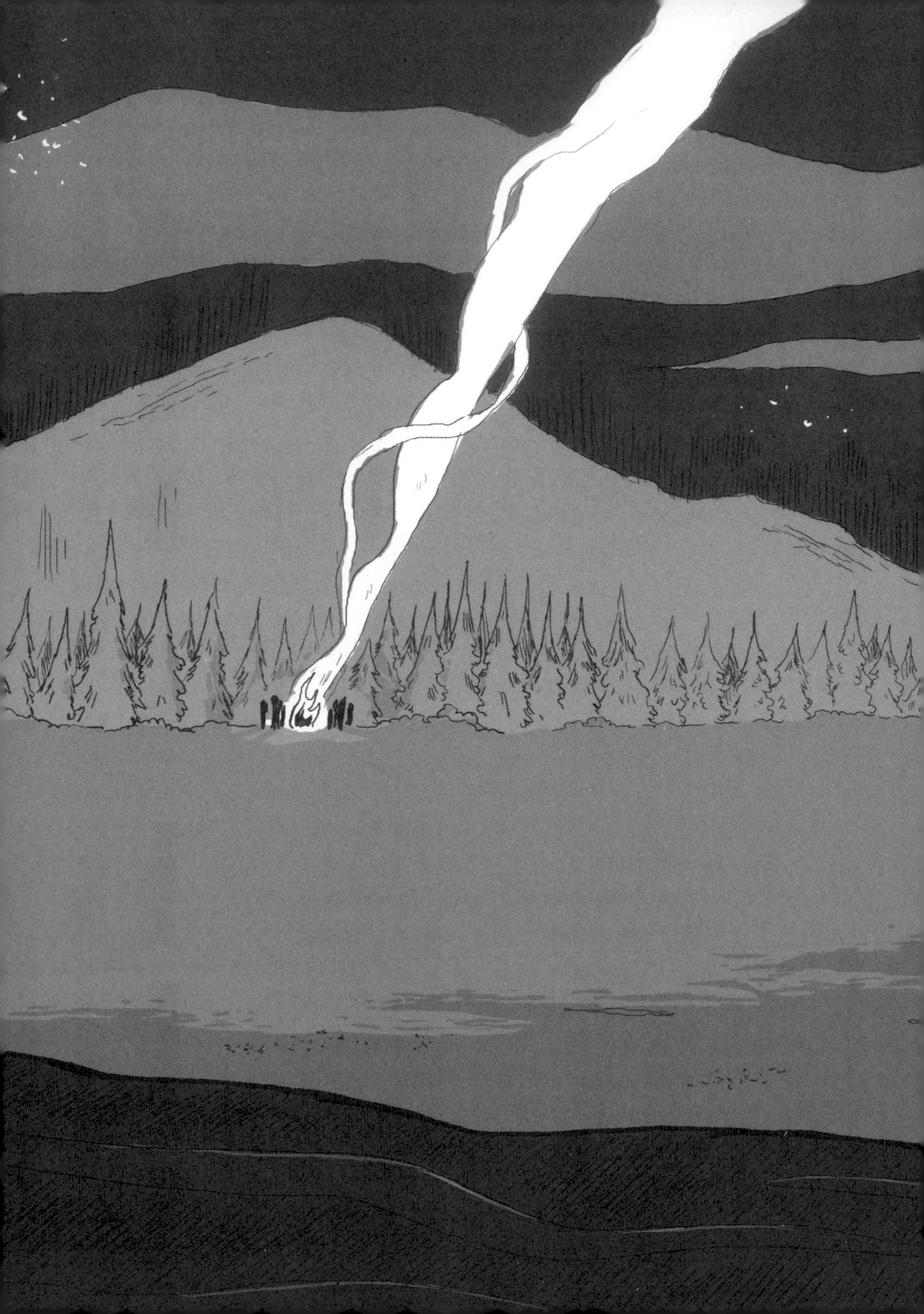

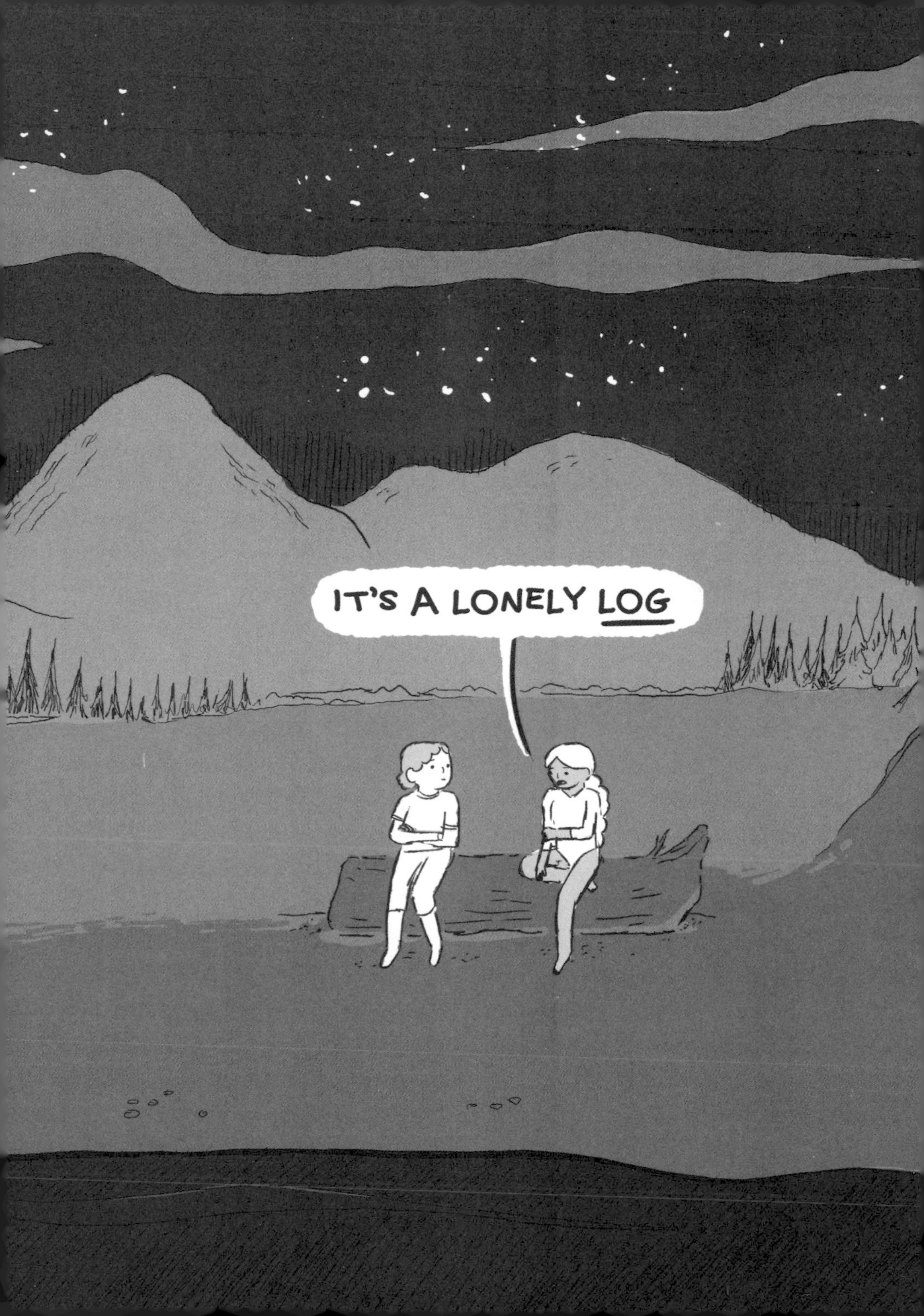
IT'S A LONELY LOG

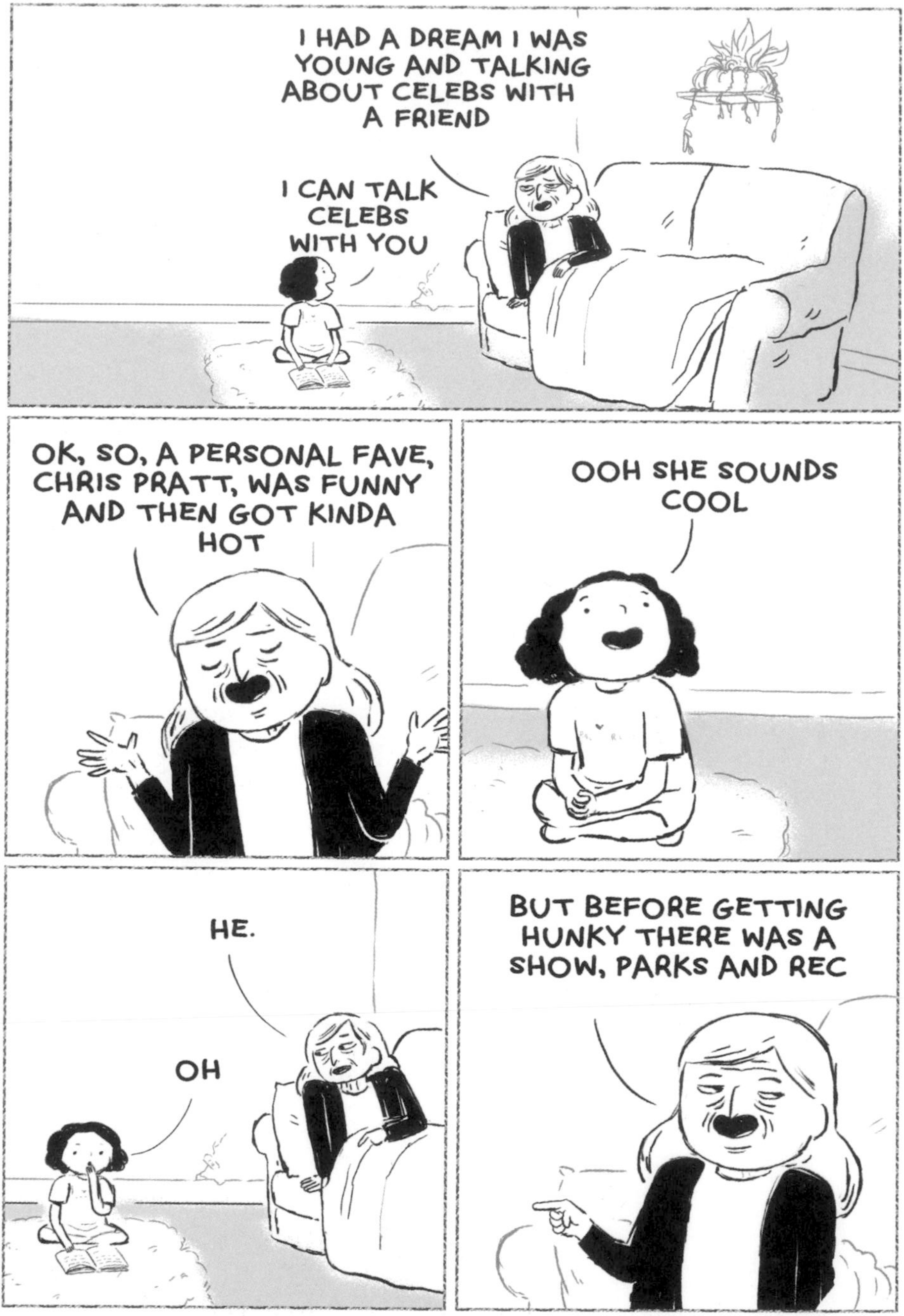
I HAD A DREAM I WAS YOUNG AND TALKING ABOUT CELEBS WITH A FRIEND
I CAN TALK CELEBS WITH YOU
OK, SO, A PERSONAL FAVE, CHRIS PRATT, WAS FUNNY AND THEN GOT KINDA HOT
OOH SHE SOUNDS COOL
HE.
OH
BUT BEFORE GETTING HUNKY THERE WAS A SHOW, PARKS AND REC

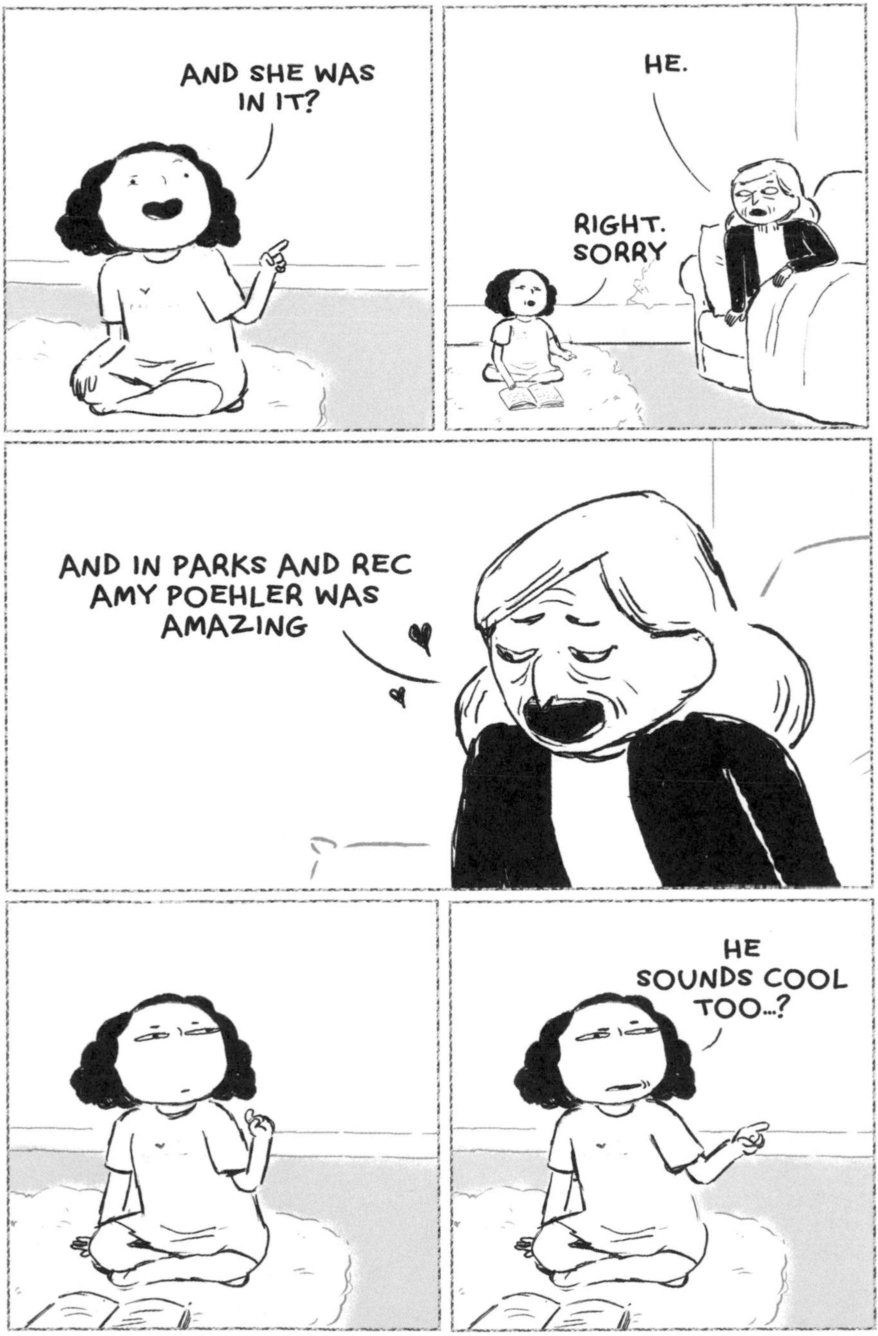
AND SHE WAS IN IT?
HE.
RIGHT. SORRY
AND IN PARKS AND REC AMY POEHLER WAS AMAZING
HE SOUNDS COOL TOO...?

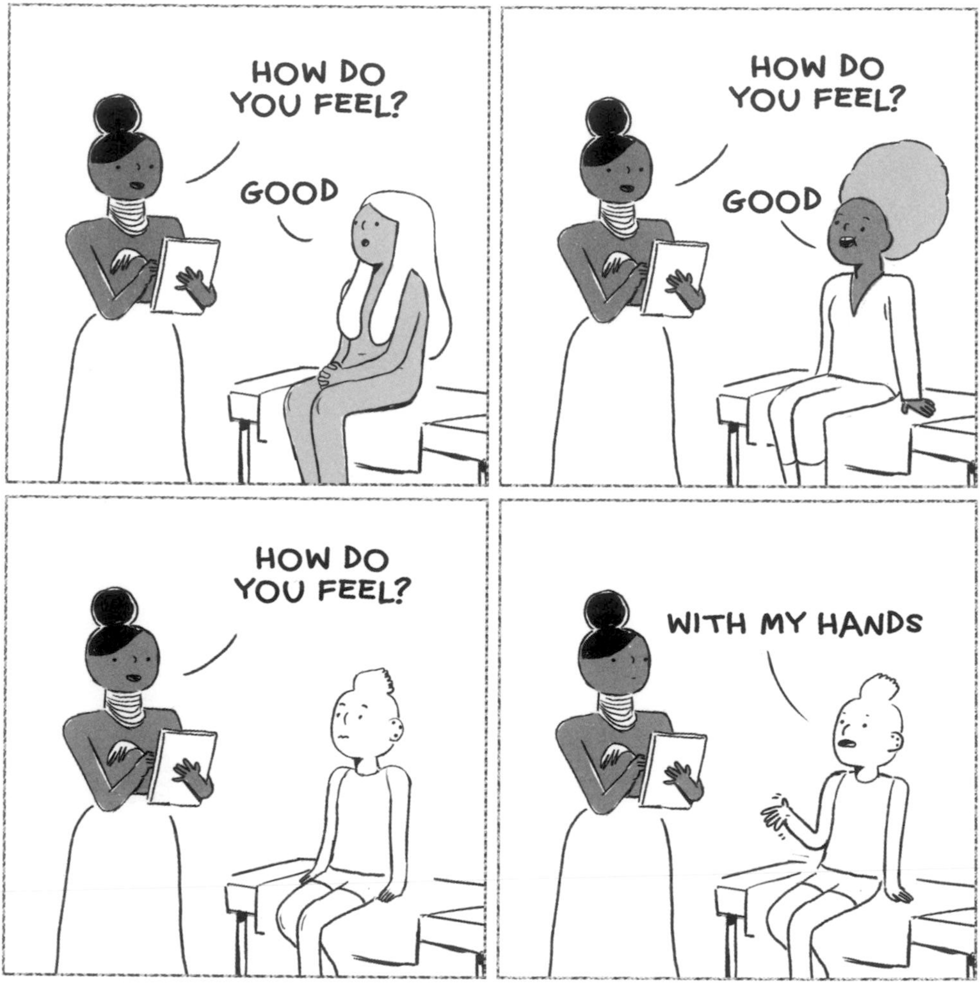
HOW DO YOU FEEL?
GOOD
HOW DO YOU FEEL?
GOOD
HOW DO YOU FEEL?
WITH MY HANDS

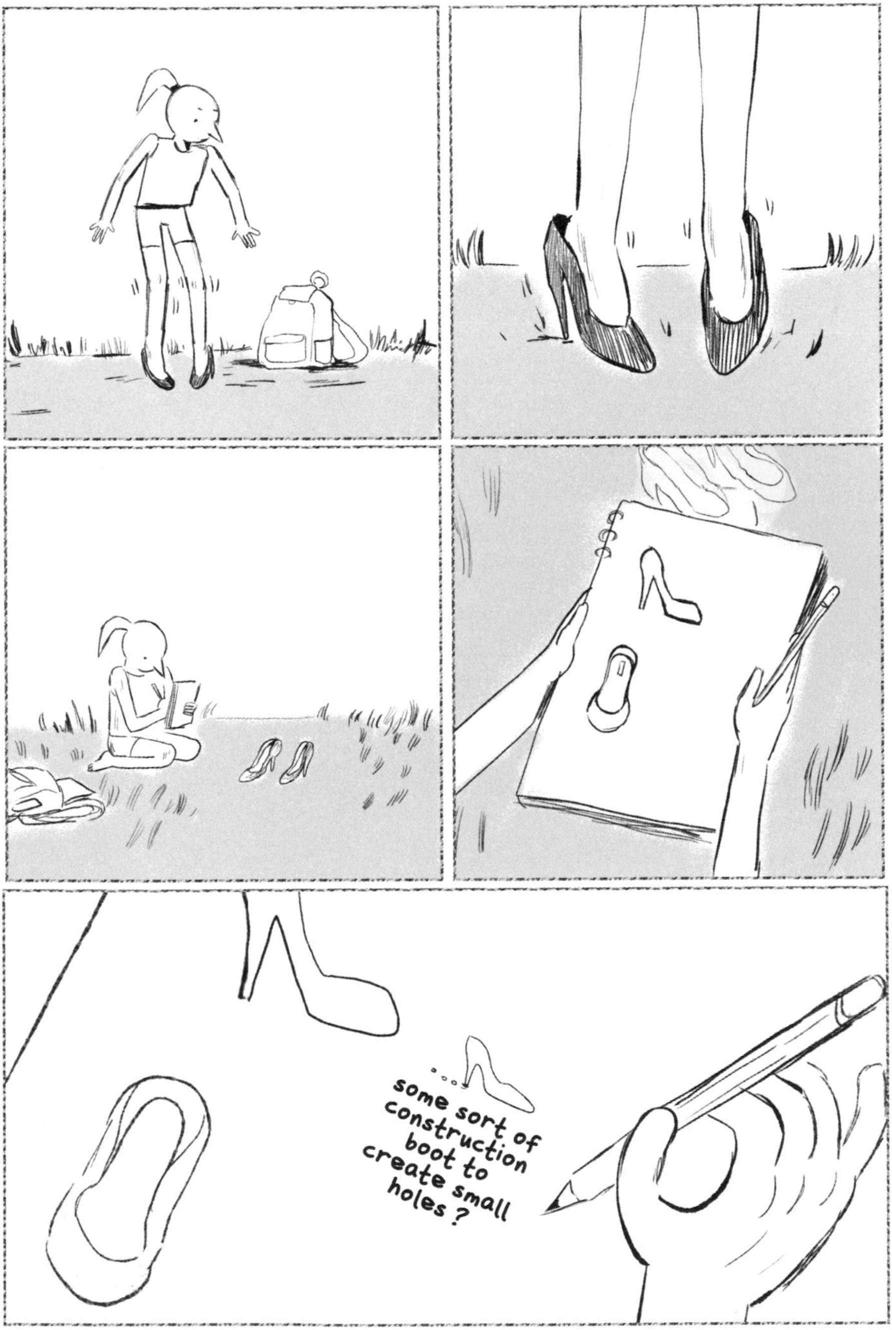
...
some sort of construction boot to create small holes ?

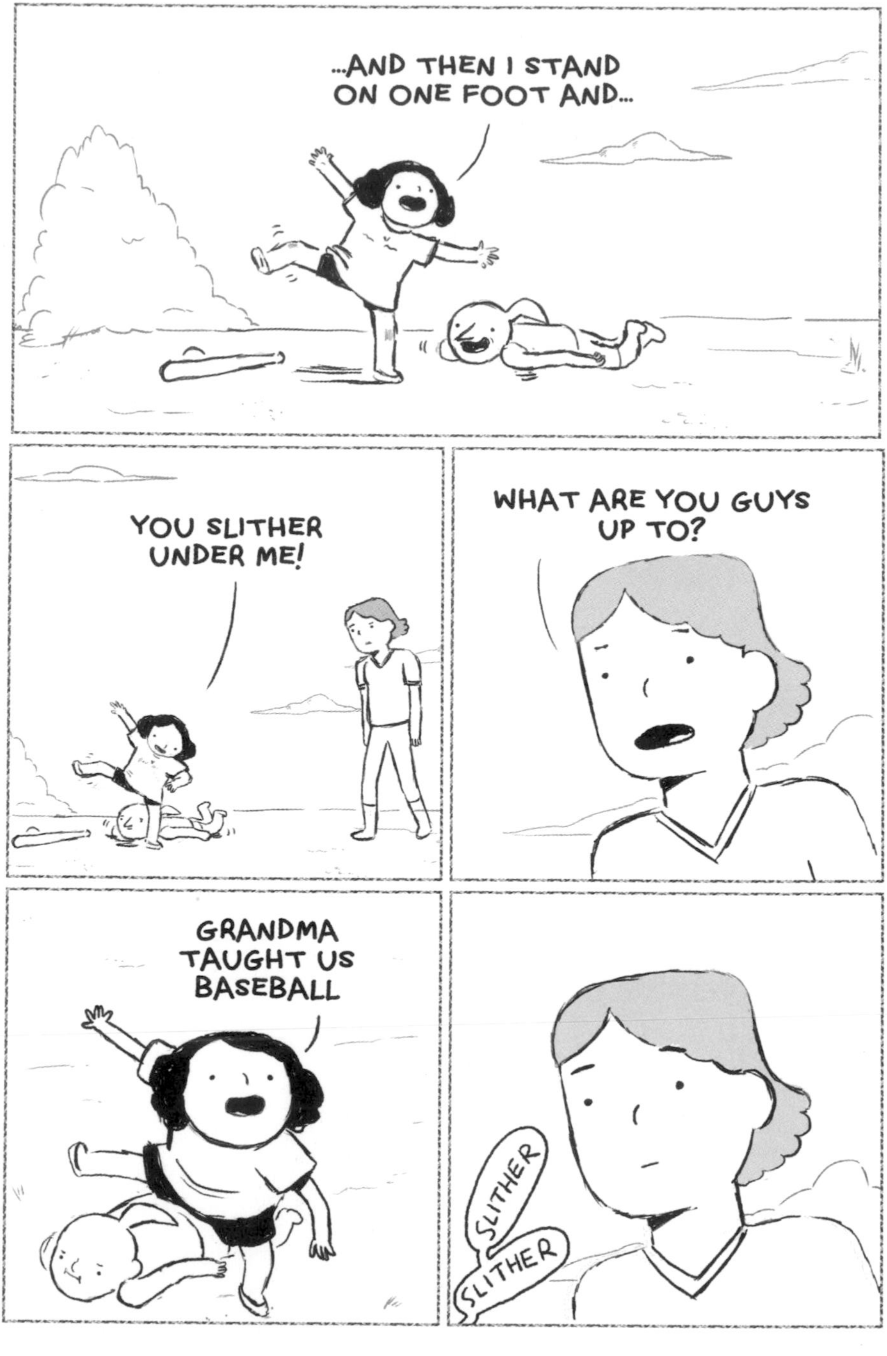
...AND THEN I STAND ON ONE FOOT AND...
YOU SLITHER UNDER ME!
WHAT ARE YOU GUYS UP TO?
GRANDMA TAUGHT US BASEBALL
SLITHER
SLITHER

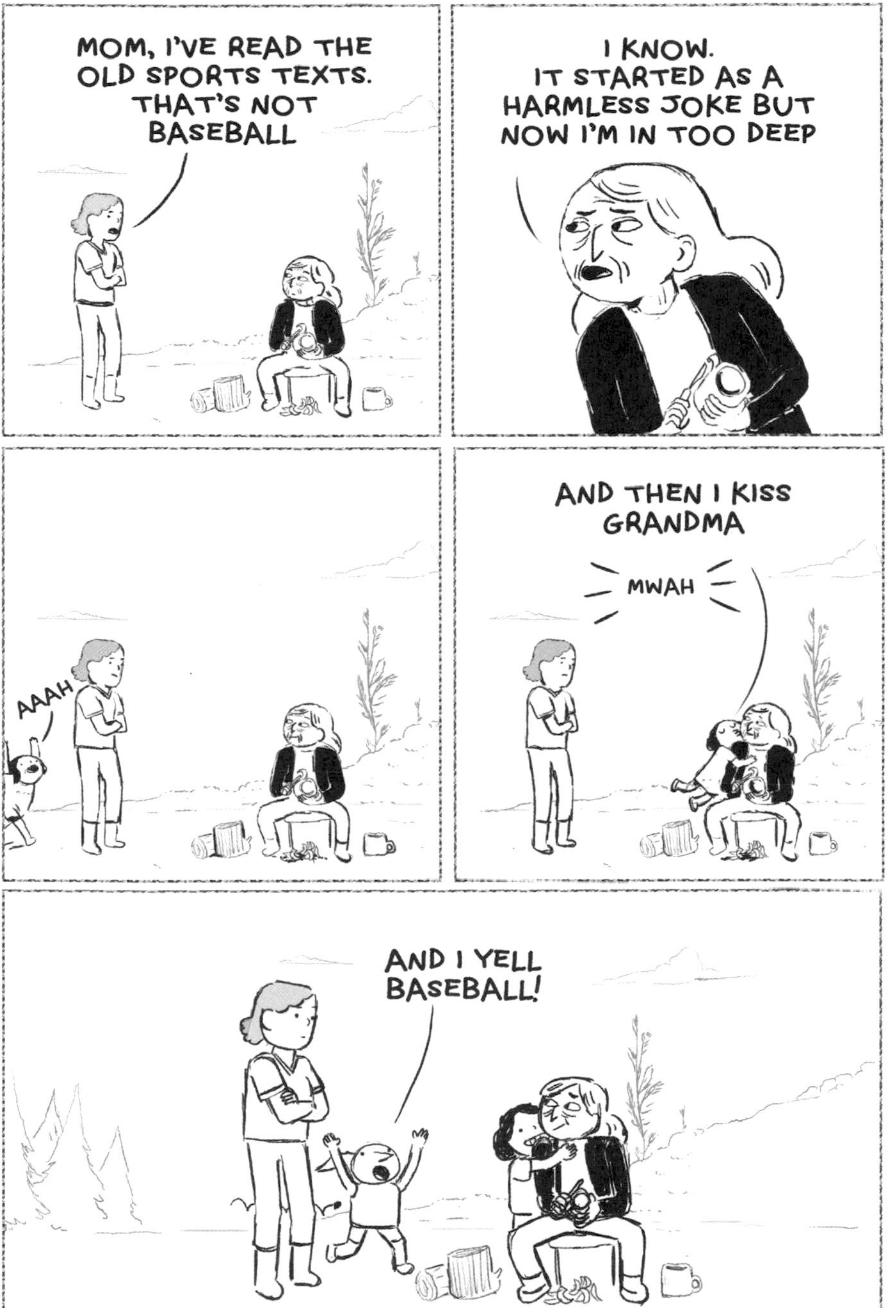
MOM, I'VE READ THE OLD SPORTS TEXTS. THAT'S NOT BASEBALL
I KNOW. IT STARTED AS A HARMLESS JOKE BUT NOW I'M IN TOO DEEP
AAAH
AND THEN I KISS GRANDMA
MWAH
AND I YELL BASEBALL!

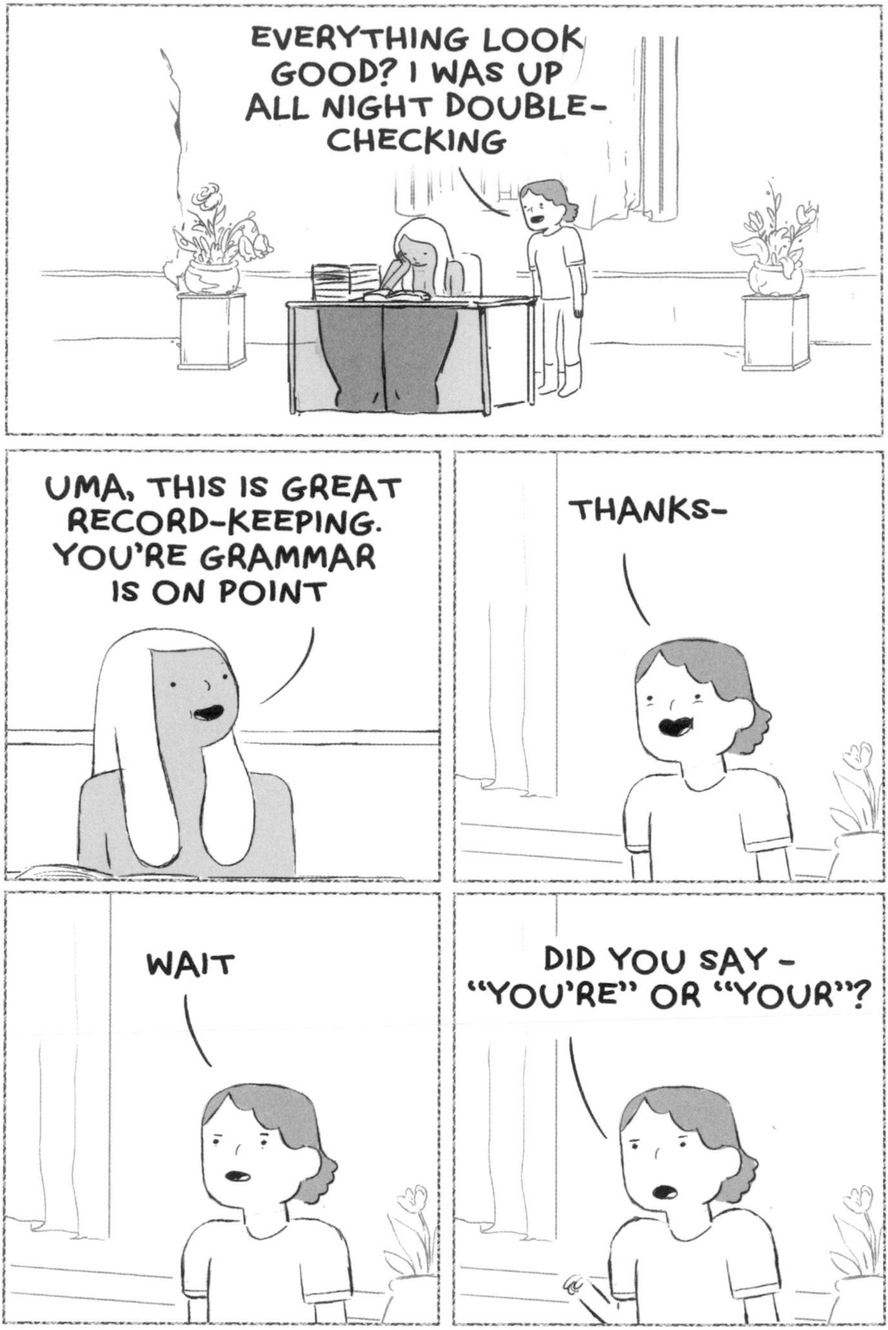
EVERYTHING LOOK GOOD? I WAS UP ALL NIGHT DOUBLE-CHECKING
UMA, THIS IS GREAT RECORD-KEEPING. YOU'RE GRAMMAR IS ON POINT
THANKS-
WAIT
DID YOU SAY - "YOU'RE" OR "YOUR"?

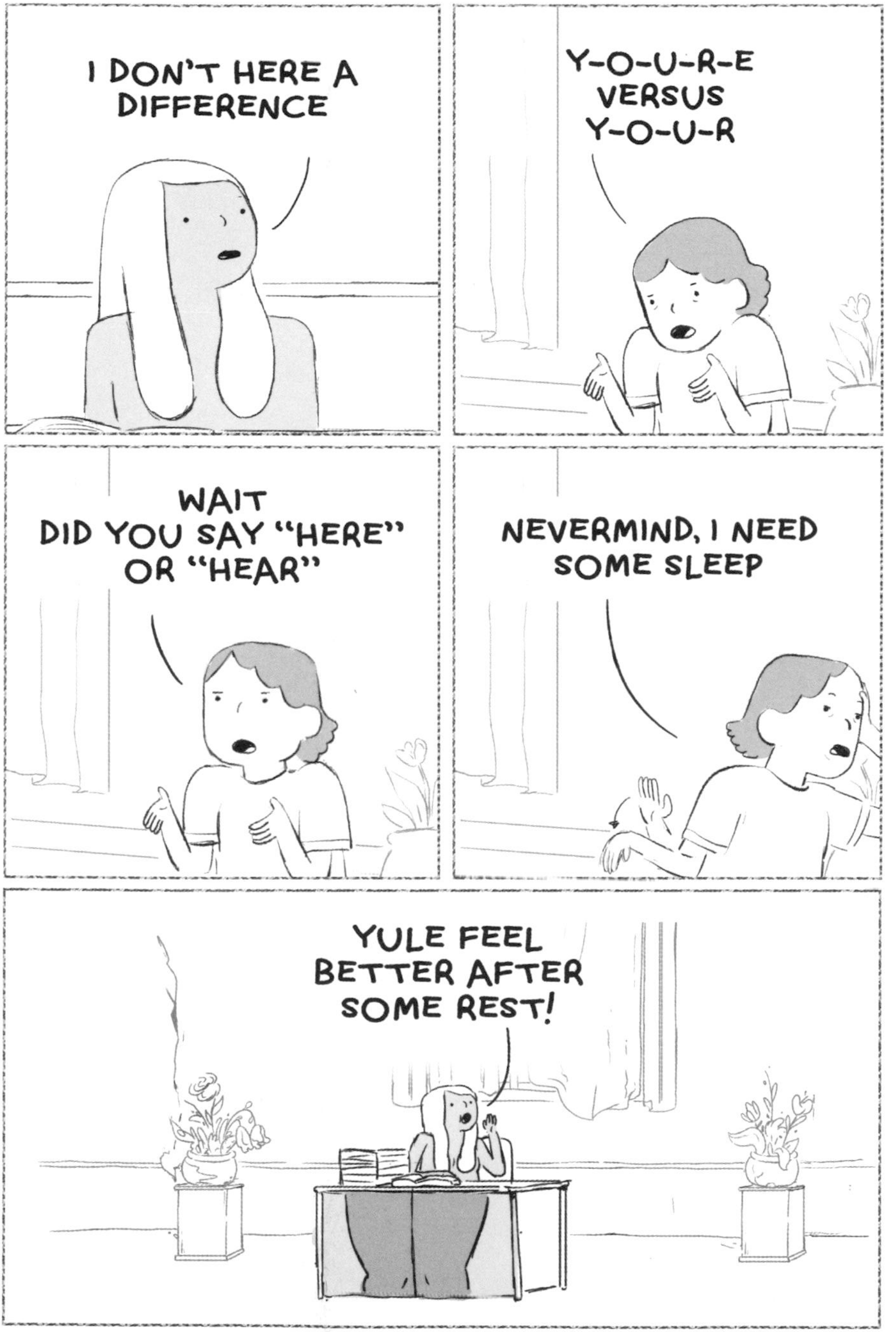
I DON'T HERE A DIFFERENCE
Y-O-U-R-E VERSUS Y-O-U-R
WAIT DID YOU SAY "HERE" OR "HEAR"
NEVERMIND, I NEED SOME SLEEP
YULE FEEL BETTER AFTER SOME REST!

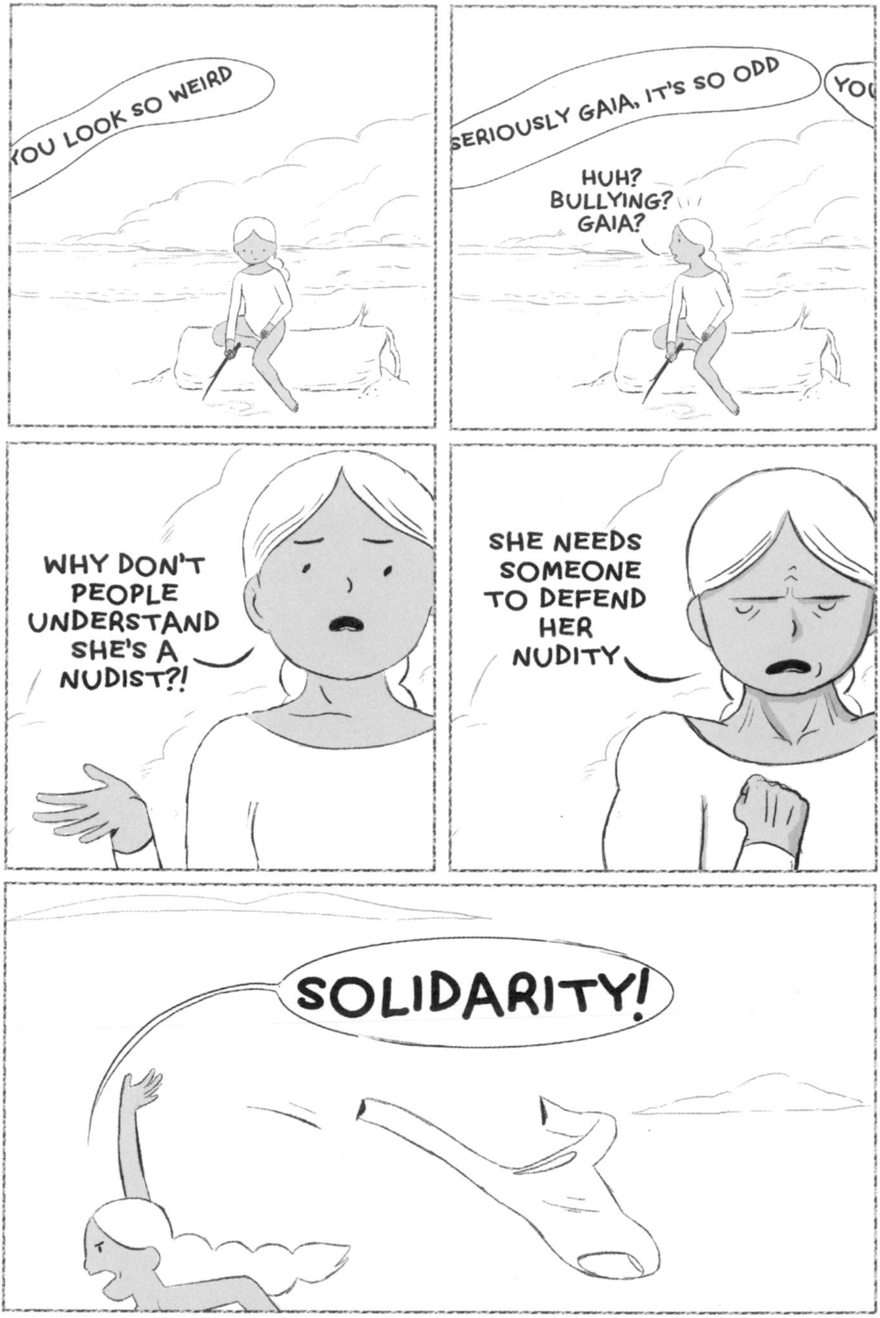
YOU LOOK SO WEIRD
SERIOUSLY GAIA, IT'S SO ODD
HUH? BULLYING? GAIA?
WHY DON'T PEOPLE UNDERSTAND SHE'S A NUDIST?!
SHE NEEDS SOMEONE TO DEFEND HER NUDITY
SOLIDARITY!

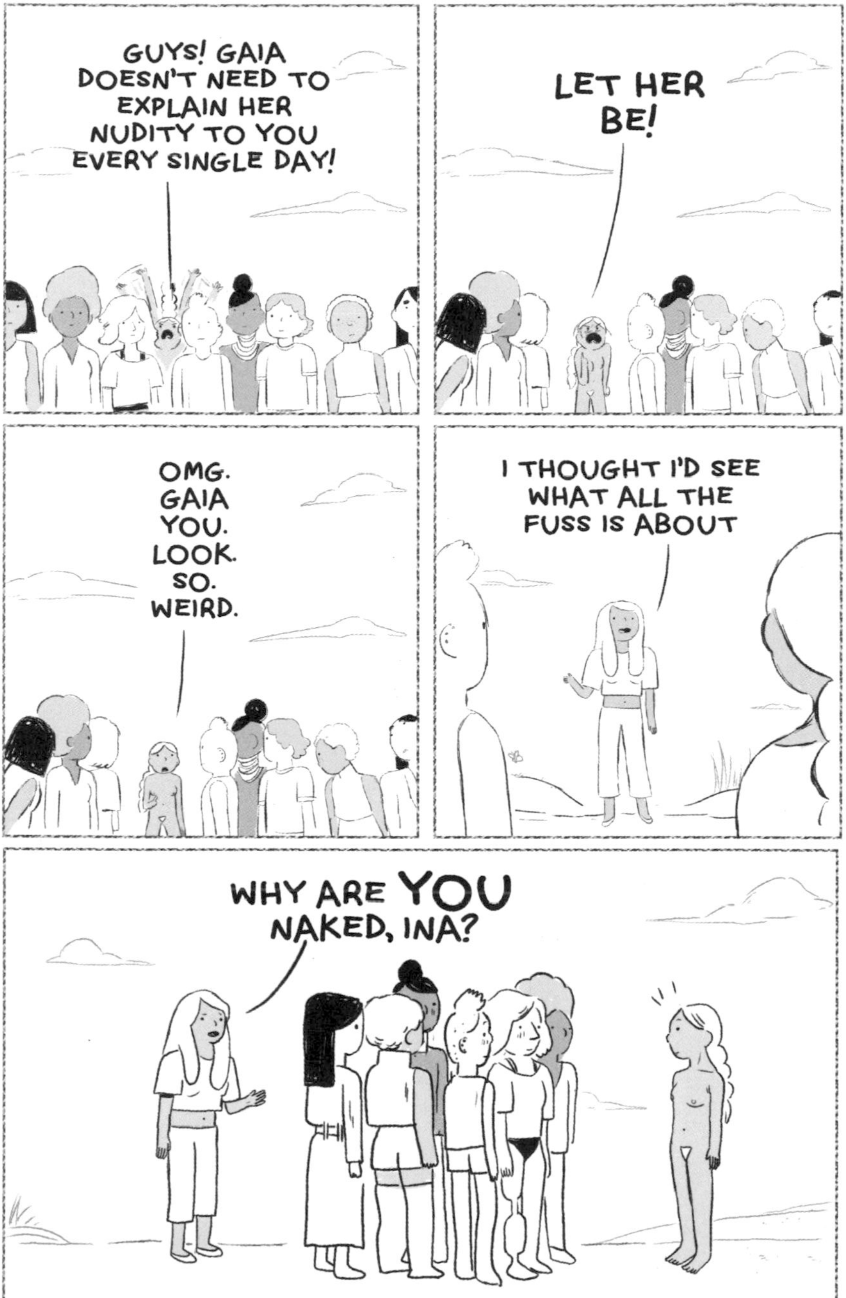
GUYS! GAIA DOESN'T NEED TO EXPLAIN HER NUDITY TO YOU EVERY SINGLE DAY!
LET HER BE!
OMG. GAIA YOU. LOOK. SO. WEIRD.
I THOUGHT I'D SEE WHAT ALL THE FUSS IS ABOUT
WHY ARE YOU NAKED, INA?

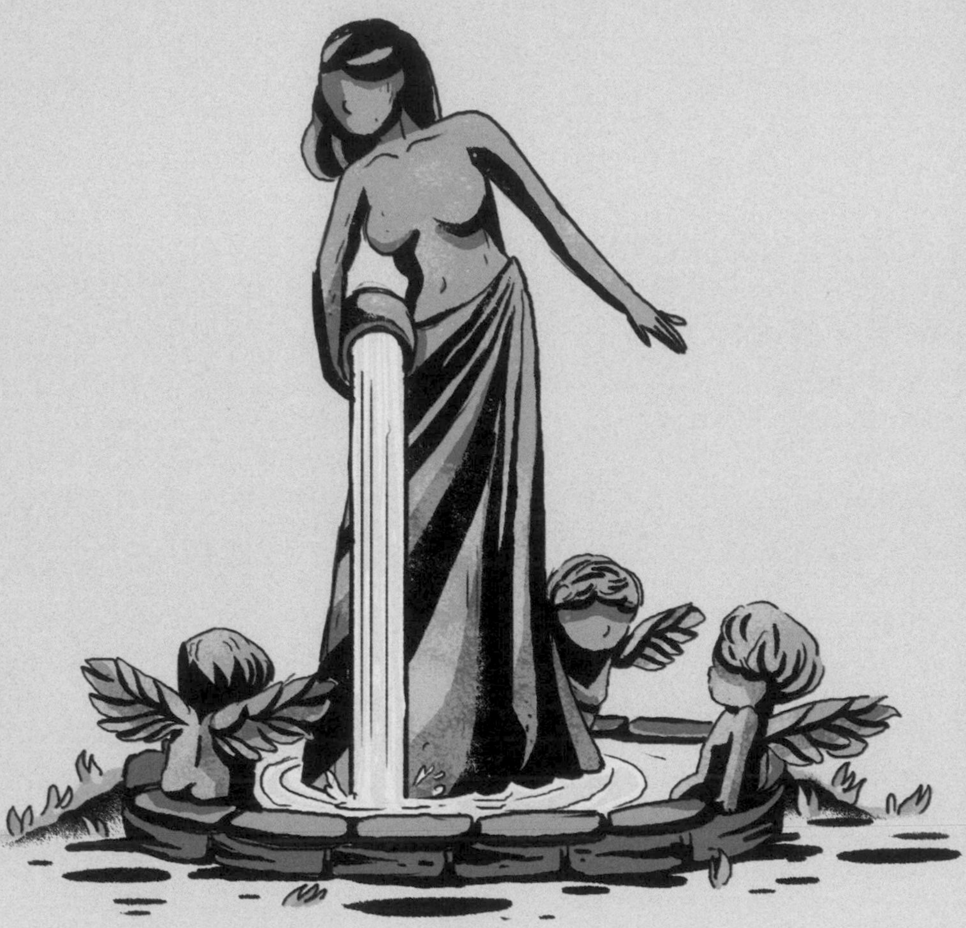

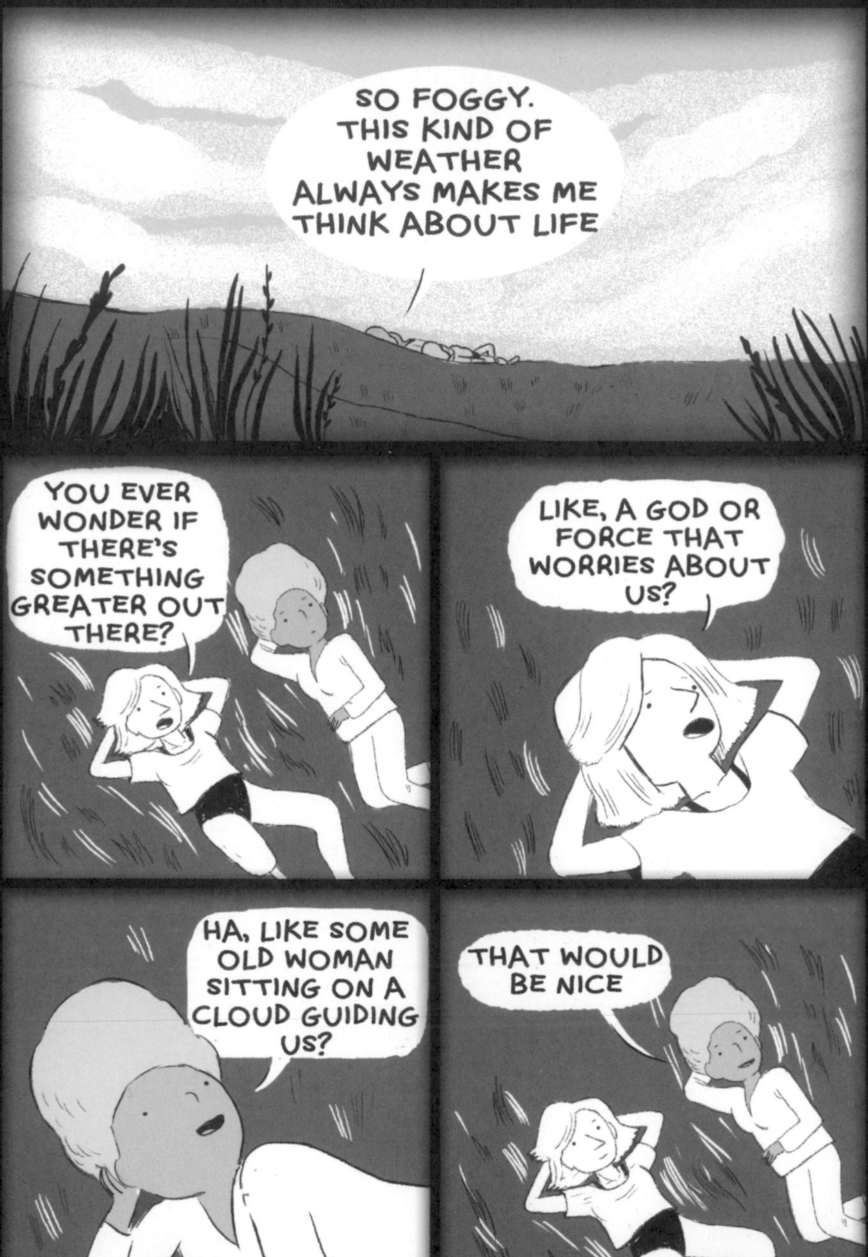
SO FOGGY. THIS KIND OF WEATHER ALWAYS MAKES ME THINK ABOUT LIFE
YOU EVER WONDER IF THERE'S SOMETHING GREATER OUT THERE?
LIKE, A GOD OR FORCE THAT WORRIES ABOUT US?
HA, LIKE SOME OLD WOMAN SITTING ON A CLOUD GUIDING US?
THAT WOULD BE NICE

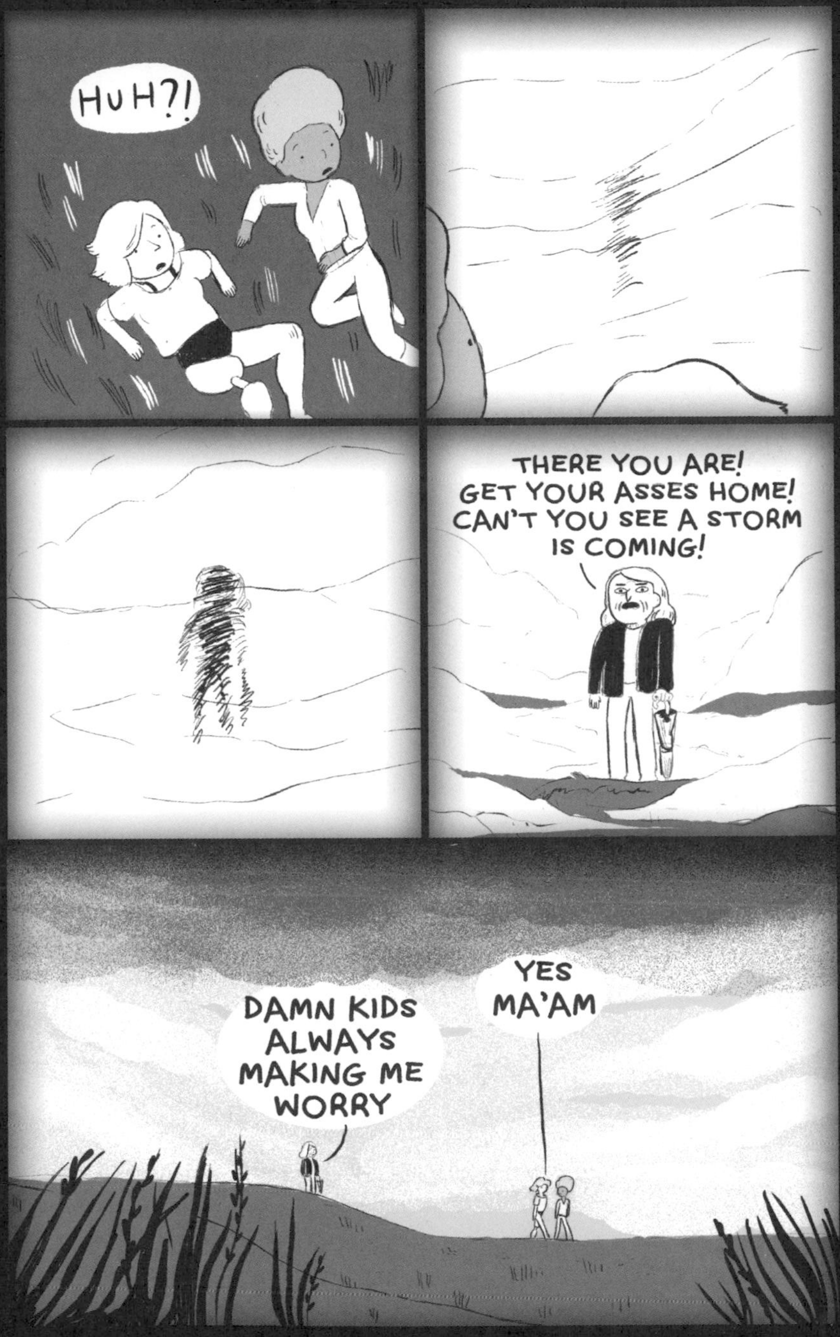
HUH?!
THERE YOU ARE! GET YOUR ASSES HOME! CAN'T YOU SEE A STORM IS COMING!
DAMN KIDS ALWAYS MAKING ME WORRY
YES MA'AM

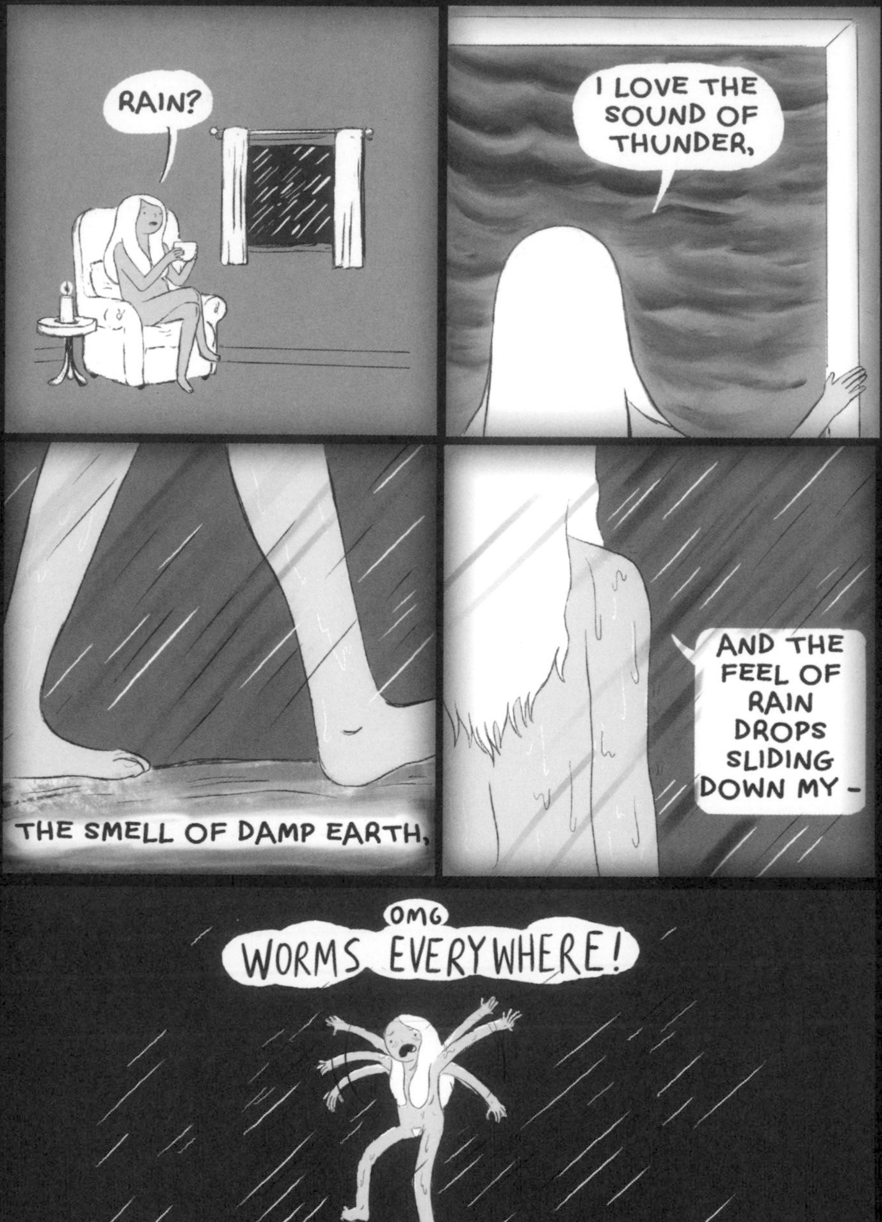
RAIN?
I LOVE THE SOUND OF THUNDER,
THE SMELL OF DAMP EARTH,
AND THE FEEL OF RAIN DROPS SLIDING DOWN MY -
OMG
WORMS EVERYWHERE!

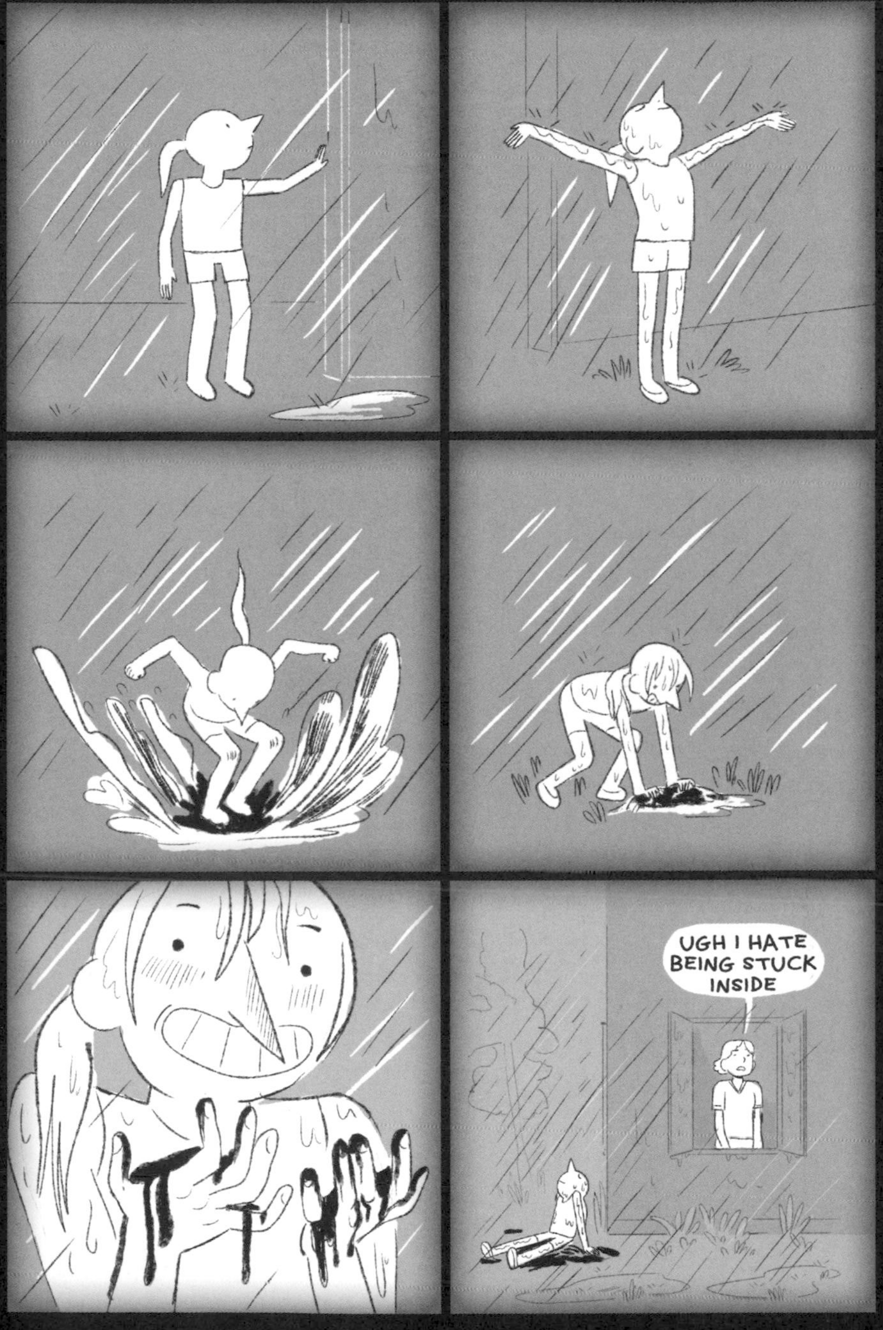
UGH I HATE BEING STUCK INSIDE

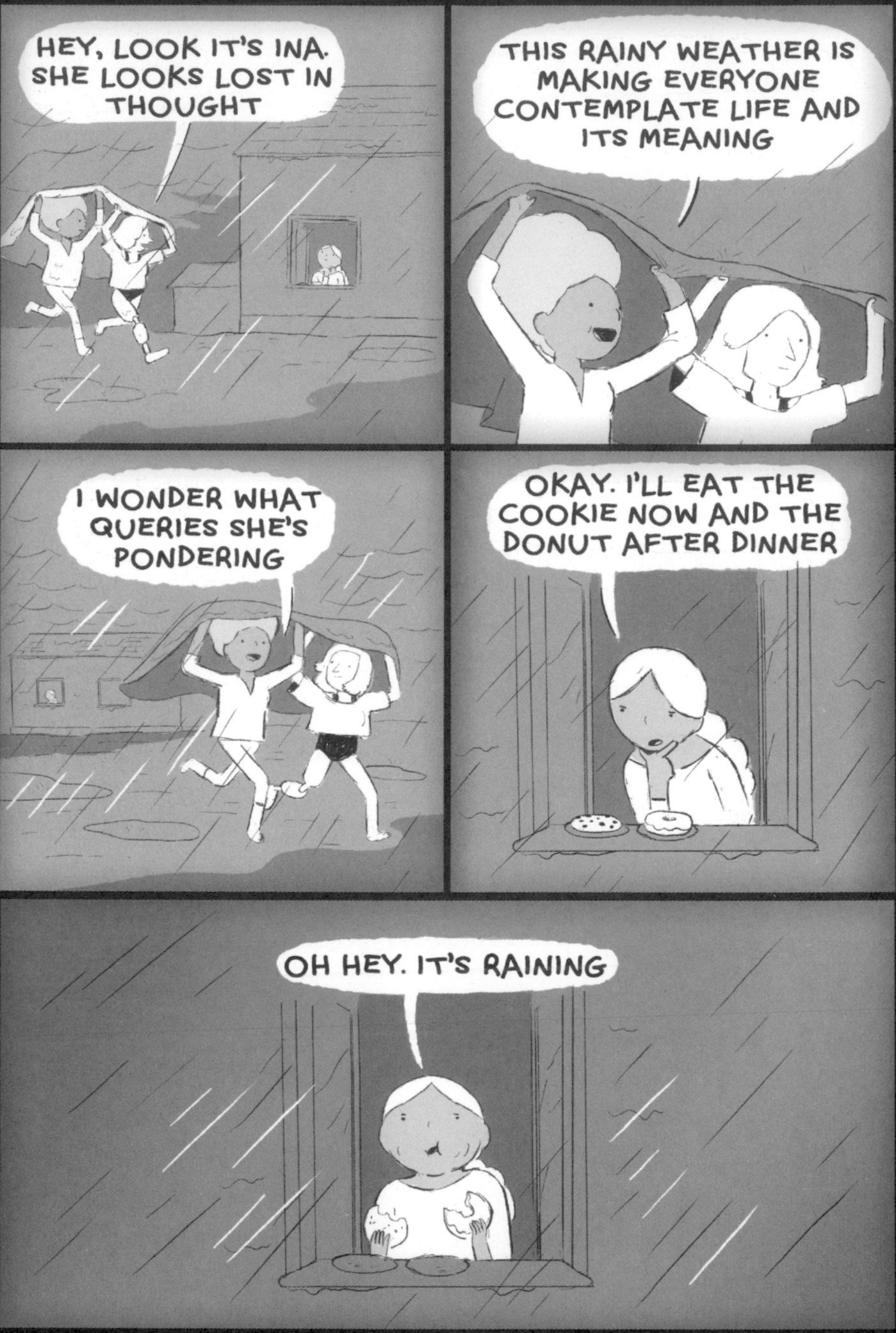
HEY, LOOK IT'S INA. SHE LOOKS LOST IN THOUGHT
THIS RAINY WEATHER IS MAKING EVERYONE CONTEMPLATE LIFE AND ITS MEANING
I WONDER WHAT QUERIES SHE'S PONDERING
OKAY. I'LL EAT THE COOKIE NOW AND THE DONUT AFTER DINNER
OH HEY. IT'S RAINING

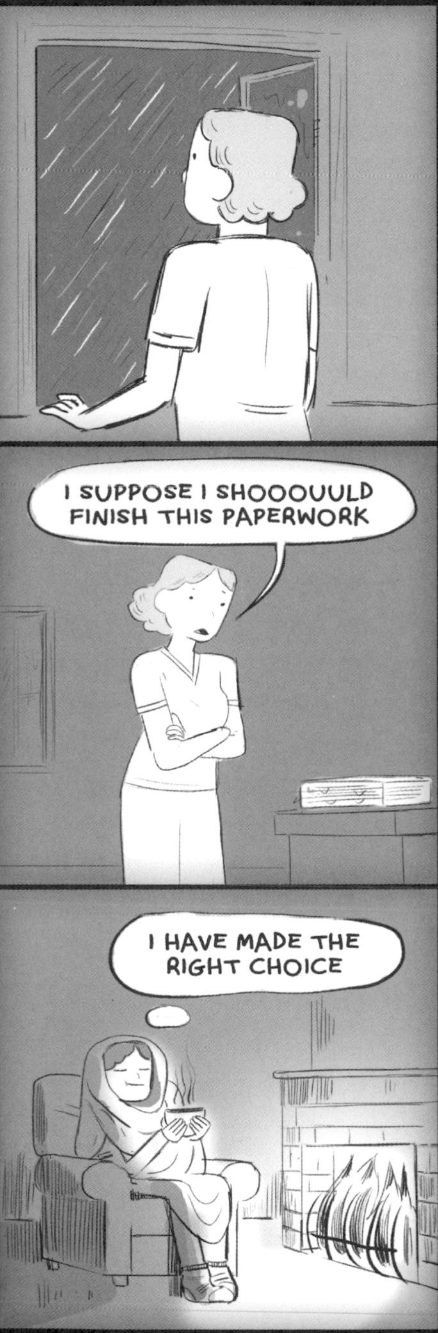
I SUPPOSE I SHOOOUULD FINISH THIS PAPERWORK
I HAVE MADE THE RIGHT CHOICE

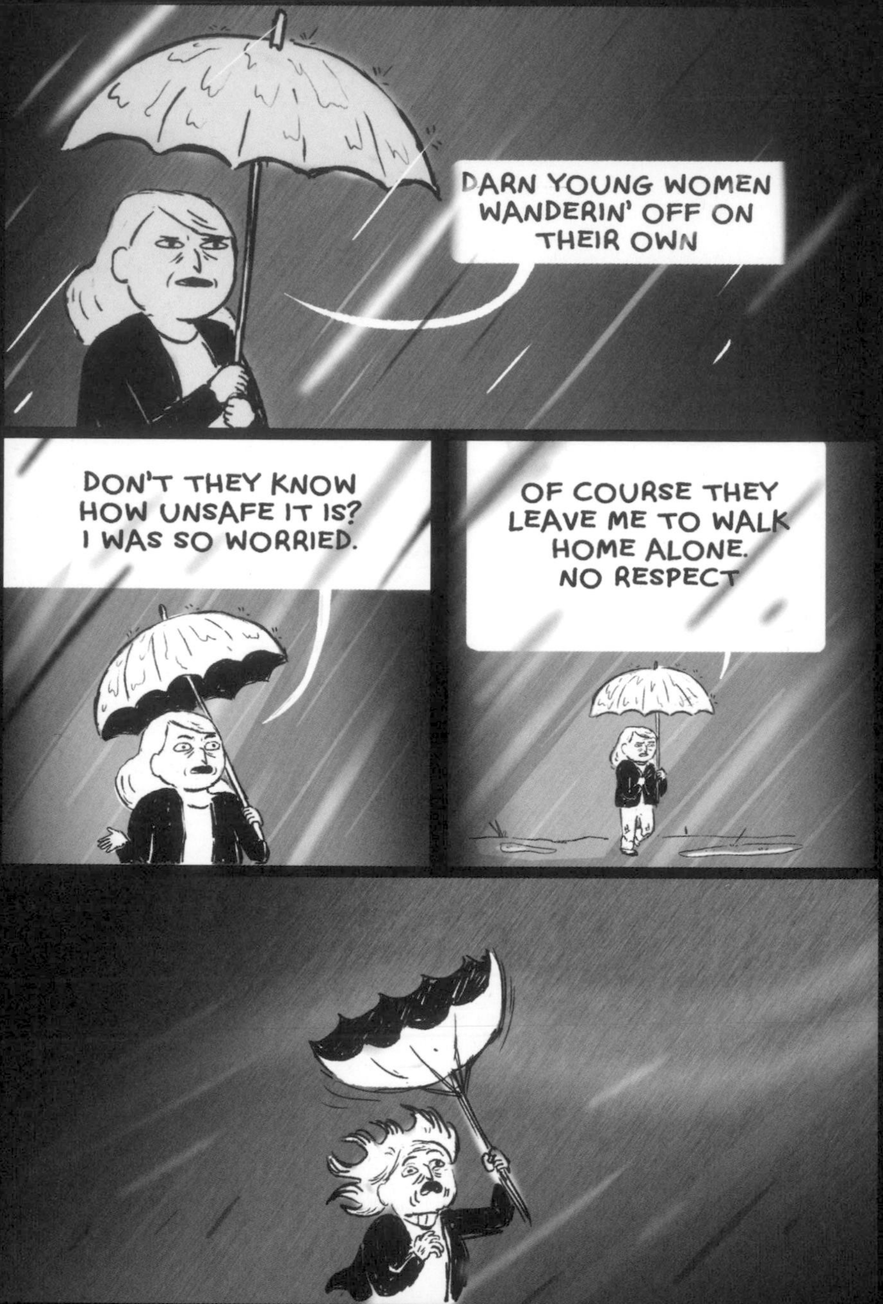
DARN YOUNG WOMEN WANDERIN' OFF ON THEIR OWN
DON'T THEY KNOW HOW UNSAFE IT IS? I WAS SO WORRIED.
OF COURSE THEY LEAVE ME TO WALK HOME ALONE. NO RESPECT

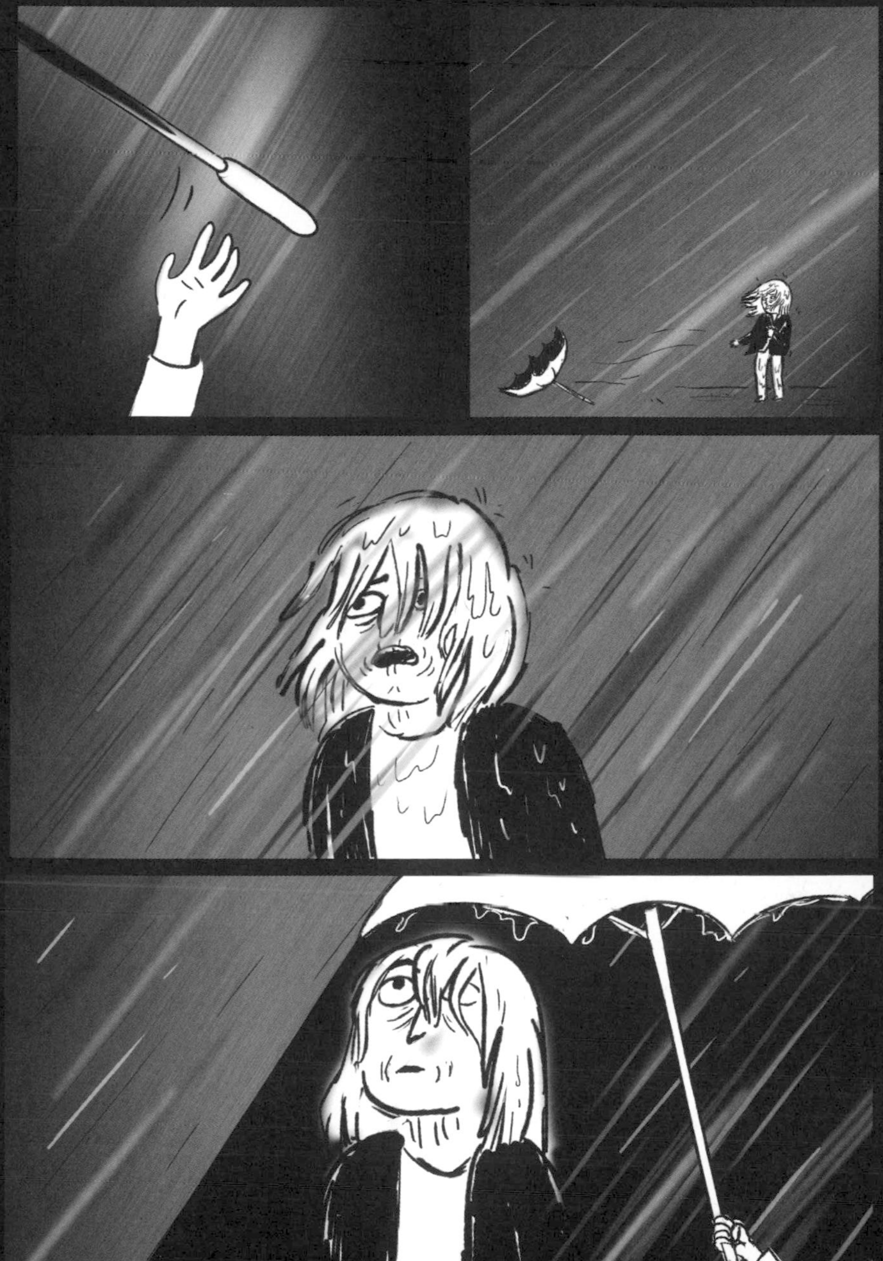

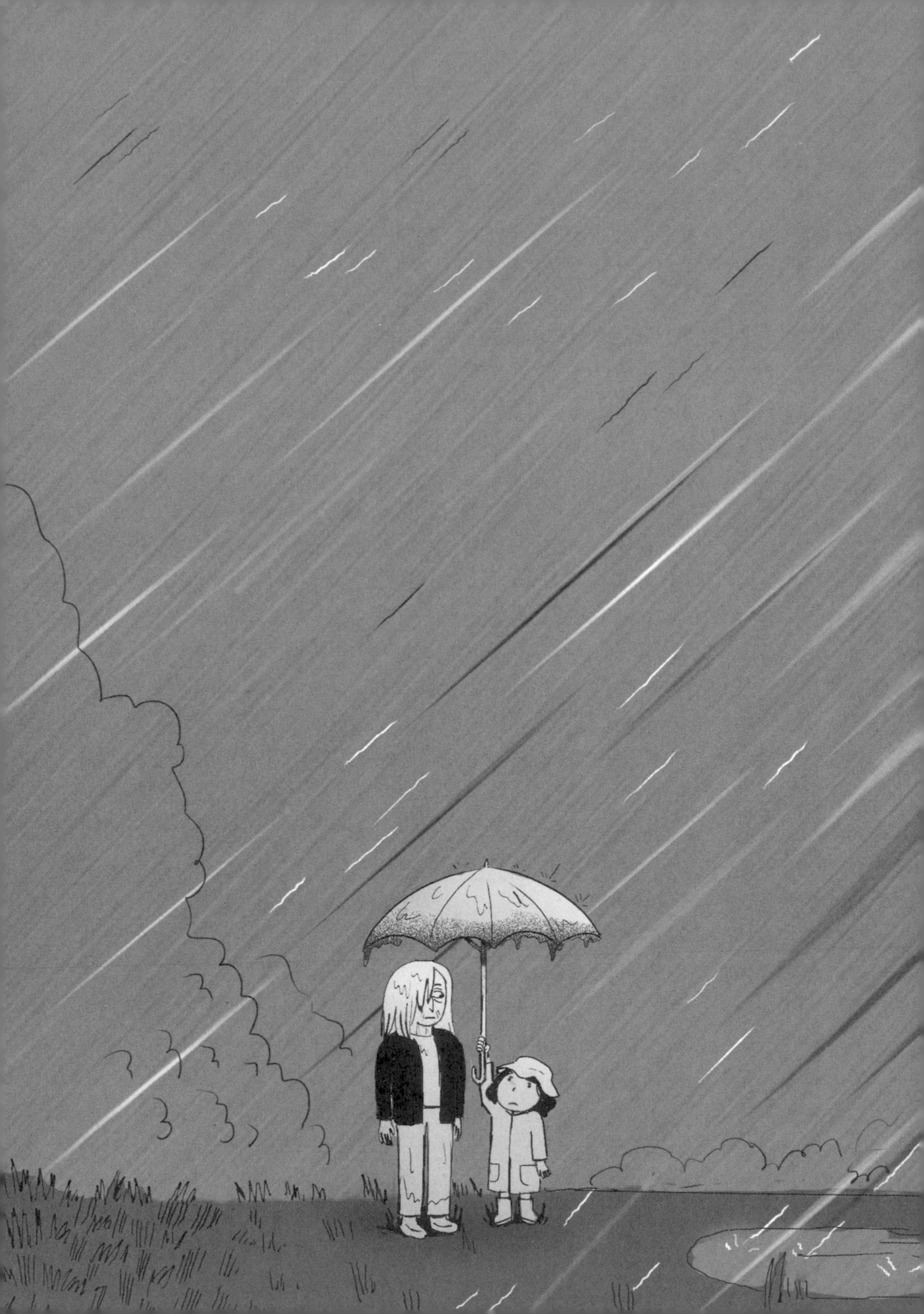

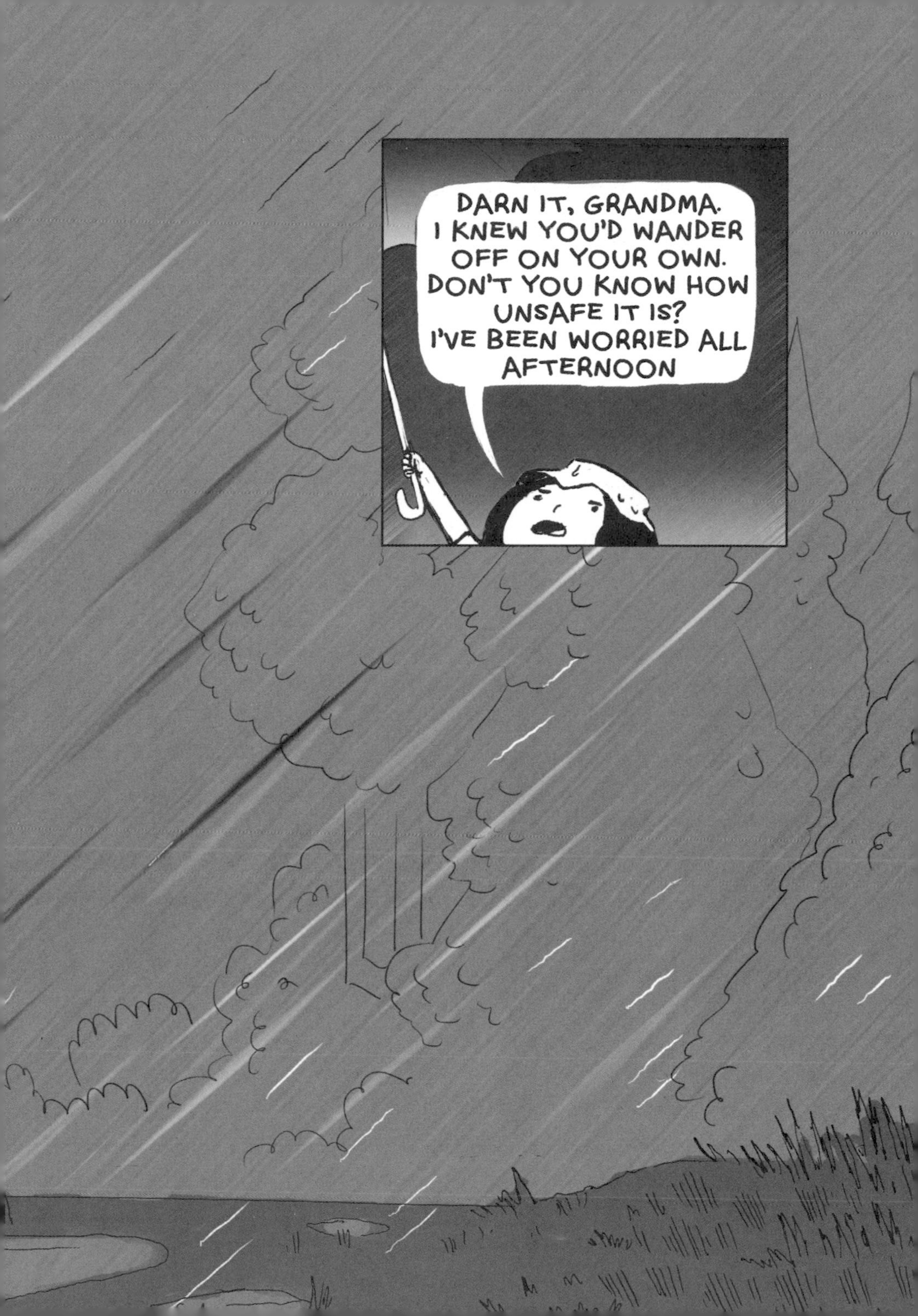
DARN IT, GRANDMA. I KNEW YOU'D WANDER OFF ON YOUR OWN. DON'T YOU KNOW HOW UNSAFE IT IS? I'VE BEEN WORRIED ALL AFTERNOON

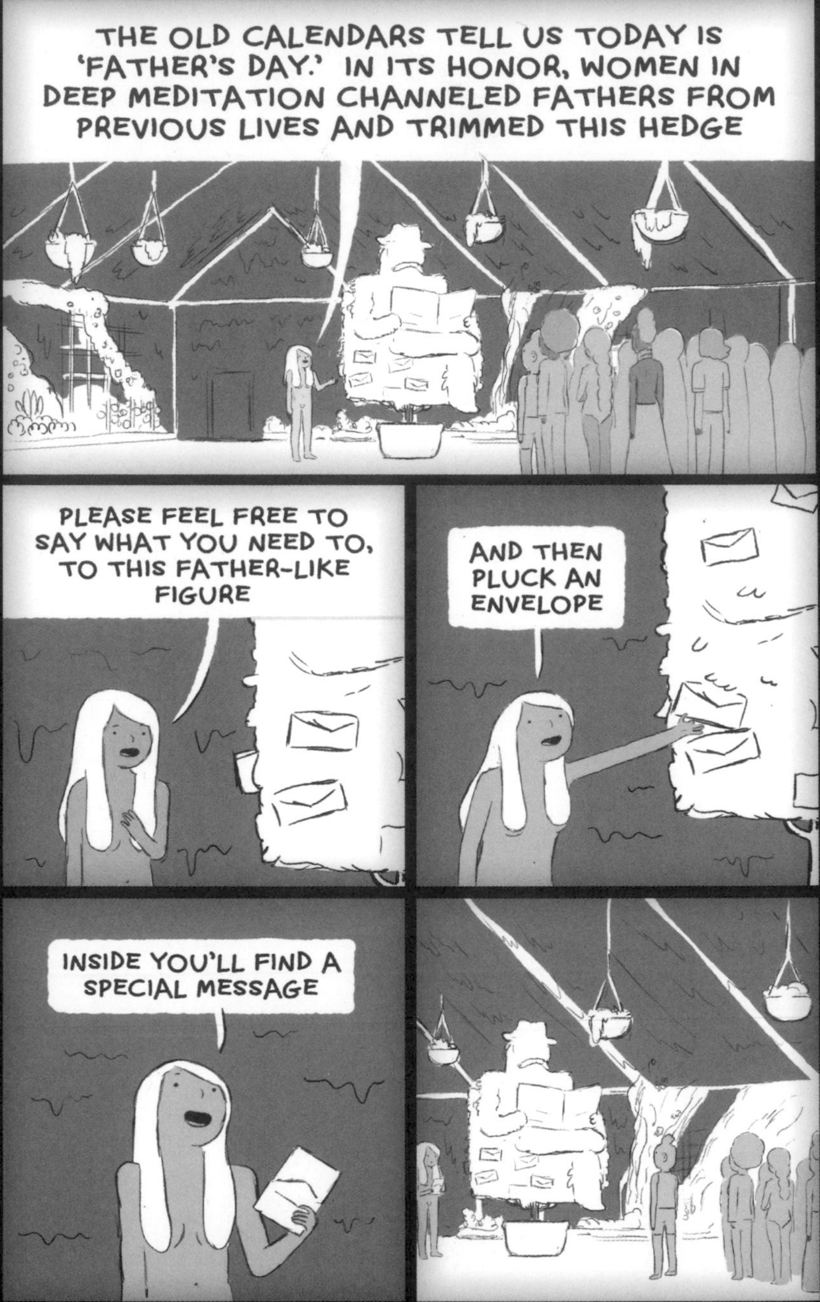
THE OLD CALENDARS TELL US TODAY IS 'FATHER'S DAY.' IN ITS HONOR, WOMEN IN DEEP MEDITATION CHANNELED FATHERS FROM PREVIOUS LIVES AND TRIMMED THIS HEDGE
PLEASE FEEL FREE TO SAY WHAT YOU NEED TO, TO THIS FATHER-LIKE FIGURE
AND THEN PLUCK AN ENVELOPE
INSIDE YOU'LL FIND A SPECIAL MESSAGE

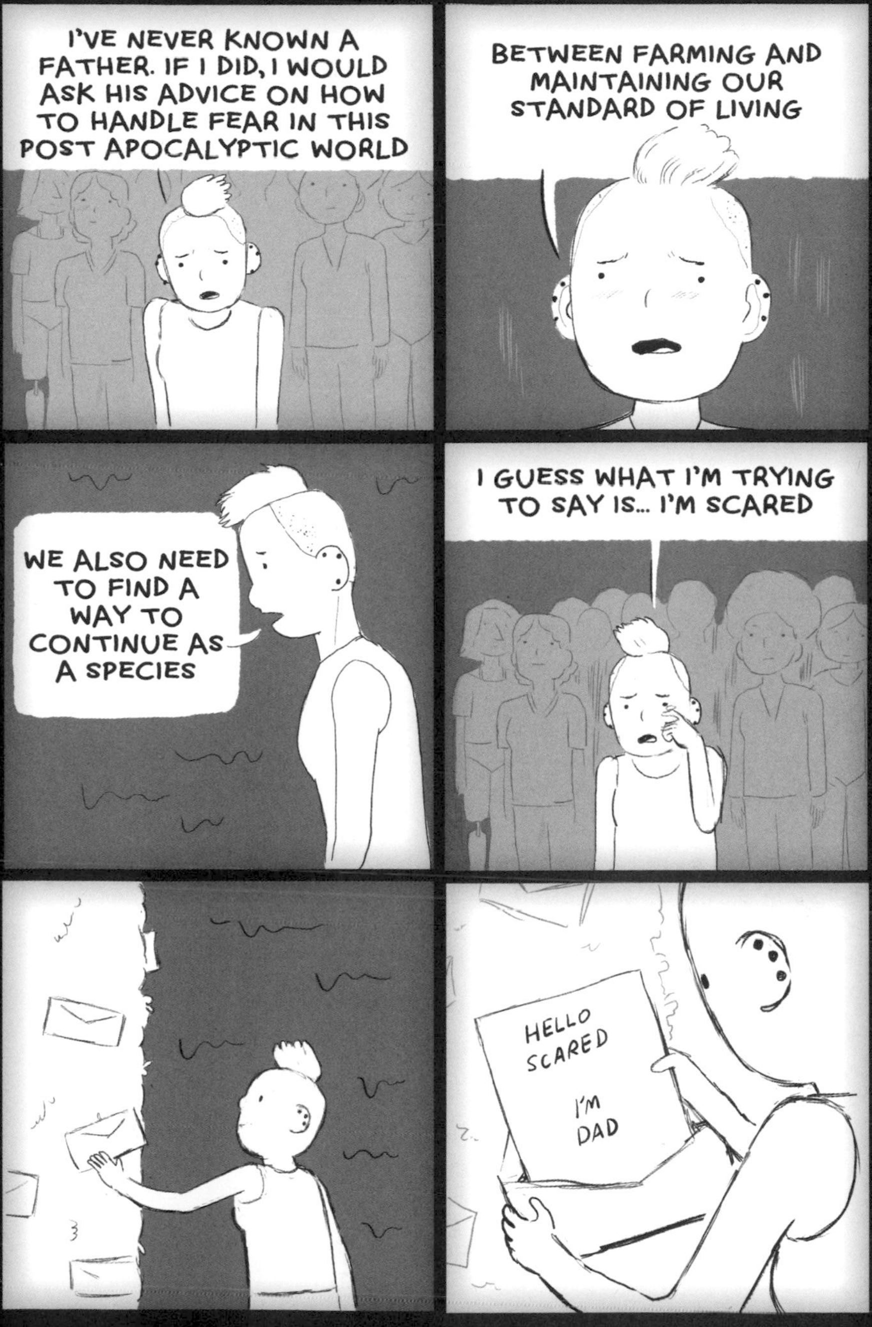
I'VE NEVER KNOWN A FATHER. IF I DID, I WOULD ASK HIS ADVICE ON HOW TO HANDLE FEAR IN THIS POST APOCALYPTIC WORLD
BETWEEN FARMING AND MAINTAINING OUR STANDARD OF LIVING
WE ALSO NEED TO FIND A WAY TO CONTINUE AS A SPECIES
I GUESS WHAT I'M TRYING TO SAY IS... I'M SCARED
HELLO SCARED
I'M DAD

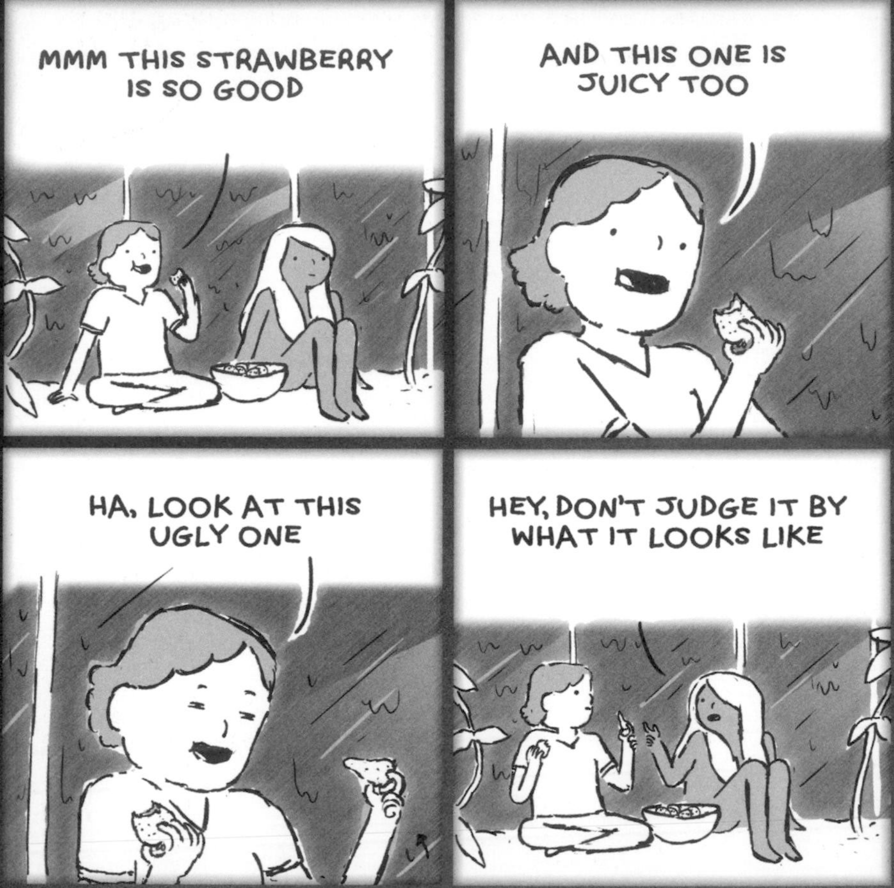
MMM THIS STRAWBERRY IS SO GOOD
AND THIS ONE IS JUICY TOO
HA, LOOK AT THIS UGLY ONE
HEY, DON'T JUDGE IT BY WHAT IT LOOKS LIKE

SEE, IT'S EVERY BIT AS TASTY
TERRIBLE TIME FOR AN ALLERGIC REACTION
LIKE, YOU REALLY HAD A POINT FOR A MOMENT

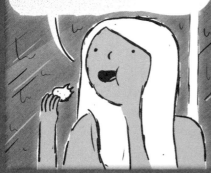

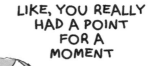

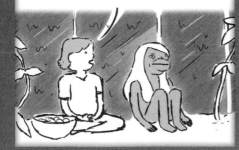

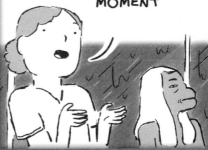

THANKS FOR HOLDING THE BASKET
NO PROBLEM
I FAILED YOU

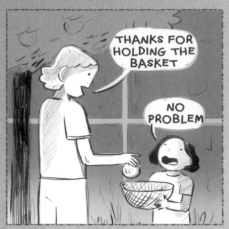

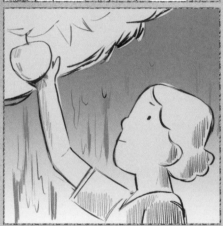

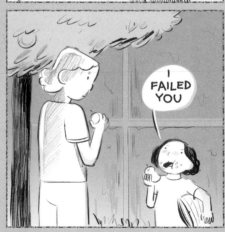

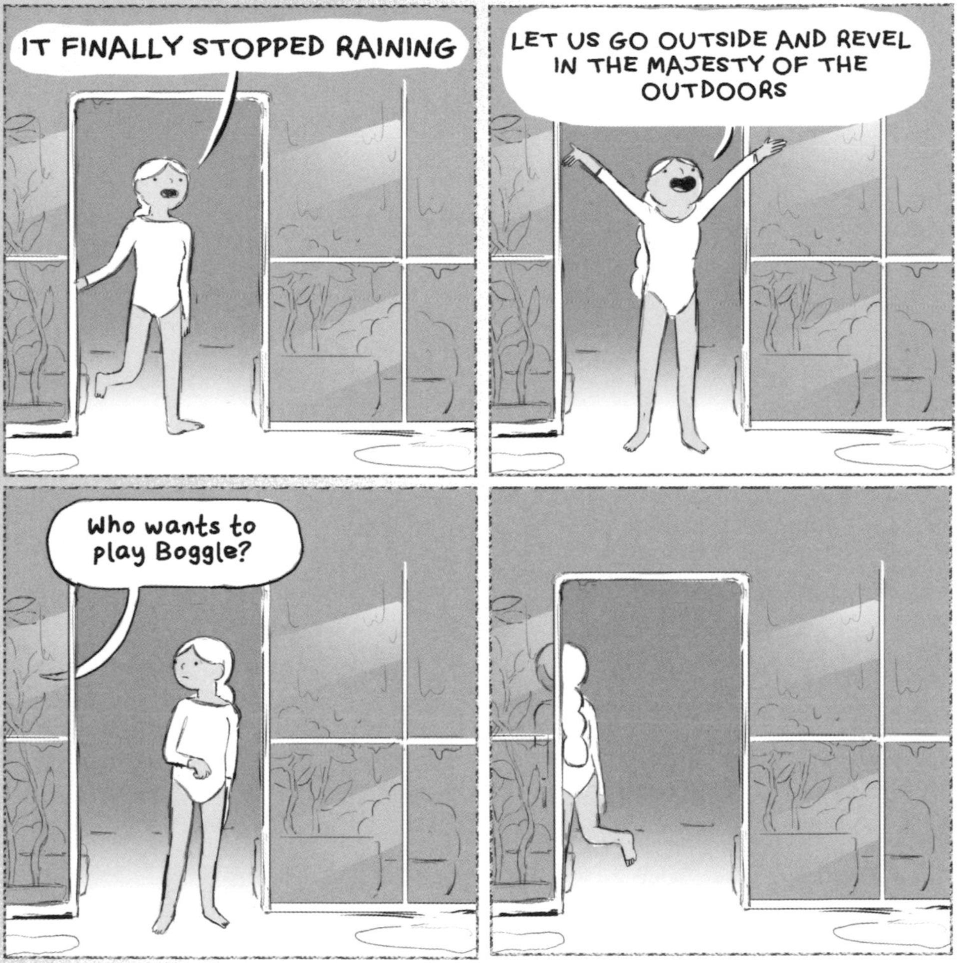
IT FINALLY STOPPED RAINING
LET US GO OUTSIDE AND REVEL IN THE MAJESTY OF THE OUTDOORS
Who wants to play Boggle?

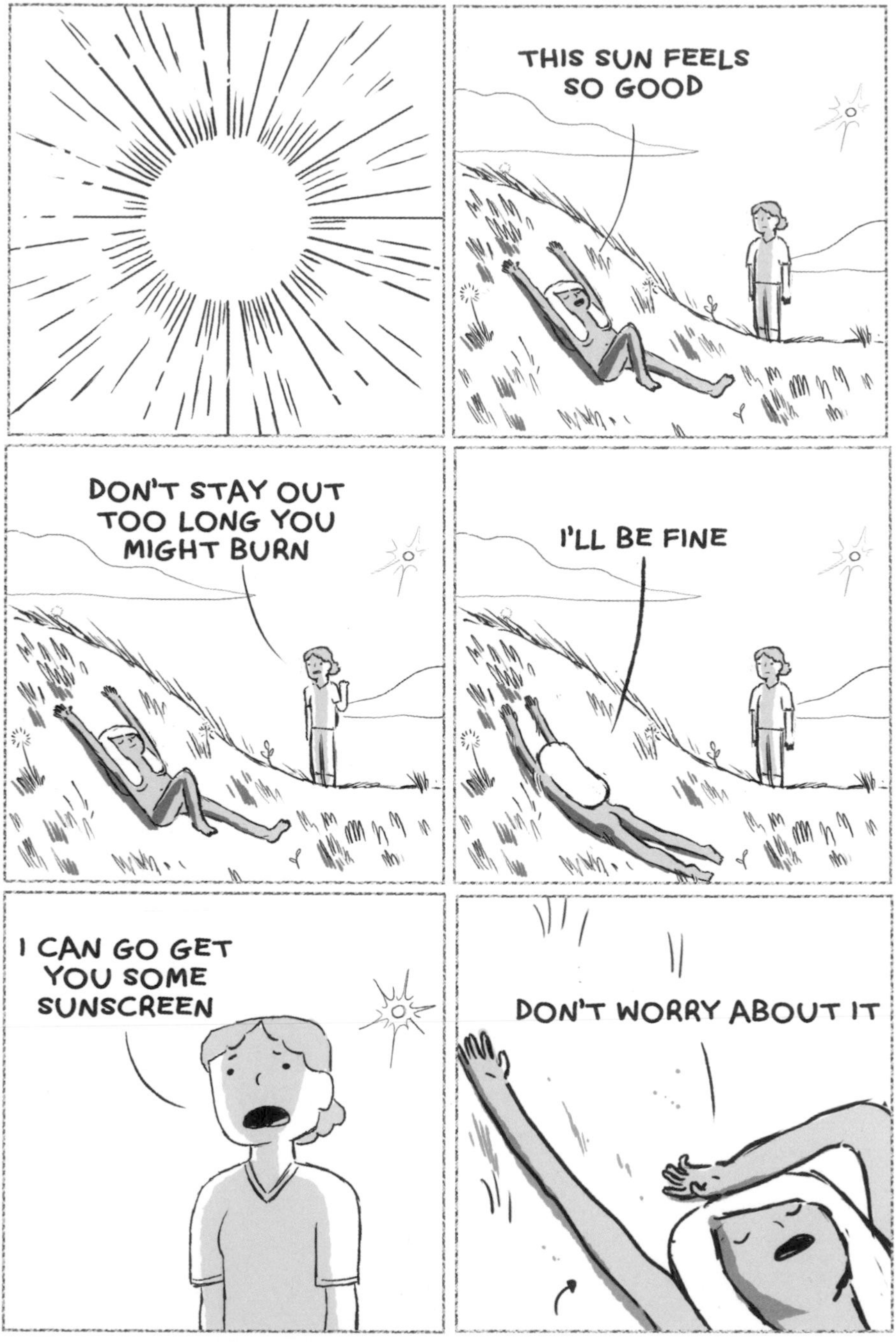
THIS SUN FEELS SO GOOD
DON'T STAY OUT TOO LONG YOU MIGHT BURN
I'LL BE FINE
I CAN GO GET YOU SOME SUNSCREEN
DON'T WORRY ABOUT IT

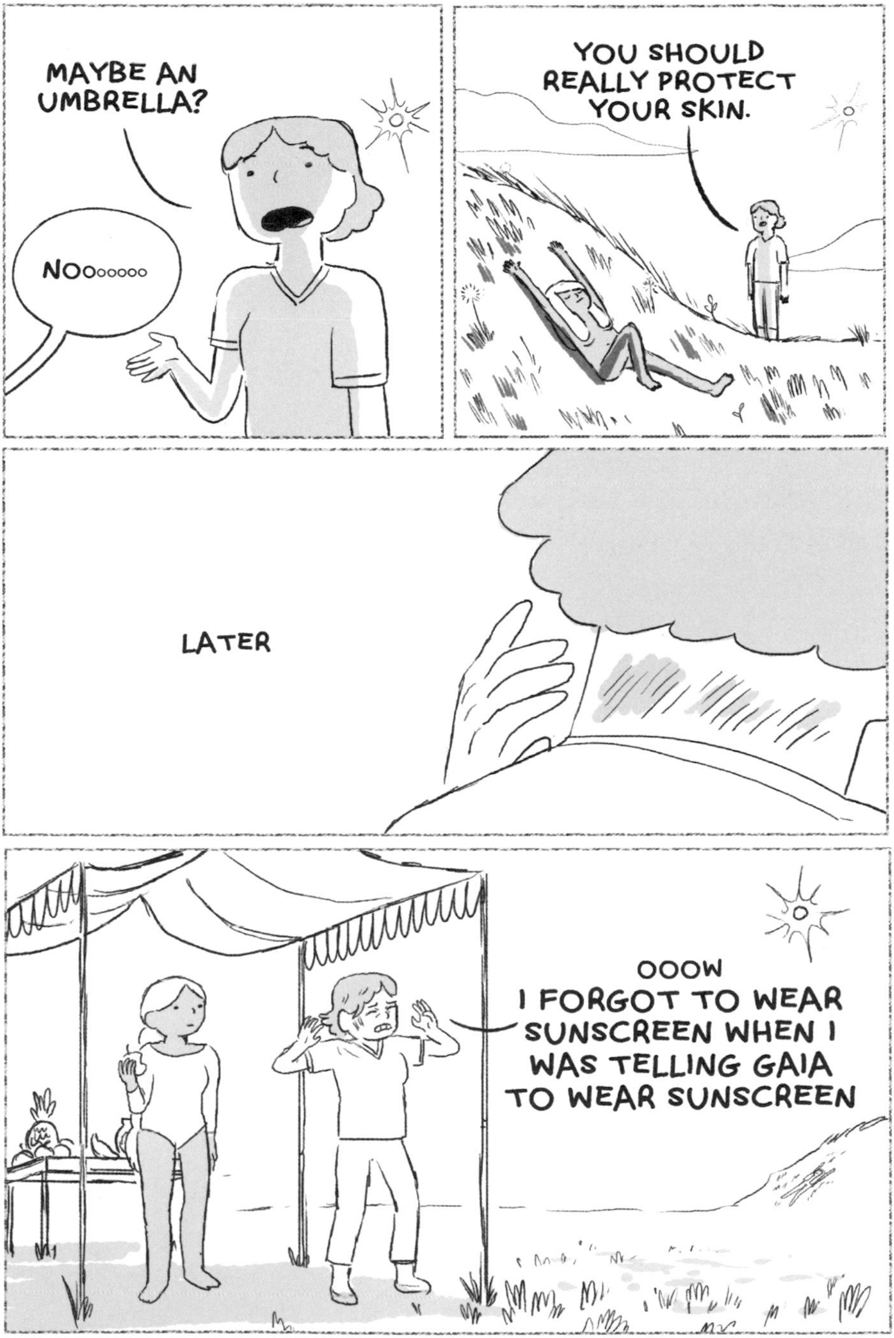
MAYBE AN UMBRELLA?
NOoooooo
YOU SHOULD REALLY PROTECT YOUR SKIN.
LATER
OOOW I FORGOT TO WEAR SUNSCREEN WHEN I WAS TELLING GAIA TO WEAR SUNSCREEN

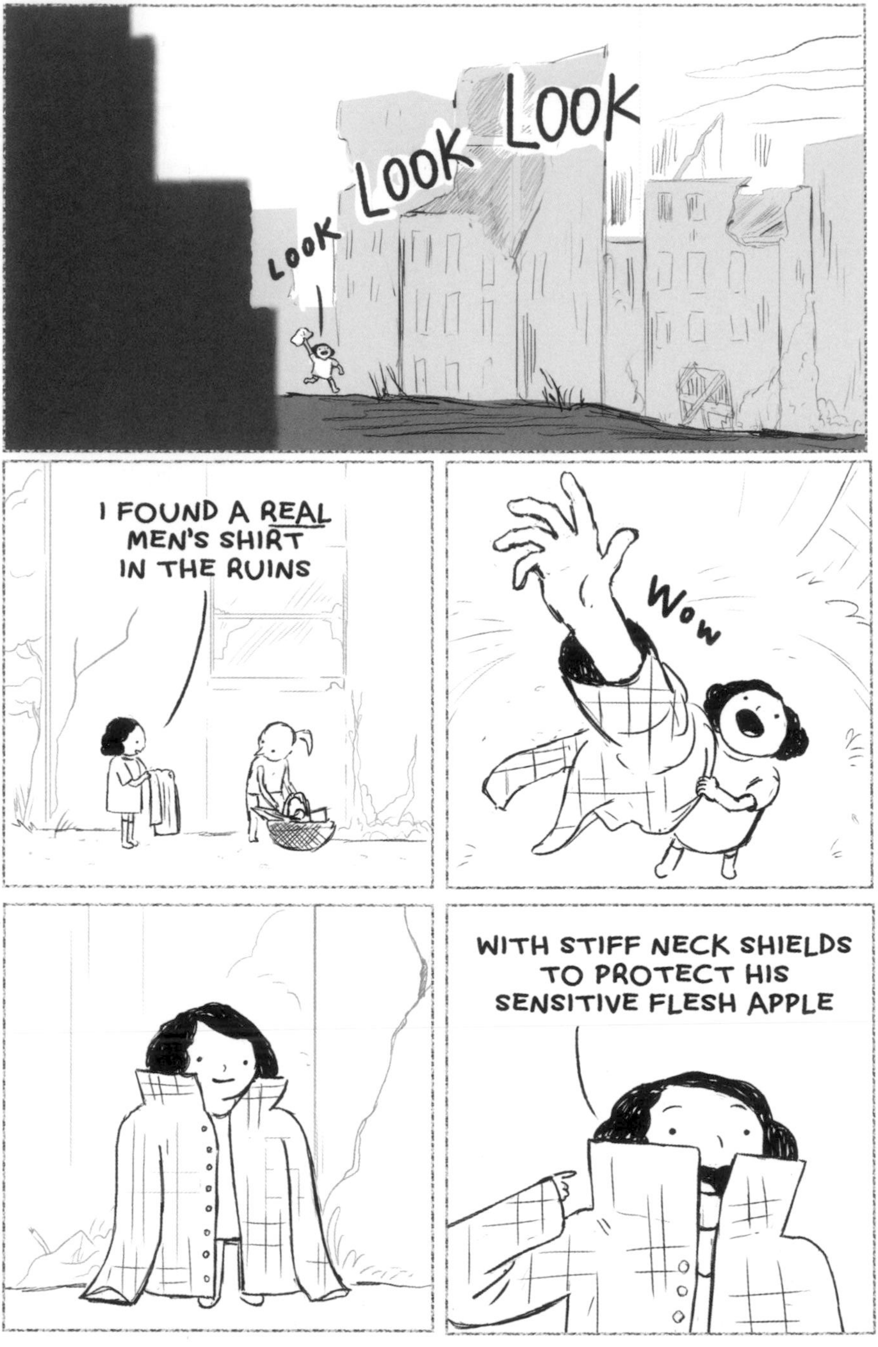
LOOK
LOOK
LOOK
I FOUND A REAL MEN'S SHIRT IN THE RUINS
WOW
WITH STIFF NECK SHIELDS TO PROTECT HIS SENSITIVE FLESH APPLE

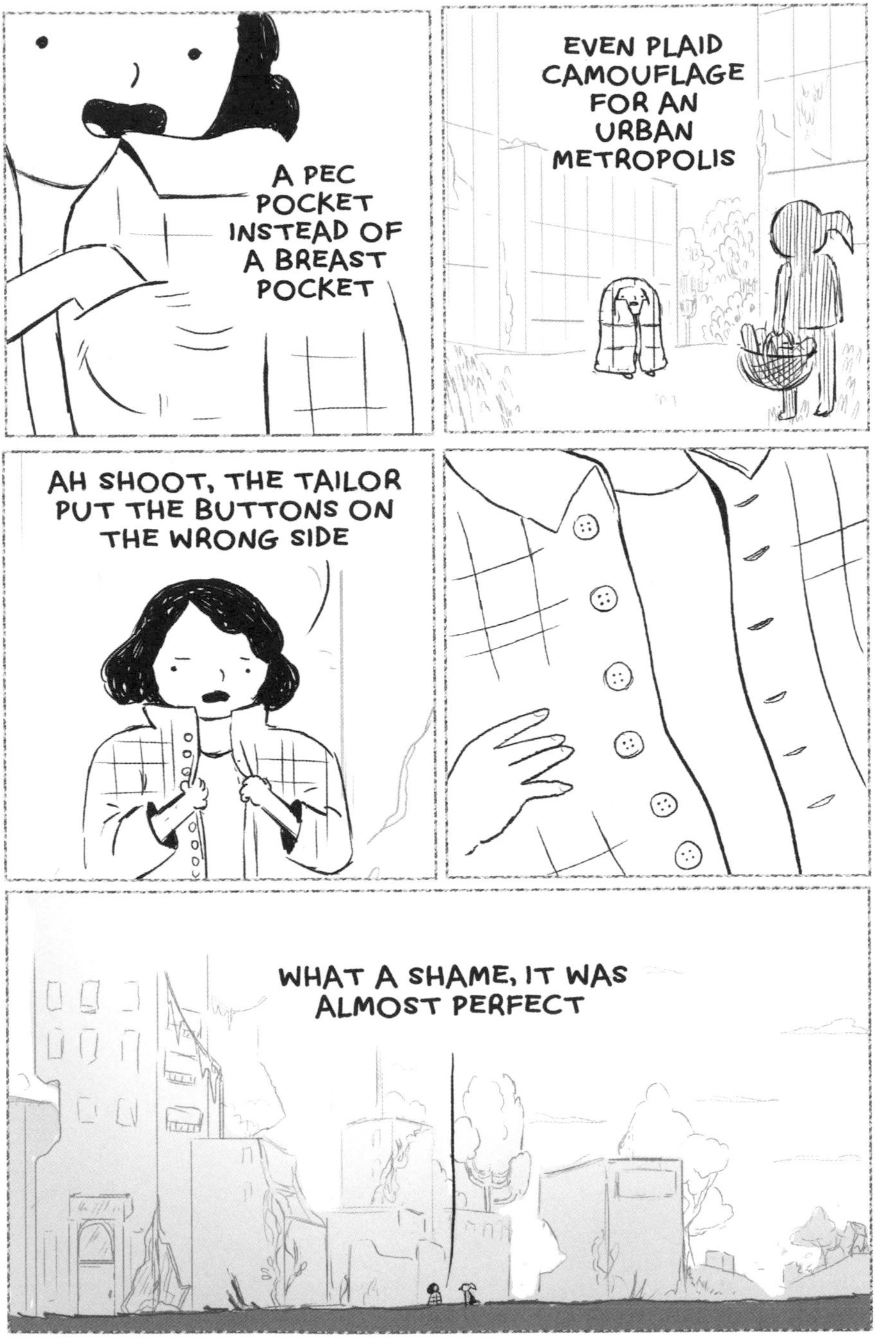
A PEC POCKET INSTEAD OF A BREAST POCKET
EVEN PLAID CAMOUFLAGE FOR AN URBAN METROPOLIS
AH SHOOT, THE TAILOR PUT THE BUTTONS ON THE WRONG SIDE
WHAT A SHAME, IT WAS ALMOST PERFECT

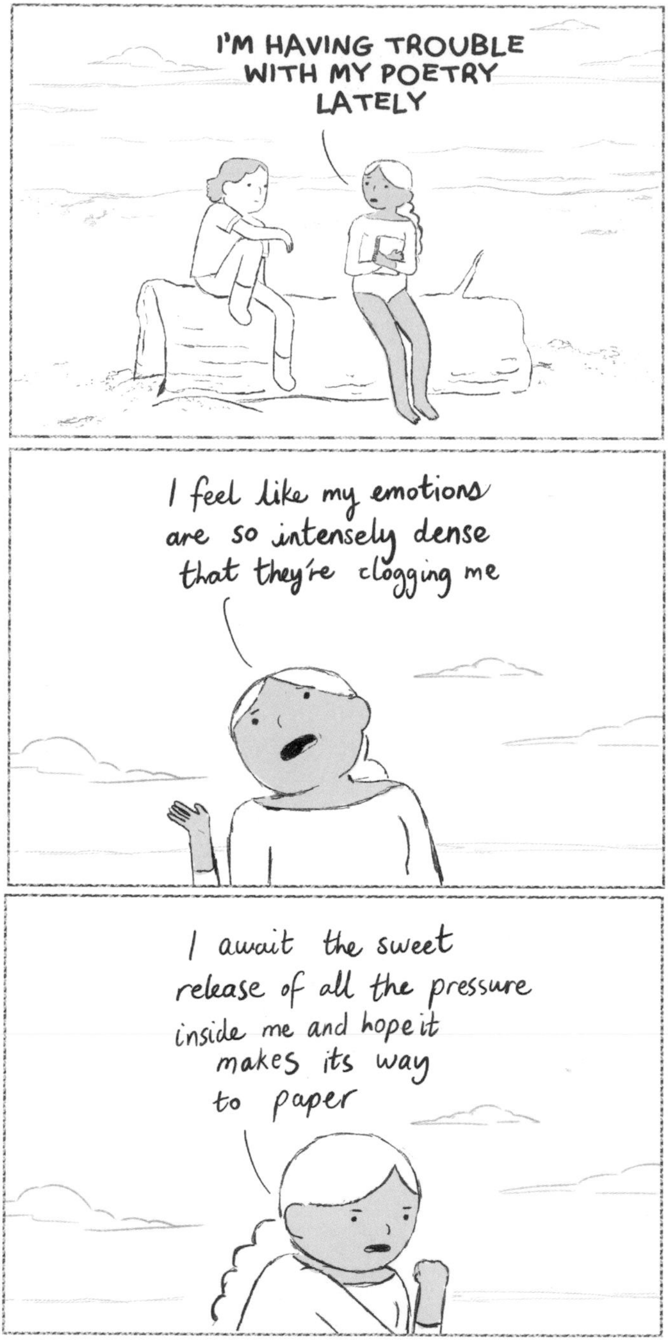
I'M HAVING TROUBLE WITH MY POETRY LATELY
I feel like my emotions are so intensely dense that they're clogging me
I await the sweet release of all the pressure inside me and hope it makes its way to paper

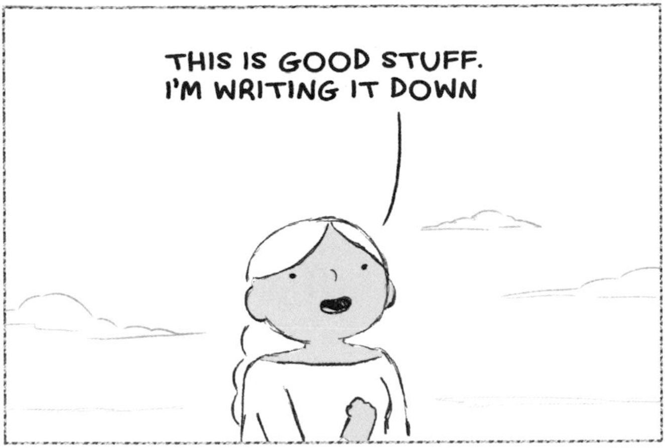
THIS IS GOOD STUFF.
I'M WRITING IT DOWN

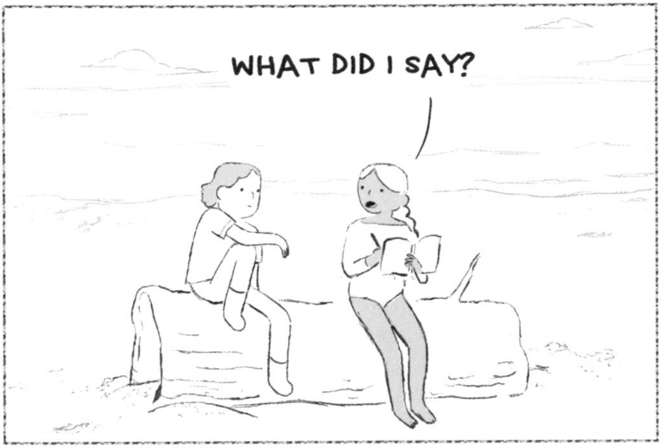
WHAT DID I SAY?

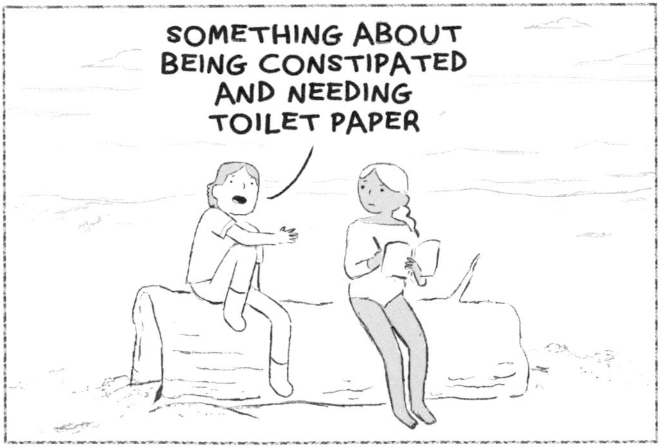
SOMETHING ABOUT BEING CONSTIPATED AND NEEDING TOILET PAPER

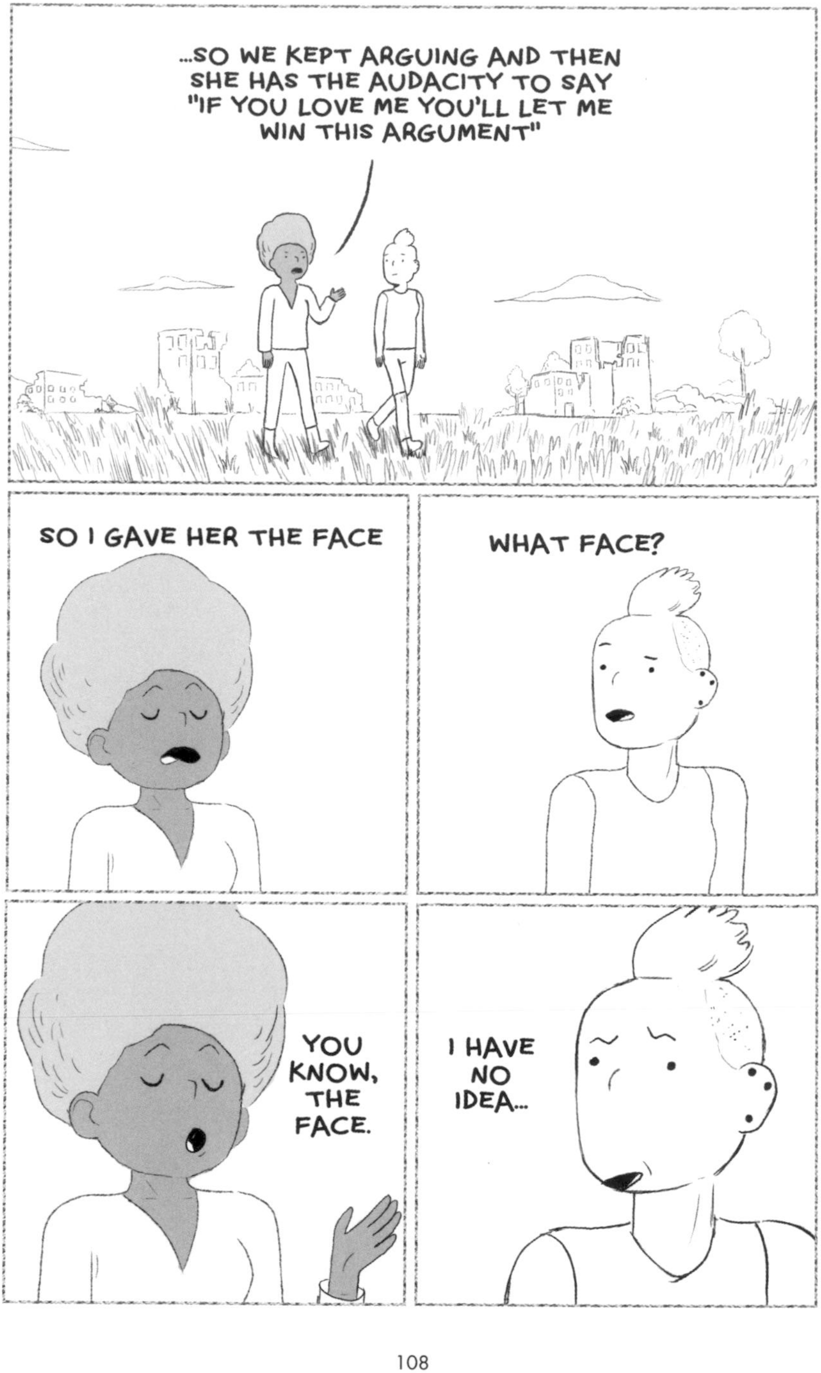
...SO WE KEPT ARGUING AND THEN SHE HAS THE AUDACITY TO SAY "IF YOU LOVE ME YOU'LL LET ME WIN THIS ARGUMENT"
SO I GAVE HER THE FACE
WHAT FACE?
YOU KNOW, THE FACE.
I HAVE NO IDEA...

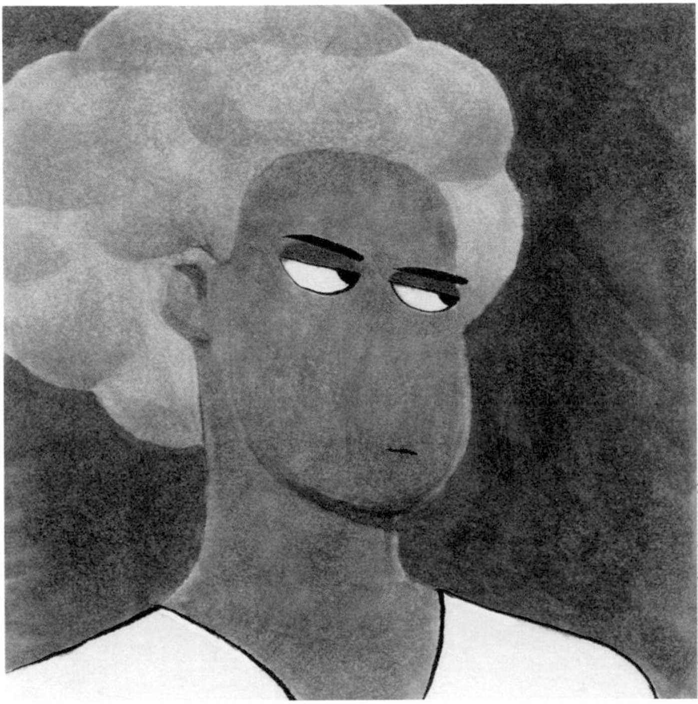

guest panel by Miranda Tacchia

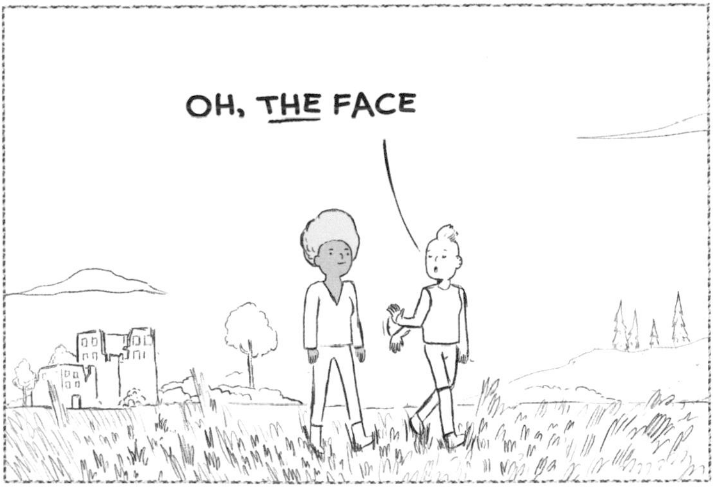
OH, THE FACE

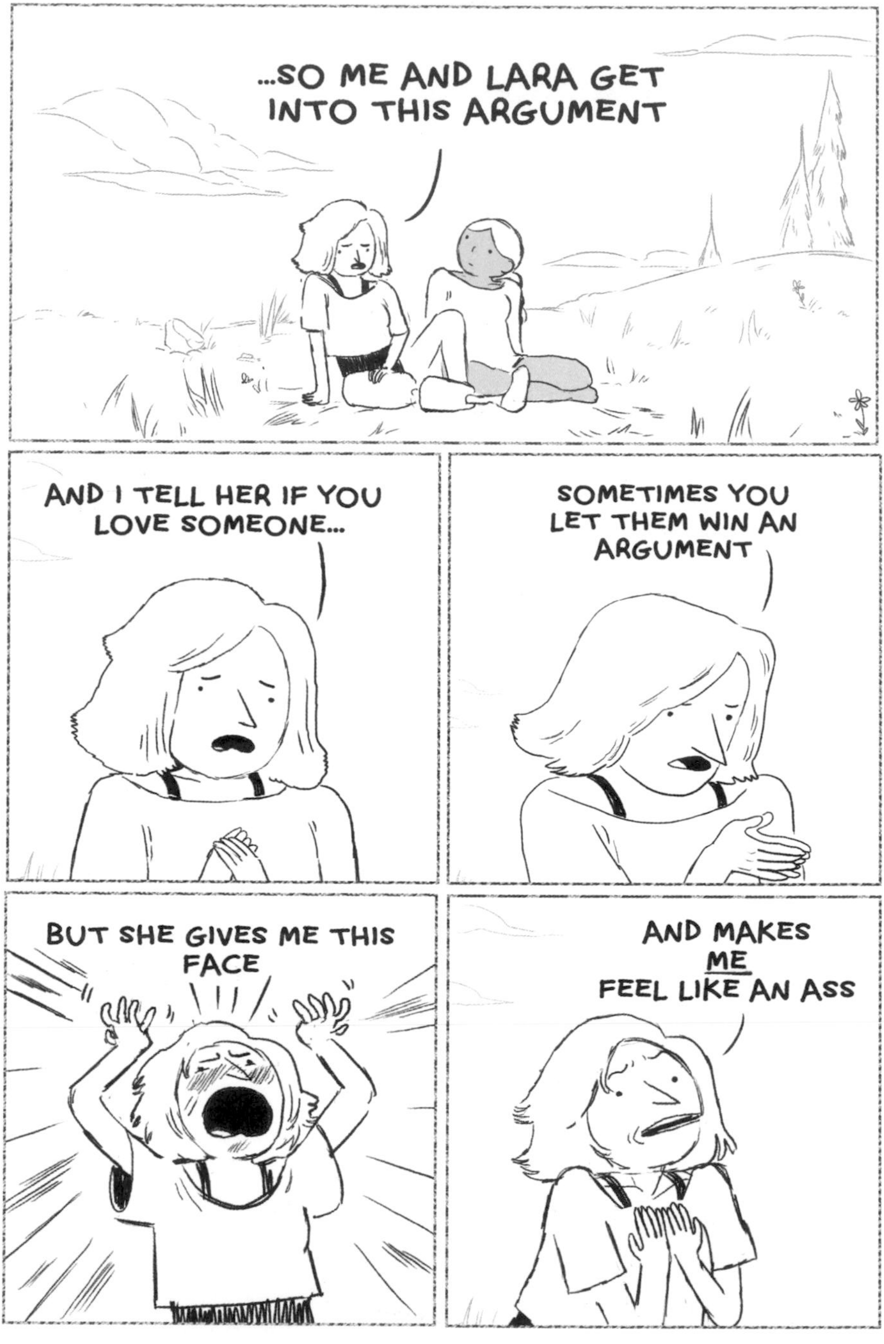
...SO ME AND LARA GET INTO THIS ARGUMENT
AND I TELL HER IF YOU LOVE SOMEONE...
SOMETIMES YOU LET THEM WIN AN ARGUMENT
BUT SHE GIVES ME THIS FACE
AND MAKES ME FEEL LIKE AN ASS

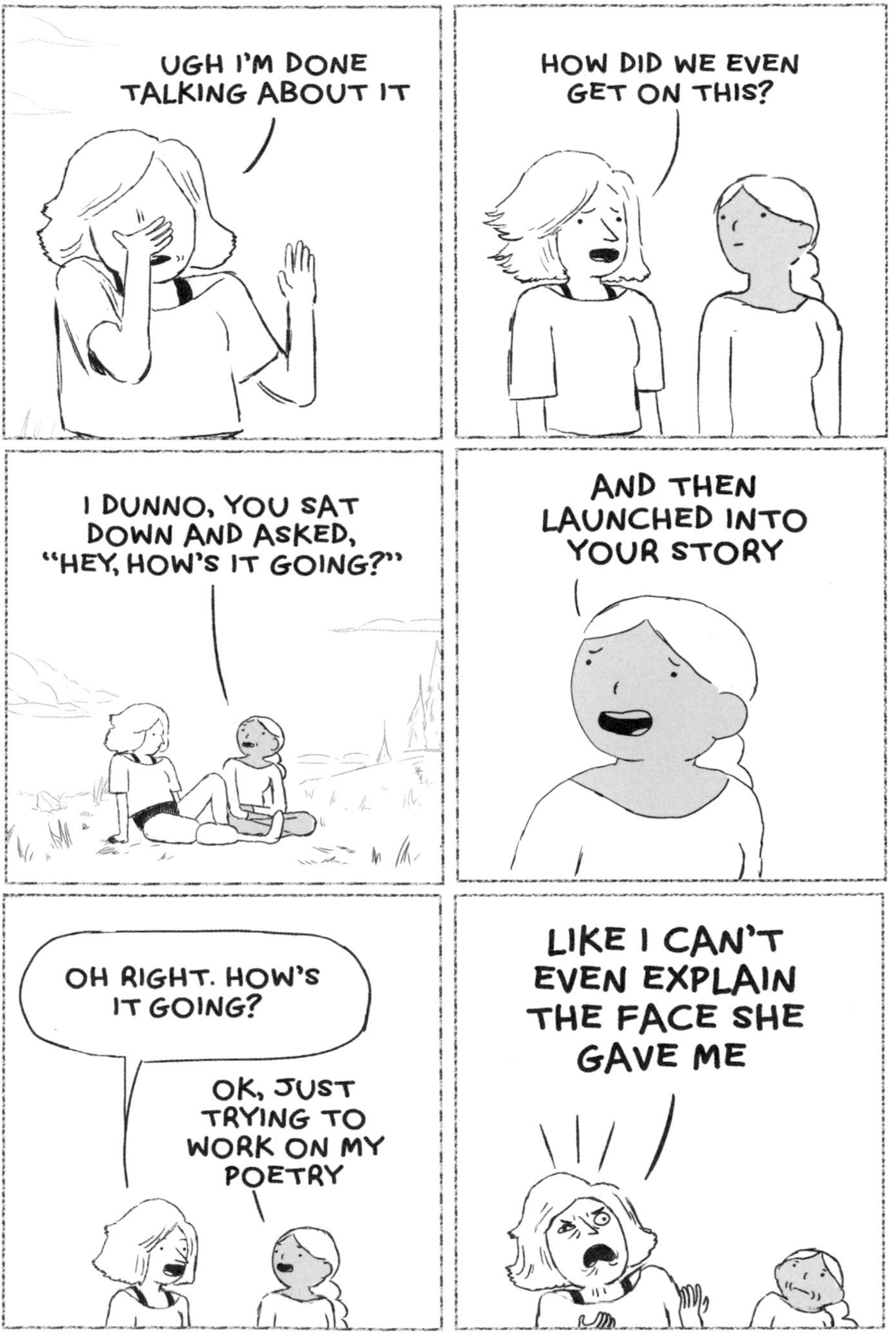
UGH I'M DONE TALKING ABOUT IT
HOW DID WE EVEN GET ON THIS?
I DUNNO, YOU SAT DOWN AND ASKED, "HEY, HOW'S IT GOING?"
AND THEN LAUNCHED INTO YOUR STORY
OH RIGHT. HOW'S IT GOING?
OK, JUST TRYING TO WORK ON MY POETRY
LIKE I CAN'T EVEN EXPLAIN THE FACE SHE GAVE ME

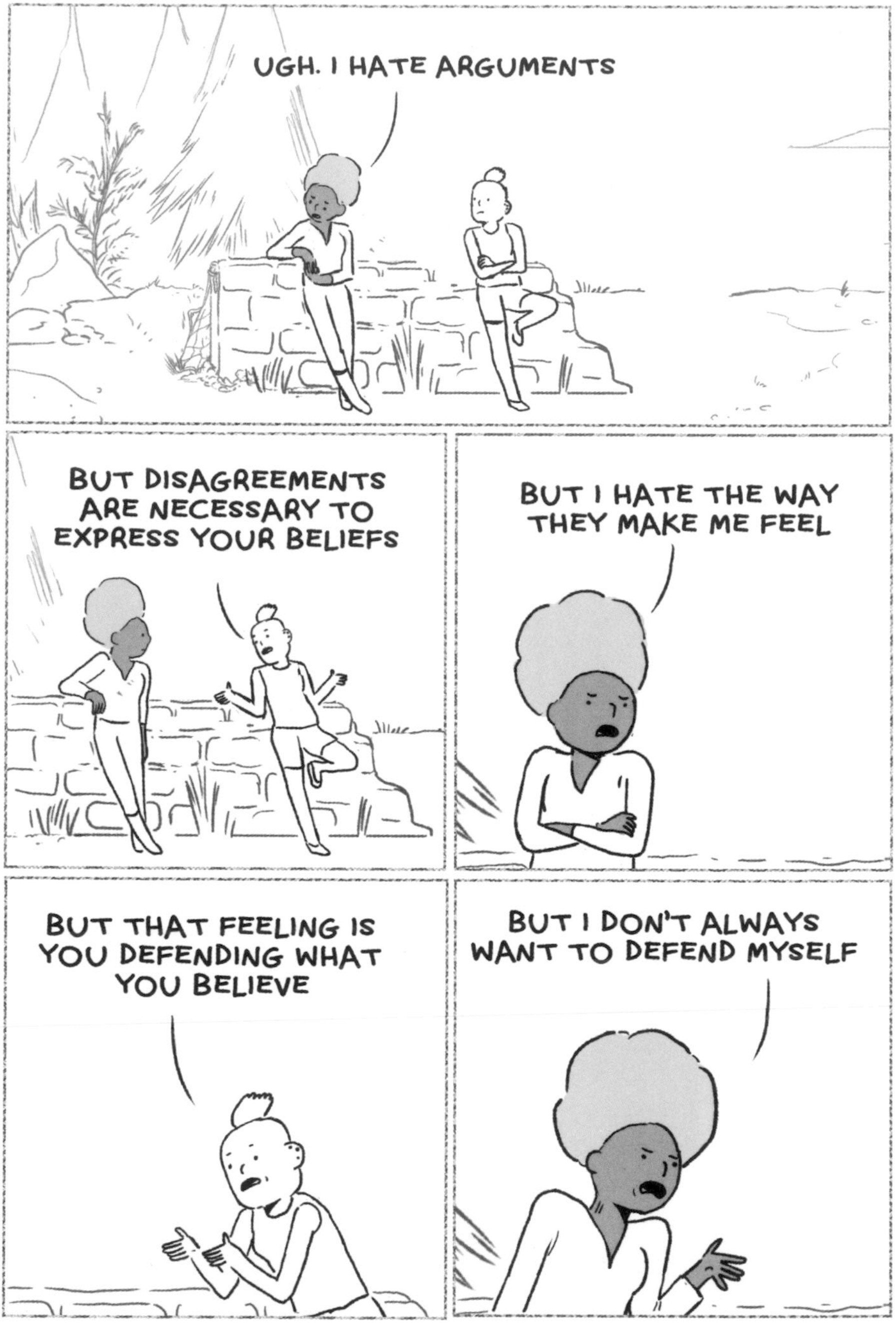
UGH. I HATE ARGUMENTS
BUT DISAGREEMENTS ARE NECESSARY TO EXPRESS YOUR BELIEFS
BUT I HATE THE WAY THEY MAKE ME FEEL
BUT THAT FEELING IS YOU DEFENDING WHAT YOU BELIEVE
BUT I DON'T ALWAYS WANT TO DEFEND MYSELF

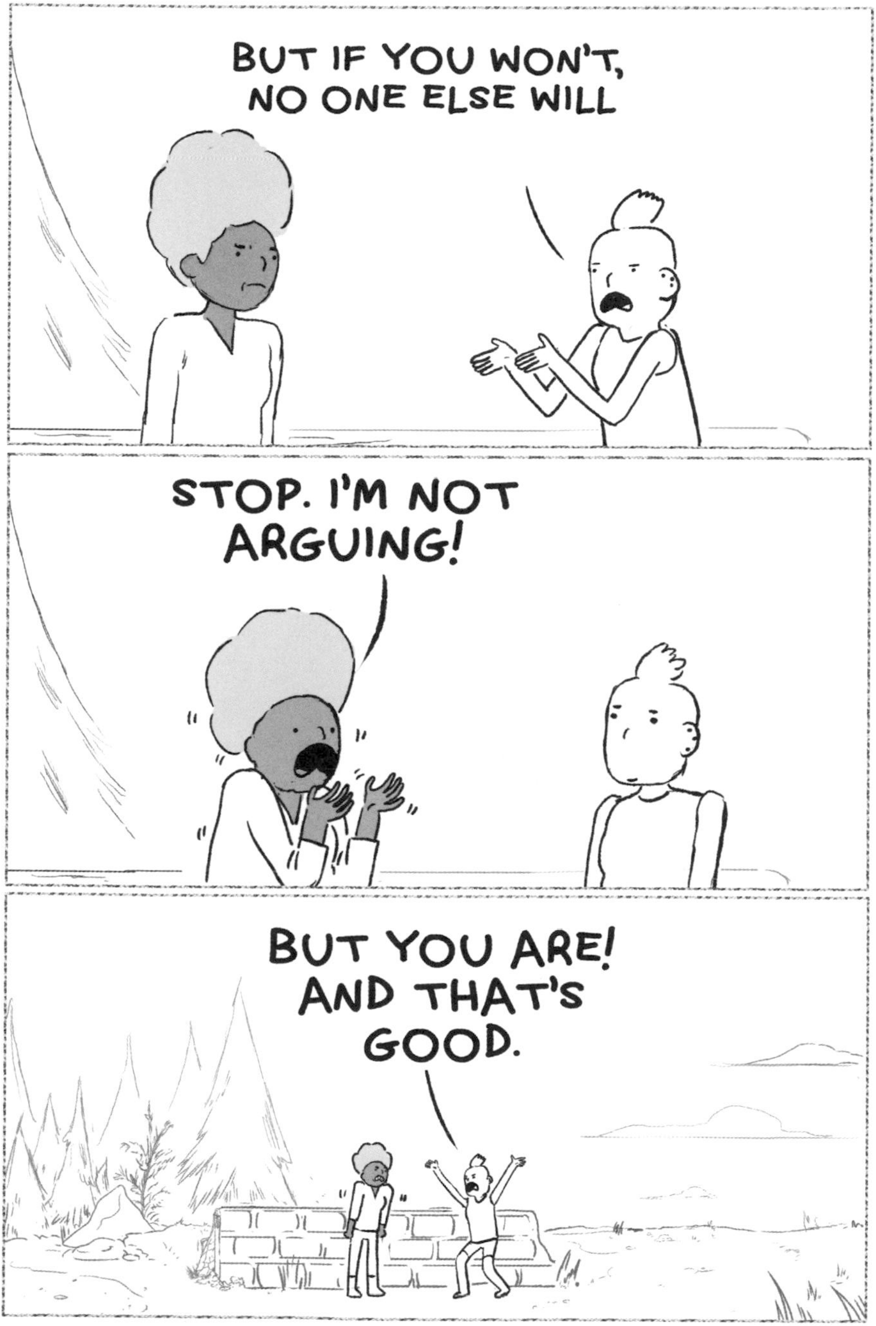
BUT IF YOU WON'T, NO ONE ELSE WILL
STOP. I'M NOT ARGUING!
BUT YOU ARE! AND THAT'S GOOD.

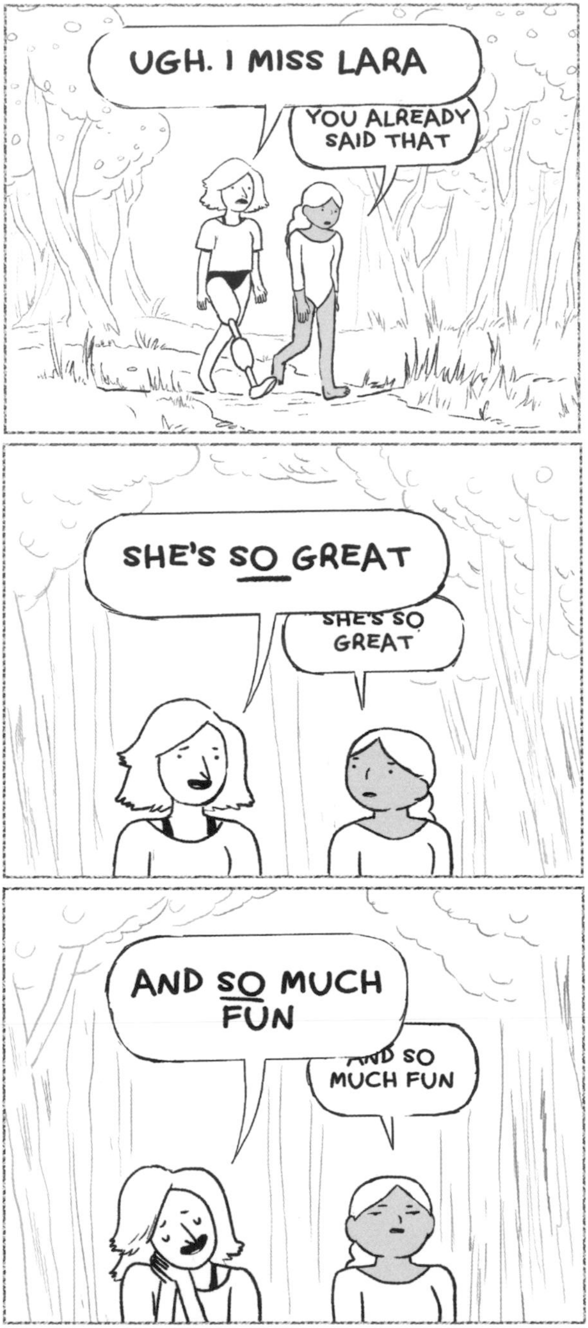
UGH. I MISS LARA
YOU ALREADY SAID THAT
SHE'S SO GREAT
SHE'S SO GREAT
AND SO MUCH FUN
AND SO MUCH FUN

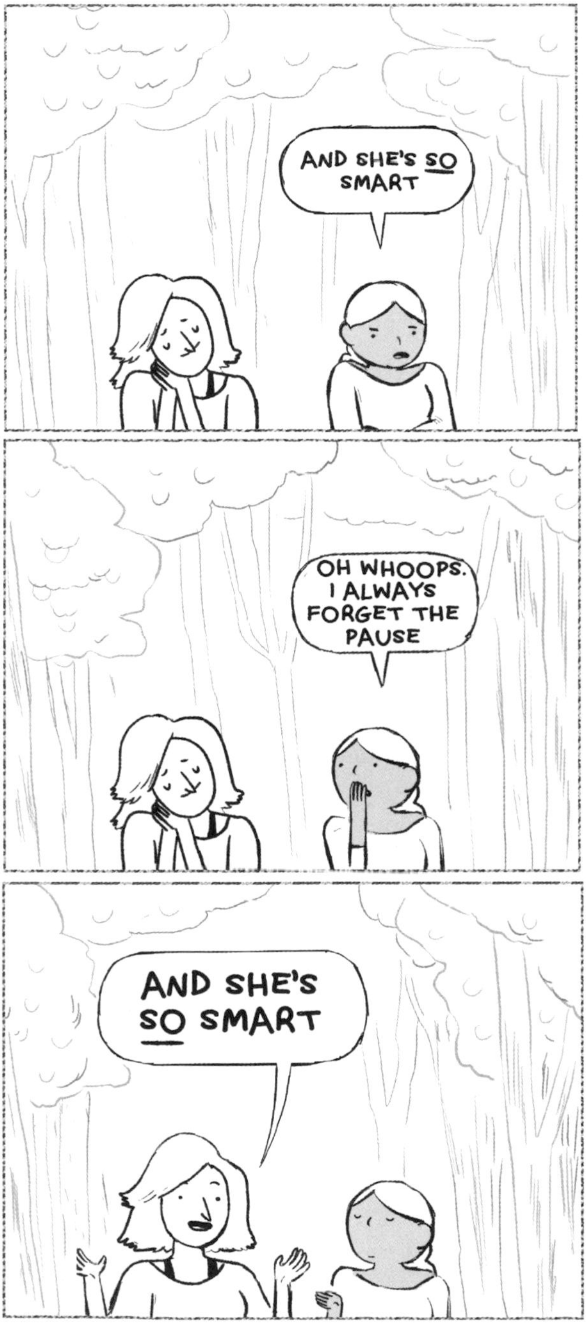
AND SHE'S SO SMART
OH WHOOPS. I ALWAYS FORGET THE PAUSE
AND SHE'S SO SMART

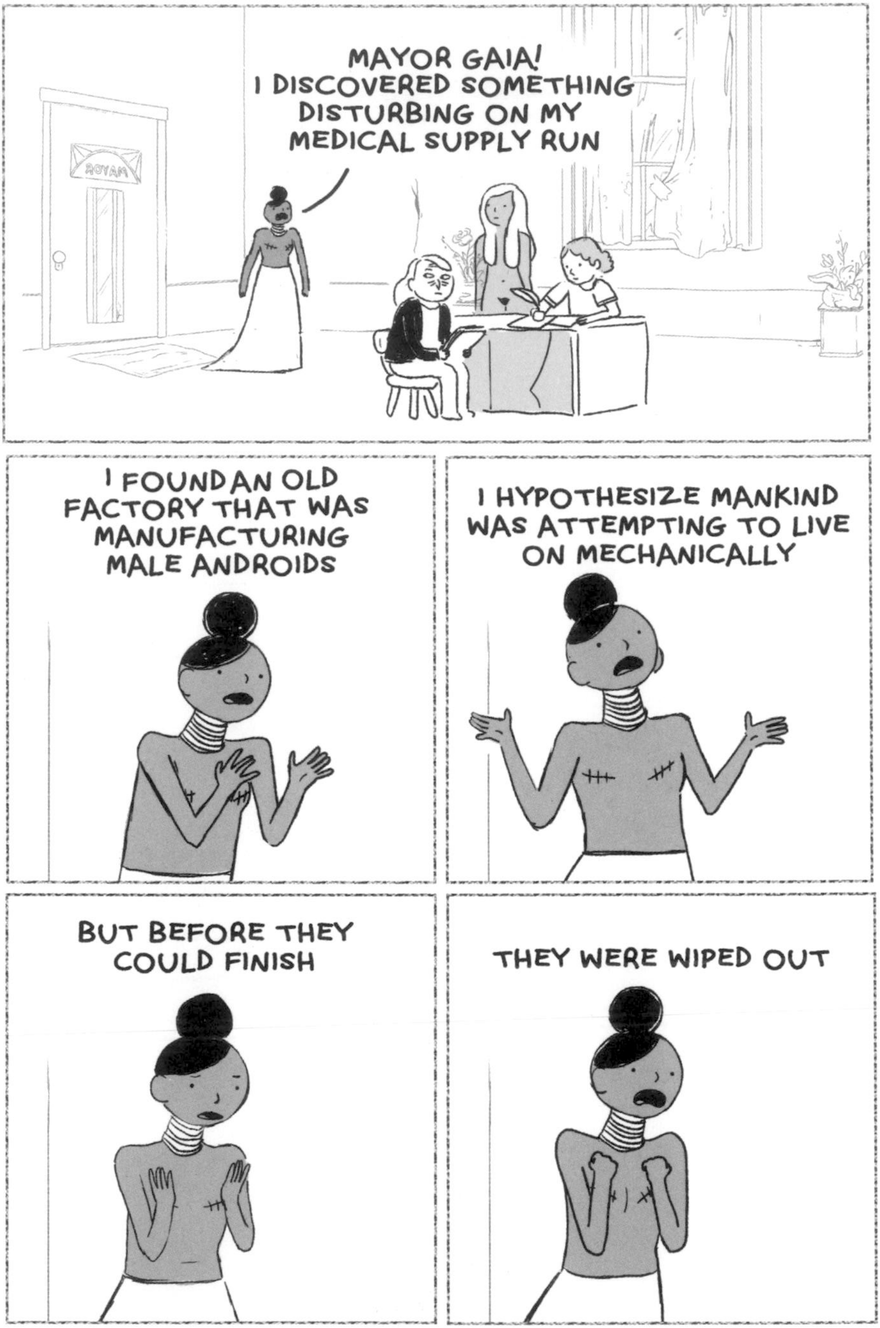
MAYOR GAIA! I DISCOVERED SOMETHING DISTURBING ON MY MEDICAL SUPPLY RUN
I FOUND AN OLD FACTORY THAT WAS MANUFACTURING MALE ANDROIDS
I HYPOTHESIZE MANKIND WAS ATTEMPTING TO LIVE ON MECHANICALLY
BUT BEFORE THEY COULD FINISH
THEY WERE WIPED OUT

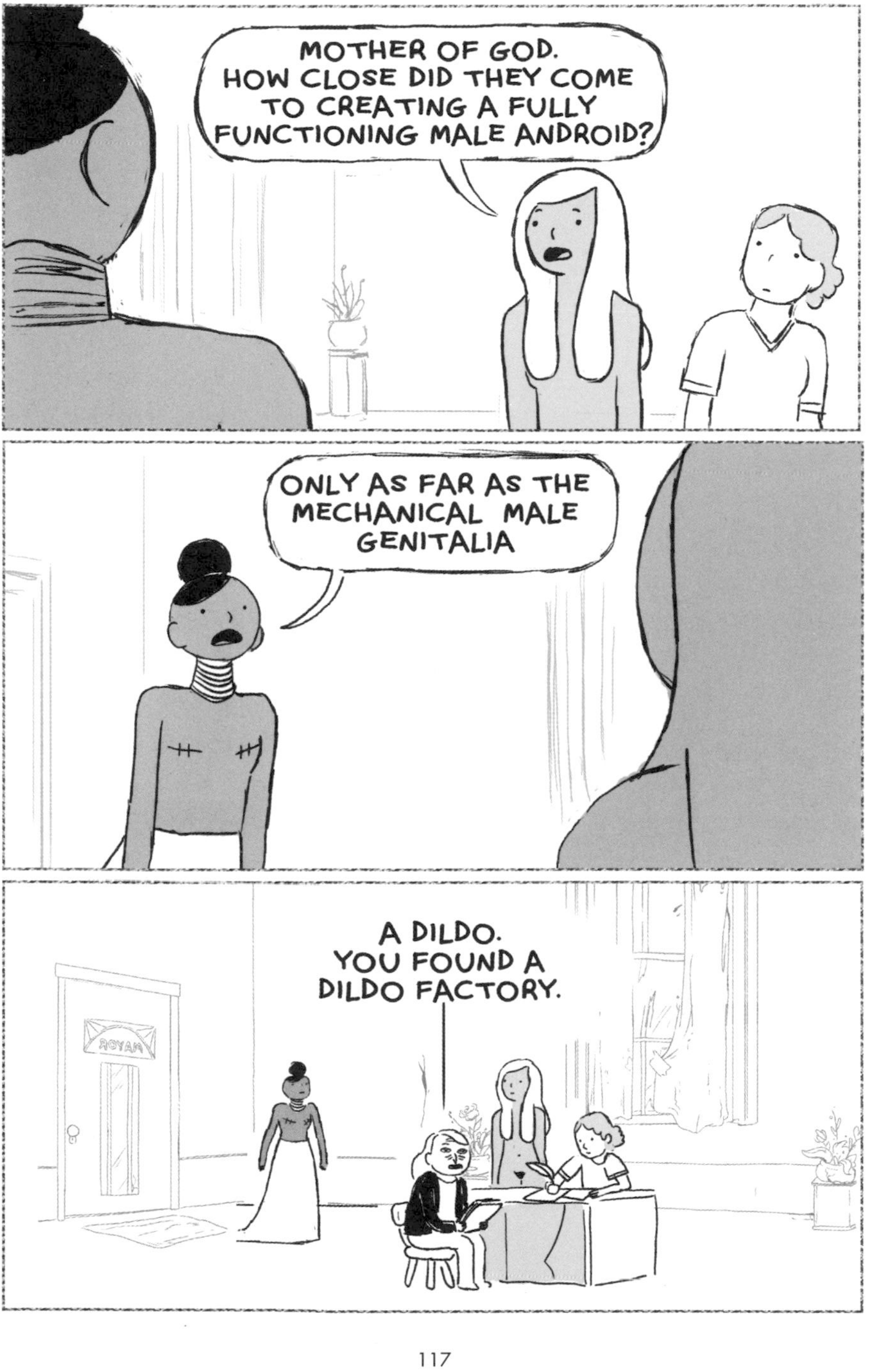
MOTHER OF GOD. HOW CLOSE DID THEY COME TO CREATING A FULLY FUNCTIONING MALE ANDROID?
ONLY AS FAR AS THE MECHANICAL MALE GENITALIA
A DILDO. YOU FOUND A DILDO FACTORY.

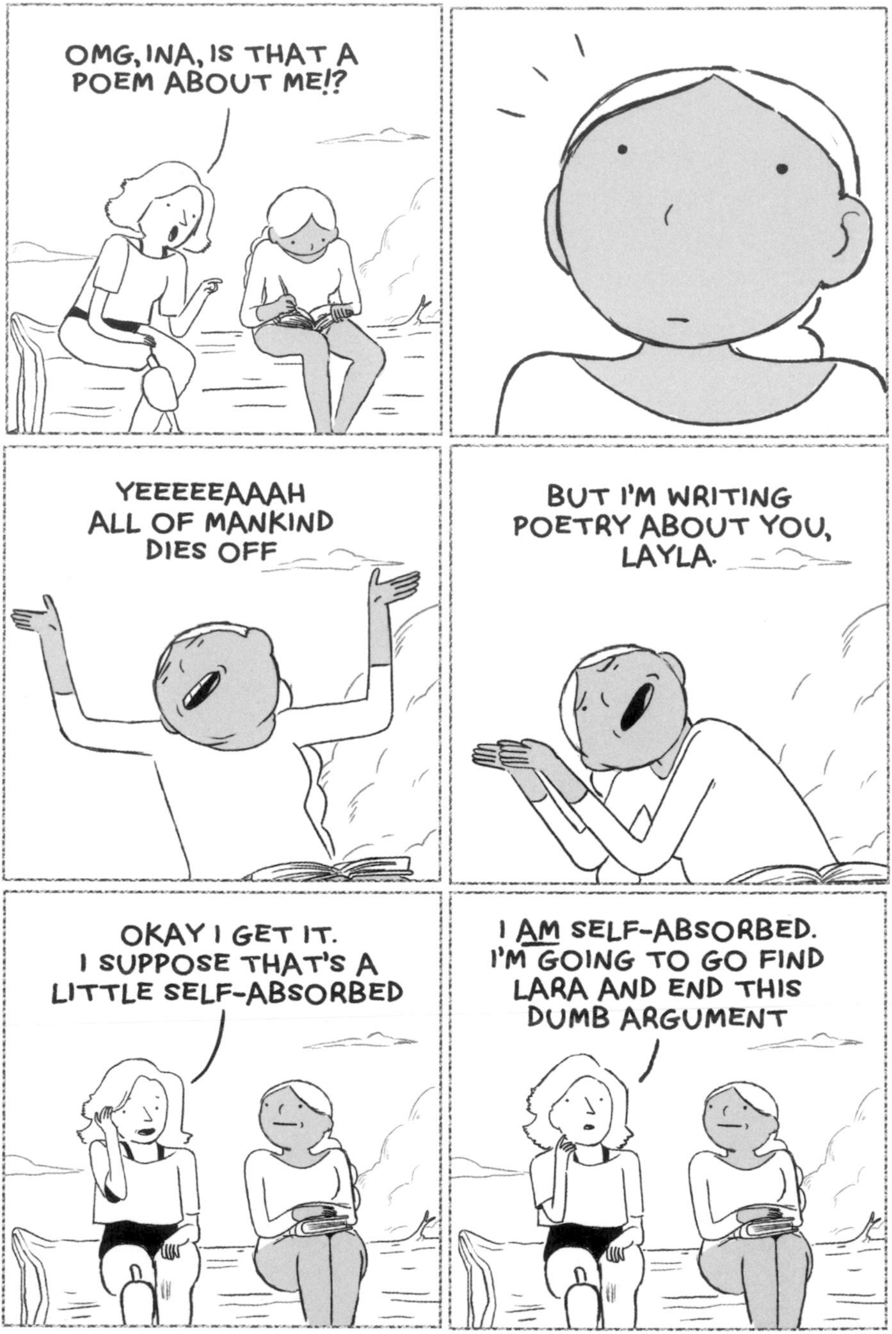
OMG, INA, IS THAT A POEM ABOUT ME!?
YEEEEEAAAH ALL OF MANKIND DIES OFF
BUT I'M WRITING POETRY ABOUT YOU, LAYLA.
OKAY I GET IT. I SUPPOSE THAT'S A LITTLE SELF-ABSORBED
I AM SELF-ABSORBED. I'M GOING TO GO FIND LARA AND END THIS DUMB ARGUMENT

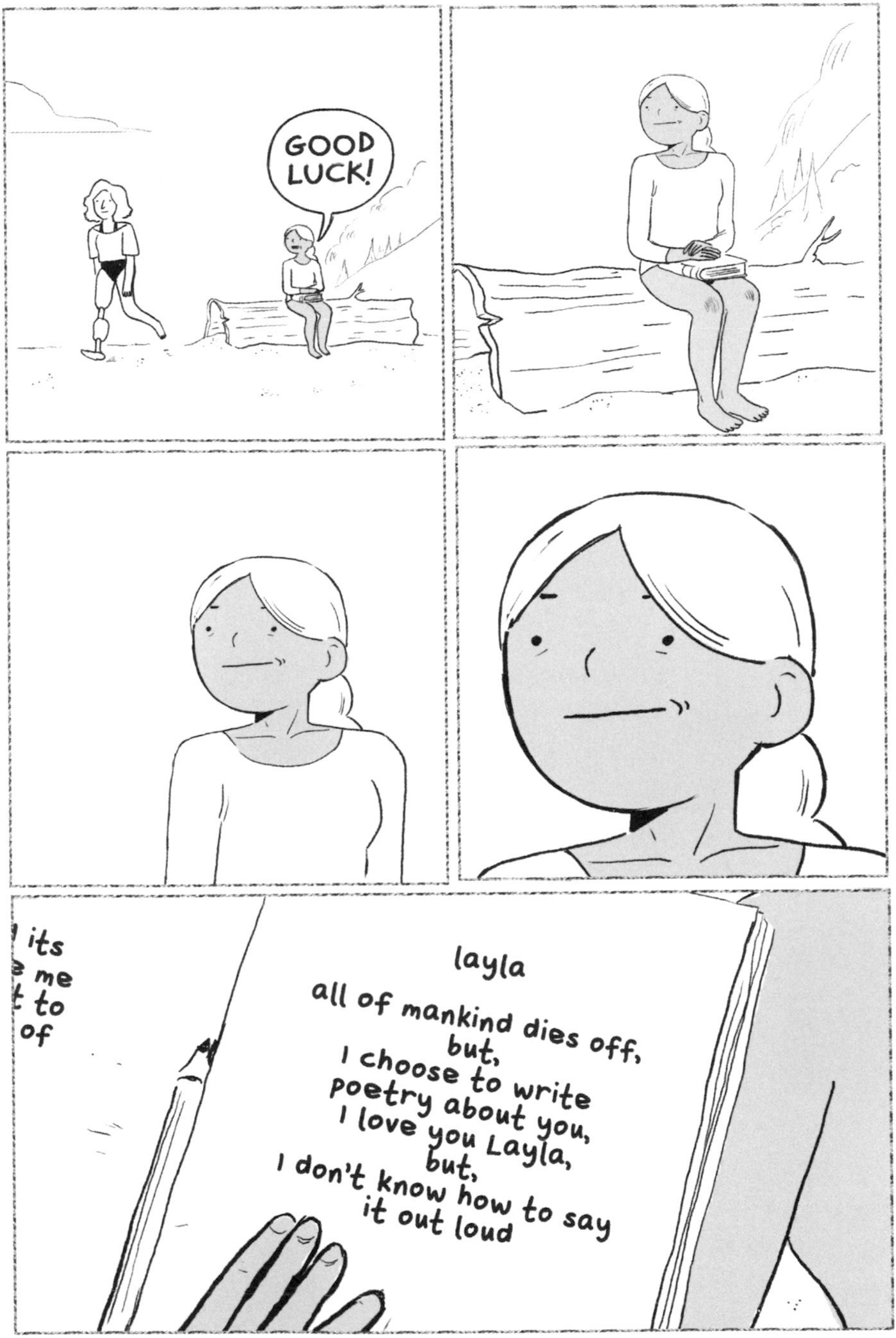
GOOD LUCK!
layla
all of mankind dies off,
but,
I choose to write
poetry about you,
I love you Layla,
but,
I don't know how to say
it out loud

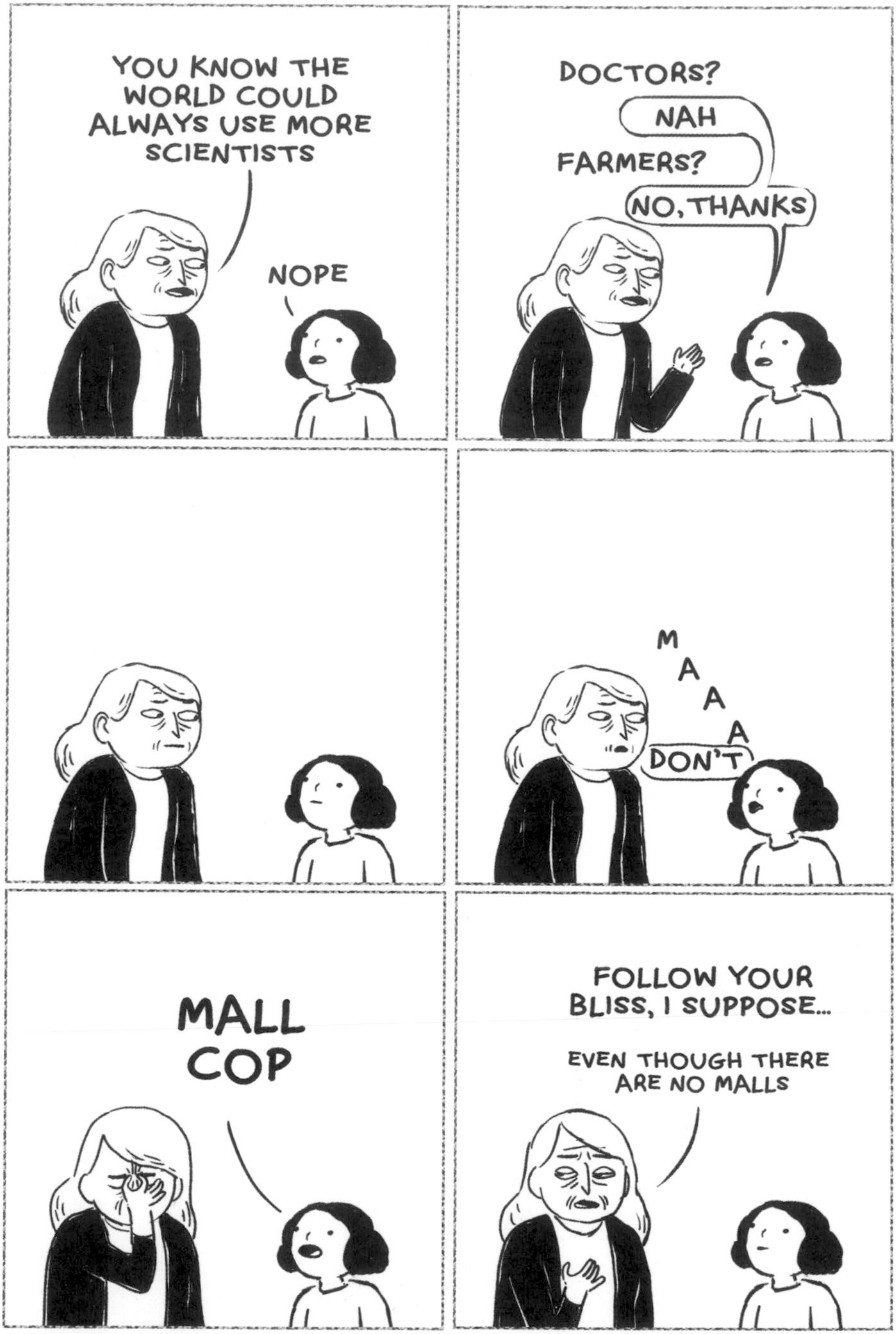
YOU KNOW THE WORLD COULD ALWAYS USE MORE SCIENTISTS
NOPE
DOCTORS?
NAH
FARMERS?
NO, THANKS
M A A A
DON'T
MALL COP
FOLLOW YOUR BLISS, I SUPPOSE...
EVEN THOUGH THERE ARE NO MALLS

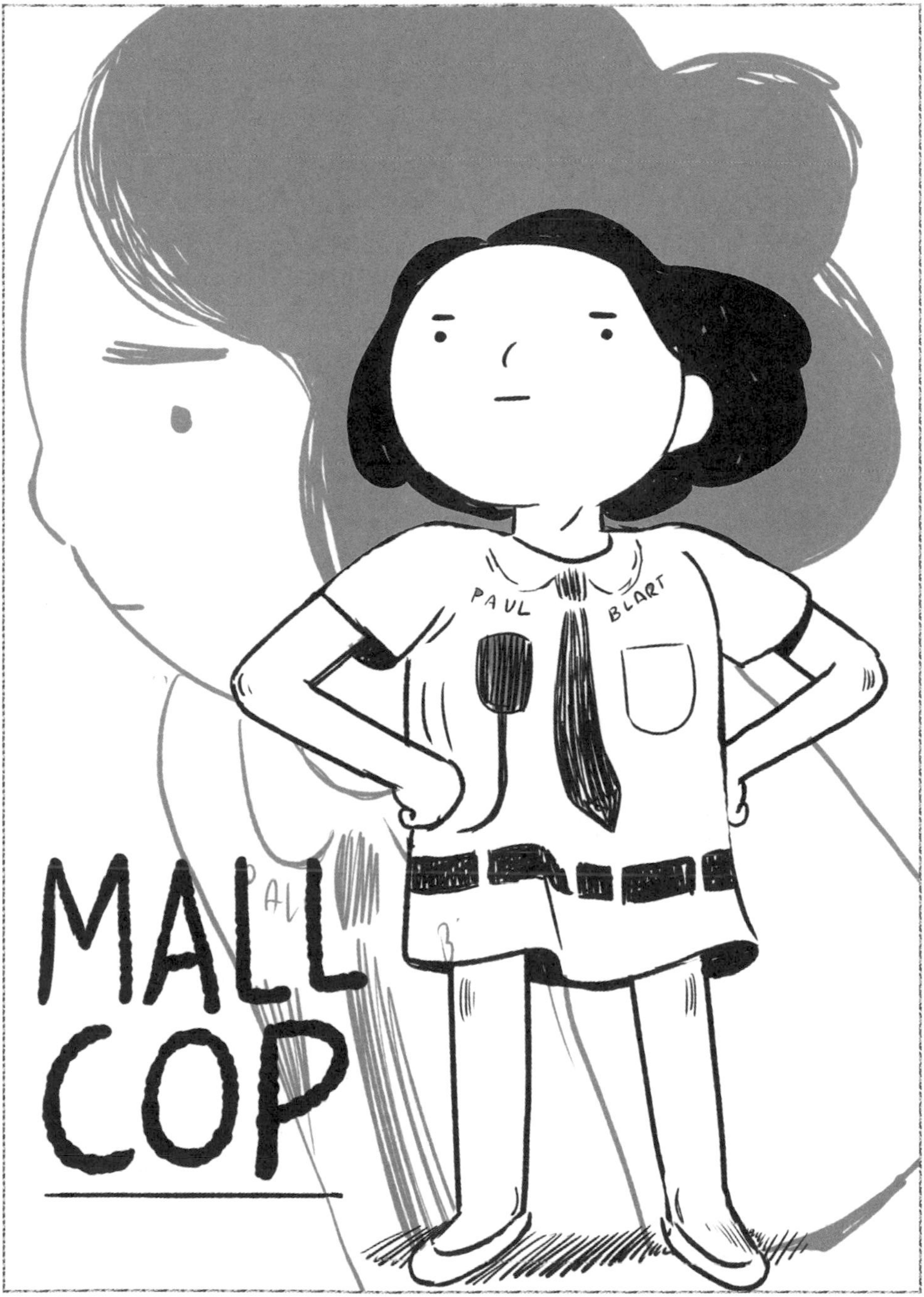

PAUL BLART
MALL COP

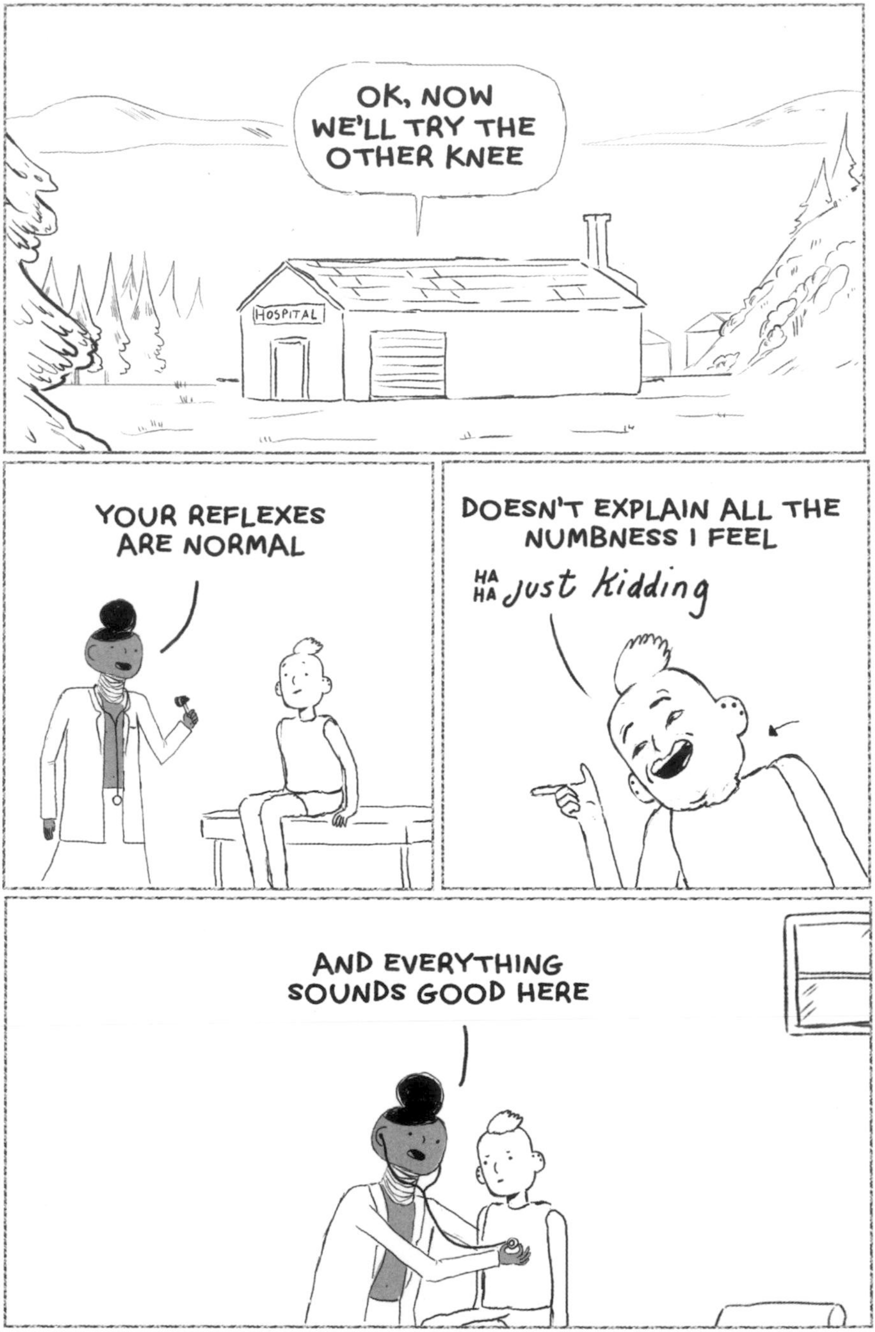

OK, NOW WE'LL TRY THE OTHER KNEE
HOSPITAL
YOUR REFLEXES ARE NORMAL
DOESN'T EXPLAIN ALL THE NUMBNESS I FEEL
HA HA just kidding
AND EVERYTHING SOUNDS GOOD HERE

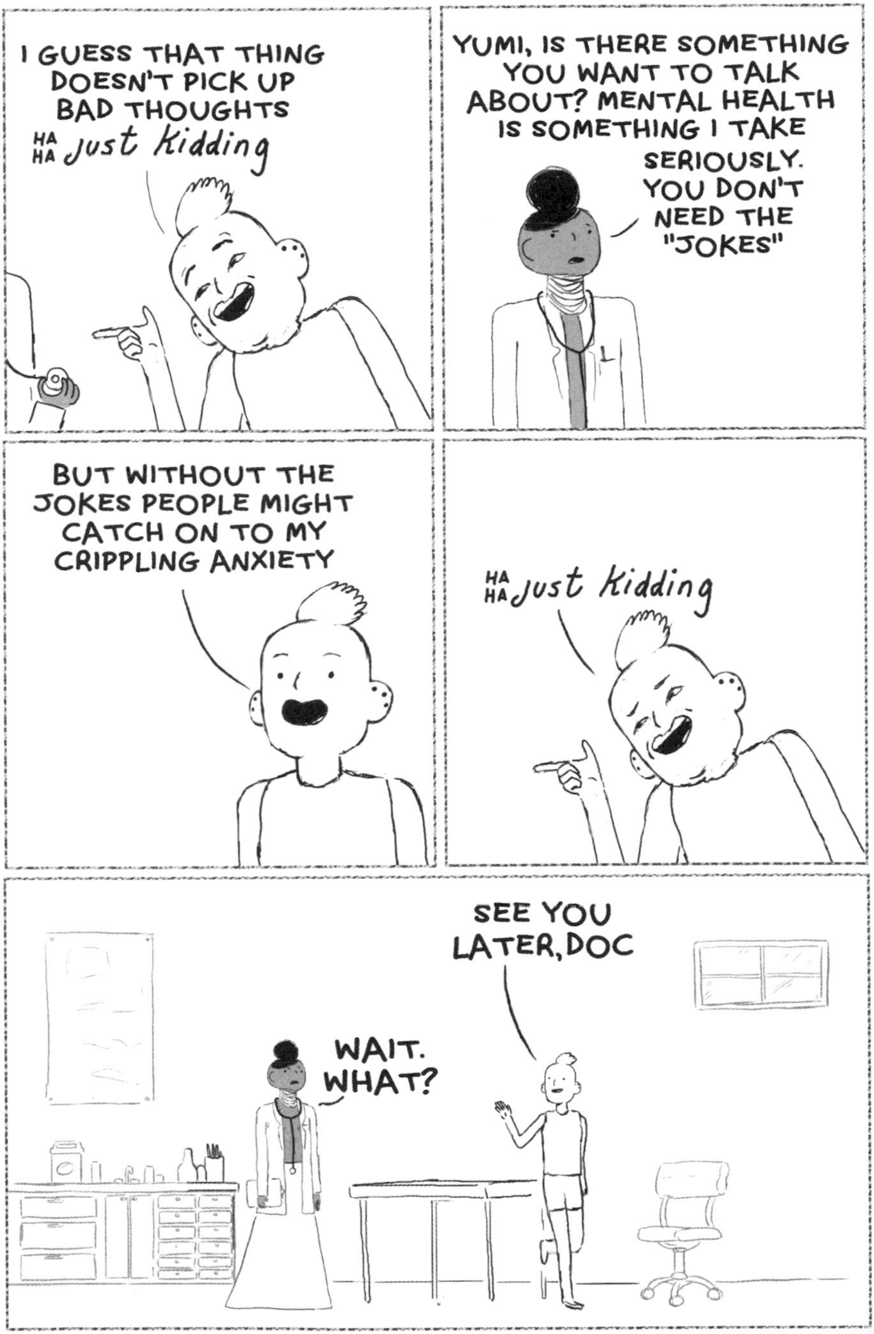
I GUESS THAT THING DOESN'T PICK UP BAD THOUGHTS
HA HA just kidding
YUMI, IS THERE SOMETHING YOU WANT TO TALK ABOUT? MENTAL HEALTH IS SOMETHING I TAKE SERIOUSLY. YOU DON'T NEED THE "JOKES"
BUT WITHOUT THE JOKES PEOPLE MIGHT CATCH ON TO MY CRIPPLING ANXIETY
HA HA just kidding
SEE YOU LATER, DOC
WAIT. WHAT?

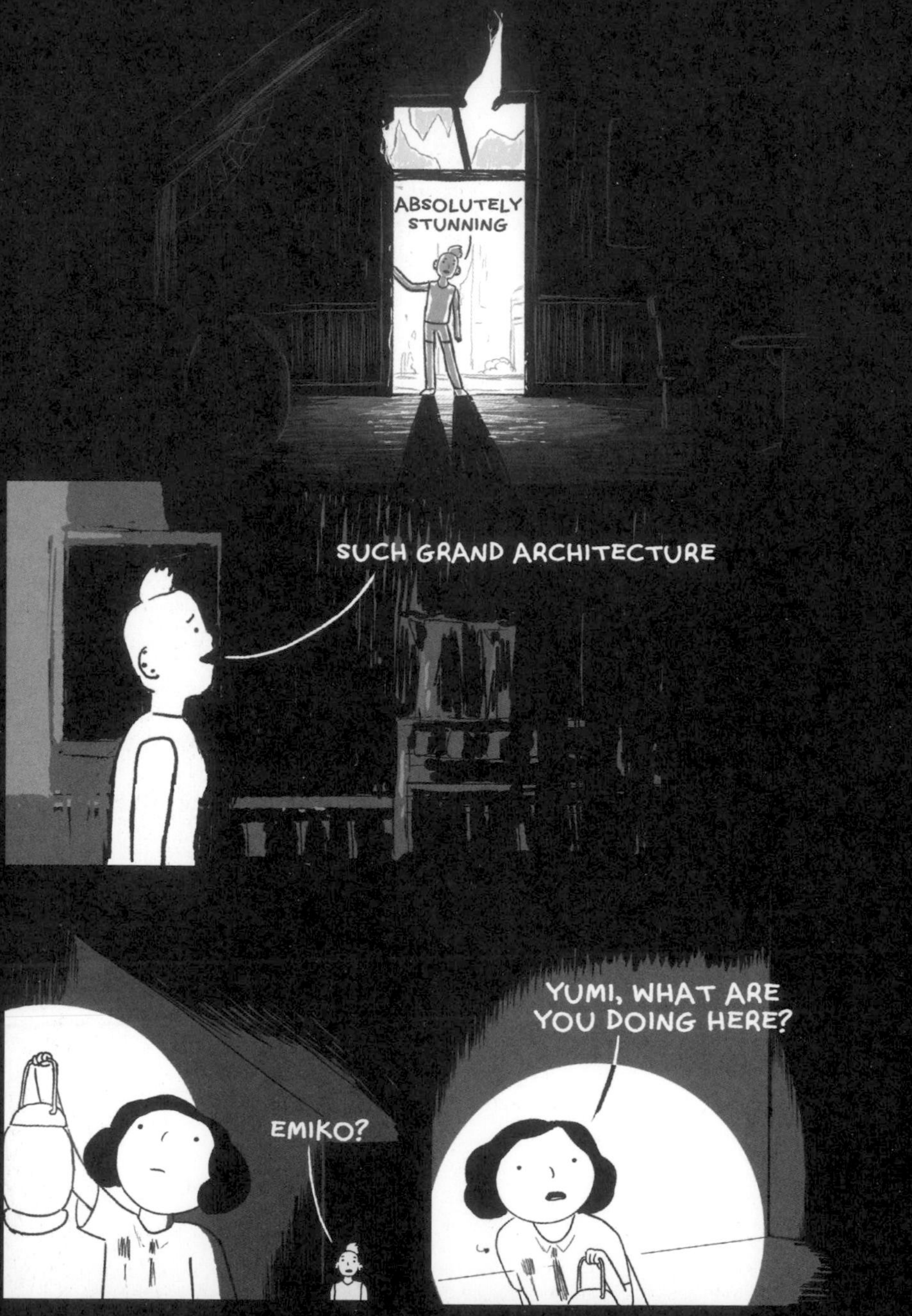
ABSOLUTELY STUNNING
SUCH GRAND ARCHITECTURE
EMIKO?
YUMI, WHAT ARE YOU DOING HERE?

I FELT AN URGE TO
EXPLORE THE RUINS

TO SEEK ANSWERS
FROM THE PAST

THERE'S SO MUCH
WISDOM TRAPPED
IN THESE WALLS

S BUCKS COFFEE

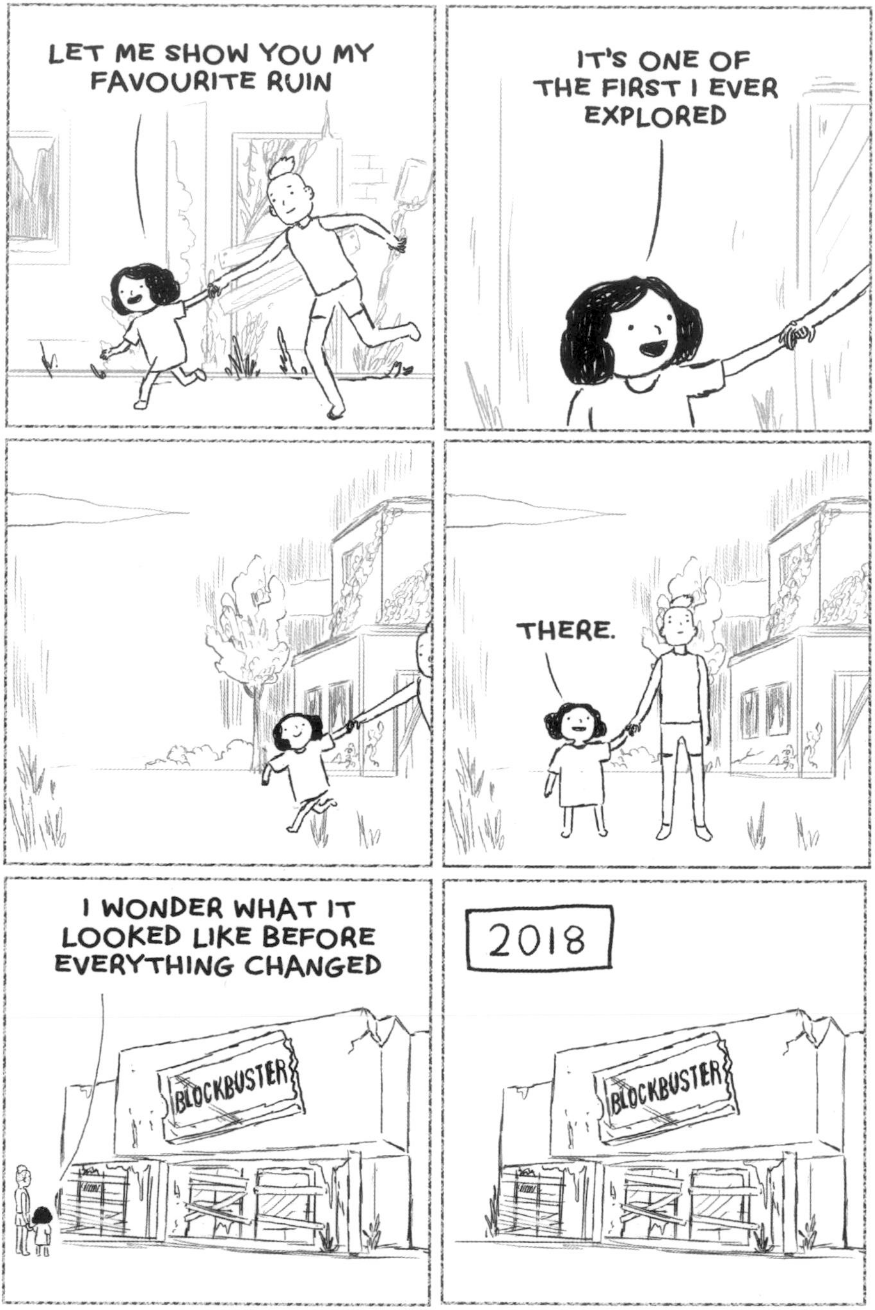
LET ME SHOW YOU MY FAVOURITE RUIN
IT'S ONE OF THE FIRST I EVER EXPLORED
THERE.
I WONDER WHAT IT LOOKED LIKE BEFORE EVERYTHING CHANGED
BLOCKBUSTER
2018
BLOCKBUSTER

I DUNNO IF I COULD BAND WOMEN TOGETHER LIKE YOU DO
I DON'T HAVE YOUR CONFIDENCE
OH! YOU SHOULD DO WHAT I DO!
NOPE. NUH-UH. NOT FEELING MORE CONFIDENT.

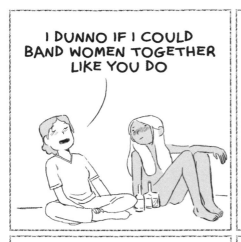

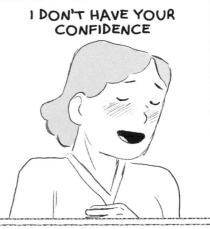

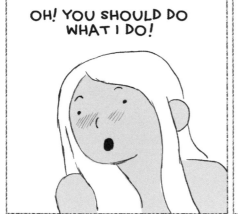

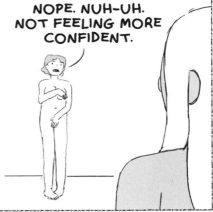

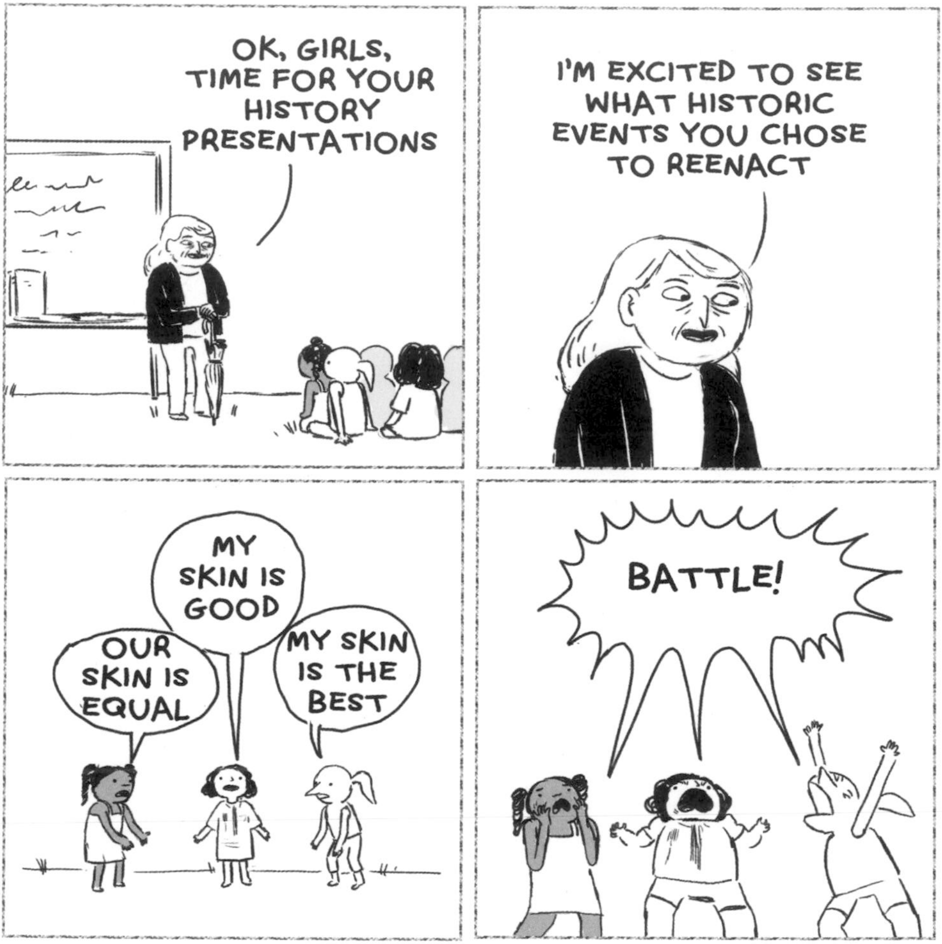
OK, GIRLS, TIME FOR YOUR HISTORY PRESENTATIONS
I'M EXCITED TO SEE WHAT HISTORIC EVENTS YOU CHOSE TO REENACT
OUR SKIN IS EQUAL
MY SKIN IS GOOD
MY SKIN IS THE BEST
BATTLE!

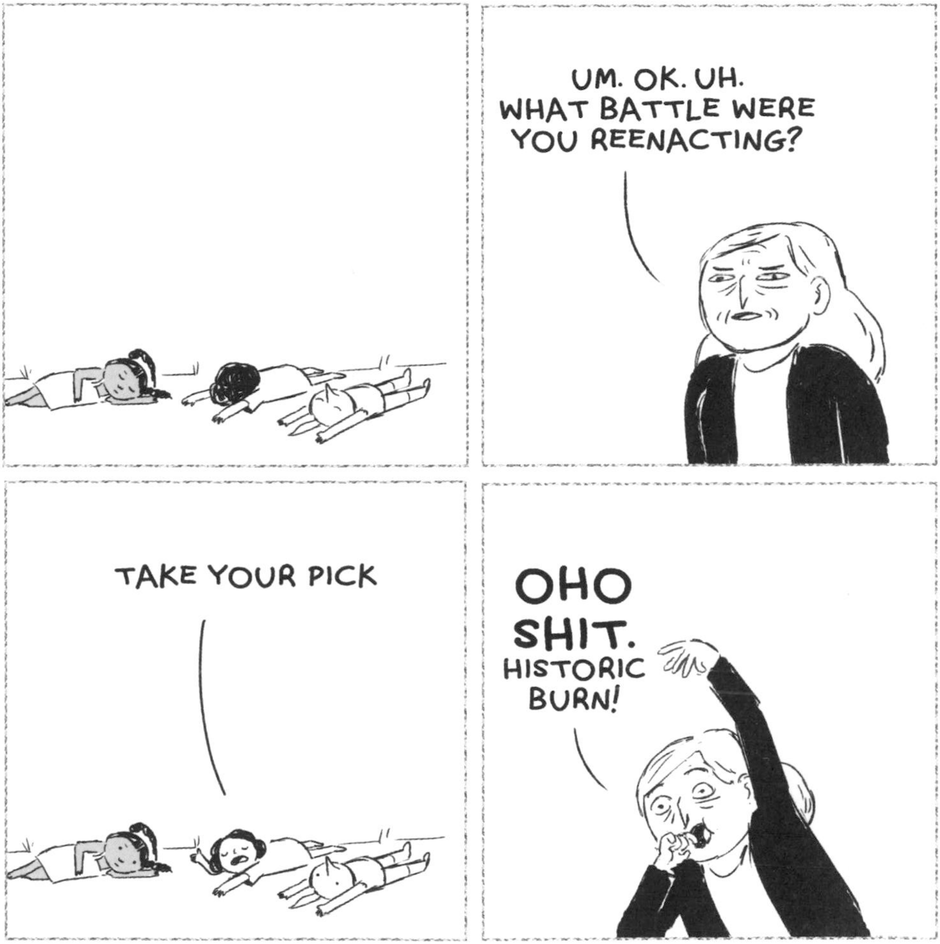
UM. OK. UH.
WHAT BATTLE WERE
YOU REENACTING?
TAKE YOUR PICK
OHO
SHIT.
HISTORIC
BURN!

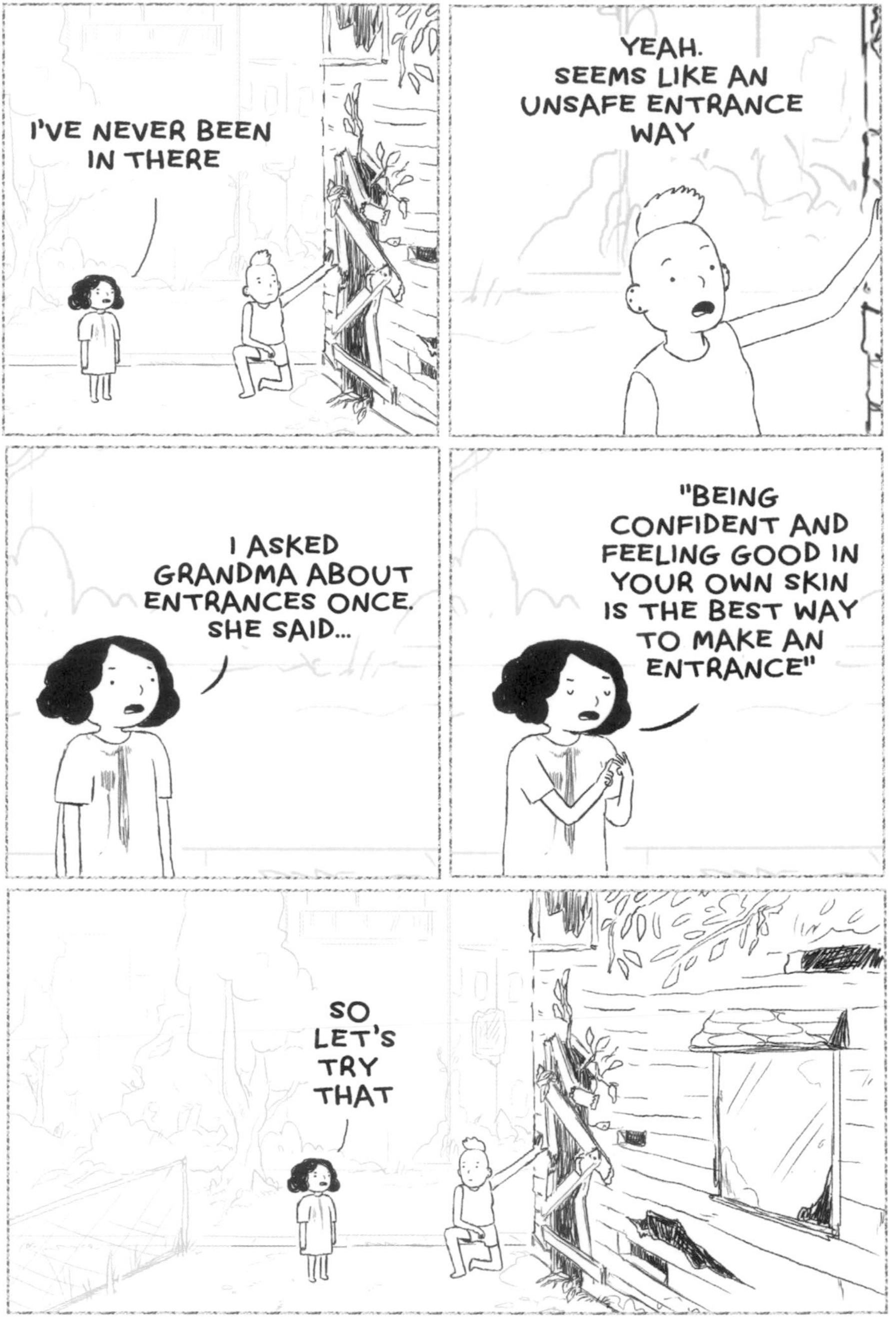
I'VE NEVER BEEN IN THERE
YEAH. SEEMS LIKE AN UNSAFE ENTRANCE WAY
I ASKED GRANDMA ABOUT ENTRANCES ONCE. SHE SAID...
"BEING CONFIDENT AND FEELING GOOD IN YOUR OWN SKIN IS THE BEST WAY TO MAKE AN ENTRANCE"
SO LET'S TRY THAT

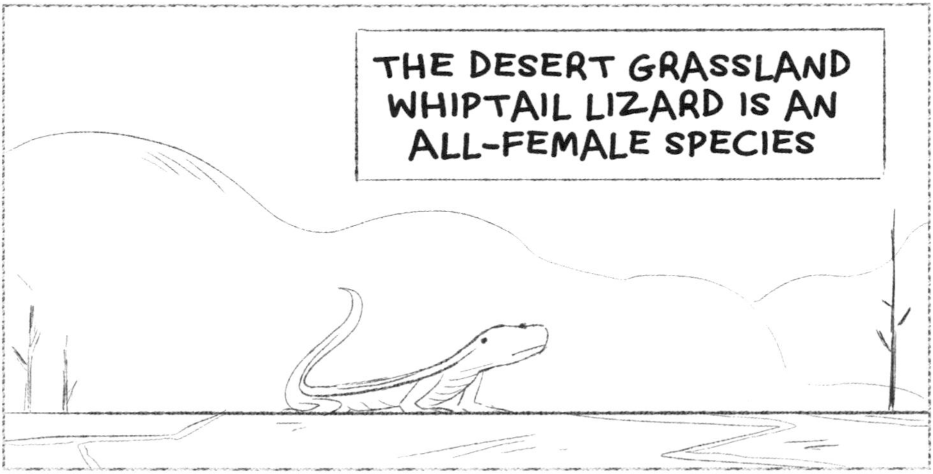
THE DESERT GRASSLAND WHIPTAIL LIZARD IS AN ALL-FEMALE SPECIES

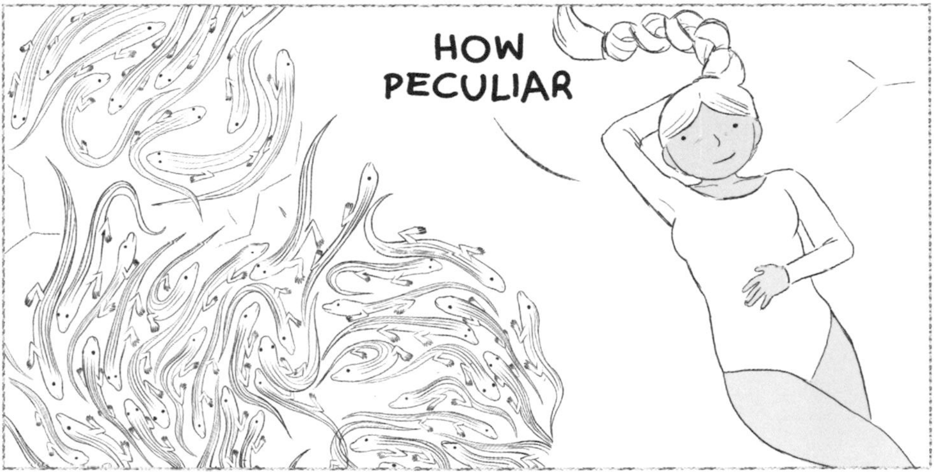
HOW PECULIAR

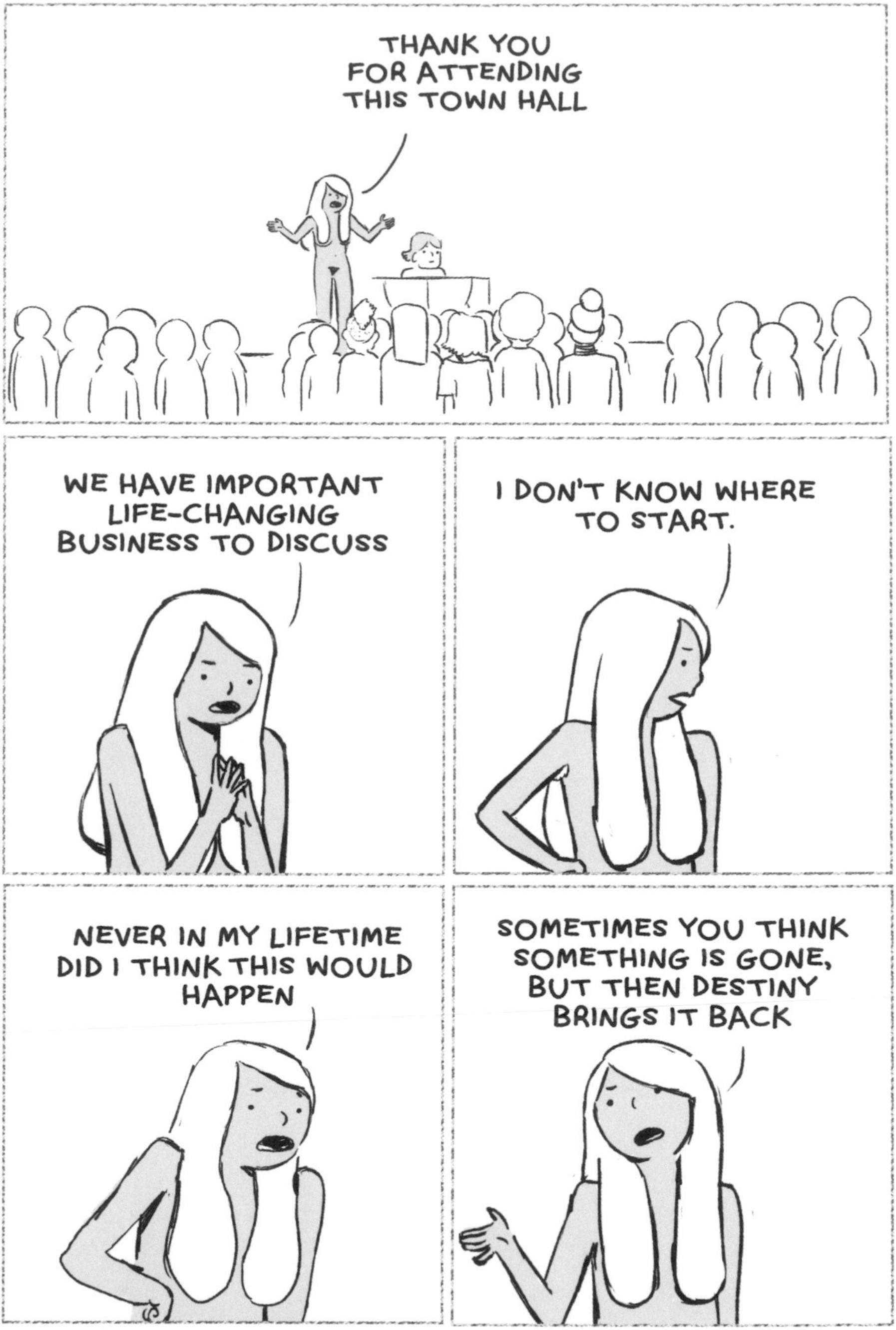
THANK YOU FOR ATTENDING THIS TOWN HALL
WE HAVE IMPORTANT LIFE-CHANGING BUSINESS TO DISCUSS
I DON'T KNOW WHERE TO START.
NEVER IN MY LIFETIME DID I THINK THIS WOULD HAPPEN
SOMETIMES YOU THINK SOMETHING IS GONE, BUT THEN DESTINY BRINGS IT BACK

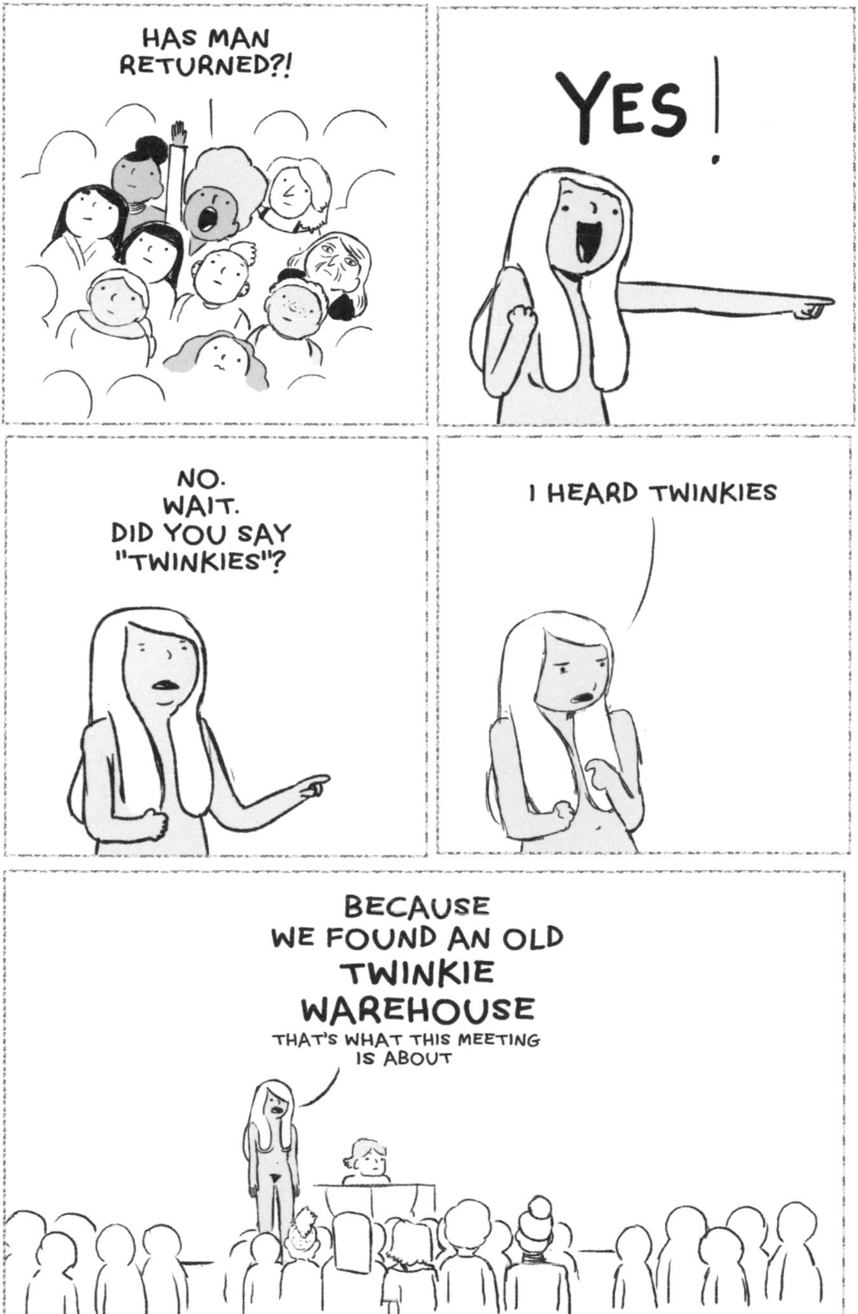
HAS MAN RETURNED?!
YES!
NO.
WAIT.
DID YOU SAY "TWINKIES"?
I HEARD TWINKIES
BECAUSE WE FOUND AN OLD TWINKIE WAREHOUSE
THAT'S WHAT THIS MEETING IS ABOUT

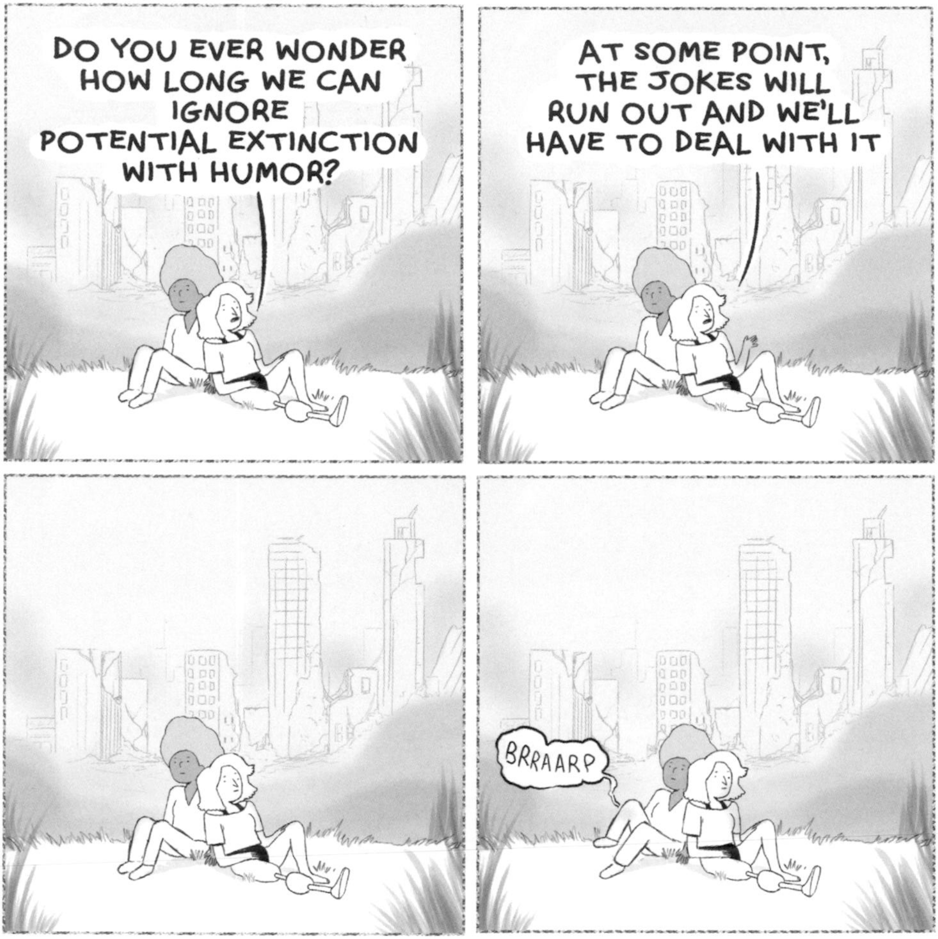
DO YOU EVER WONDER HOW LONG WE CAN IGNORE POTENTIAL EXTINCTION WITH HUMOR?
AT SOME POINT, THE JOKES WILL RUN OUT AND WE'LL HAVE TO DEAL WITH IT
BRRAARP

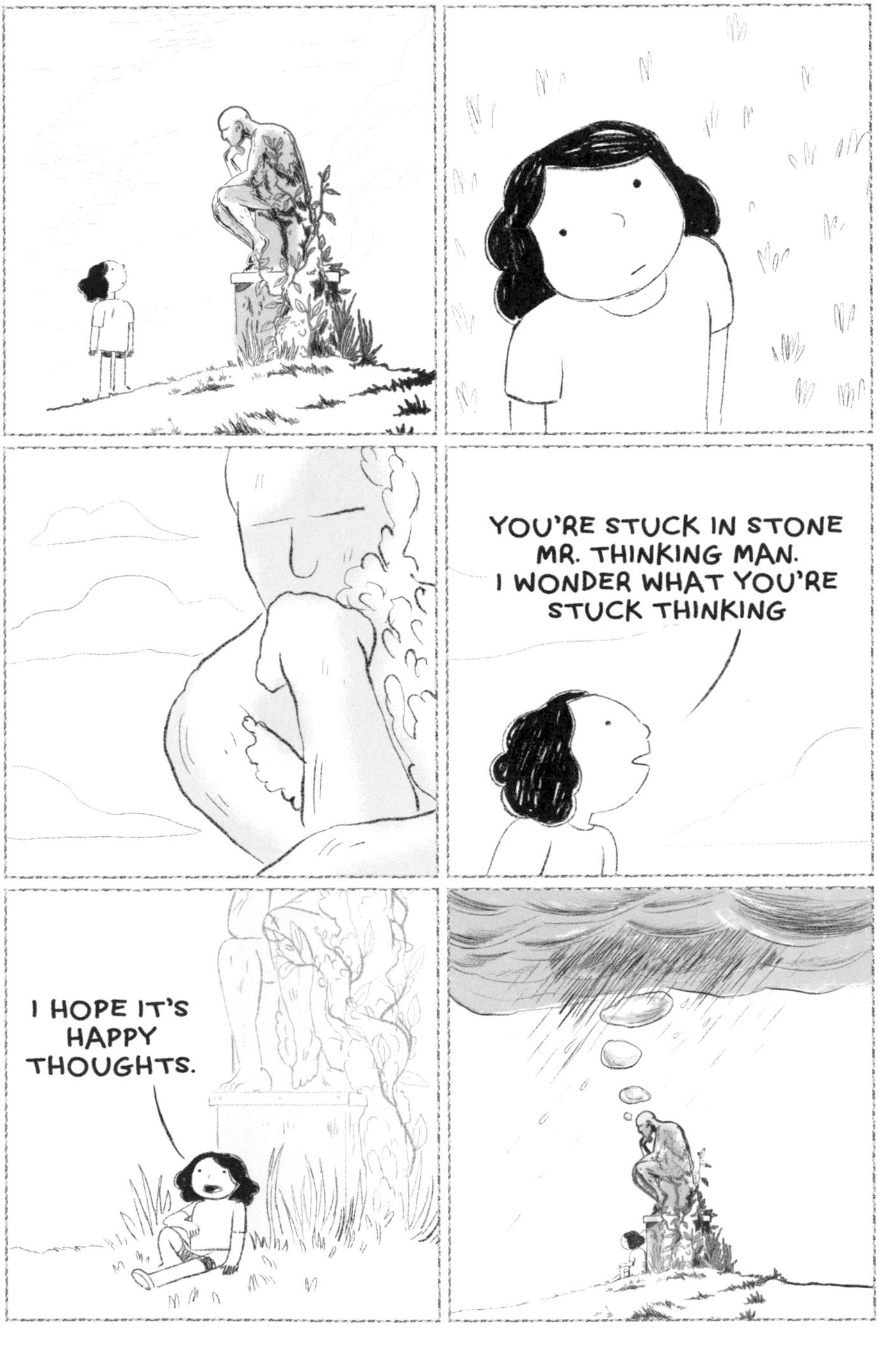
YOU'RE STUCK IN STONE MR. THINKING MAN. I WONDER WHAT YOU'RE STUCK THINKING
I HOPE IT'S HAPPY THOUGHTS.

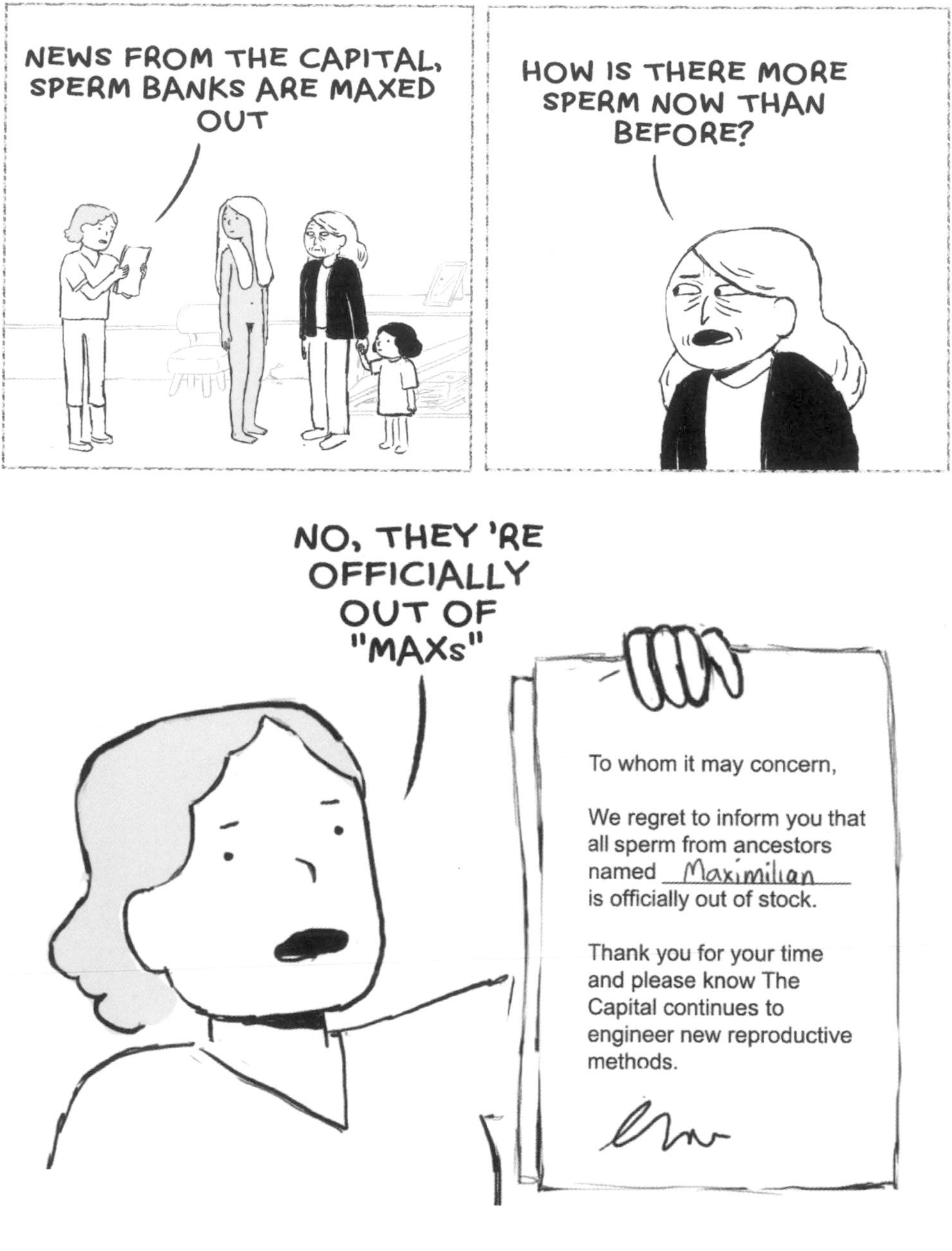
NEWS FROM THE CAPITAL, SPERM BANKS ARE MAXED OUT
HOW IS THERE MORE SPERM NOW THAN BEFORE?
NO, THEY 'RE OFFICIALLY OUT OF "MAXs"
To whom it may concern,
We regret to inform you that all sperm from ancestors named Maximilian is officially out of stock.
Thank you for your time and please know The Capital continues to engineer new reproductive methods.

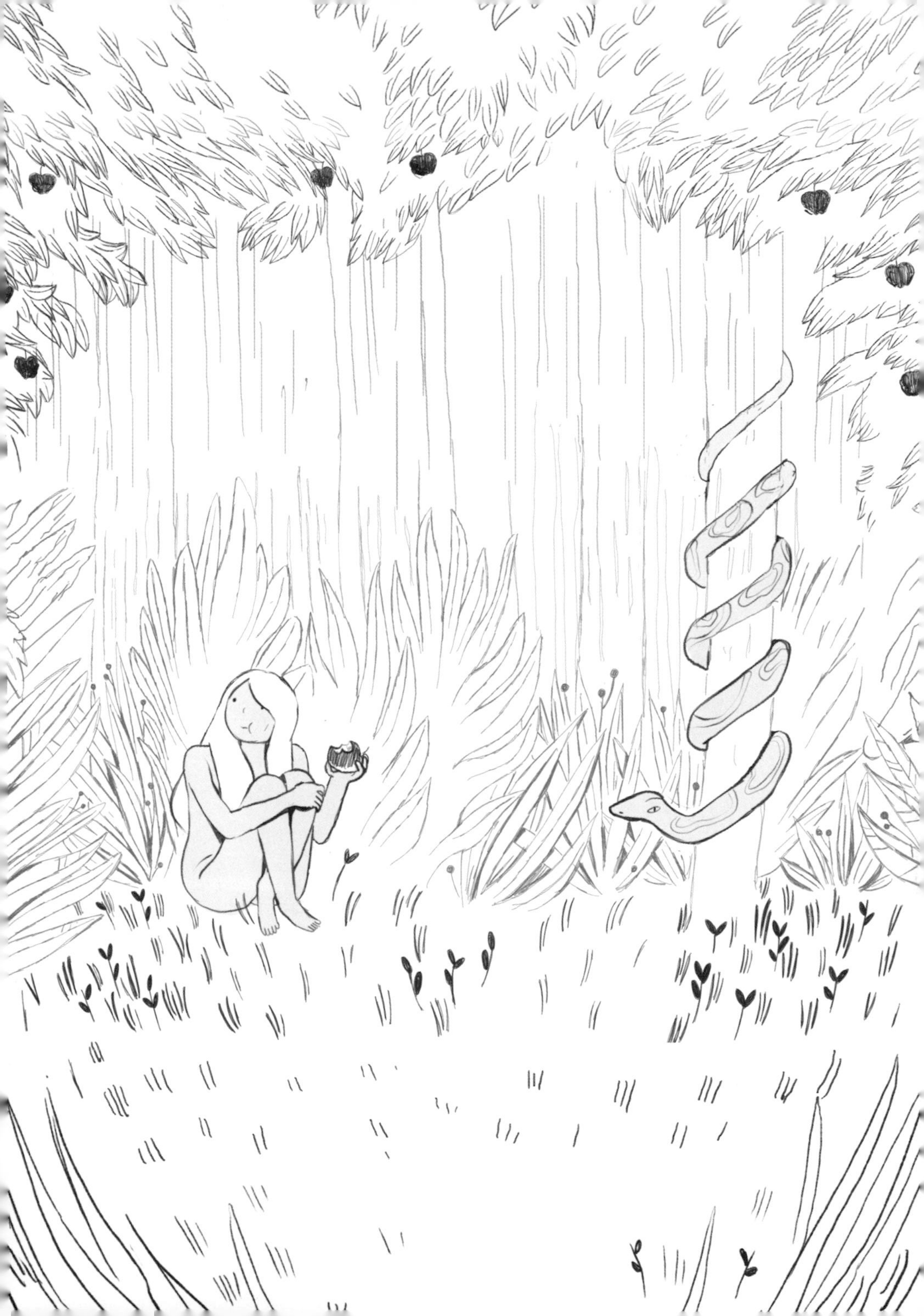

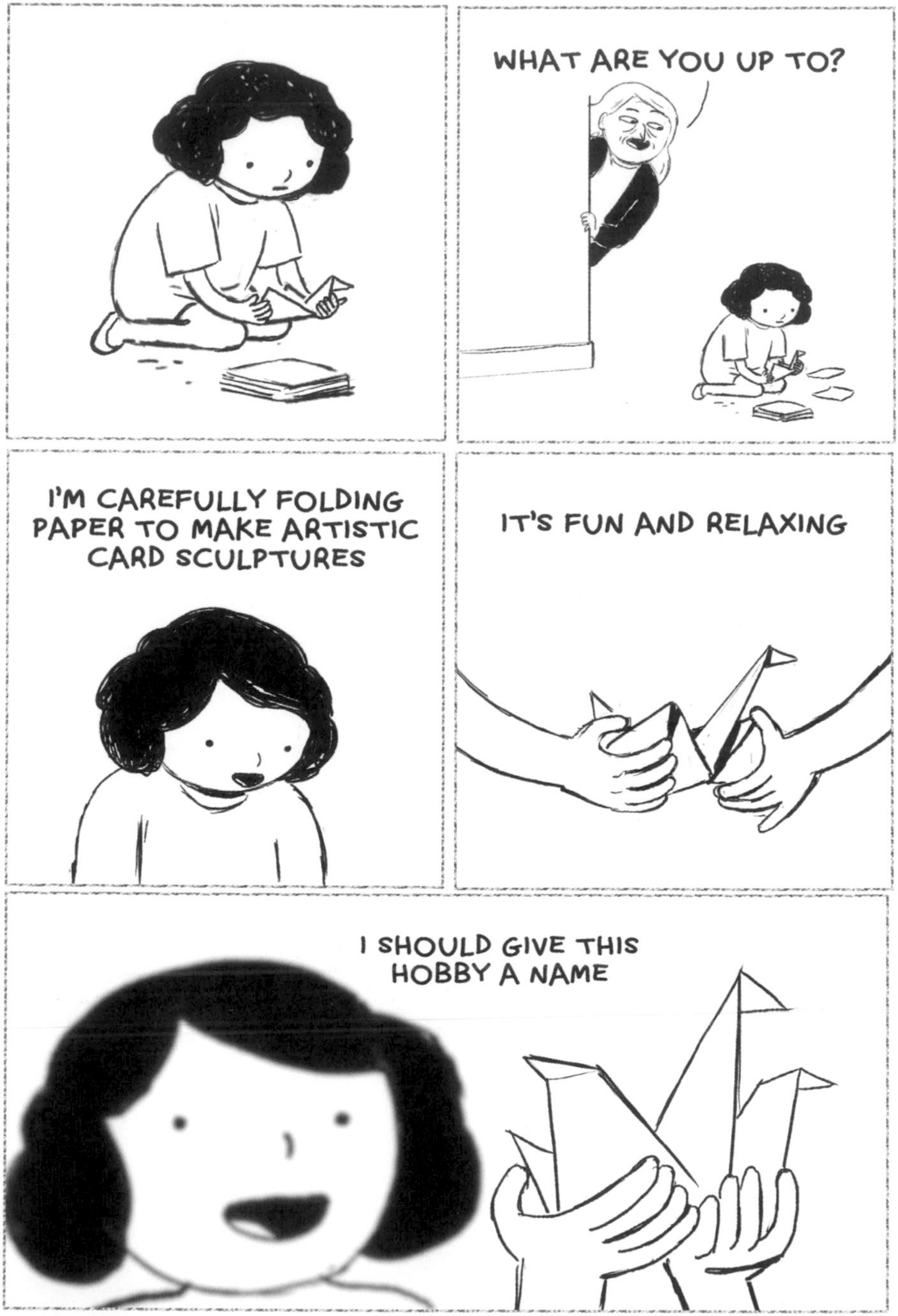
WHAT ARE YOU UP TO?
I'M CAREFULLY FOLDING PAPER TO MAKE ARTISTIC CARD SCULPTURES
IT'S FUN AND RELAXING
I SHOULD GIVE THIS HOBBY A NAME

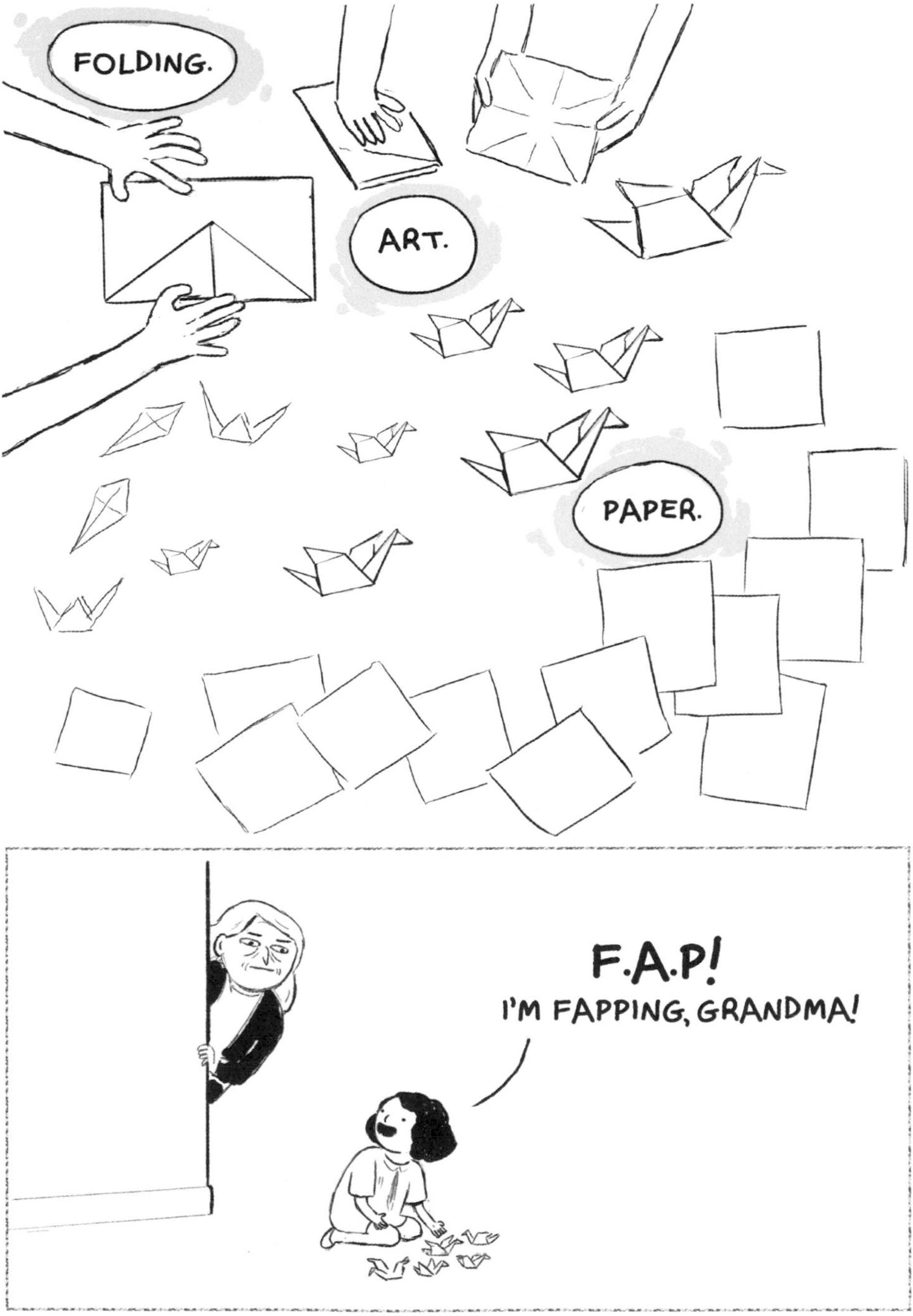
FOLDING.
ART.
PAPER.
F.A.P!
I'M FAPPING, GRANDMA!

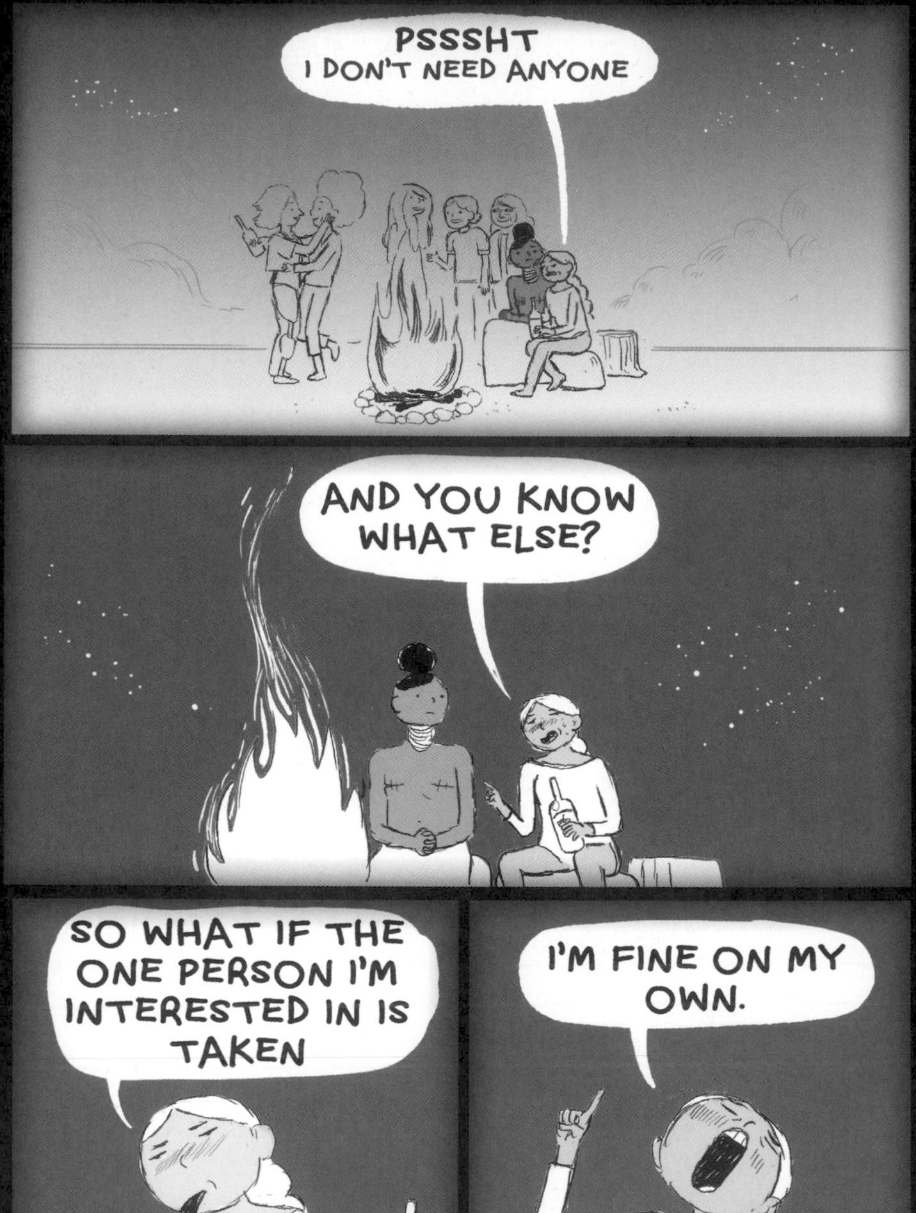
PSSSHT
I DON'T NEED ANYONE
AND YOU KNOW WHAT ELSE?
SO WHAT IF THE ONE PERSON I'M INTERESTED IN IS TAKEN
I'M FINE ON MY OWN.

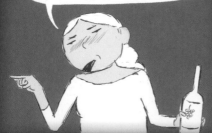

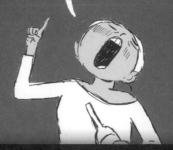

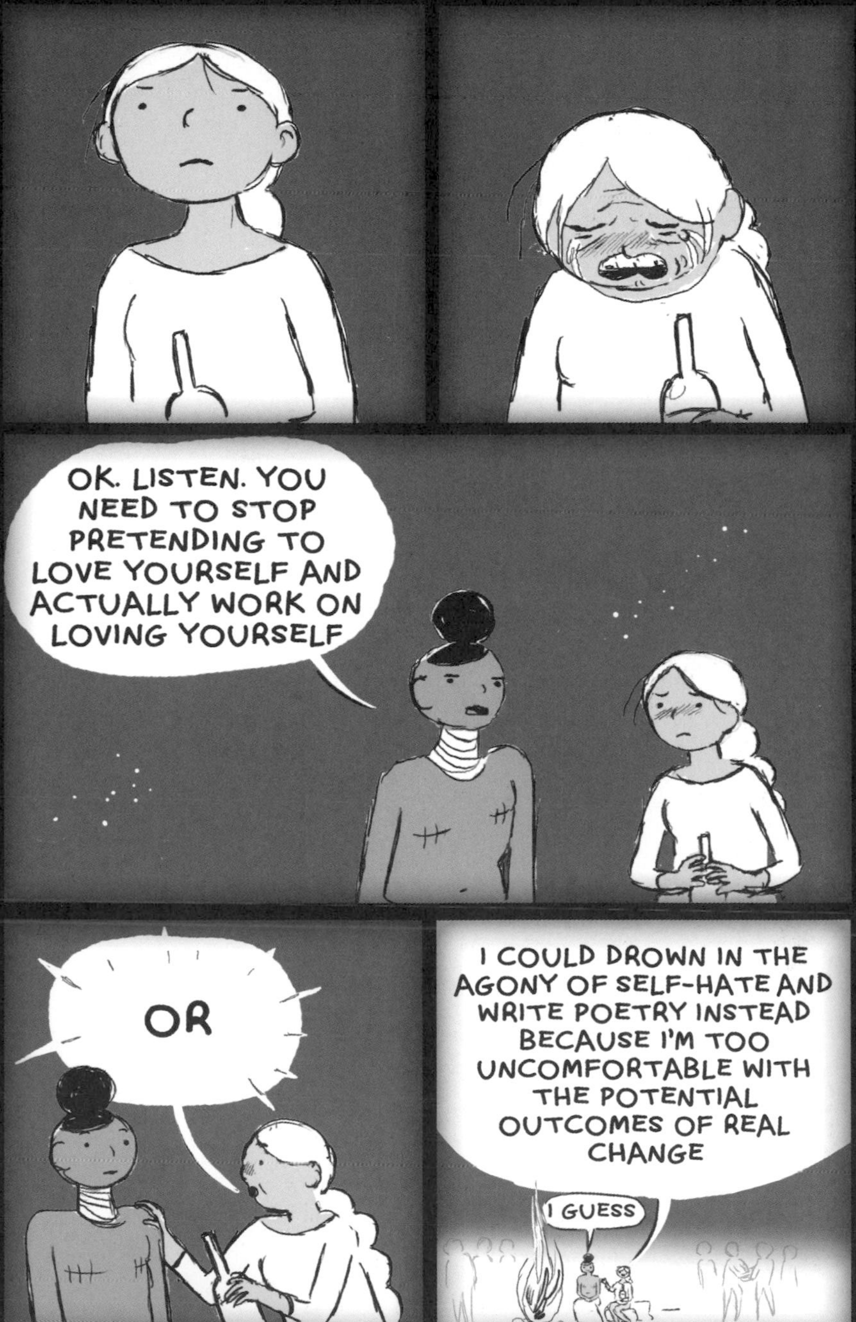

OK. LISTEN. YOU NEED TO STOP PRETENDING TO LOVE YOURSELF AND ACTUALLY WORK ON LOVING YOURSELF
OR
I COULD DROWN IN THE AGONY OF SELF-HATE AND WRITE POETRY INSTEAD BECAUSE I'M TOO UNCOMFORTABLE WITH THE POTENTIAL OUTCOMES OF REAL CHANGE
I GUESS

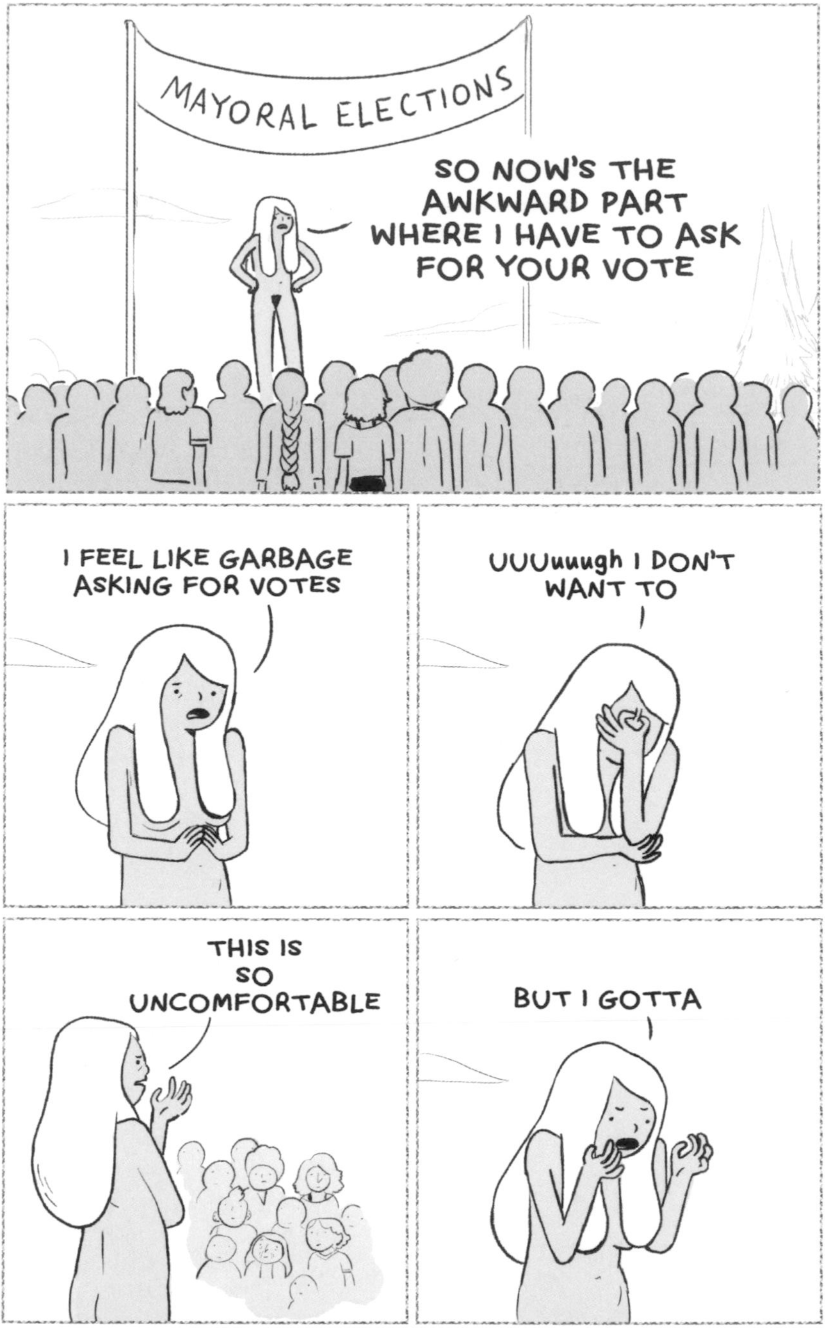
MAYORAL ELECTIONS
SO NOW'S THE AWKWARD PART WHERE I HAVE TO ASK FOR YOUR VOTE
I FEEL LIKE GARBAGE ASKING FOR VOTES
UUUuuugh I DON'T WANT TO
THIS IS SO UNCOMFORTABLE
BUT I GOTTA

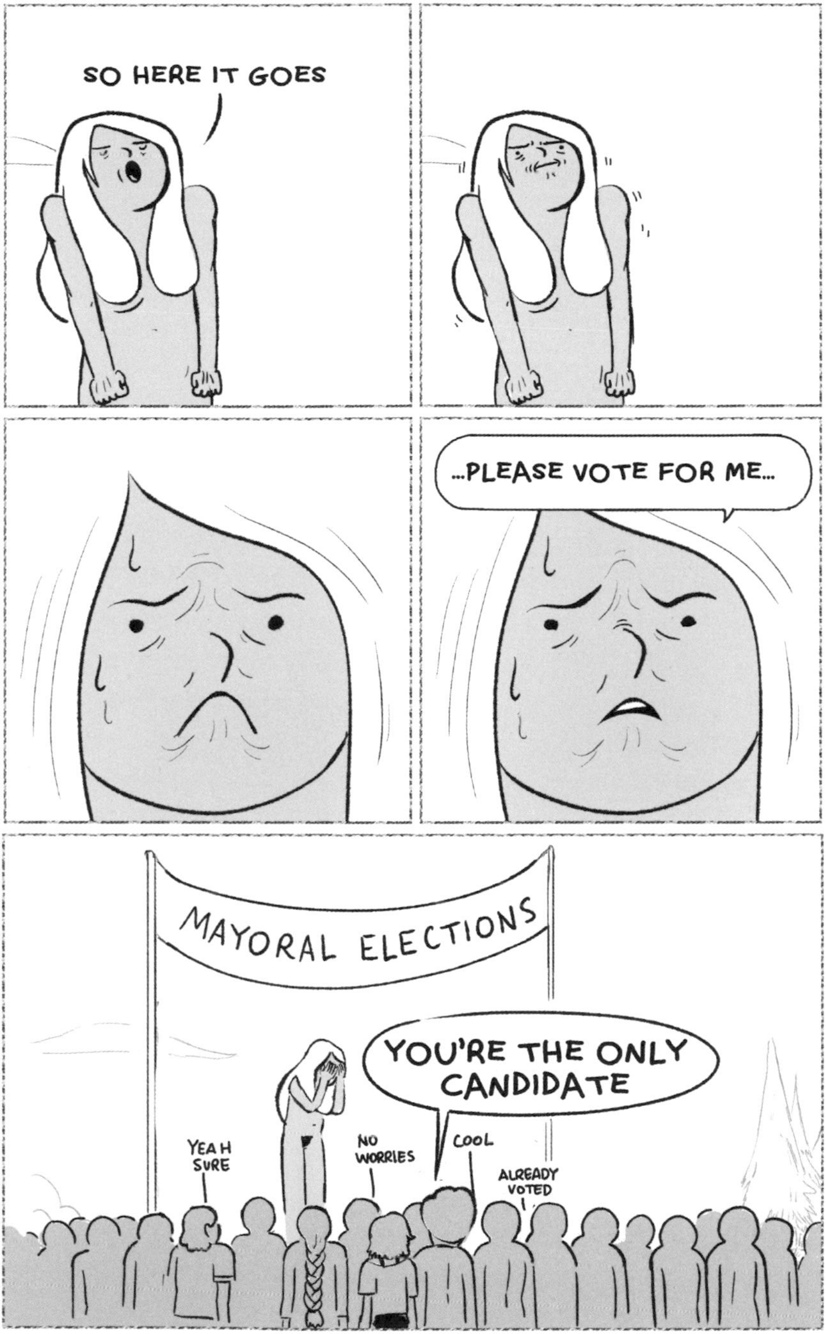
SO HERE IT GOES
...PLEASE VOTE FOR ME...
MAYORAL ELECTIONS
YOU'RE THE ONLY CANDIDATE
YEAH SURE
NO WORRIES
COOL
ALREADY VOTED

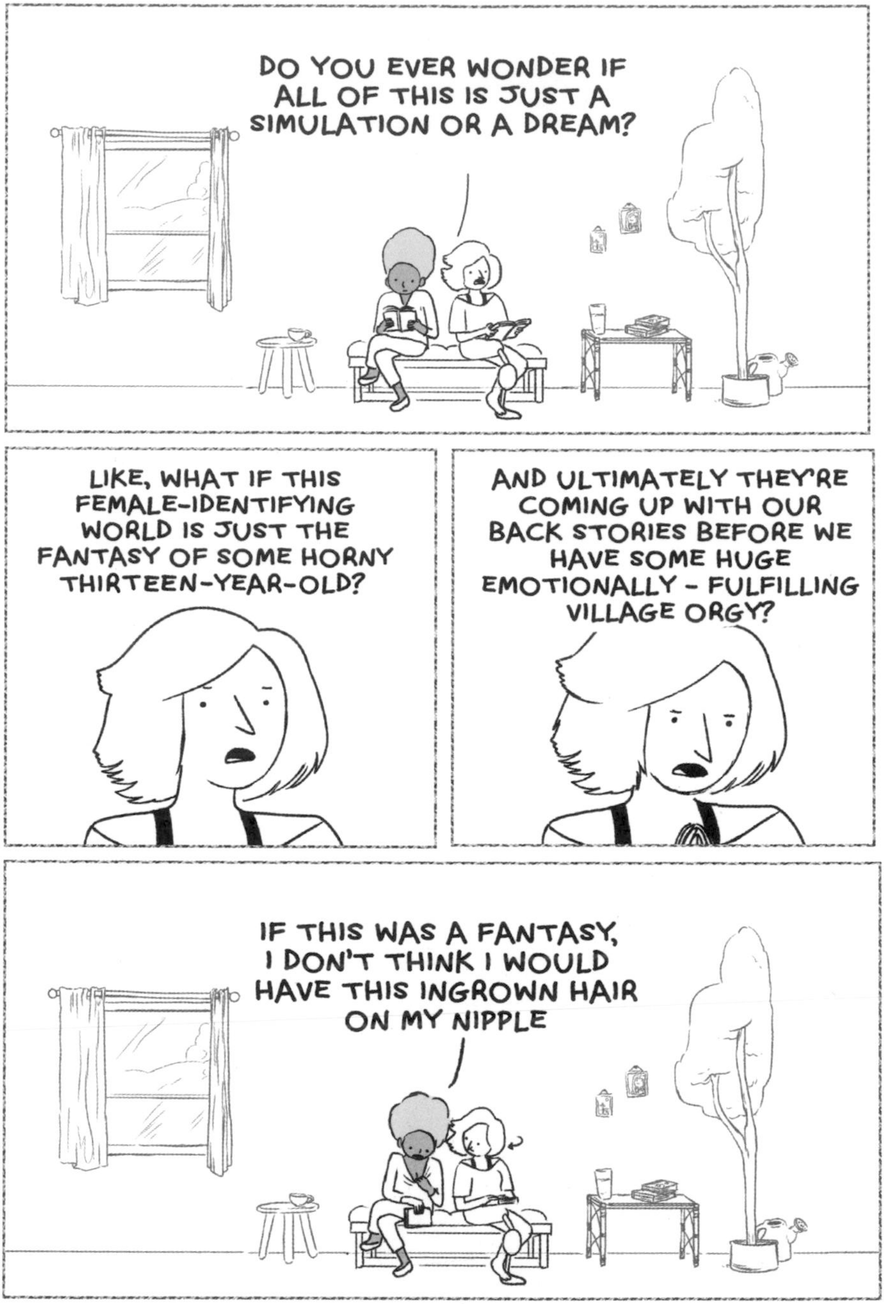
DO YOU EVER WONDER IF ALL OF THIS IS JUST A SIMULATION OR A DREAM?
LIKE, WHAT IF THIS FEMALE-IDENTIFYING WORLD IS JUST THE FANTASY OF SOME HORNY THIRTEEN-YEAR-OLD?
AND ULTIMATELY THEY'RE COMING UP WITH OUR BACK STORIES BEFORE WE HAVE SOME HUGE EMOTIONALLY - FULFILLING VILLAGE ORGY?
IF THIS WAS A FANTASY, I DON'T THINK I WOULD HAVE THIS INGROWN HAIR ON MY NIPPLE

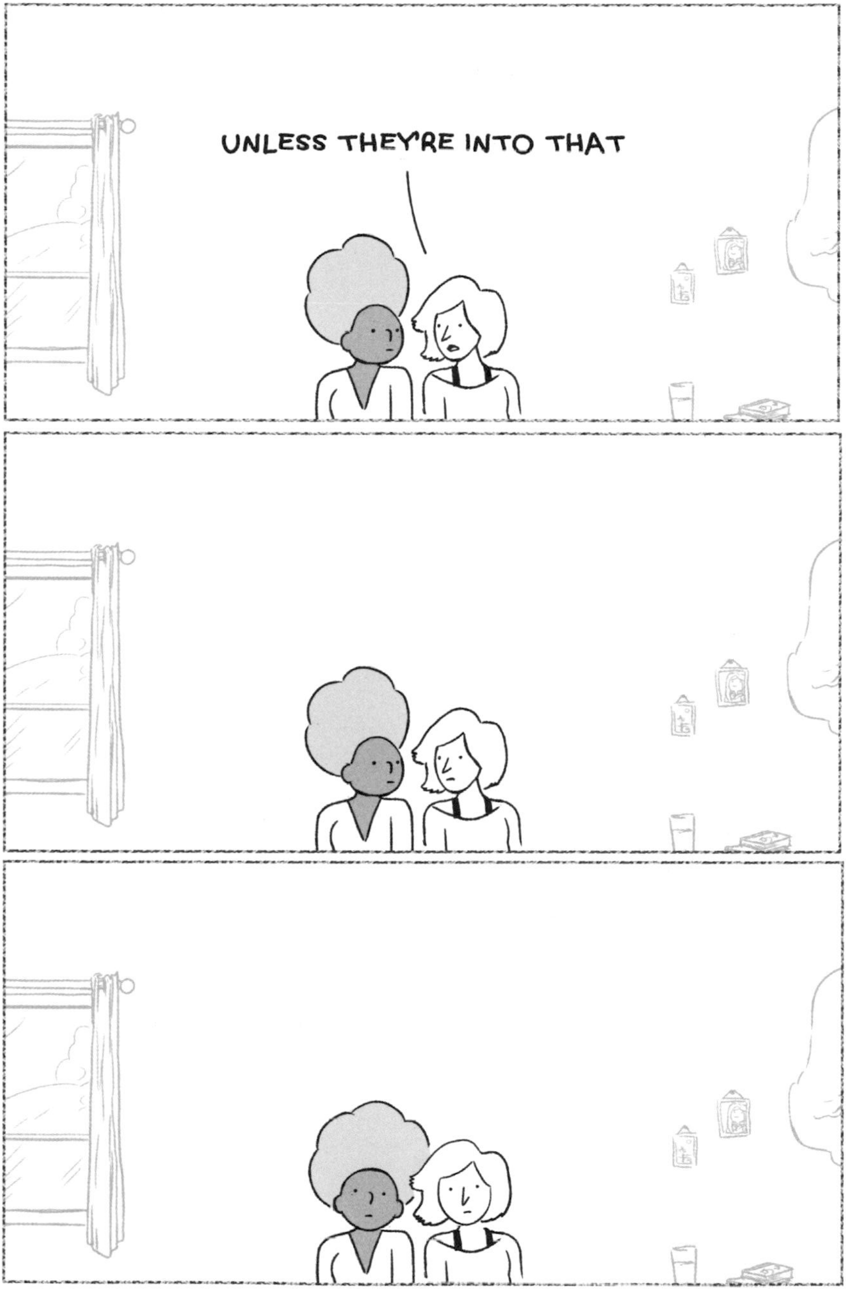
UNLESS THEY'RE INTO THAT

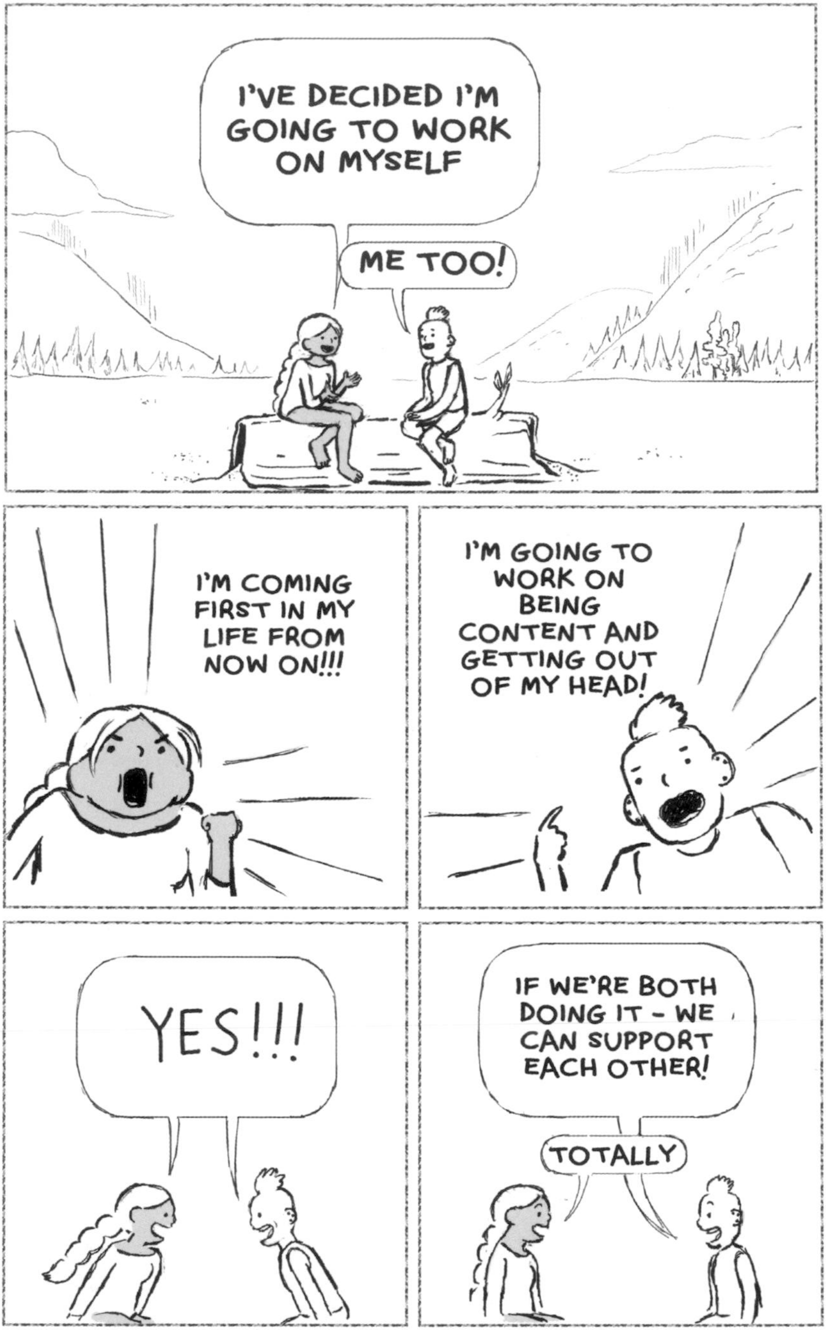
I'VE DECIDED I'M GOING TO WORK ON MYSELF
ME TOO!
I'M COMING FIRST IN MY LIFE FROM NOW ON!!!
I'M GOING TO WORK ON BEING CONTENT AND GETTING OUT OF MY HEAD!
YES!!!
IF WE'RE BOTH DOING IT - WE CAN SUPPORT EACH OTHER!
TOTALLY

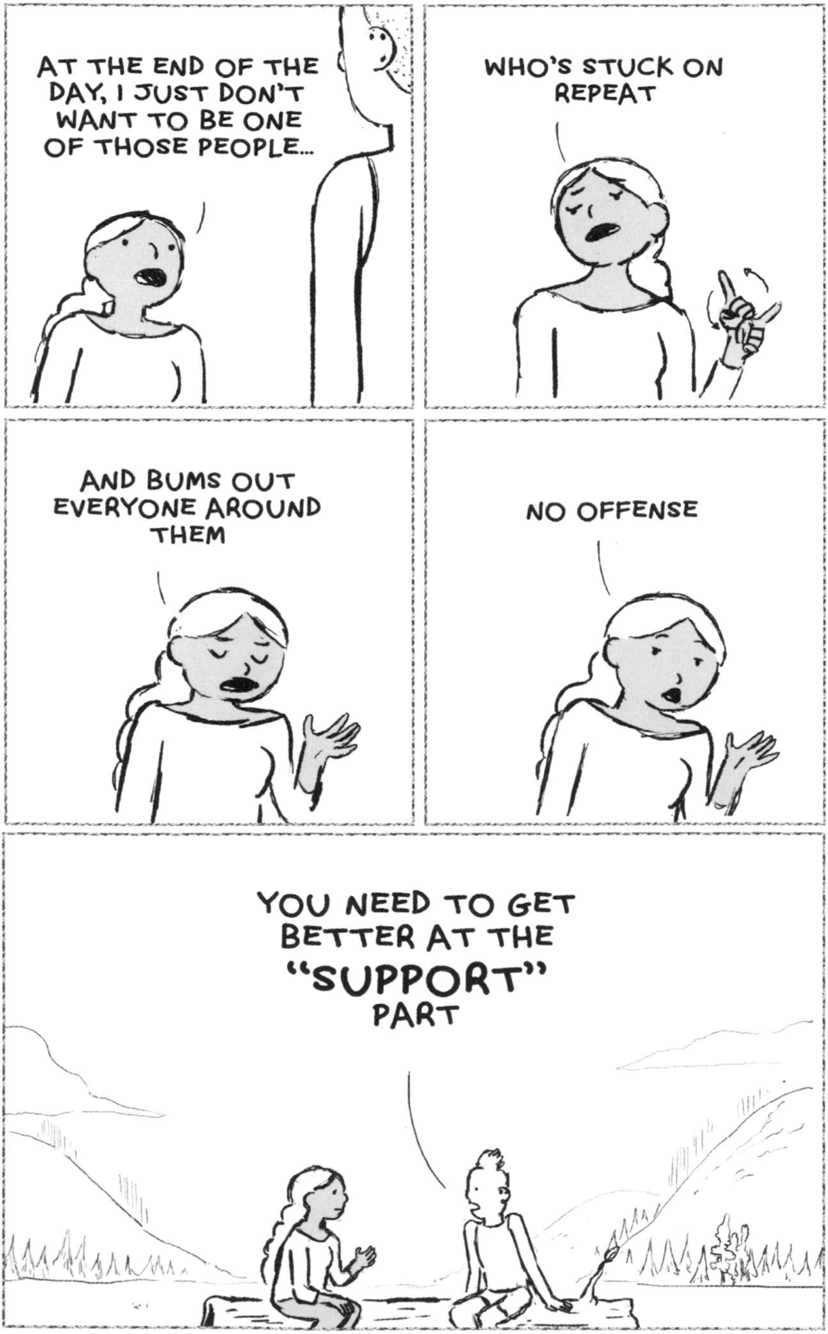
AT THE END OF THE DAY, I JUST DON'T WANT TO BE ONE OF THOSE PEOPLE...
WHO'S STUCK ON REPEAT
AND BUMS OUT EVERYONE AROUND THEM
NO OFFENSE
YOU NEED TO GET BETTER AT THE "SUPPORT" PART

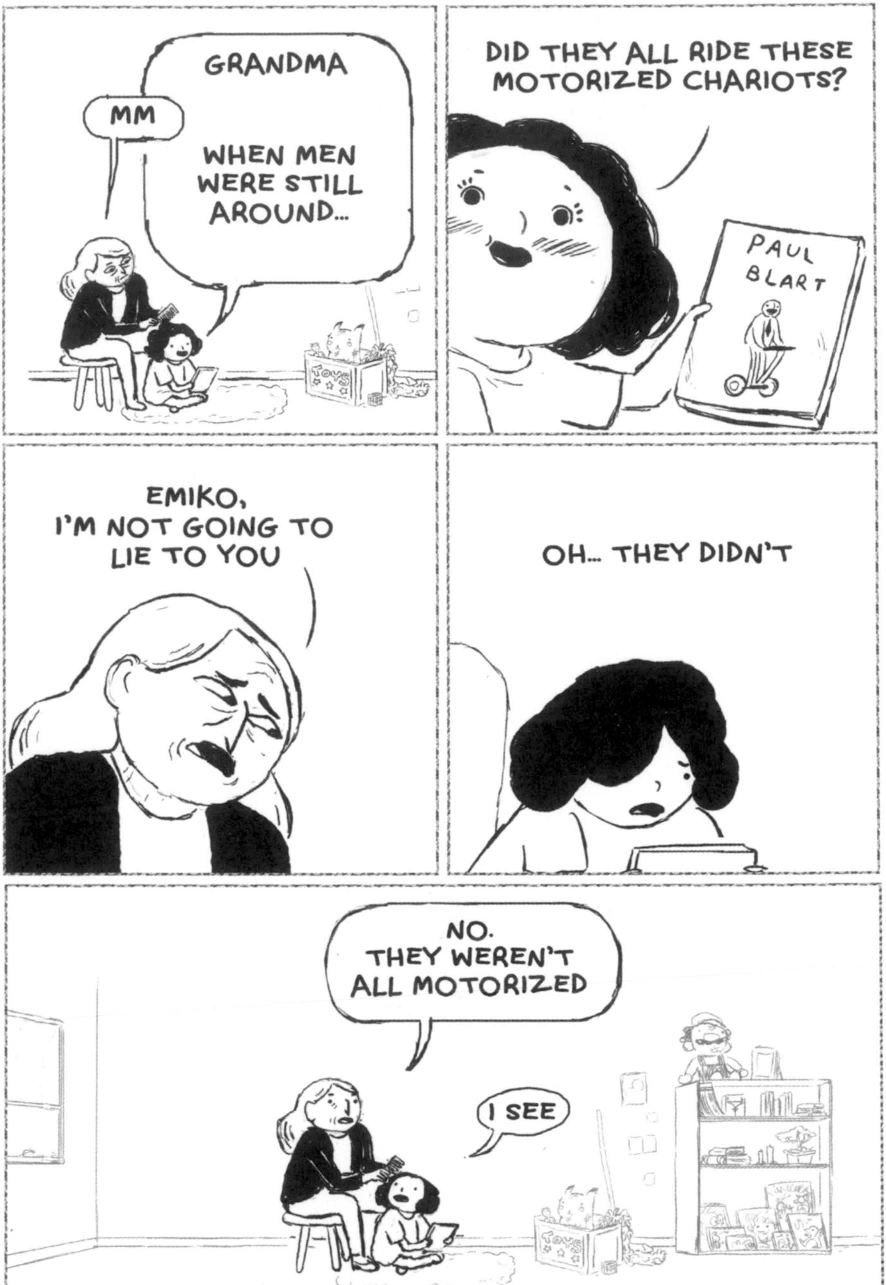
MM
GRANDMA
WHEN MEN WERE STILL AROUND...
DID THEY ALL RIDE THESE MOTORIZED CHARIOTS?
PAUL BLART
EMIKO, I'M NOT GOING TO LIE TO YOU
OH... THEY DIDN'T
NO. THEY WEREN'T ALL MOTORIZED
I SEE
TOYS

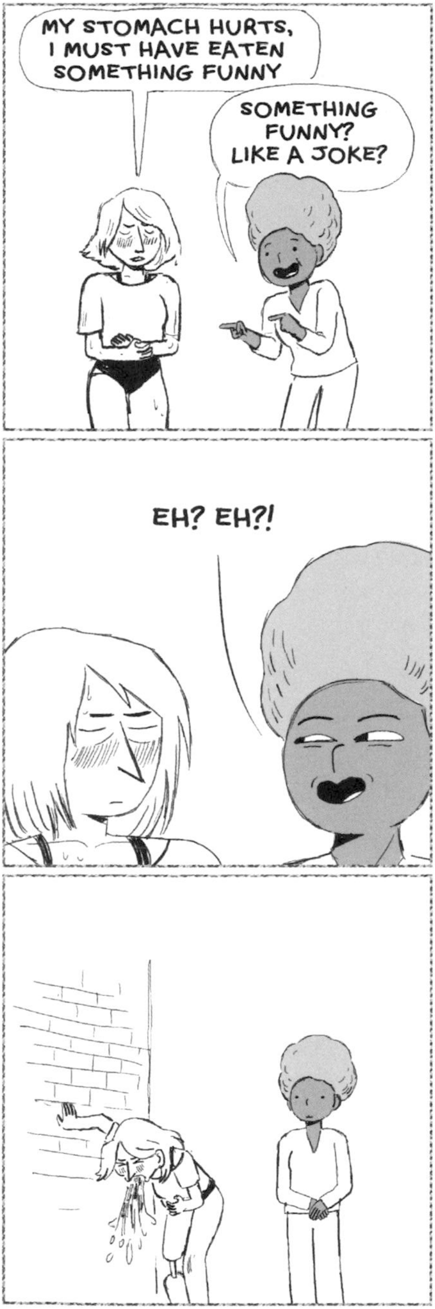
MY STOMACH HURTS, I MUST HAVE EATEN SOMETHING FUNNY
SOMETHING FUNNY? LIKE A JOKE?
EH? EH?!

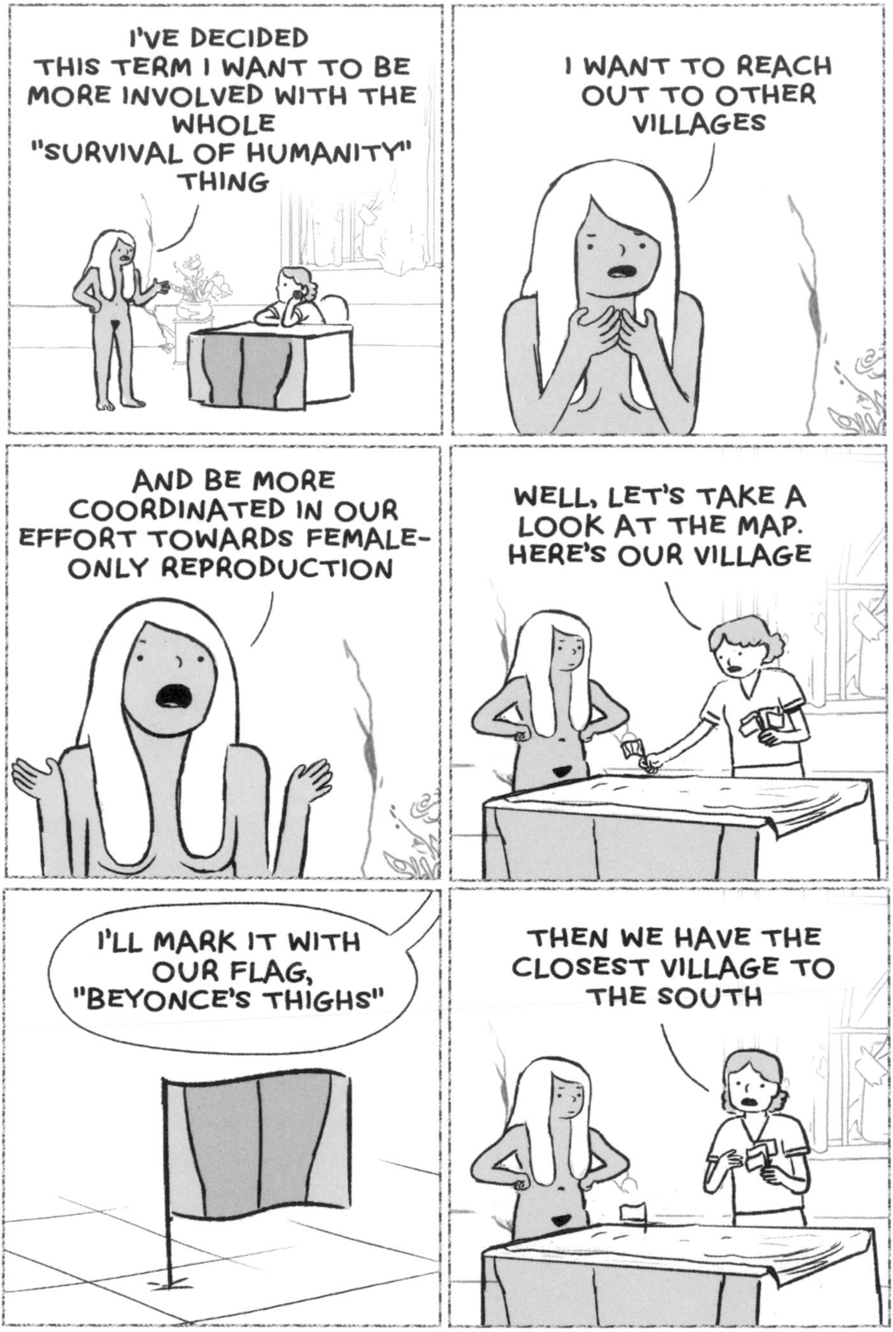
I'VE DECIDED THIS TERM I WANT TO BE MORE INVOLVED WITH THE WHOLE "SURVIVAL OF HUMANITY" THING
I WANT TO REACH OUT TO OTHER VILLAGES
AND BE MORE COORDINATED IN OUR EFFORT TOWARDS FEMALE-ONLY REPRODUCTION
WELL, LET'S TAKE A LOOK AT THE MAP. HERE'S OUR VILLAGE
I'LL MARK IT WITH OUR FLAG, "BEYONCE'S THIGHS"
THEN WE HAVE THE CLOSEST VILLAGE TO THE SOUTH

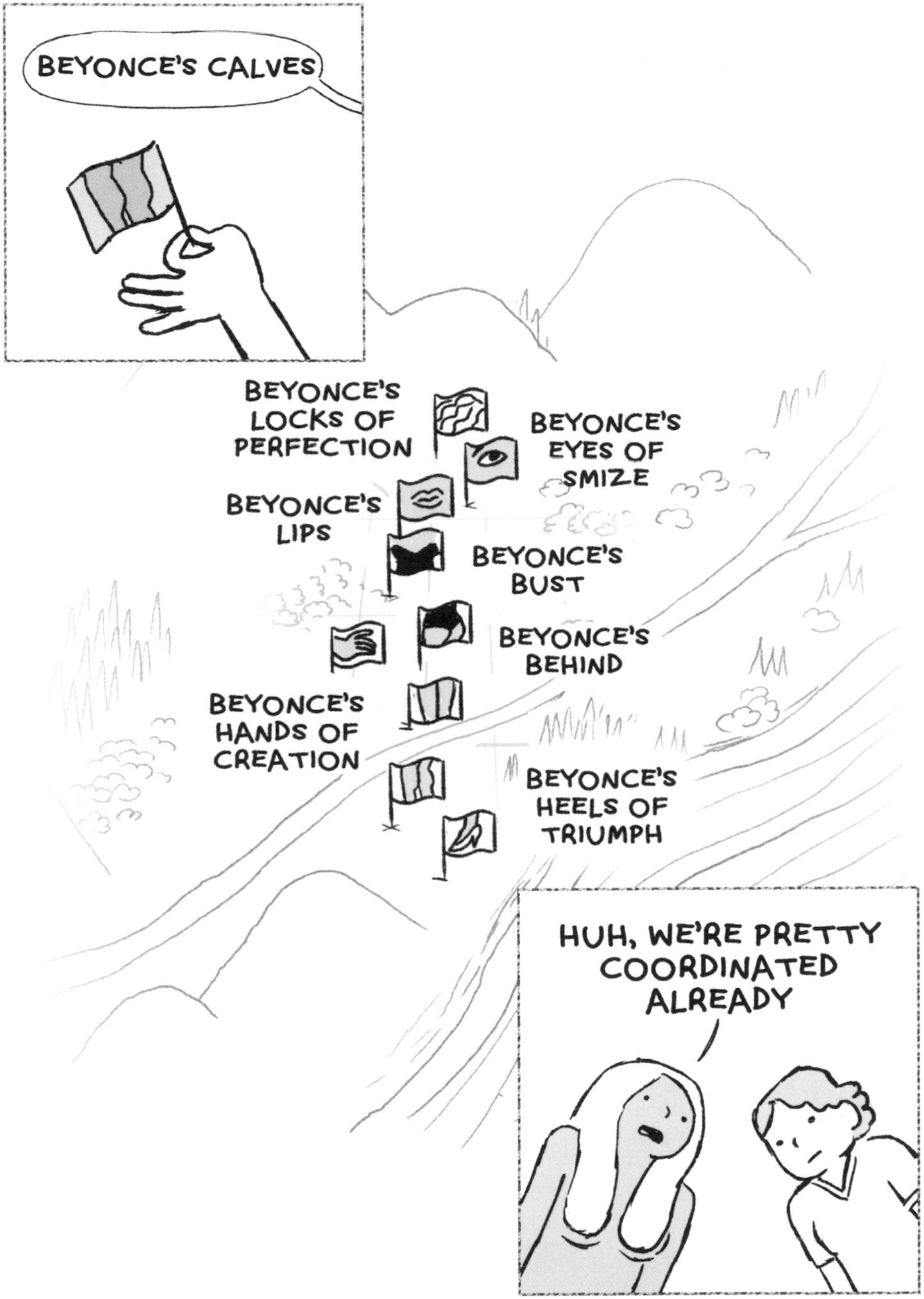
BEYONCE'S CALVES
BEYONCE'S LOCKS OF PERFECTION
BEYONCE'S EYES OF SMIZE
BEYONCE'S LIPS
BEYONCE'S BUST
BEYONCE'S BEHIND
BEYONCE'S HANDS OF CREATION
BEYONCE'S HEELS OF TRIUMPH
HUH, WE'RE PRETTY COORDINATED ALREADY

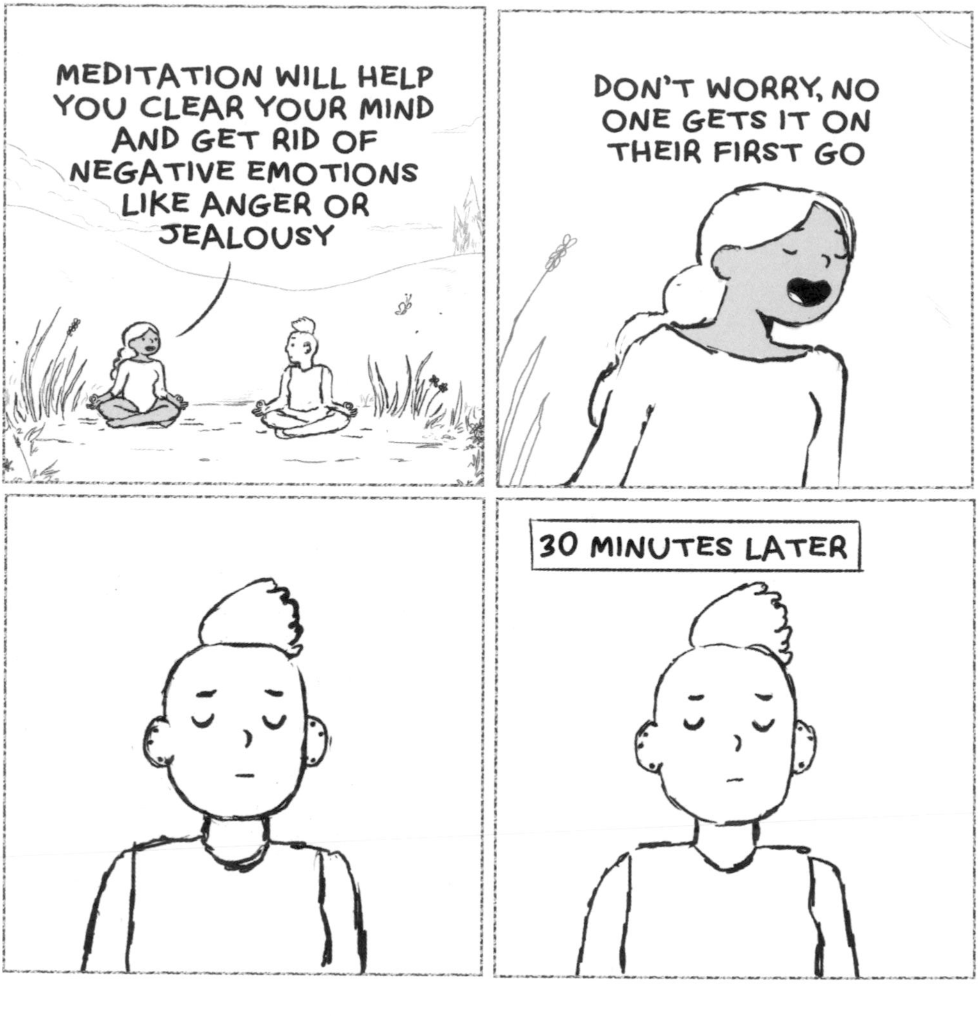
MEDITATION WILL HELP YOU CLEAR YOUR MIND AND GET RID OF NEGATIVE EMOTIONS LIKE ANGER OR JEALOUSY
DON'T WORRY, NO ONE GETS IT ON THEIR FIRST GO
30 MINUTES LATER

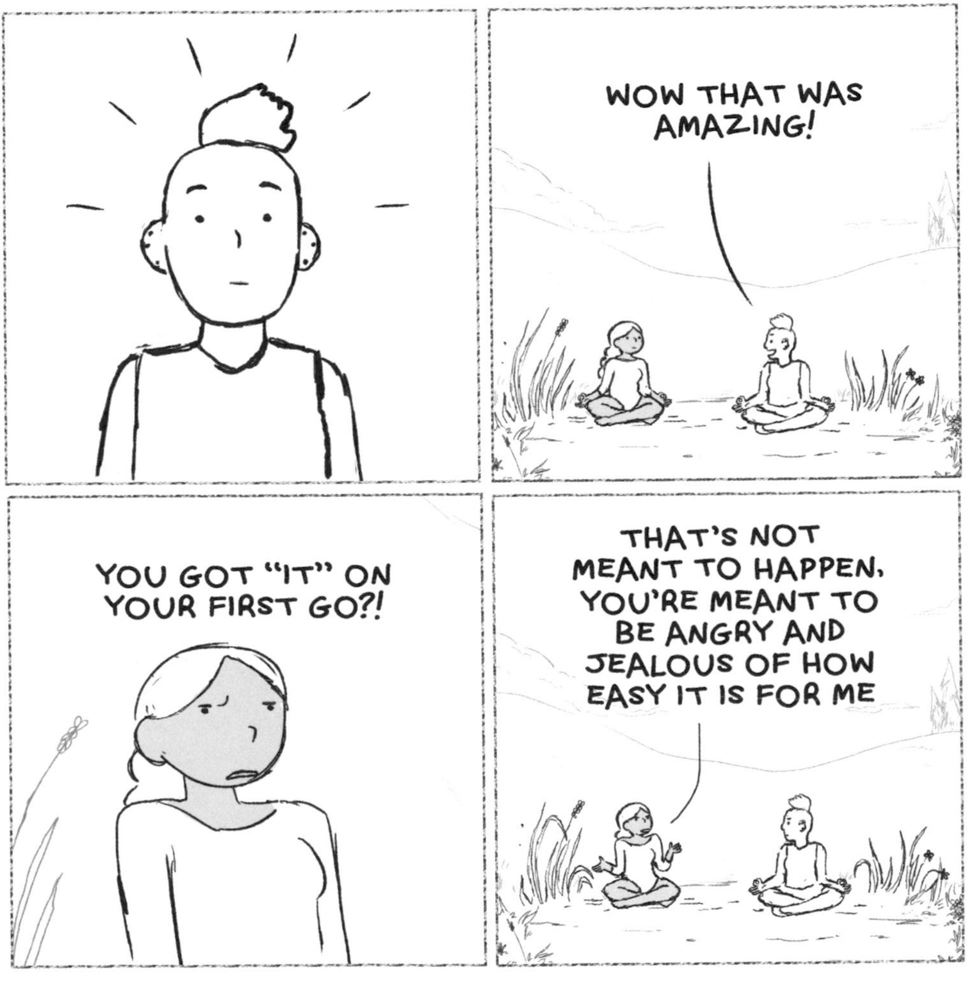
WOW THAT WAS AMAZING!
YOU GOT "IT" ON YOUR FIRST GO?!
THAT'S NOT MEANT TO HAPPEN. YOU'RE MEANT TO BE ANGRY AND JEALOUS OF HOW EASY IT IS FOR ME

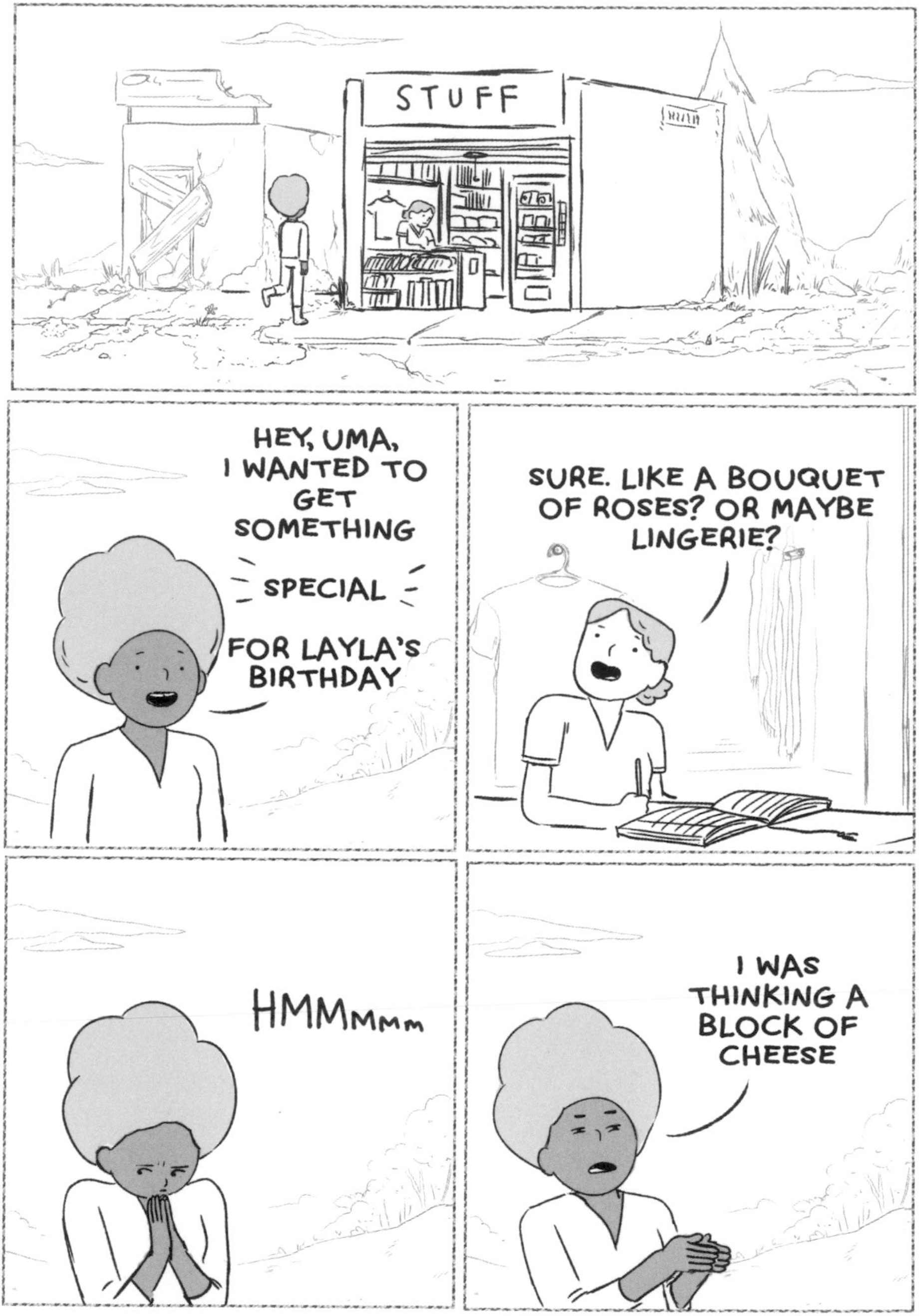
STUFF
HEY, UMA, I WANTED TO GET SOMETHING
SPECIAL
FOR LAYLA'S BIRTHDAY
SURE. LIKE A BOUQUET OF ROSES? OR MAYBE LINGERIE?
HMMMMM
I WAS THINKING A BLOCK OF CHEESE

Person
magazine
WHITENING
SOMETIMES THE PAST SEEMS TERRIFYING
Person

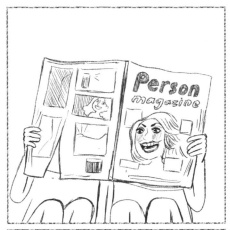

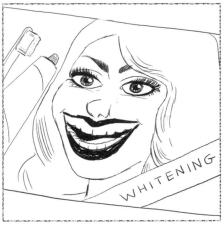

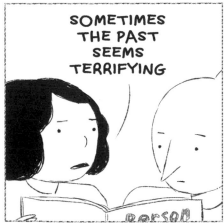

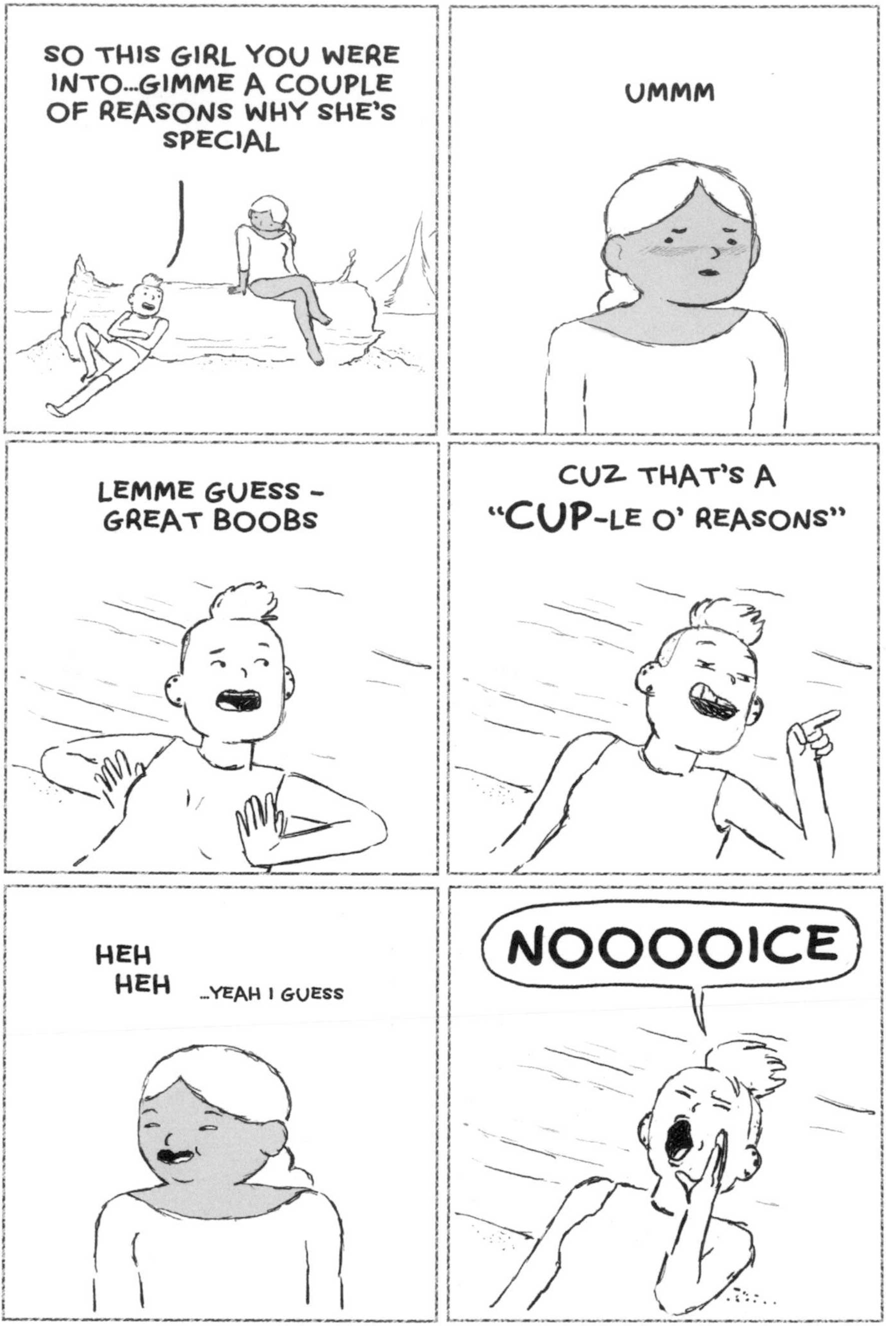

SO THIS GIRL YOU WERE INTO...GIMME A COUPLE OF REASONS WHY SHE'S SPECIAL
UMMM
LEMME GUESS - GREAT BOOBS
CUZ THAT'S A "CUP-LE O' REASONS"
HEH HEH
...YEAH I GUESS
NOOOOICE

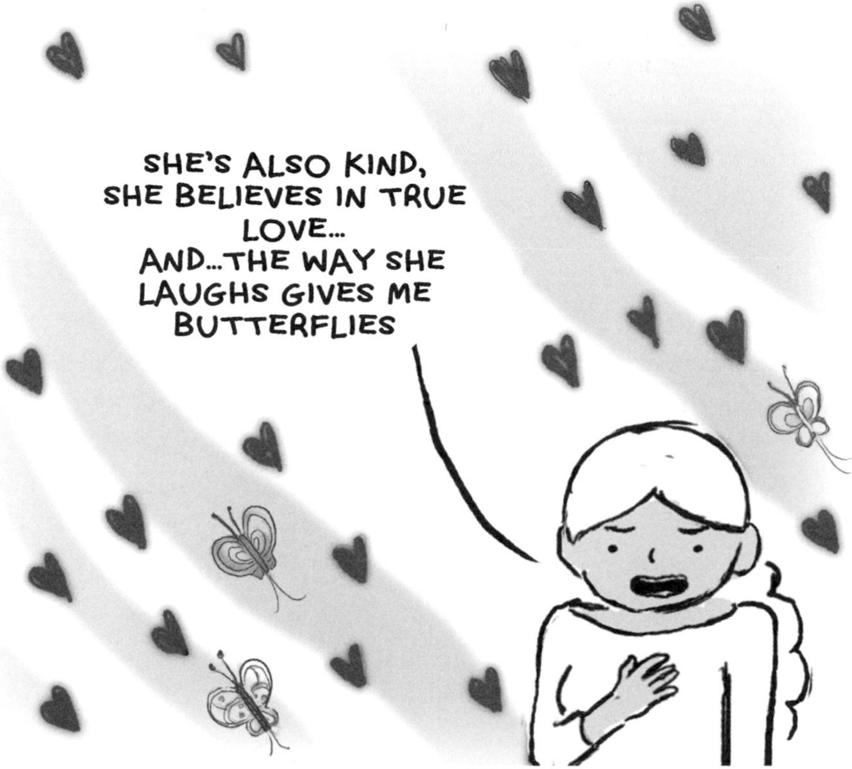
SHE'S ALSO KIND, SHE BELIEVES IN TRUE LOVE... AND...THE WAY SHE LAUGHS GIVES ME BUTTERFLIES

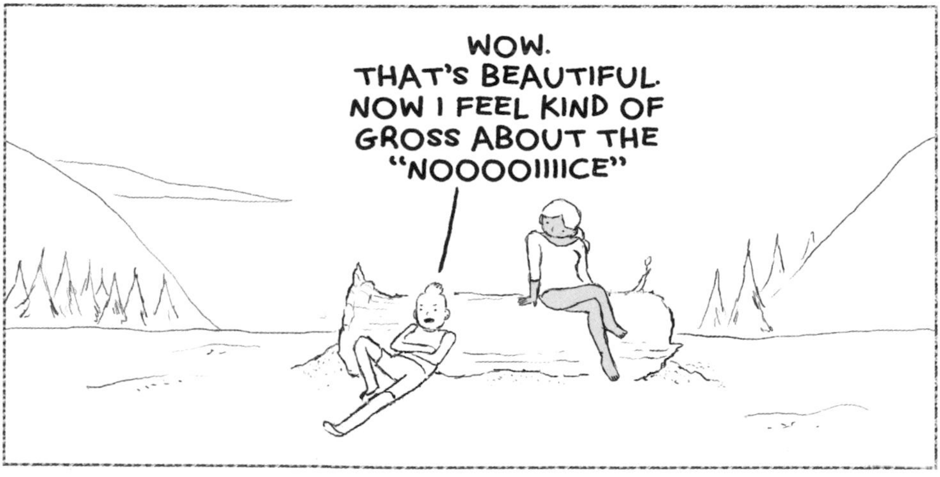
WOW. THAT'S BEAUTIFUL. NOW I FEEL KIND OF GROSS ABOUT THE "NOOOOIIIICE"

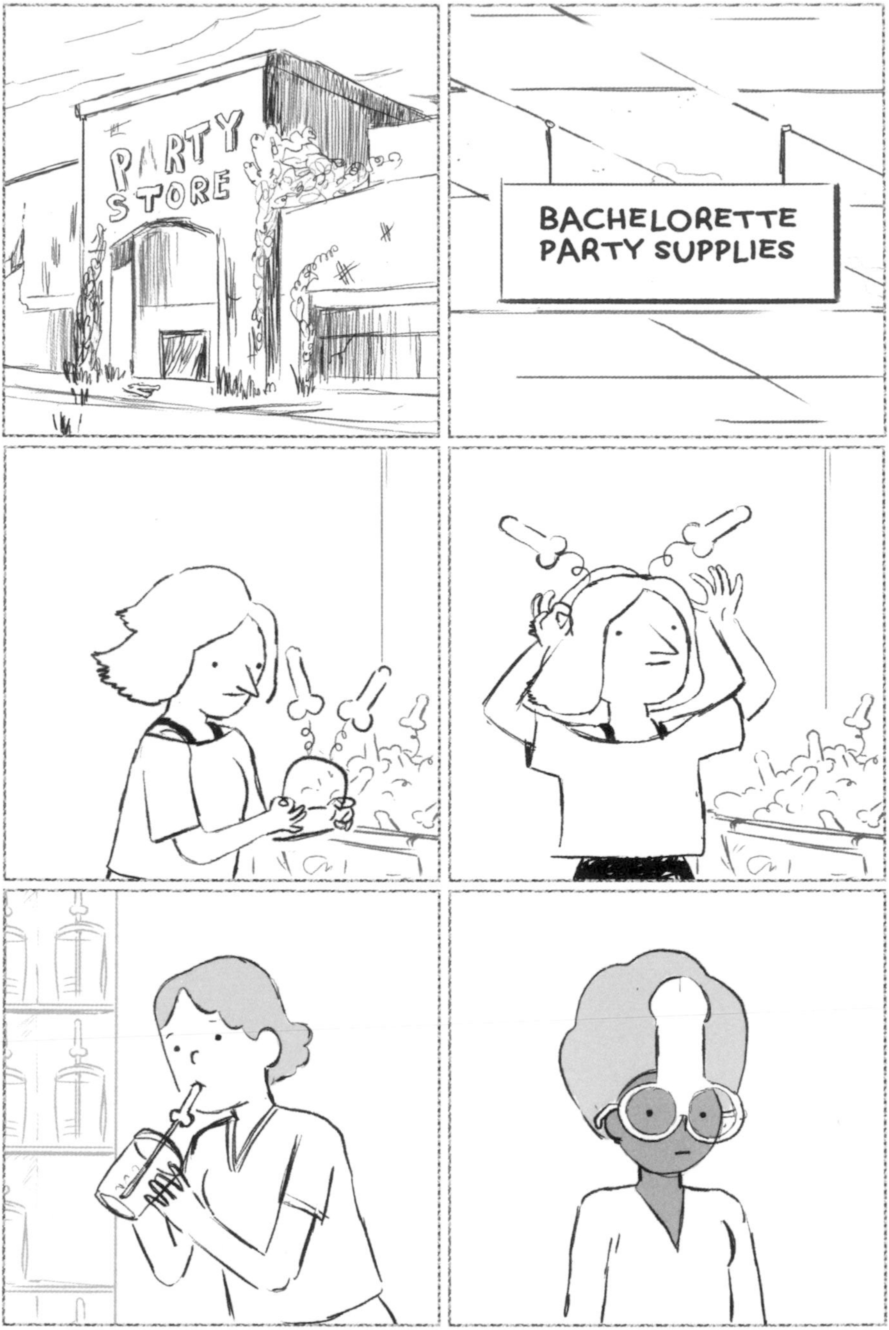
PARTY STORE
BACHELORETTE PARTY SUPPLIES

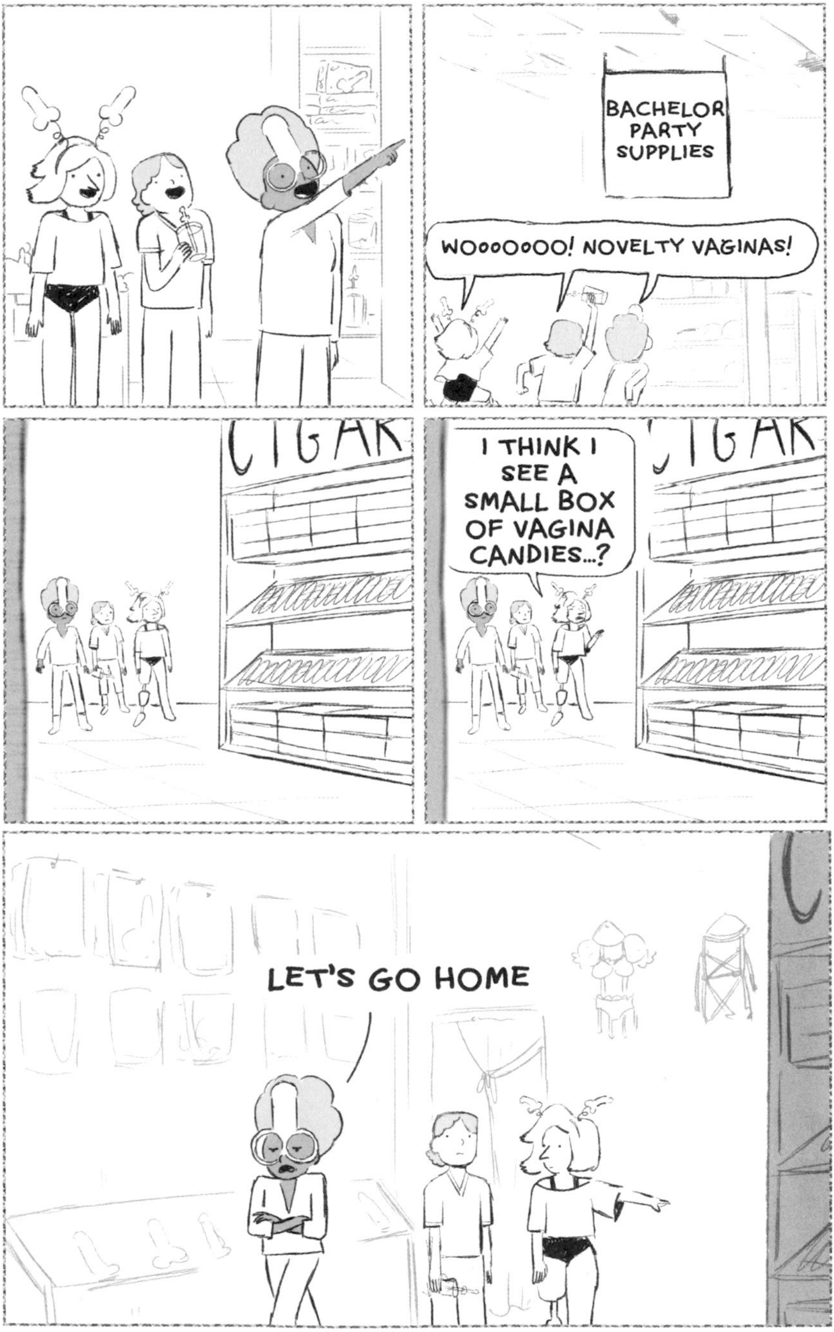
BACHELOR PARTY SUPPLIES
WOOOOOOO! NOVELTY VAGINAS!
CIGAR
CIGAR
I THINK I SEE A SMALL BOX OF VAGINA CANDIES...?
LET'S GO HOME

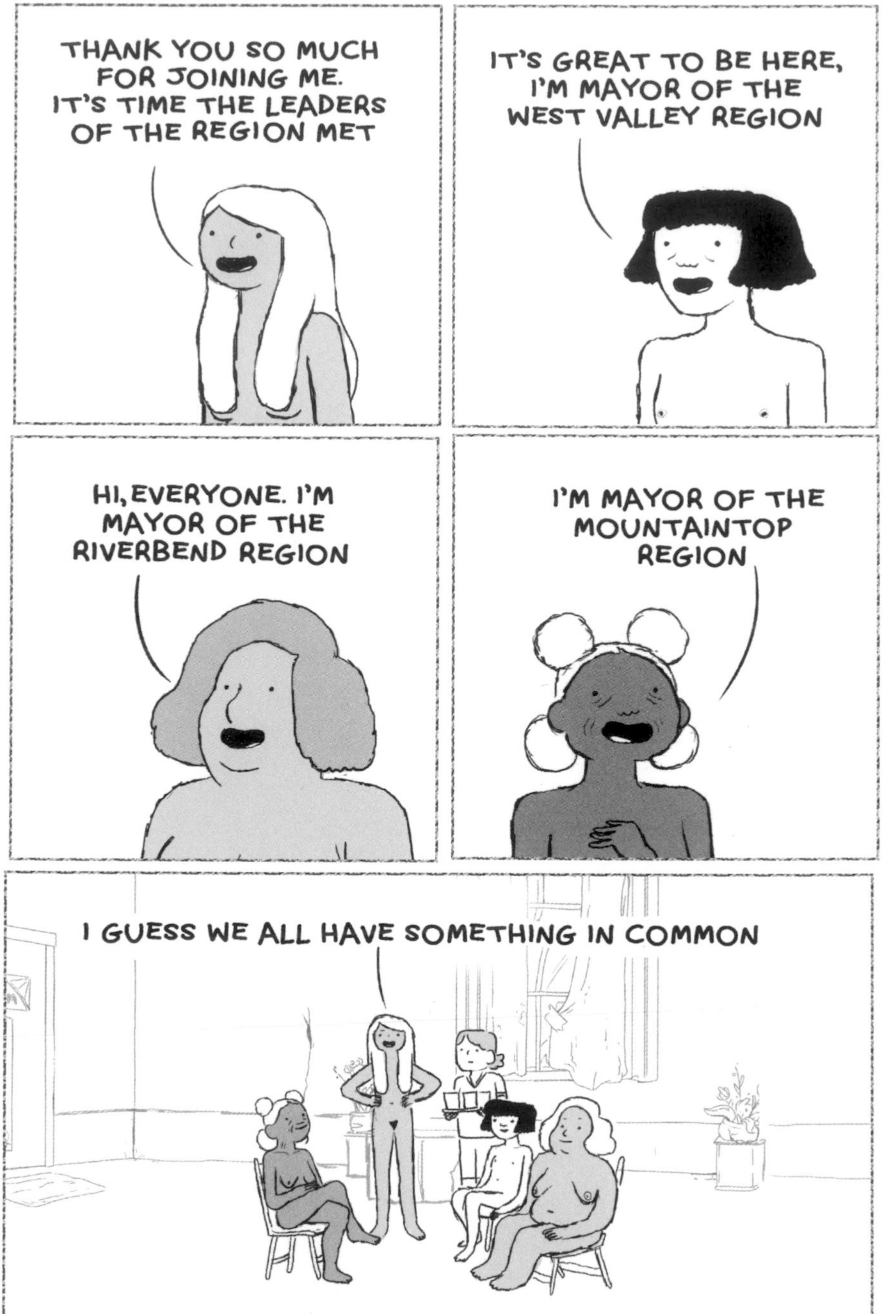
THANK YOU SO MUCH FOR JOINING ME. IT'S TIME THE LEADERS OF THE REGION MET
IT'S GREAT TO BE HERE, I'M MAYOR OF THE WEST VALLEY REGION
HI, EVERYONE. I'M MAYOR OF THE RIVERBEND REGION
I'M MAYOR OF THE MOUNTAINTOP REGION
I GUESS WE ALL HAVE SOMETHING IN COMMON

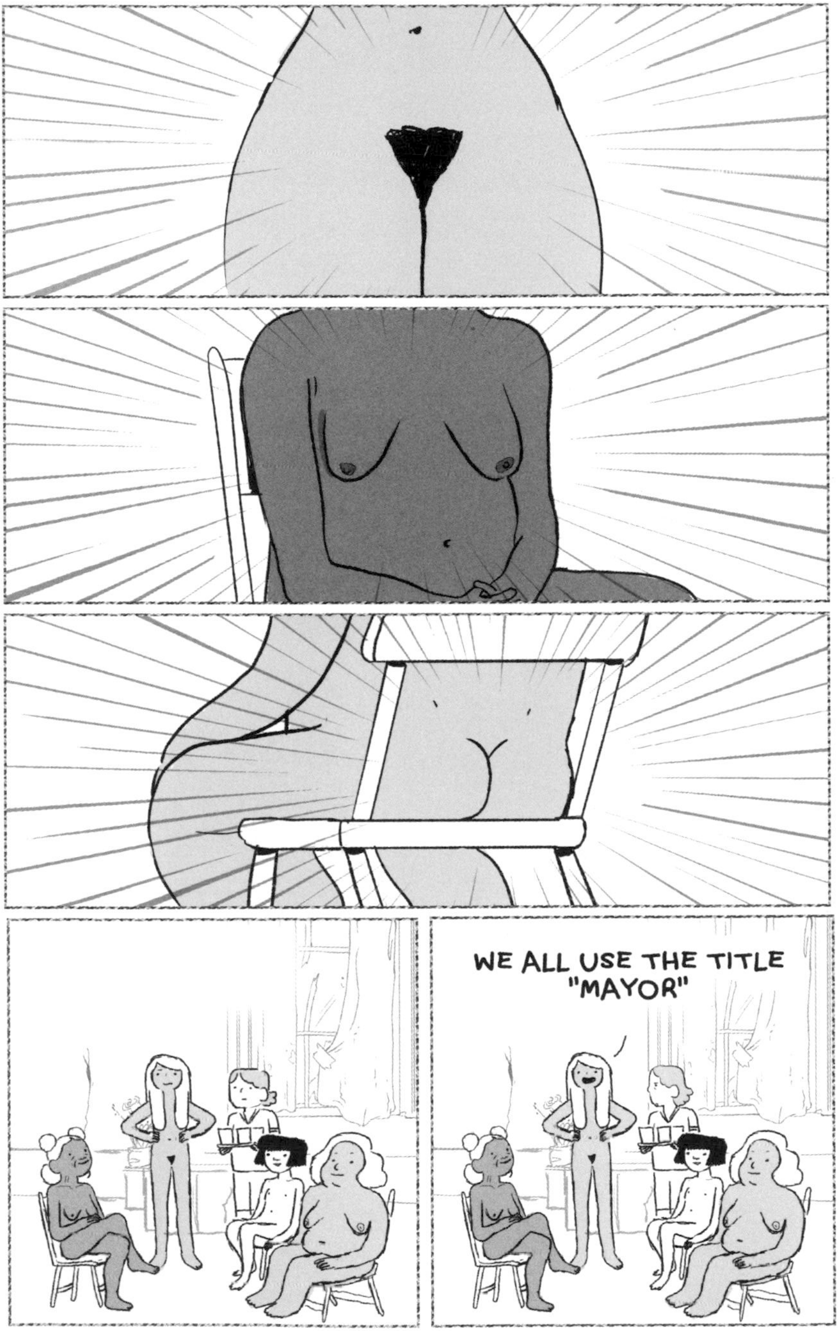
WE ALL USE THE TITLE "MAYOR"

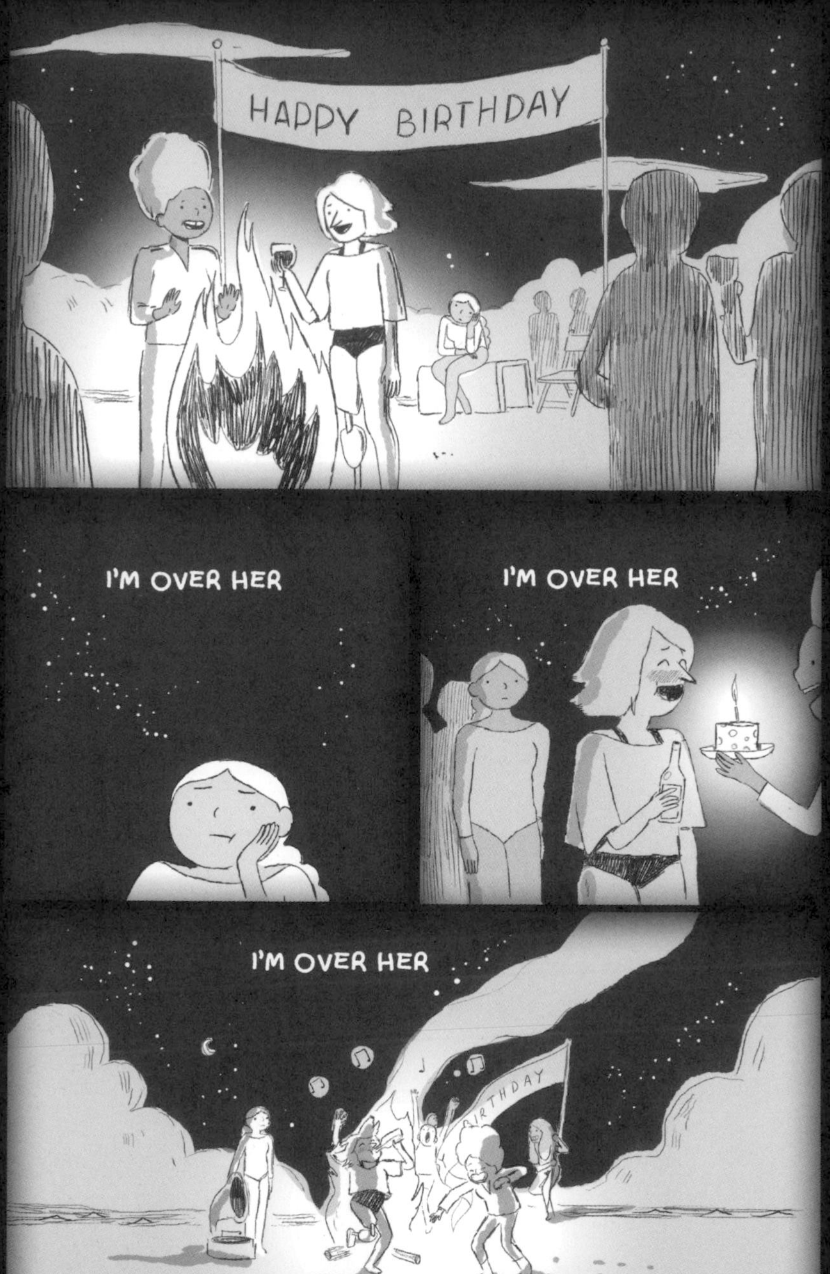
HAPPY BIRTHDAY
I'M OVER HER
I'M OVER HER
I'M OVER HER
BIRTHDAY

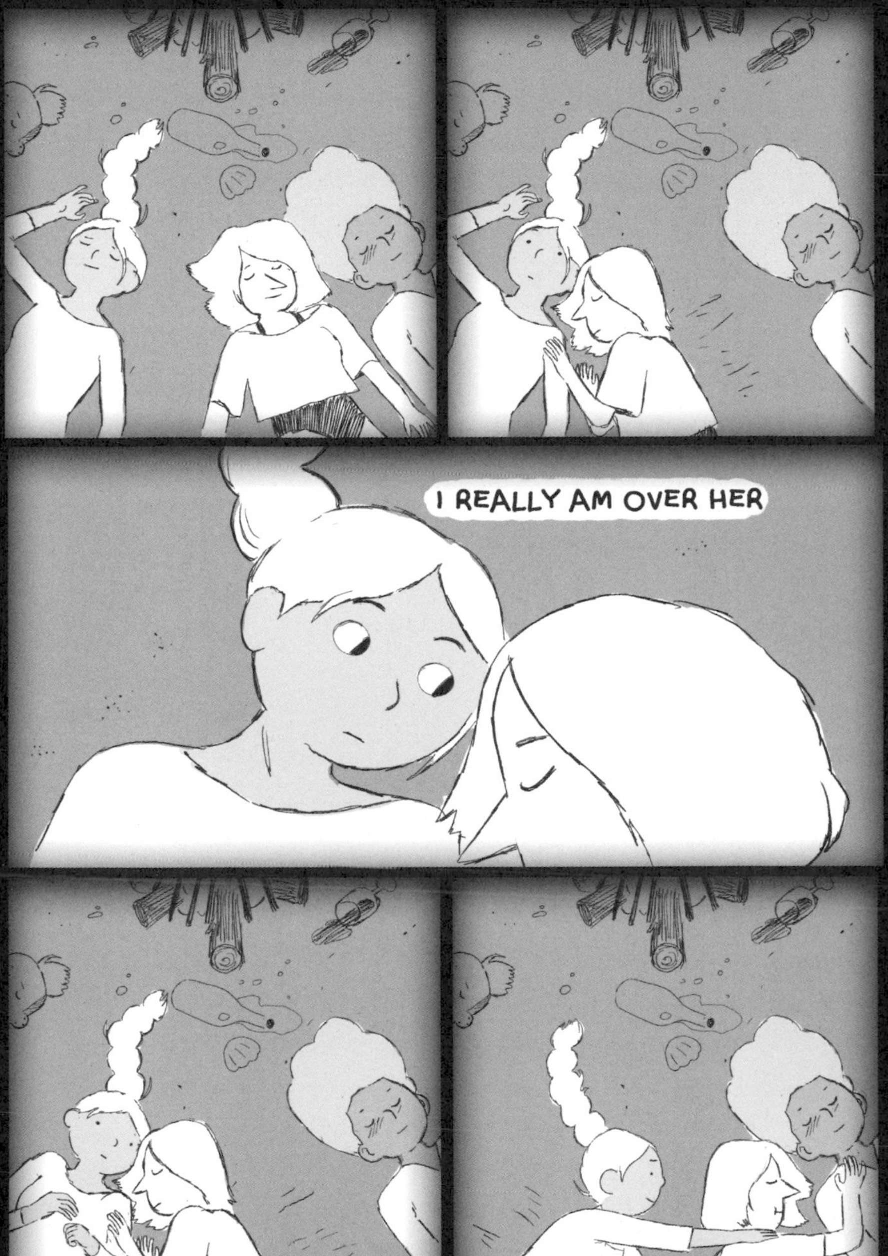
I REALLY AM OVER HER

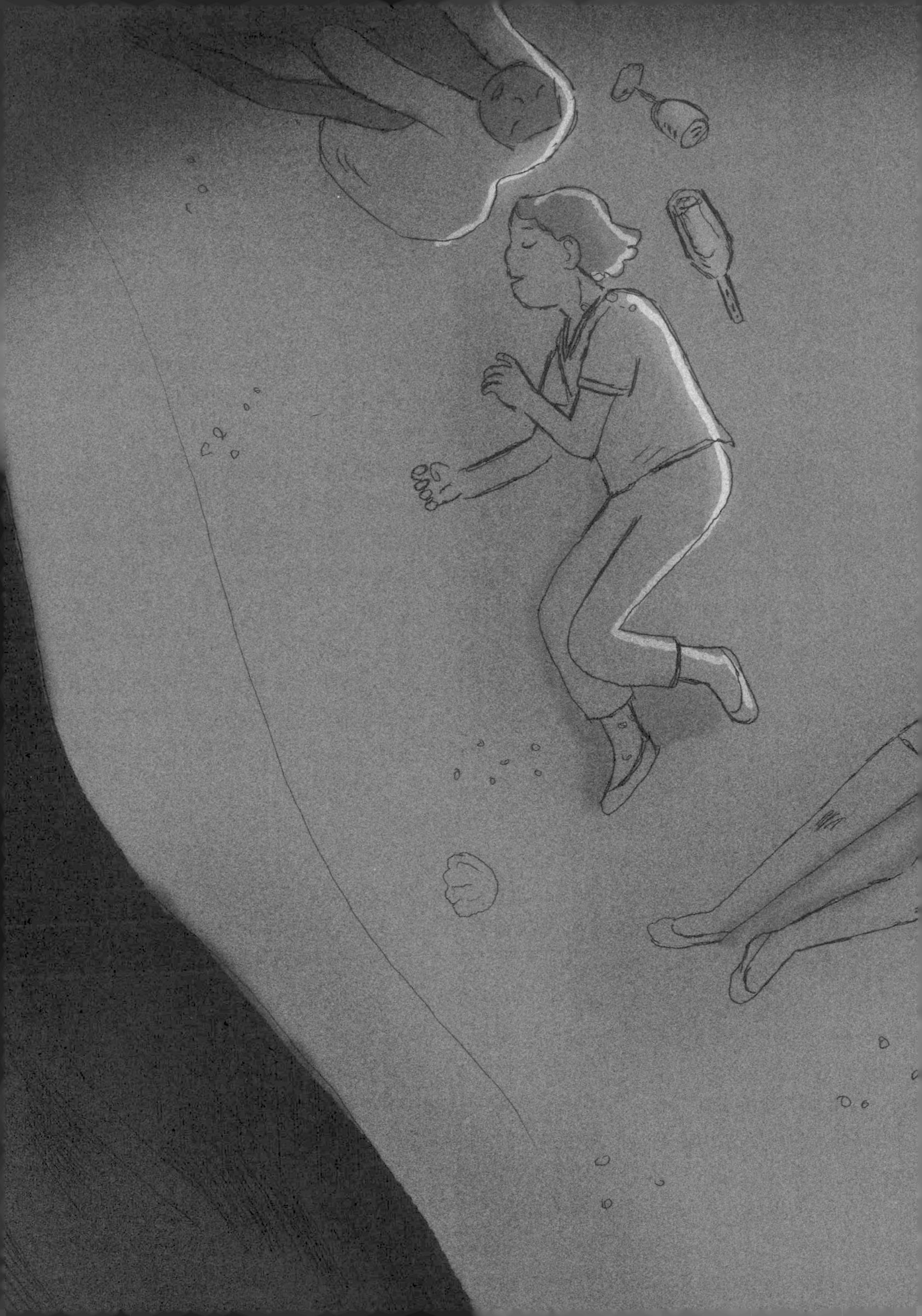

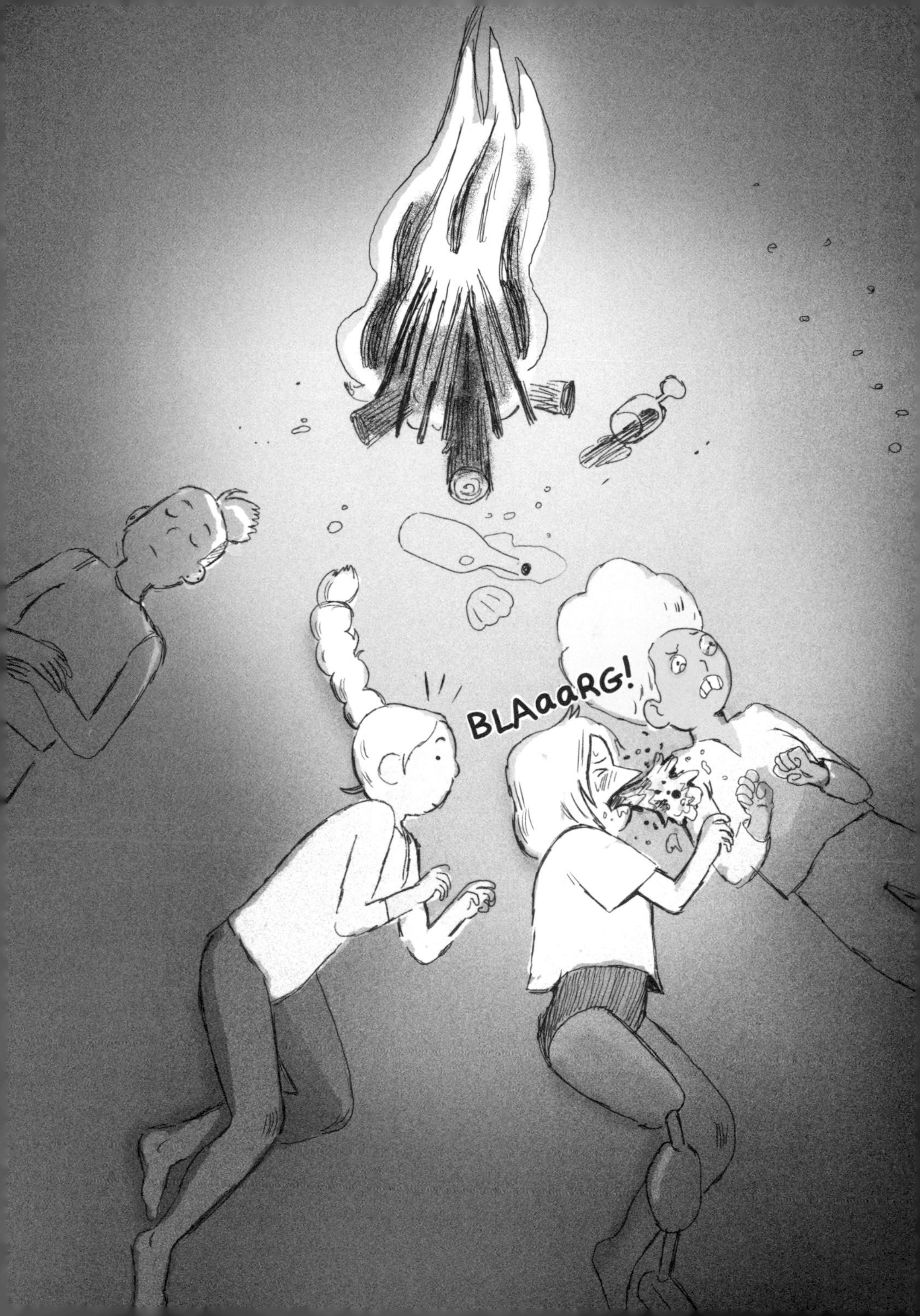
BLAaaRG!

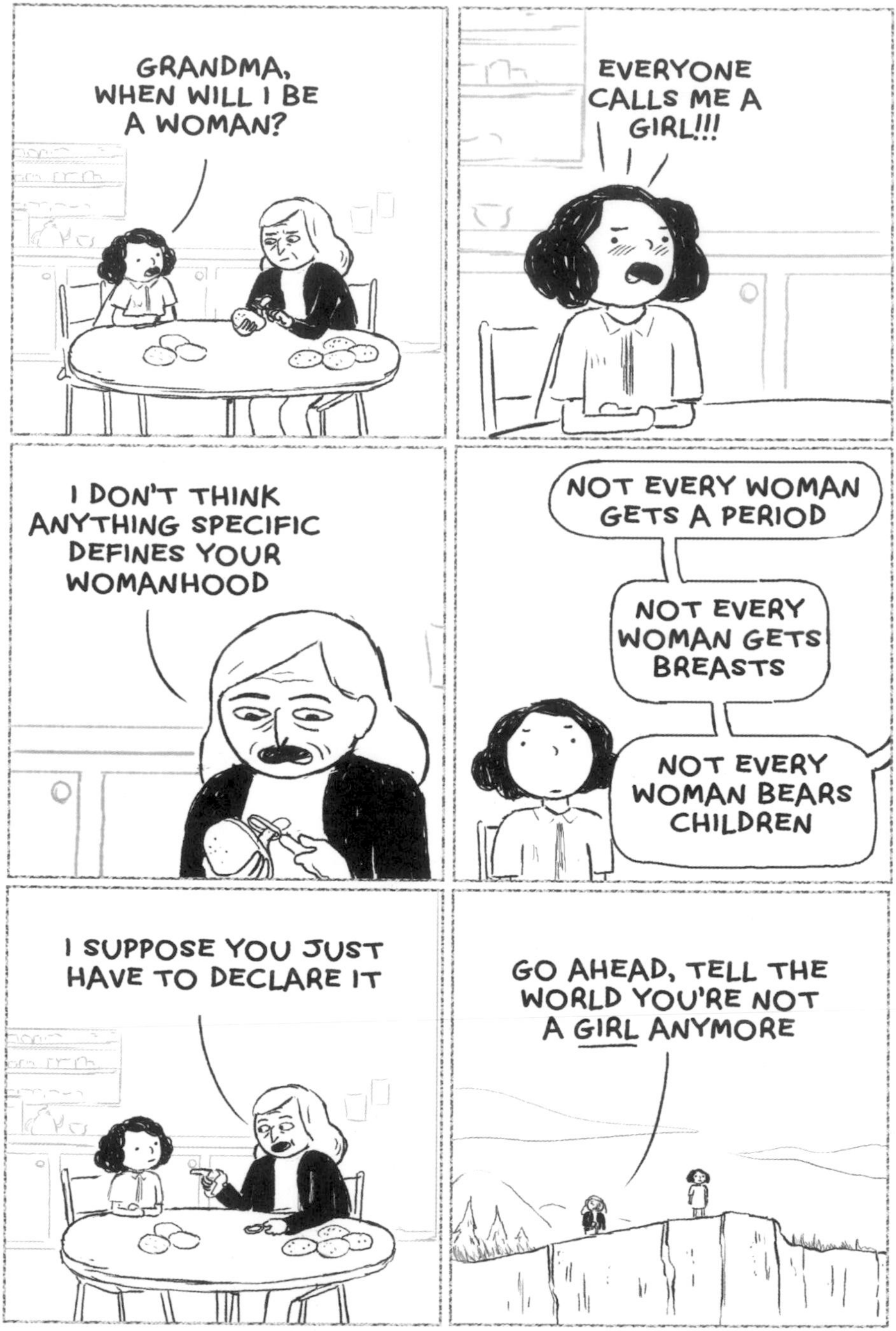
GRANDMA, WHEN WILL I BE A WOMAN?
EVERYONE CALLS ME A GIRL!!!
I DON'T THINK ANYTHING SPECIFIC DEFINES YOUR WOMANHOOD
NOT EVERY WOMAN GETS A PERIOD
NOT EVERY WOMAN GETS BREASTS
NOT EVERY WOMAN BEARS CHILDREN
I SUPPOSE YOU JUST HAVE TO DECLARE IT
GO AHEAD, TELL THE WORLD YOU'RE NOT A GIRL ANYMORE

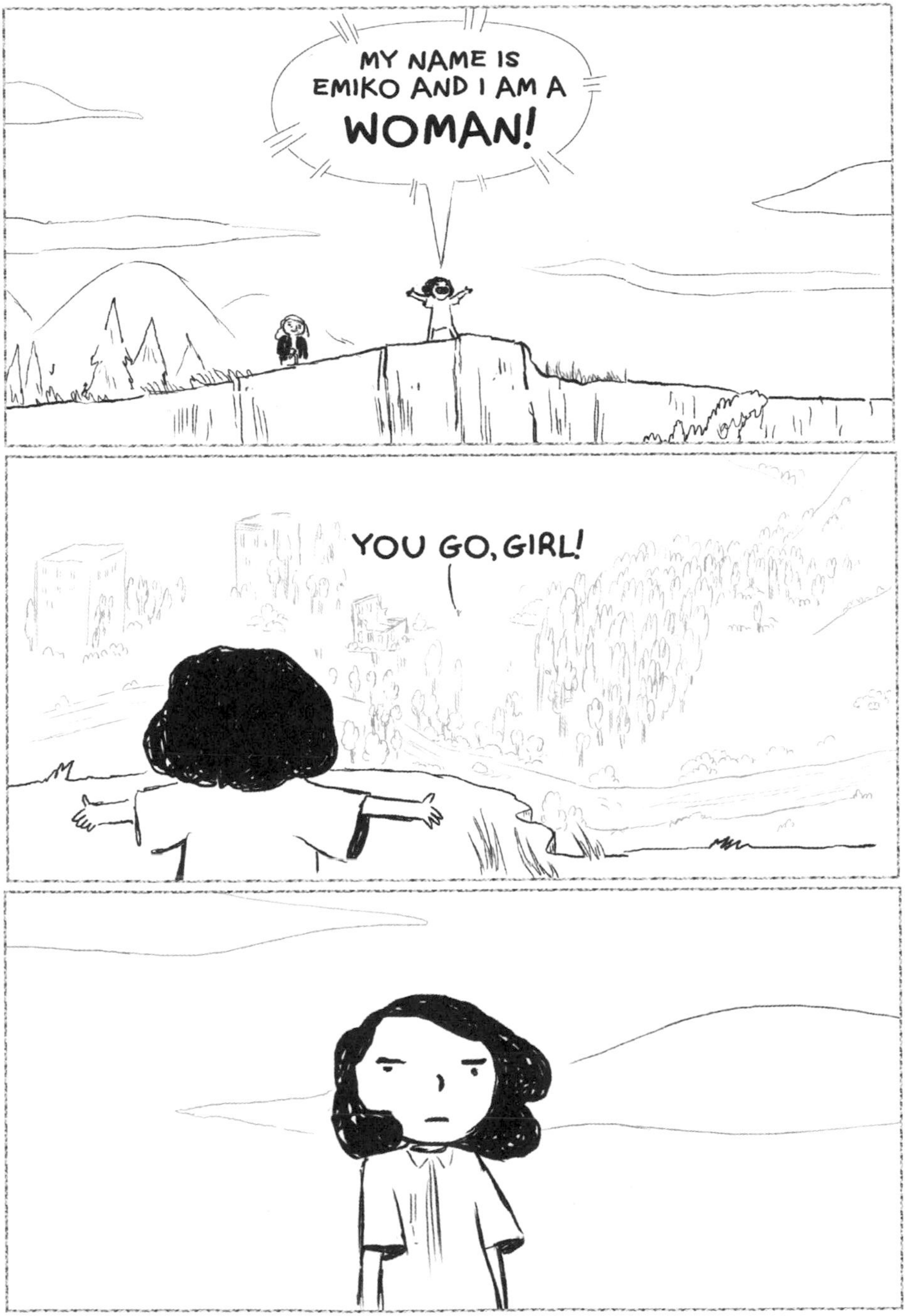
MY NAME IS EMIKO AND I AM A WOMAN!
YOU GO, GIRL!

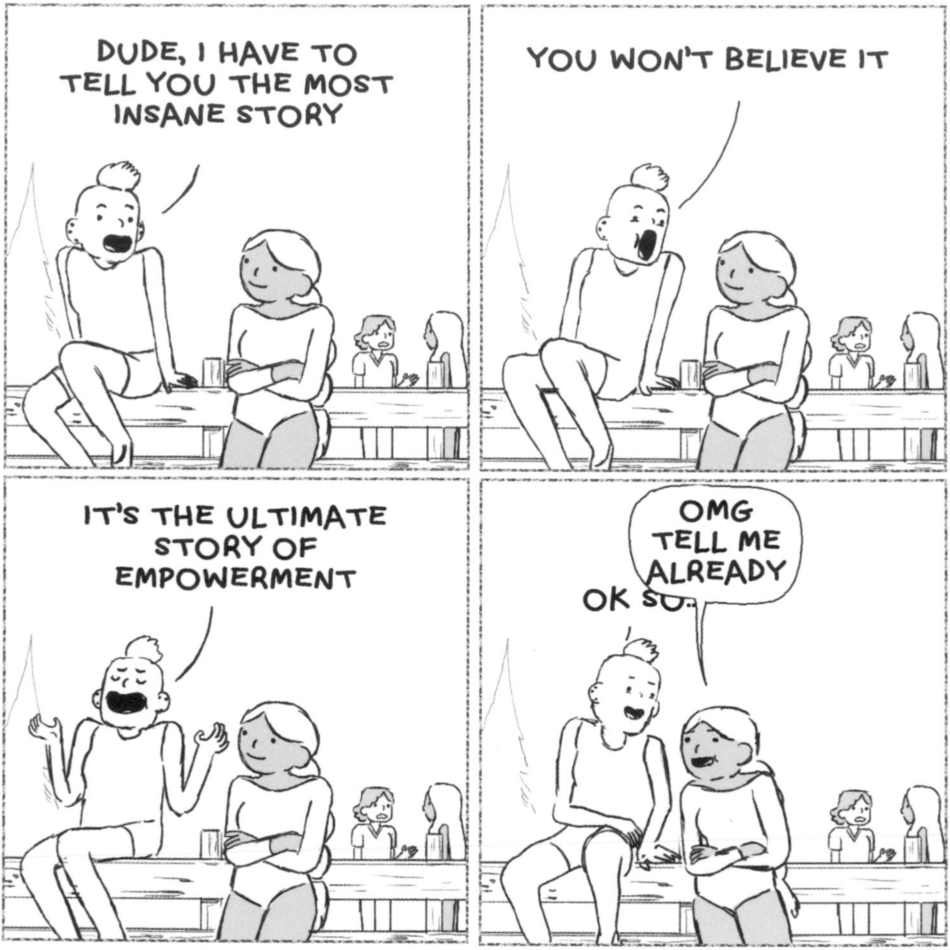
DUDE, I HAVE TO TELL YOU THE MOST INSANE STORY
YOU WON'T BELIEVE IT
IT'S THE ULTIMATE STORY OF EMPOWERMENT
OK SO..
OMG TELL ME ALREADY

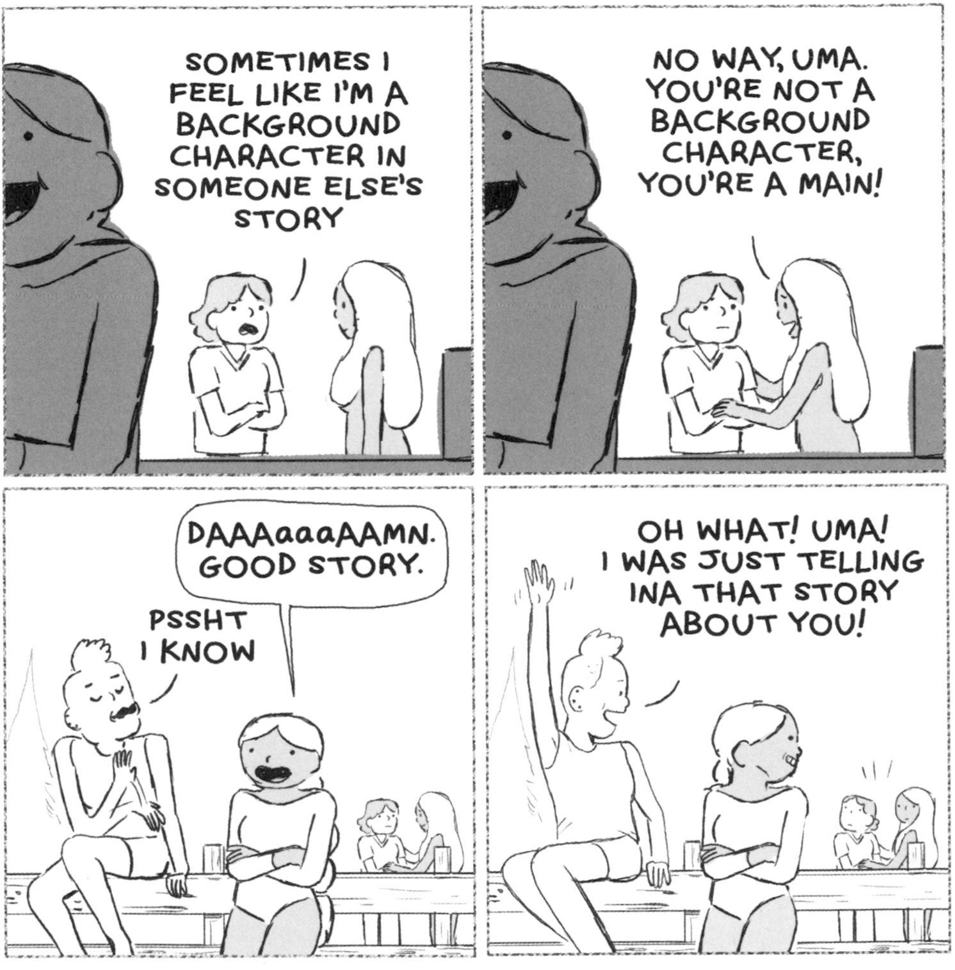
SOMETIMES I FEEL LIKE I'M A BACKGROUND CHARACTER IN SOMEONE ELSE'S STORY
NO WAY, UMA. YOU'RE NOT A BACKGROUND CHARACTER, YOU'RE A MAIN!
DAAAaaaAAMN. GOOD STORY.
PSSHT I KNOW
OH WHAT! UMA! I WAS JUST TELLING INA THAT STORY ABOUT YOU!

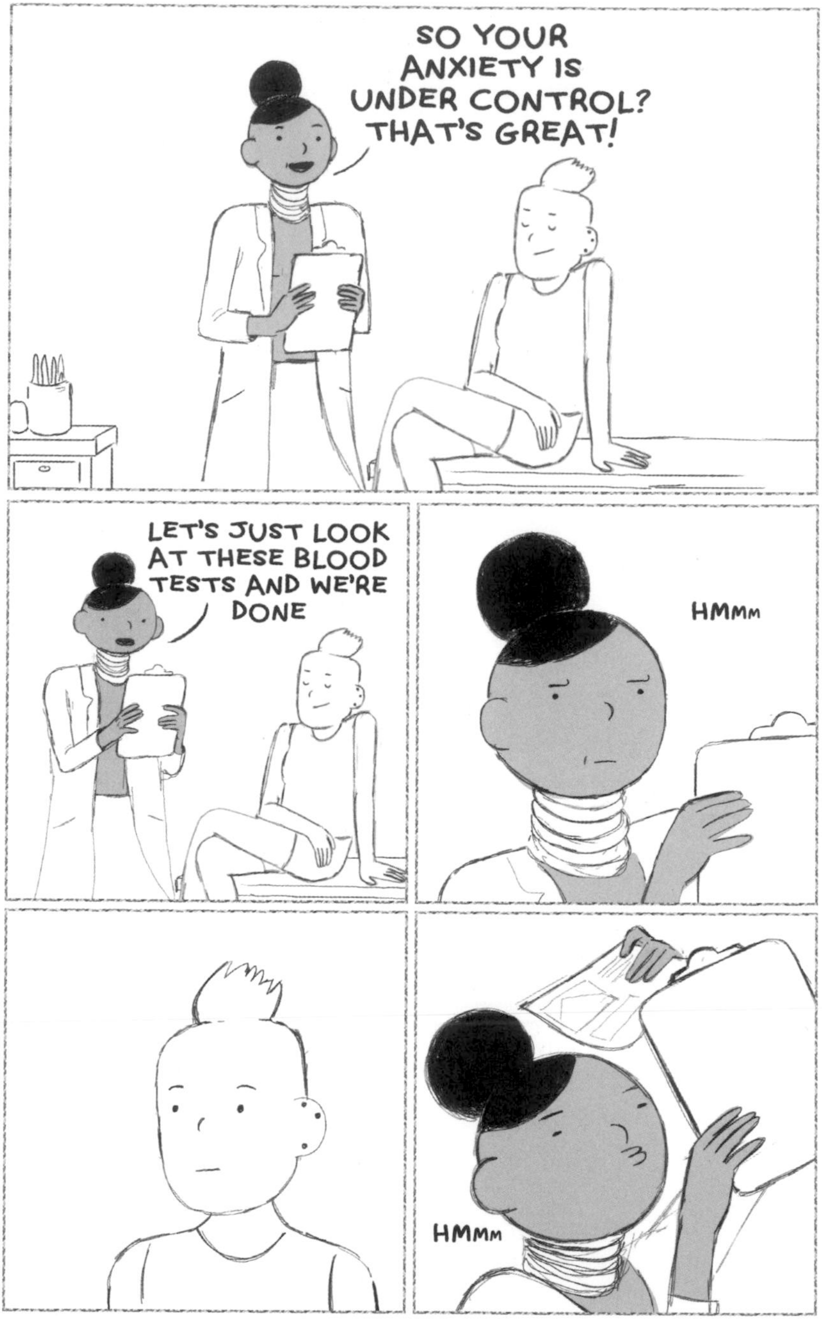

SO YOUR ANXIETY IS UNDER CONTROL? THAT'S GREAT!
LET'S JUST LOOK AT THESE BLOOD TESTS AND WE'RE DONE
HMMM
HMMM

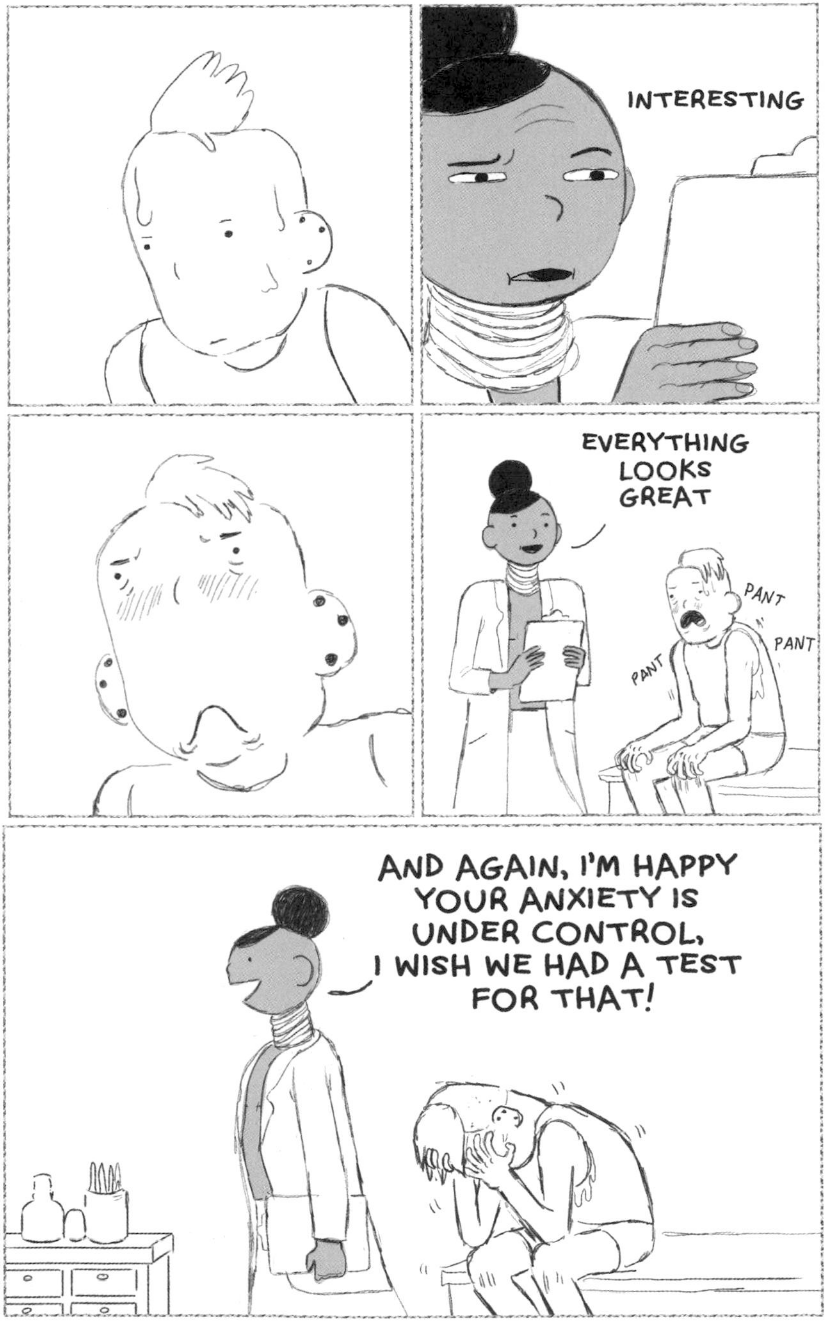
INTERESTING
EVERYTHING LOOKS GREAT
PANT
PANT
PANT
AND AGAIN, I'M HAPPY YOUR ANXIETY IS UNDER CONTROL, I WISH WE HAD A TEST FOR THAT!

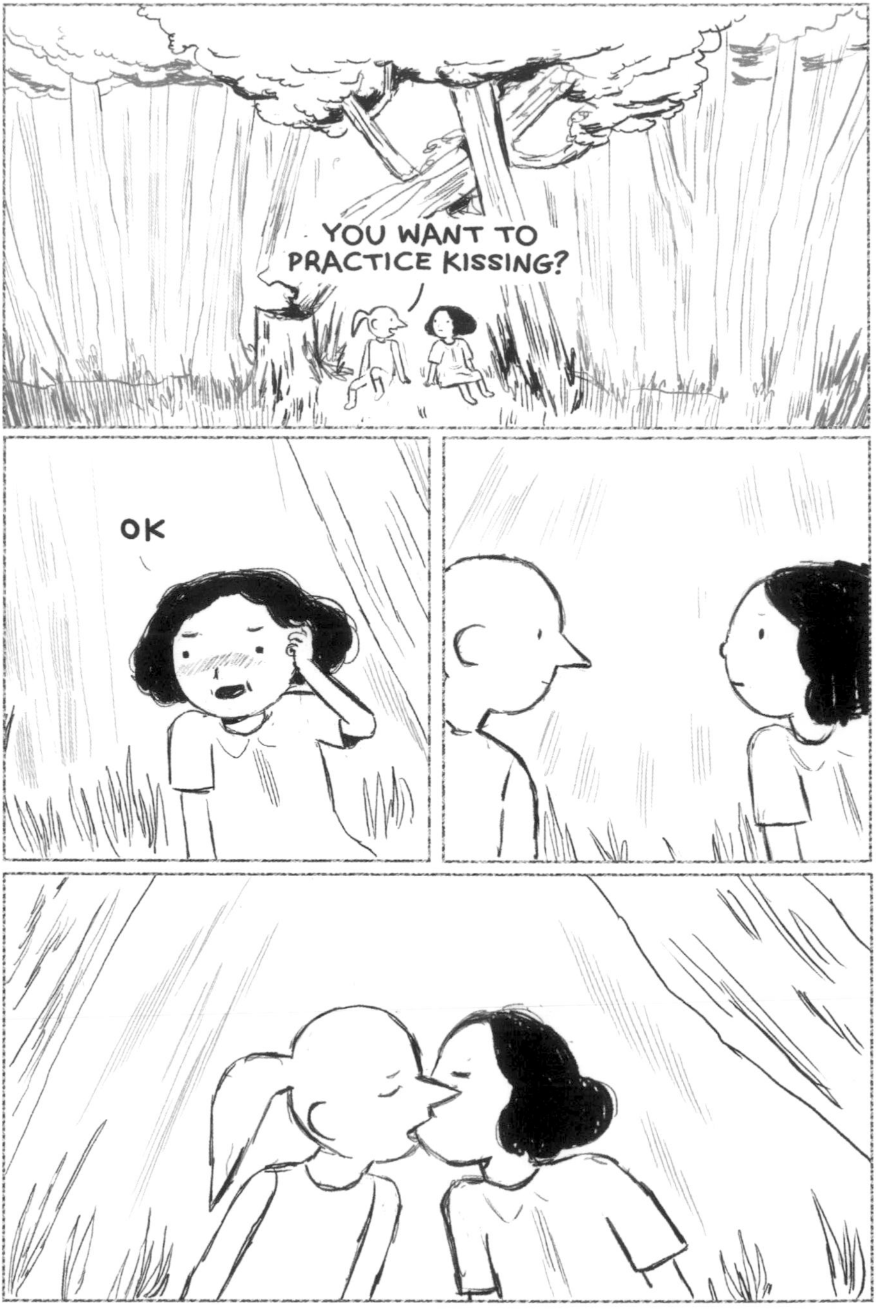
YOU WANT TO PRACTICE KISSING?
OK

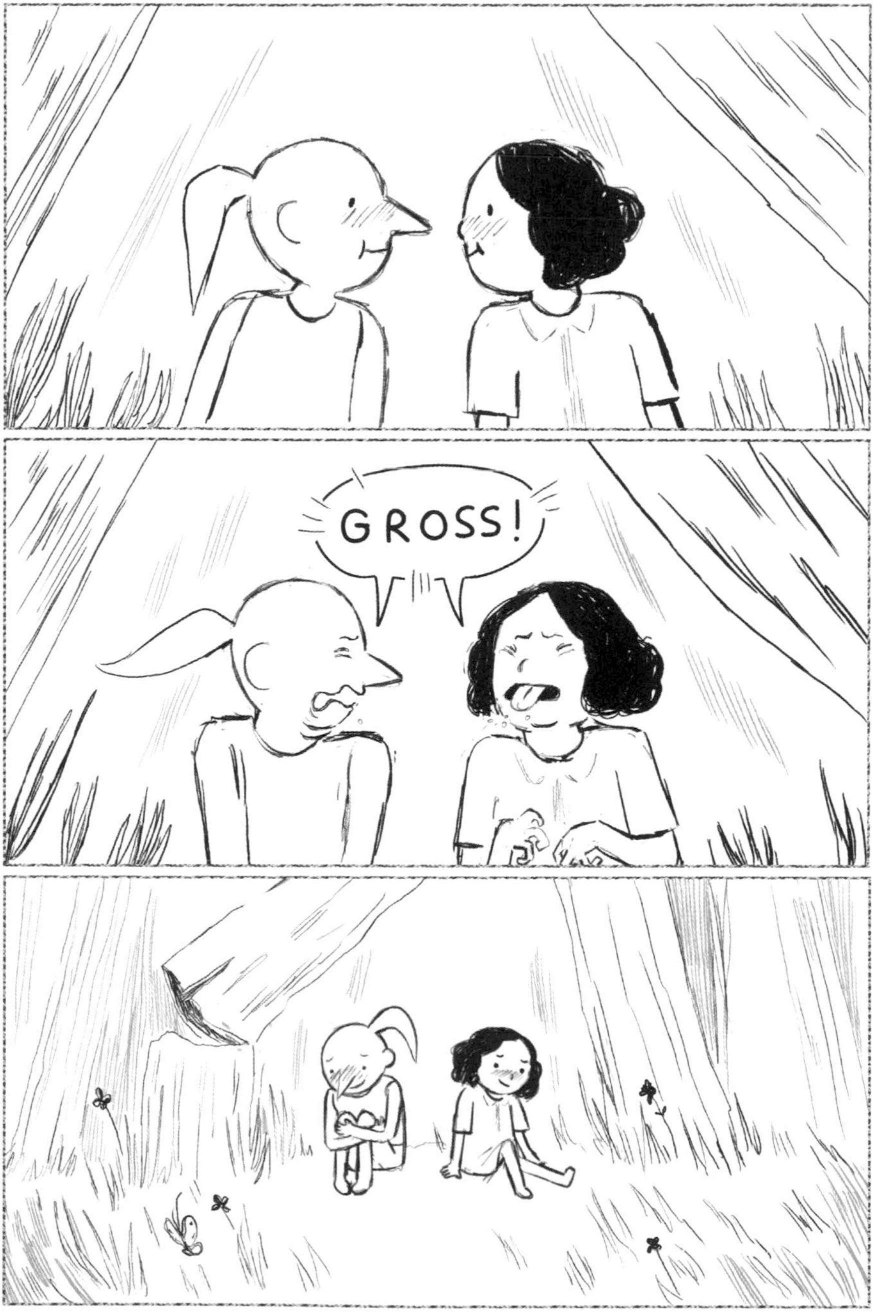
GROSS!

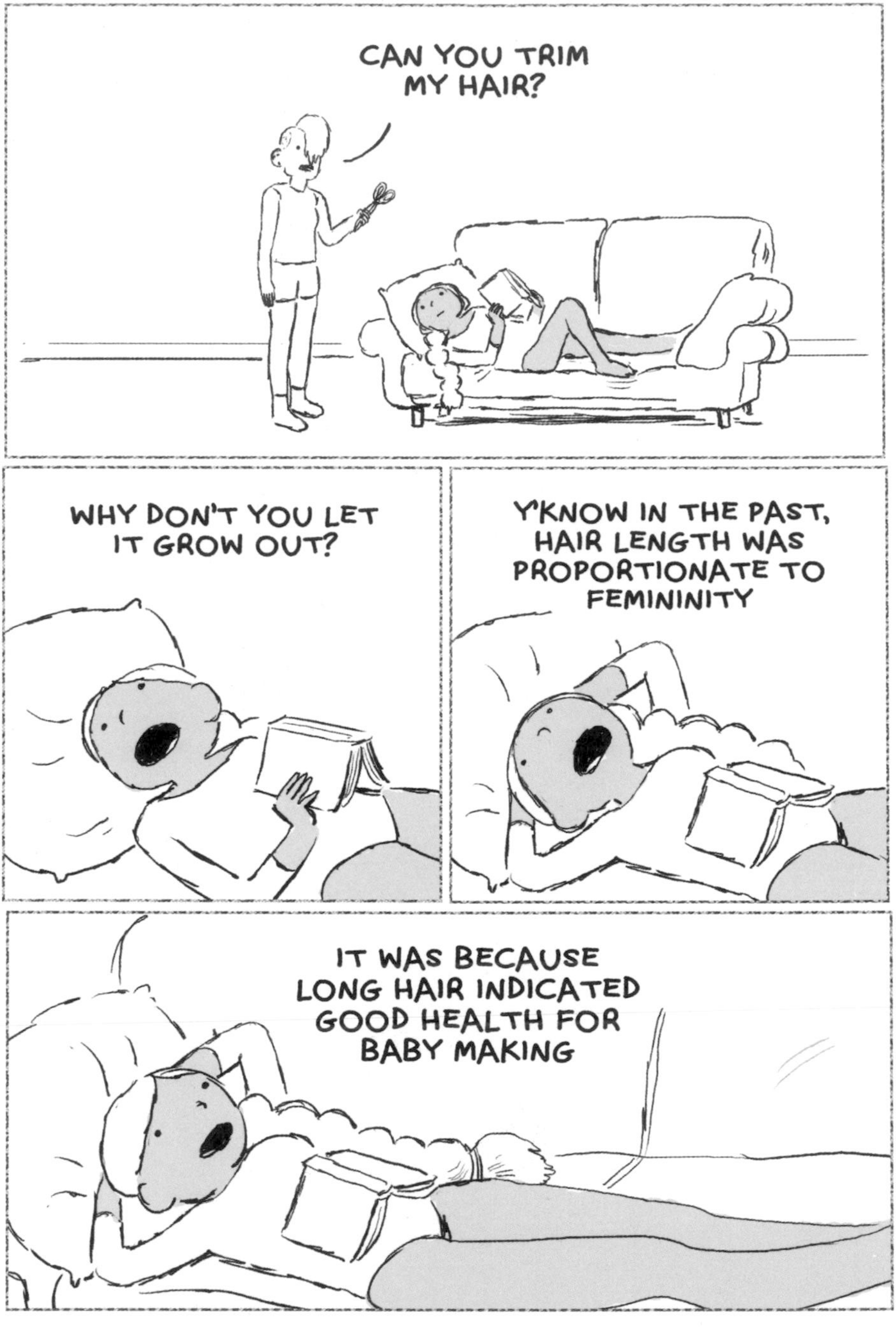
CAN YOU TRIM MY HAIR?
WHY DON'T YOU LET IT GROW OUT?
Y'KNOW IN THE PAST, HAIR LENGTH WAS PROPORTIONATE TO FEMININITY
IT WAS BECAUSE LONG HAIR INDICATED GOOD HEALTH FOR BABY MAKING

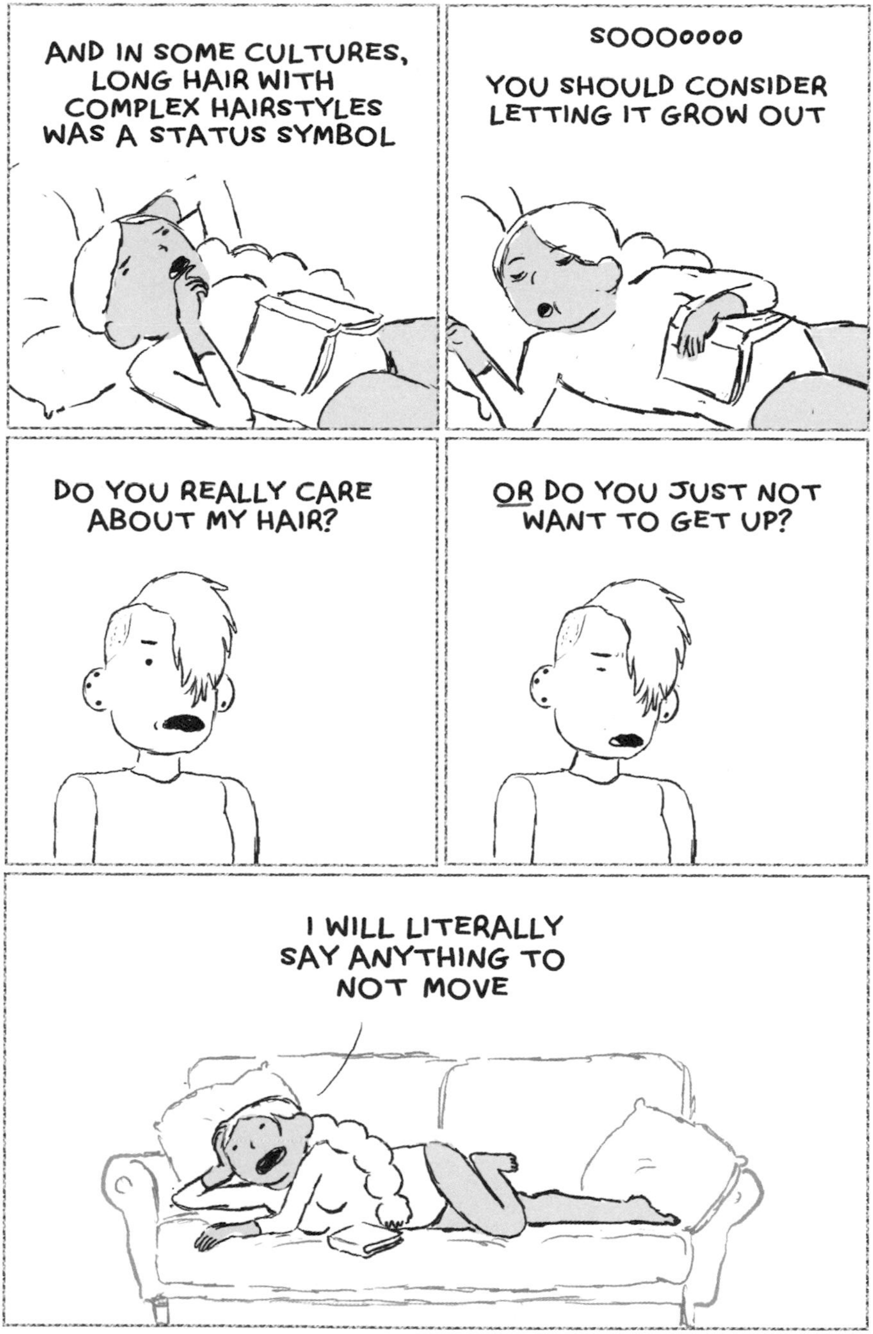
AND IN SOME CULTURES, LONG HAIR WITH COMPLEX HAIRSTYLES WAS A STATUS SYMBOL
SOOOoooo
YOU SHOULD CONSIDER LETTING IT GROW OUT
DO YOU REALLY CARE ABOUT MY HAIR?
OR DO YOU JUST NOT WANT TO GET UP?
I WILL LITERALLY SAY ANYTHING TO NOT MOVE

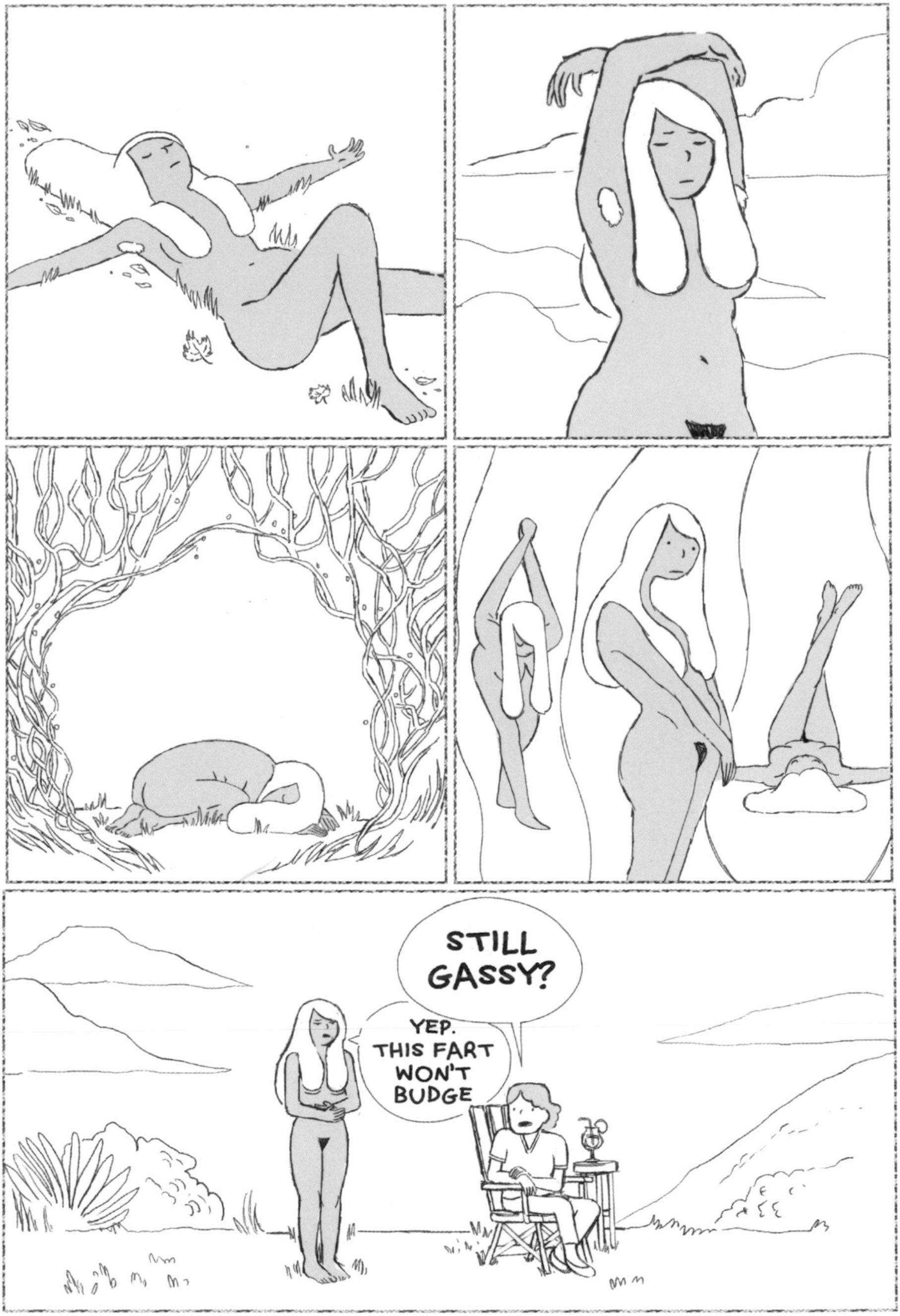
STILL GASSY?
YEP. THIS FART WON'T BUDGE

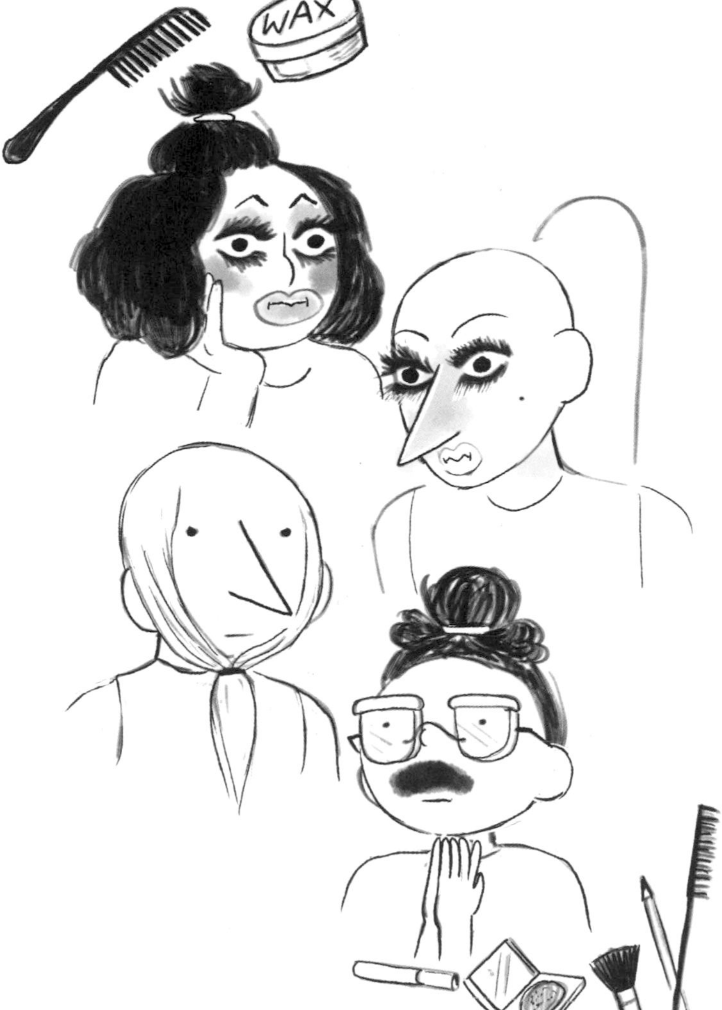
WAX

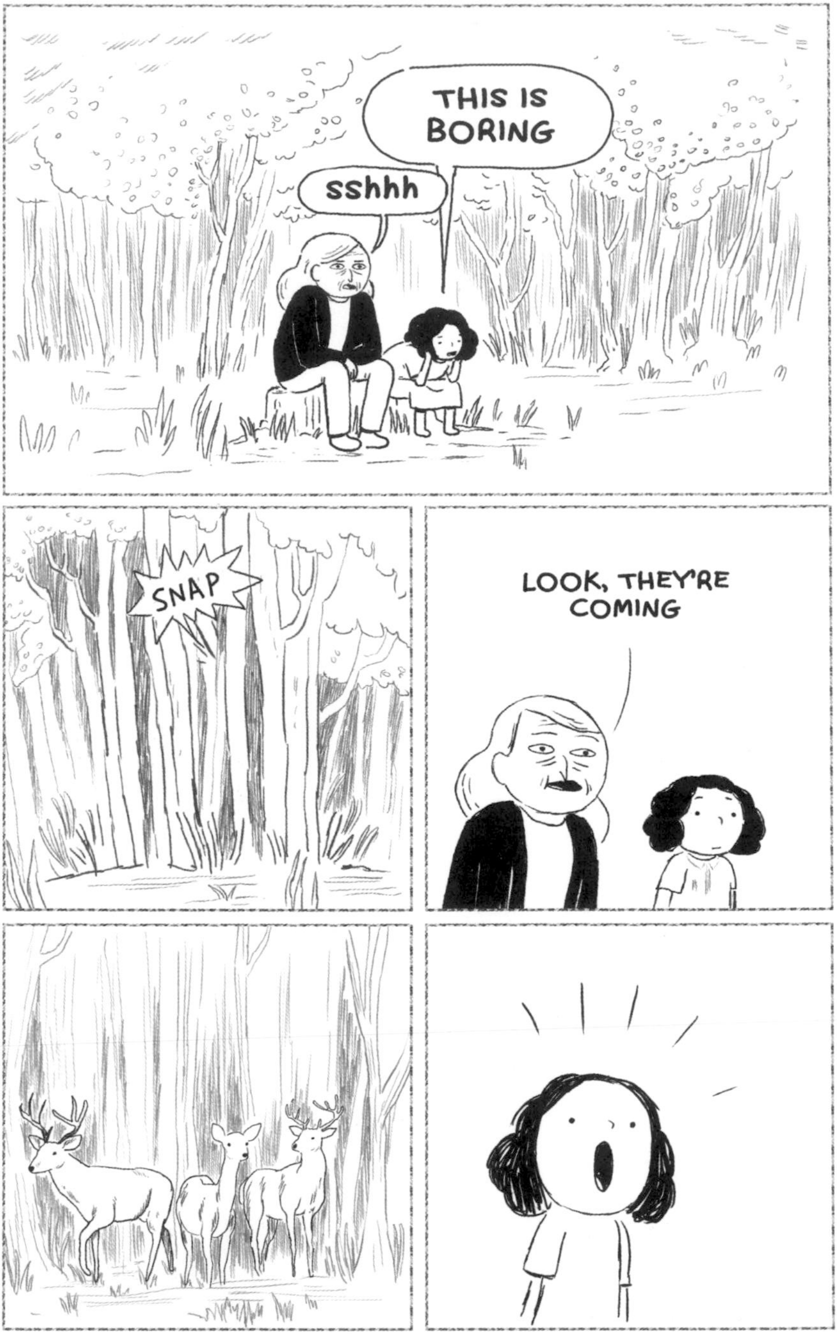
THIS IS BORING
sshhh
SNAP
LOOK, THEY'RE COMING

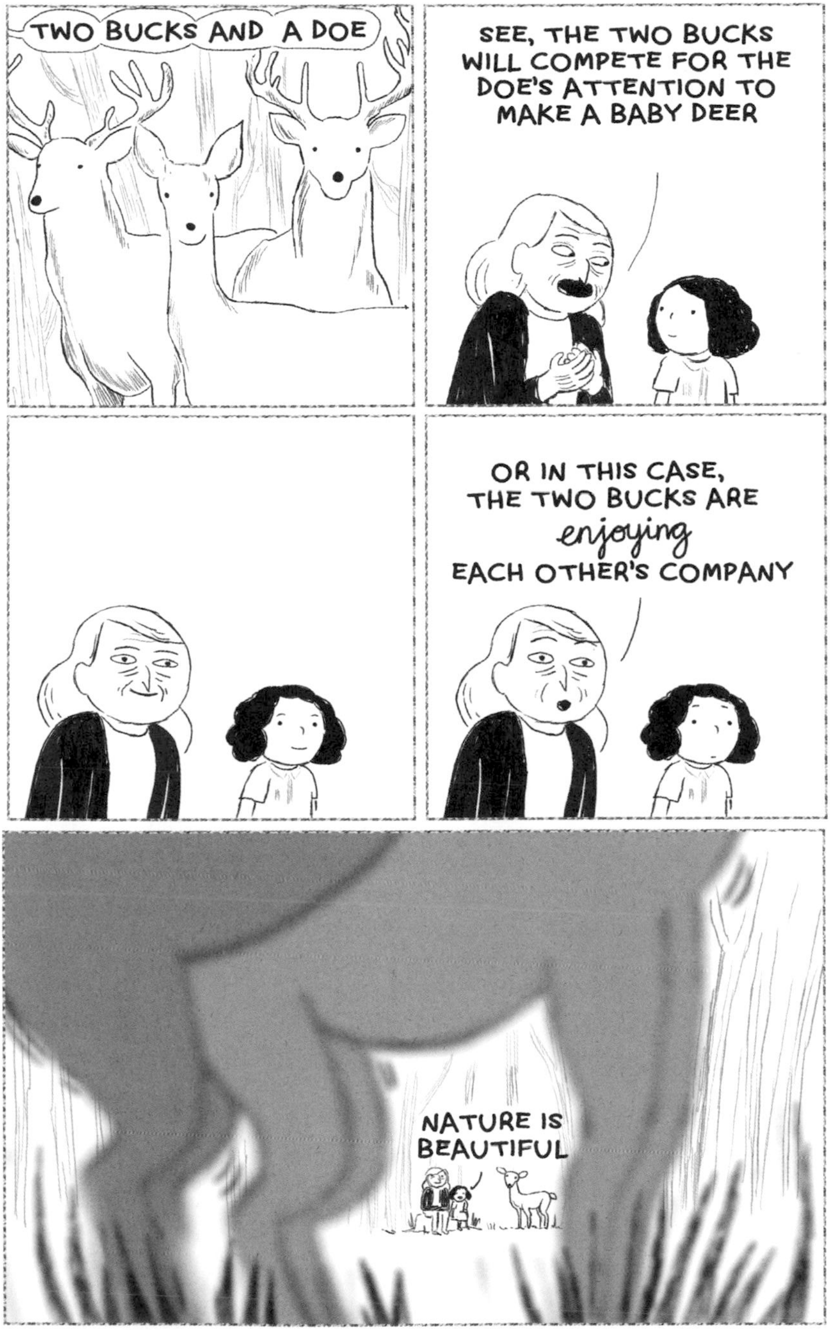
TWO BUCKS AND A DOE
SEE, THE TWO BUCKS WILL COMPETE FOR THE DOE'S ATTENTION TO MAKE A BABY DEER
OR IN THIS CASE, THE TWO BUCKS ARE *enjoying* EACH OTHER'S COMPANY
NATURE IS BEAUTIFUL

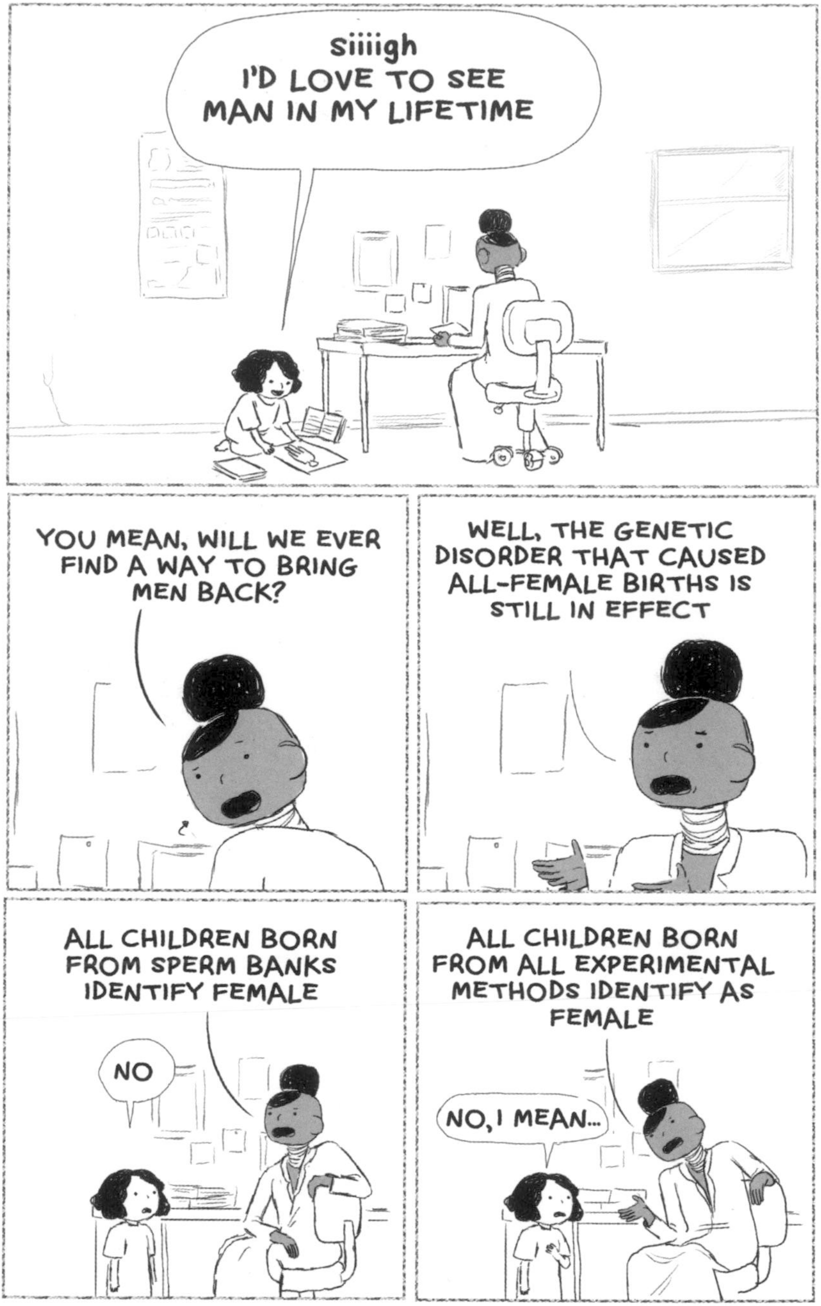
siiiigh
I'D LOVE TO SEE MAN IN MY LIFETIME
YOU MEAN, WILL WE EVER FIND A WAY TO BRING MEN BACK?
WELL, THE GENETIC DISORDER THAT CAUSED ALL-FEMALE BIRTHS IS STILL IN EFFECT
ALL CHILDREN BORN FROM SPERM BANKS IDENTIFY FEMALE
NO
ALL CHILDREN BORN FROM ALL EXPERIMENTAL METHODS IDENTIFY AS FEMALE
NO, I MEAN...

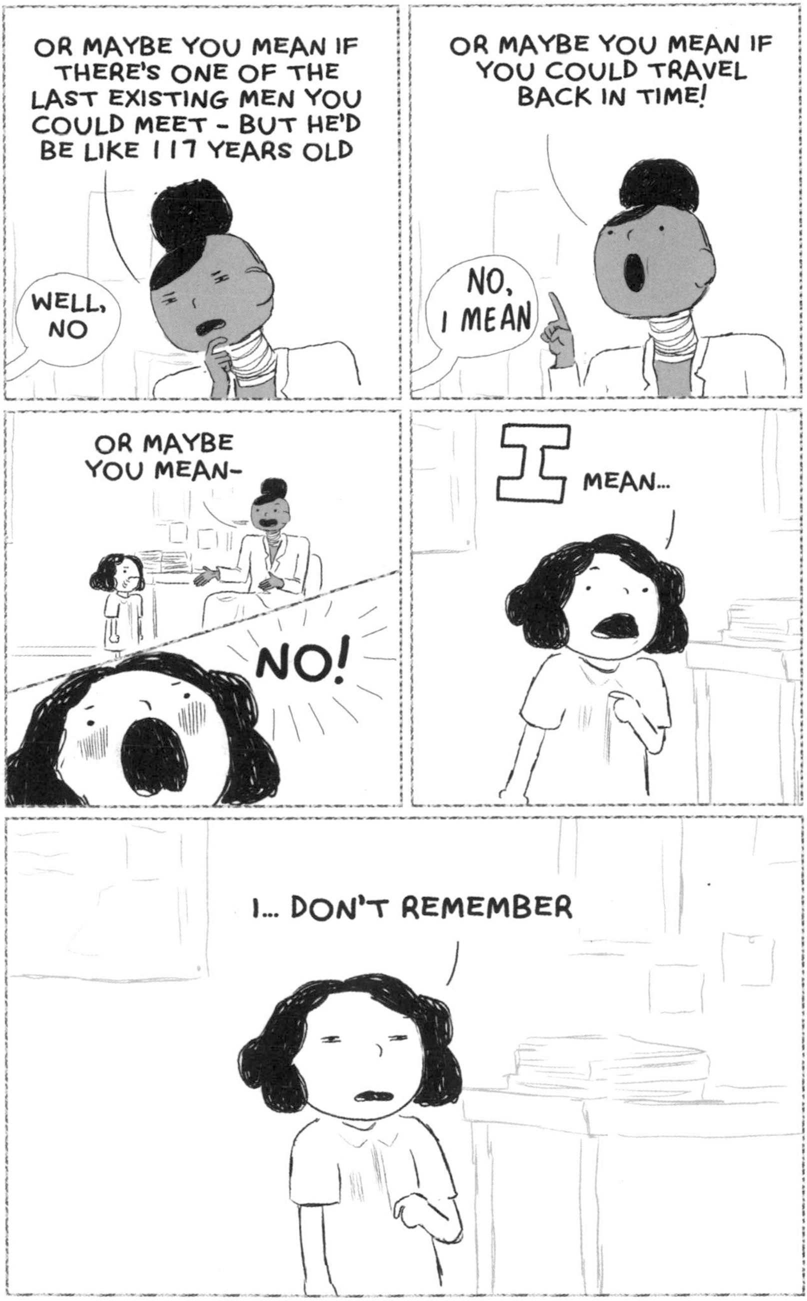
OR MAYBE YOU MEAN IF THERE'S ONE OF THE LAST EXISTING MEN YOU COULD MEET - BUT HE'D BE LIKE 117 YEARS OLD
WELL, NO
OR MAYBE YOU MEAN IF YOU COULD TRAVEL BACK IN TIME!
NO, I MEAN
OR MAYBE YOU MEAN-
NO!
I MEAN...
I... DON'T REMEMBER

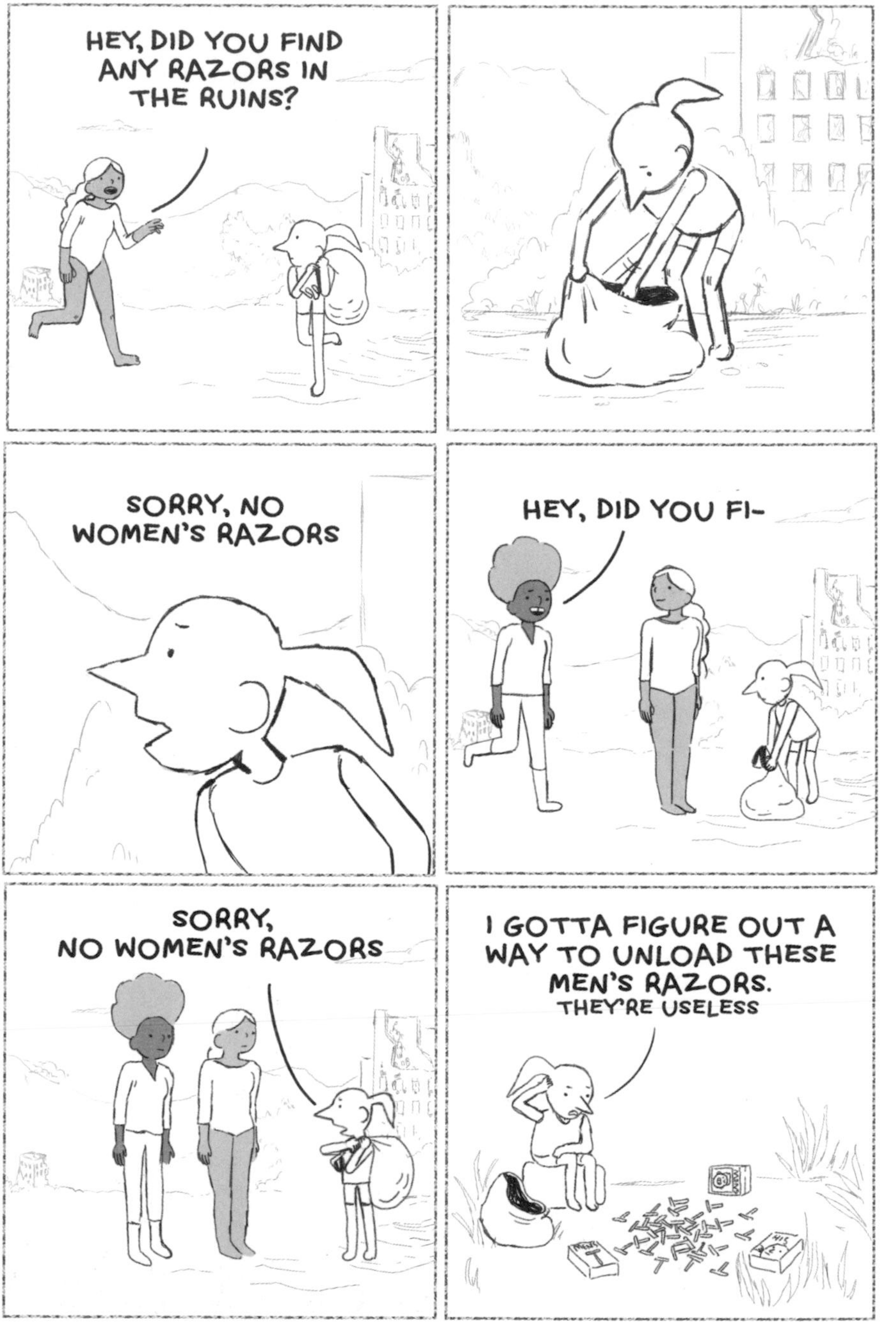
HEY, DID YOU FIND ANY RAZORS IN THE RUINS?
SORRY, NO WOMEN'S RAZORS
HEY, DID YOU FI-
SORRY, NO WOMEN'S RAZORS
I GOTTA FIGURE OUT A WAY TO UNLOAD THESE MEN'S RAZORS.
THEY'RE USELESS

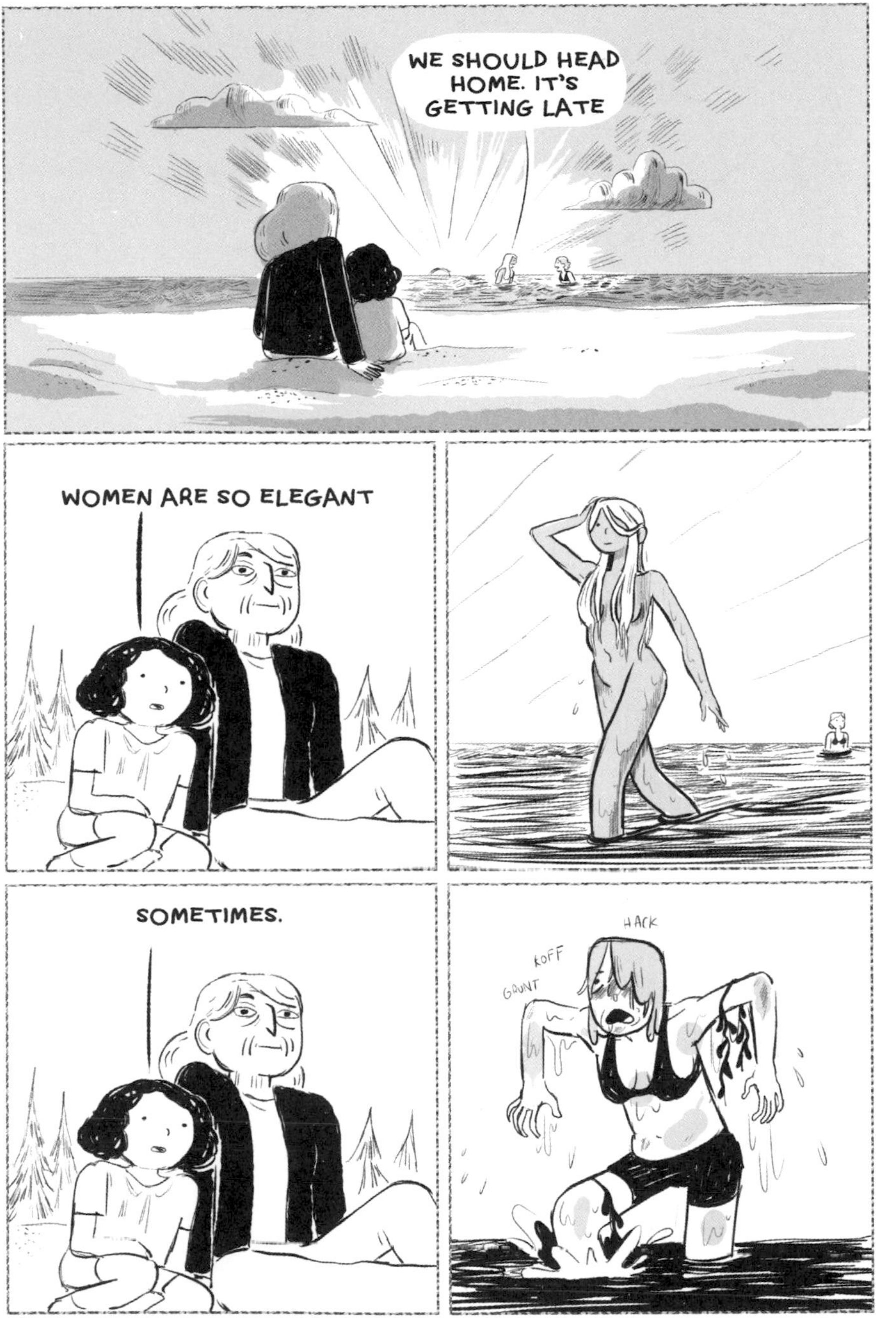
WE SHOULD HEAD HOME. IT'S GETTING LATE
WOMEN ARE SO ELEGANT
SOMETIMES.
HACK
KOFF
GRUNT

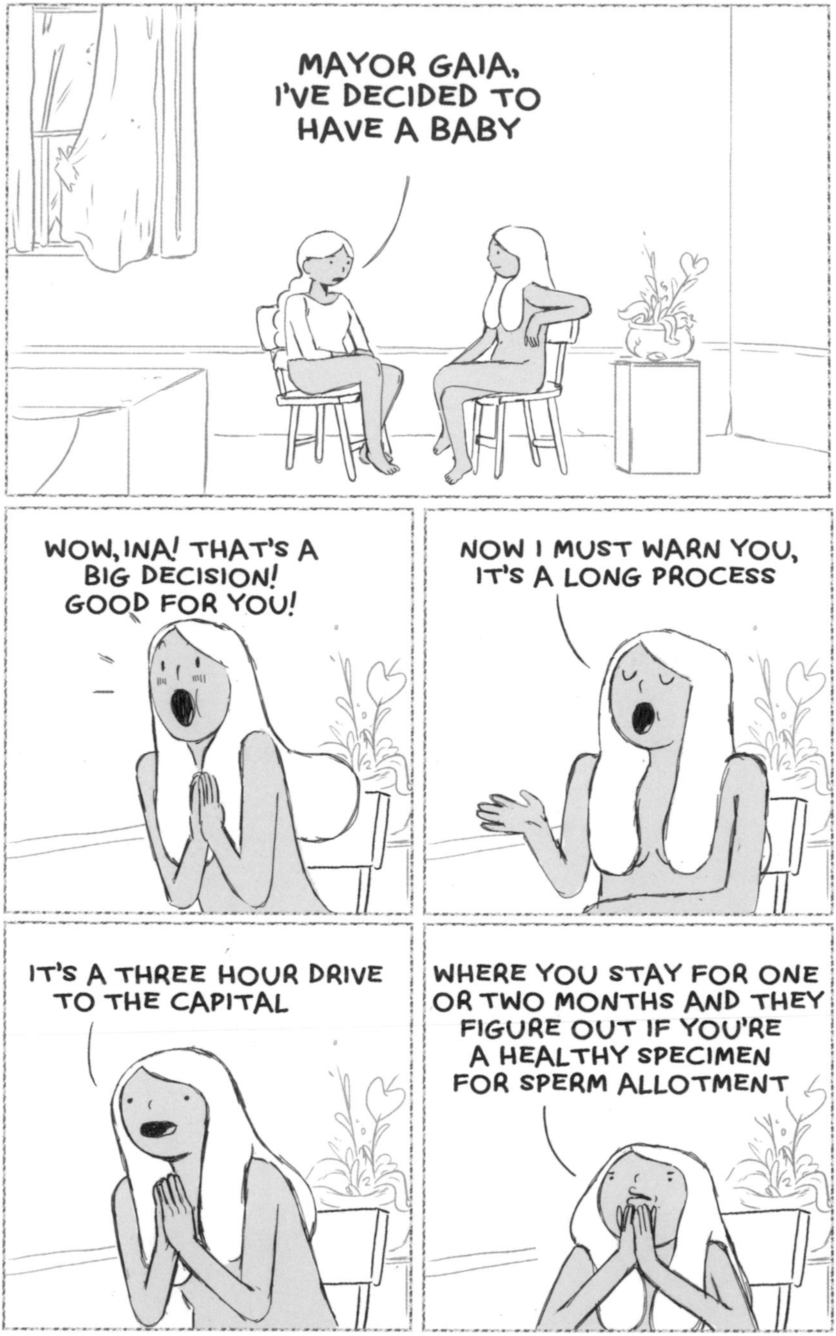
MAYOR GAIA, I'VE DECIDED TO HAVE A BABY
WOW, INA! THAT'S A BIG DECISION! GOOD FOR YOU!
NOW I MUST WARN YOU, IT'S A LONG PROCESS
IT'S A THREE HOUR DRIVE TO THE CAPITAL
WHERE YOU STAY FOR ONE OR TWO MONTHS AND THEY FIGURE OUT IF YOU'RE A HEALTHY SPECIMEN FOR SPERM ALLOTMENT

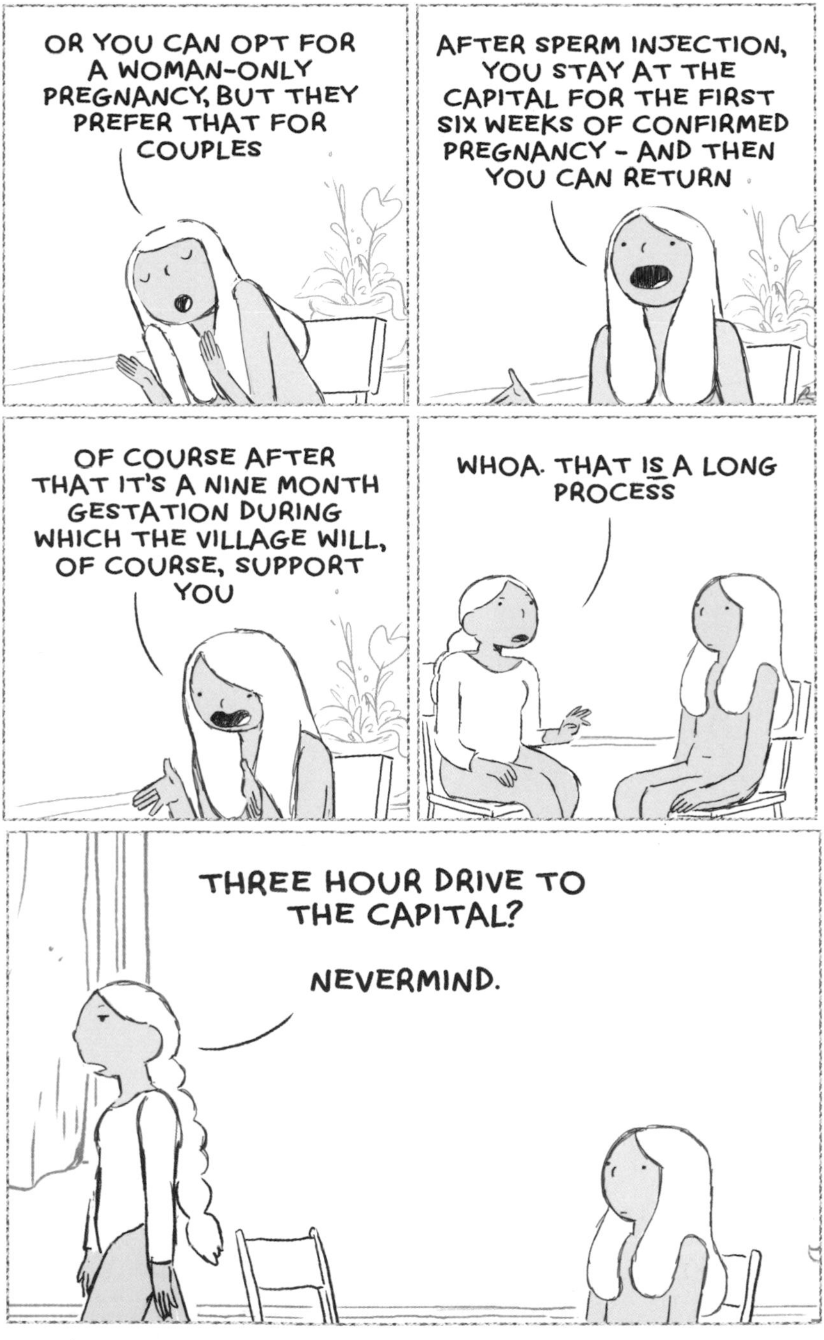
OR YOU CAN OPT FOR A WOMAN-ONLY PREGNANCY, BUT THEY PREFER THAT FOR COUPLES
AFTER SPERM INJECTION, YOU STAY AT THE CAPITAL FOR THE FIRST SIX WEEKS OF CONFIRMED PREGNANCY - AND THEN YOU CAN RETURN
OF COURSE AFTER THAT IT'S A NINE MONTH GESTATION DURING WHICH THE VILLAGE WILL, OF COURSE, SUPPORT YOU
WHOA. THAT IS A LONG PROCESS
THREE HOUR DRIVE TO THE CAPITAL?
NEVERMIND.

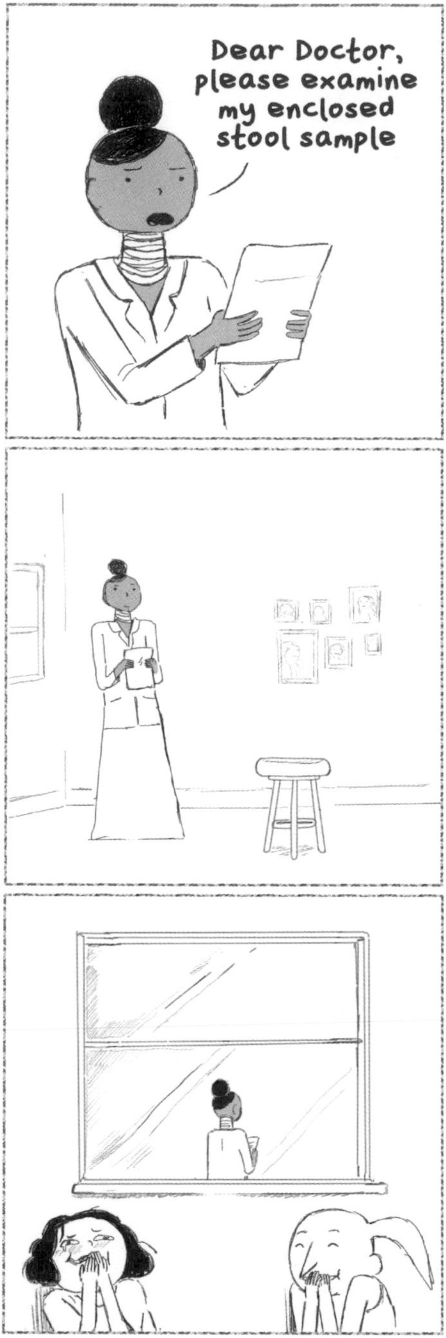
Dear Doctor, please examine my enclosed stool sample

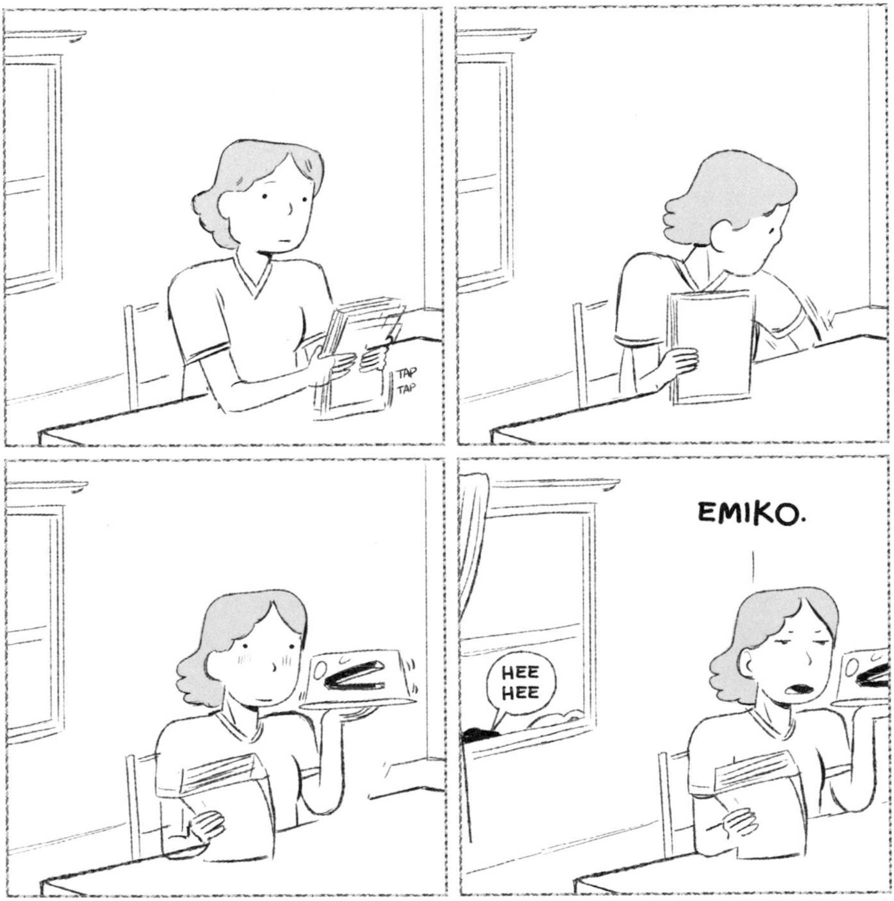
TAP
TAP
HEE
HEE
EMIKO.

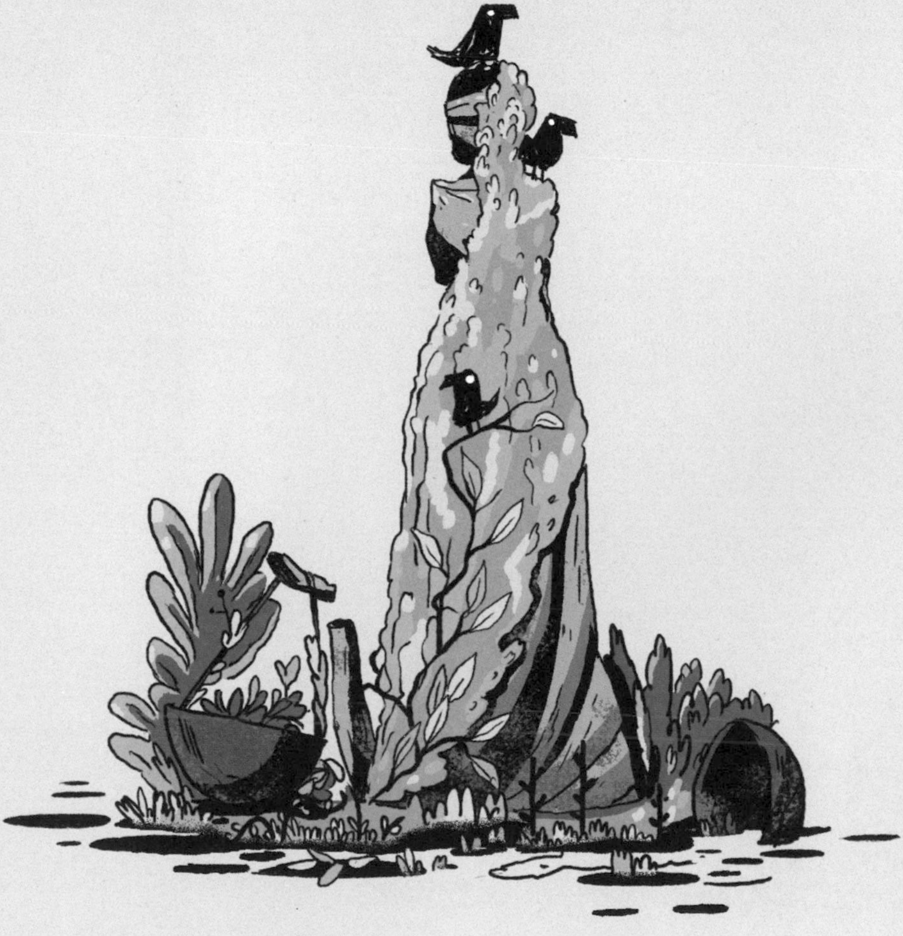

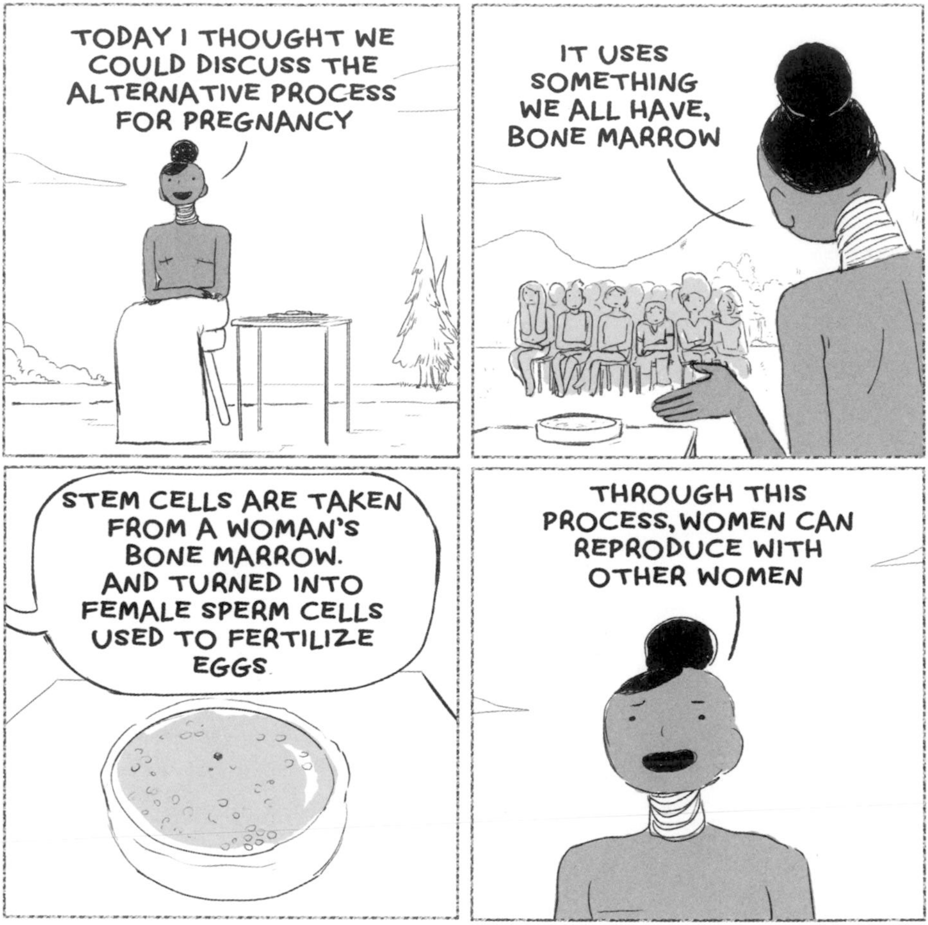
TODAY I THOUGHT WE COULD DISCUSS THE ALTERNATIVE PROCESS FOR PREGNANCY
IT USES SOMETHING WE ALL HAVE, BONE MARROW
STEM CELLS ARE TAKEN FROM A WOMAN'S BONE MARROW. AND TURNED INTO FEMALE SPERM CELLS USED TO FERTILIZE EGGS.
THROUGH THIS PROCESS, WOMEN CAN REPRODUCE WITH OTHER WOMEN

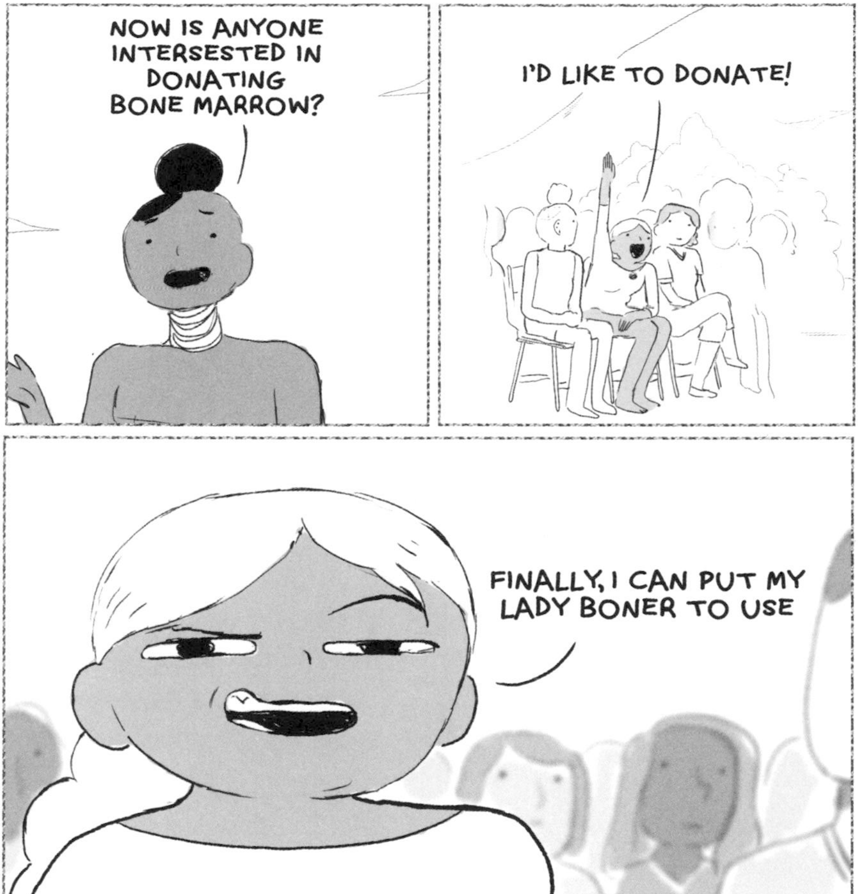
NOW IS ANYONE INTERSESTED IN DONATING BONE MARROW?
I'D LIKE TO DONATE!
FINALLY, I CAN PUT MY LADY BONER TO USE

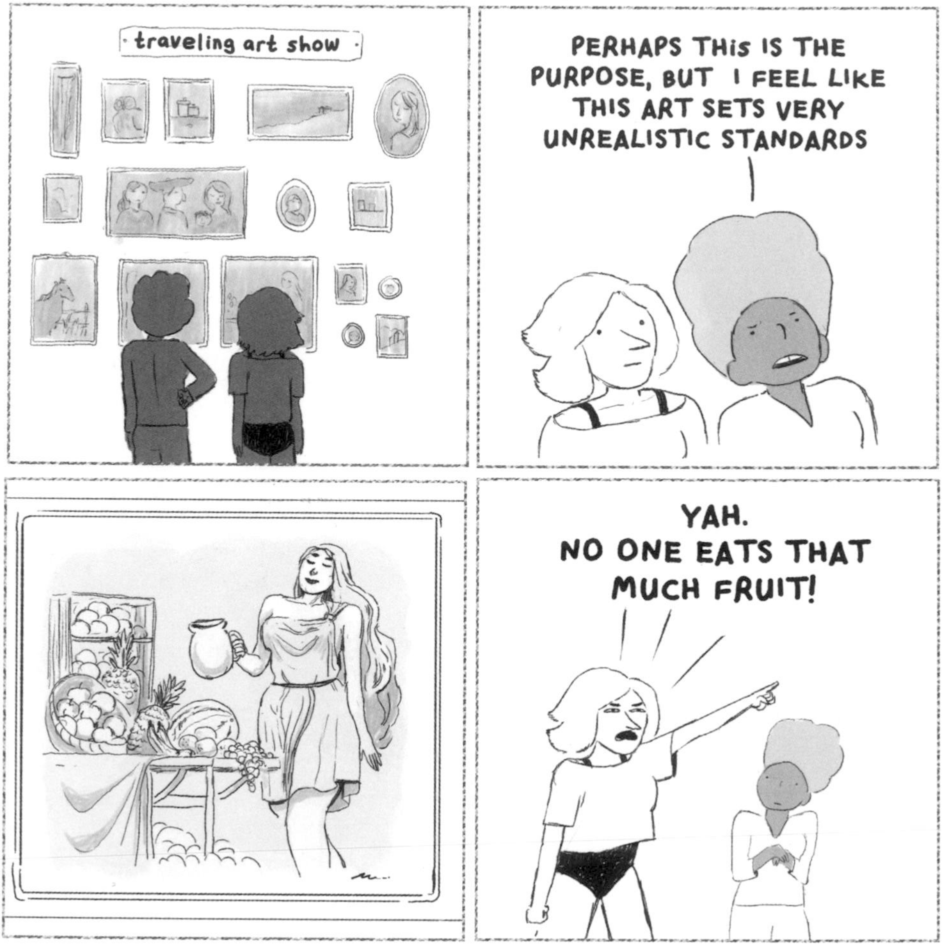
traveling art show
PERHAPS THIS IS THE PURPOSE, BUT I FEEL LIKE THIS ART SETS VERY UNREALISTIC STANDARDS
YAH. NO ONE EATS THAT MUCH FRUIT!

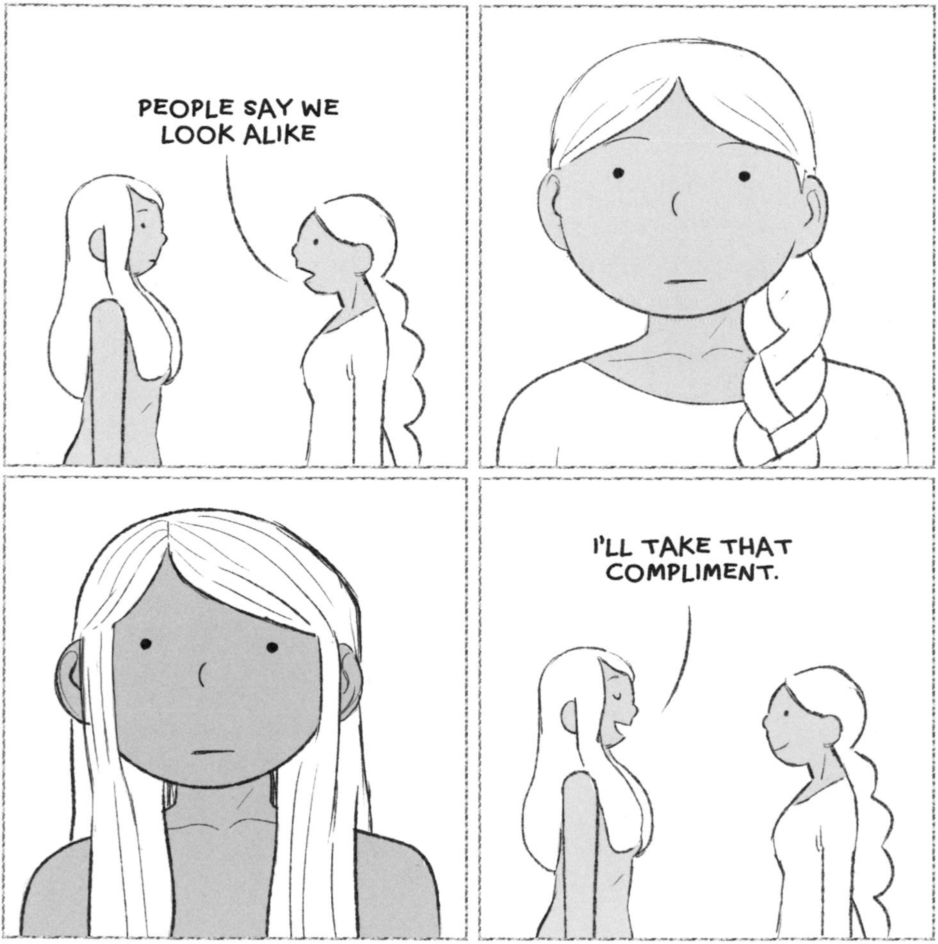
PEOPLE SAY WE LOOK ALIKE
I'LL TAKE THAT COMPLIMENT.

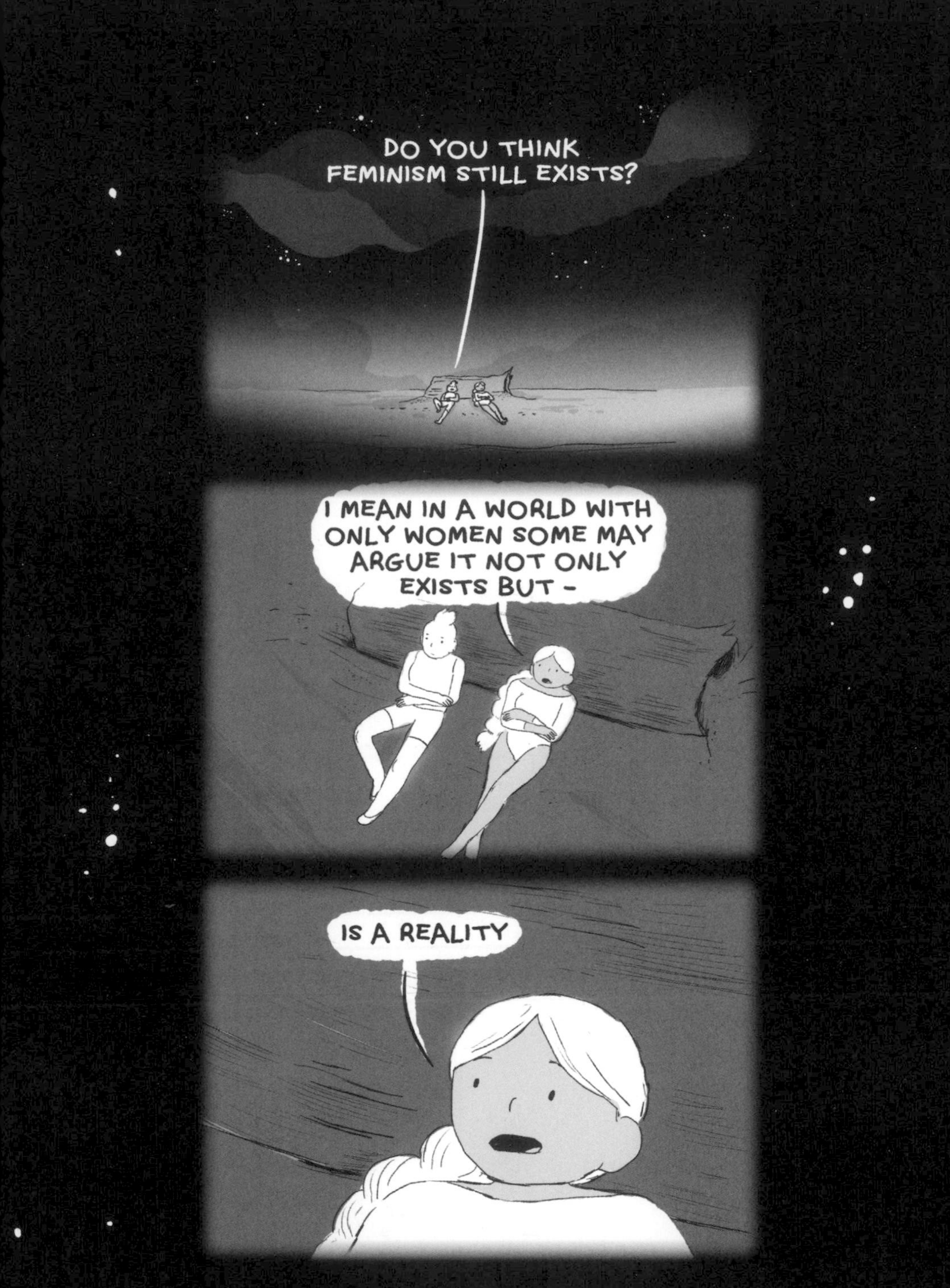
DO YOU THINK FEMINISM STILL EXISTS?
I MEAN IN A WORLD WITH ONLY WOMEN SOME MAY ARGUE IT NOT ONLY EXISTS BUT -
IS A REALITY

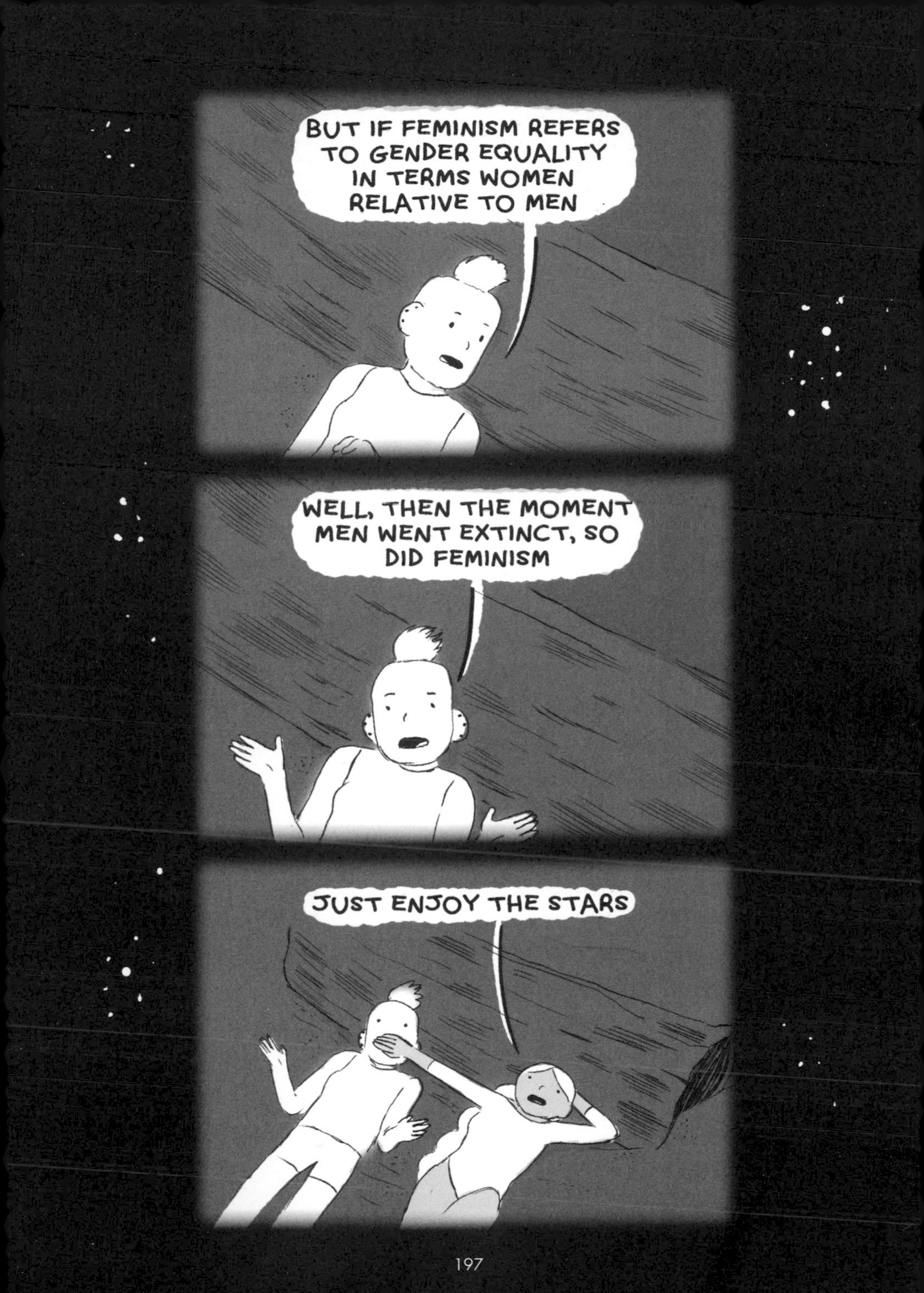
BUT IF FEMINISM REFERS TO GENDER EQUALITY IN TERMS WOMEN RELATIVE TO MEN
WELL, THEN THE MOMENT MEN WENT EXTINCT, SO DID FEMINISM
JUST ENJOY THE STARS

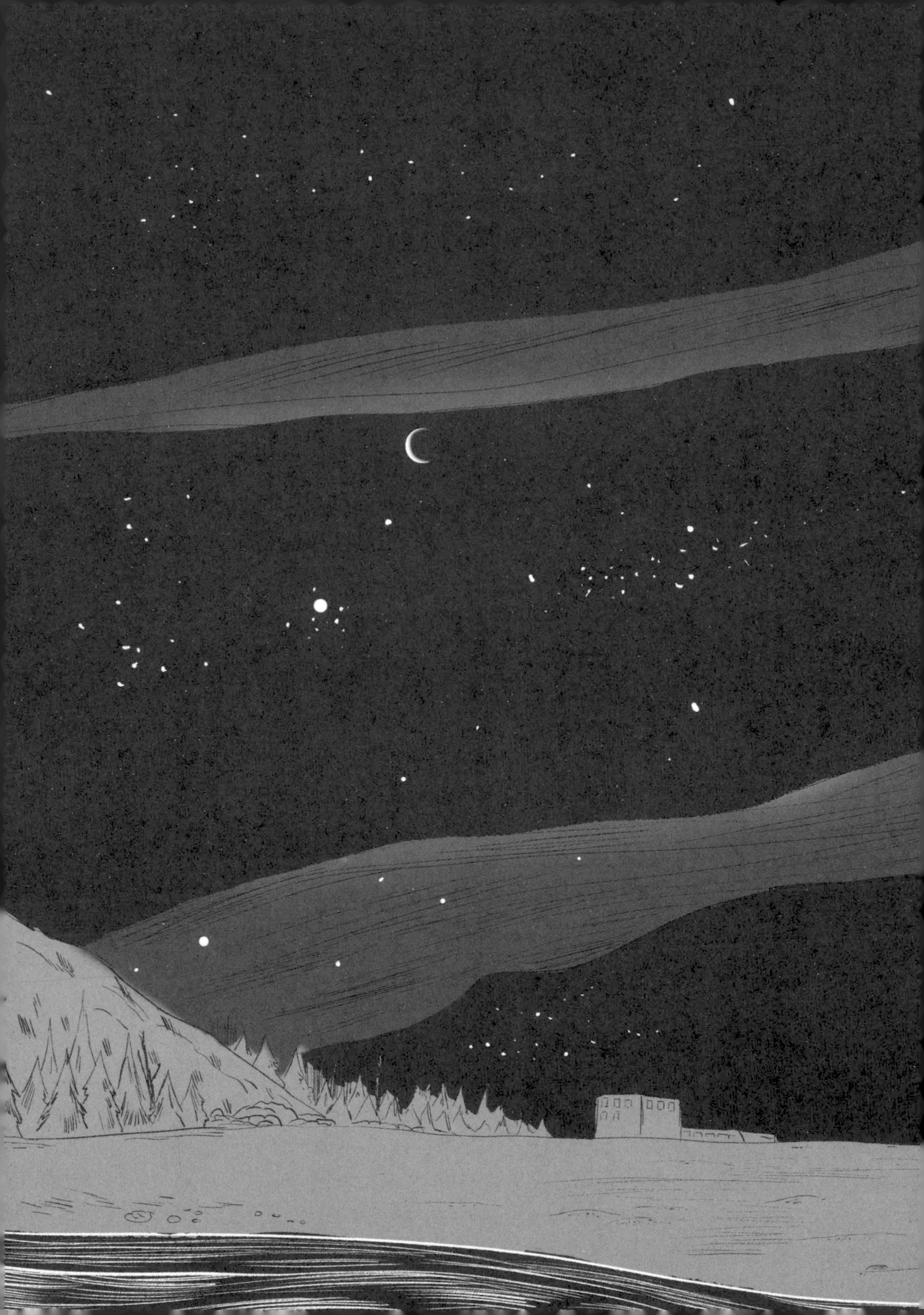

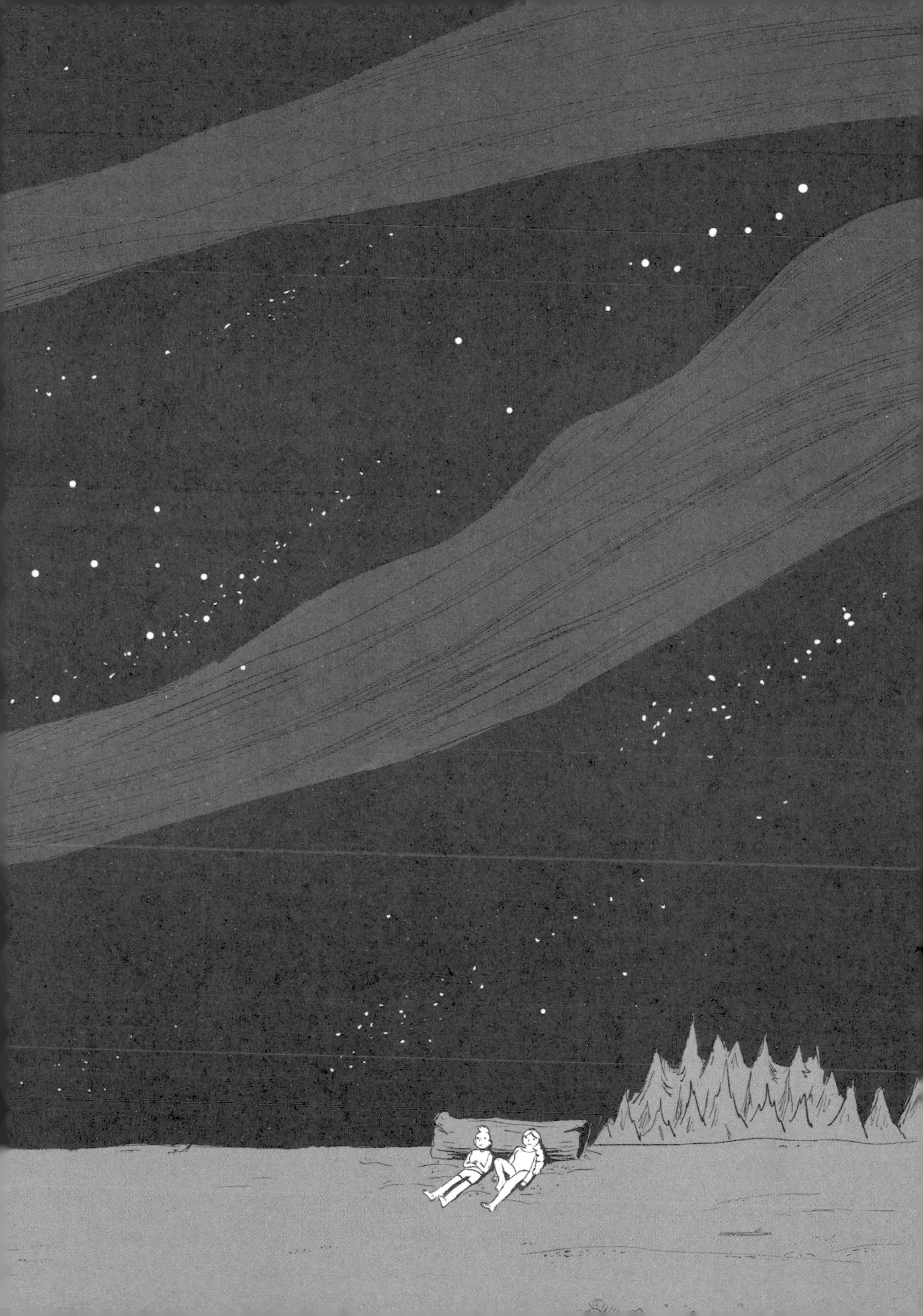

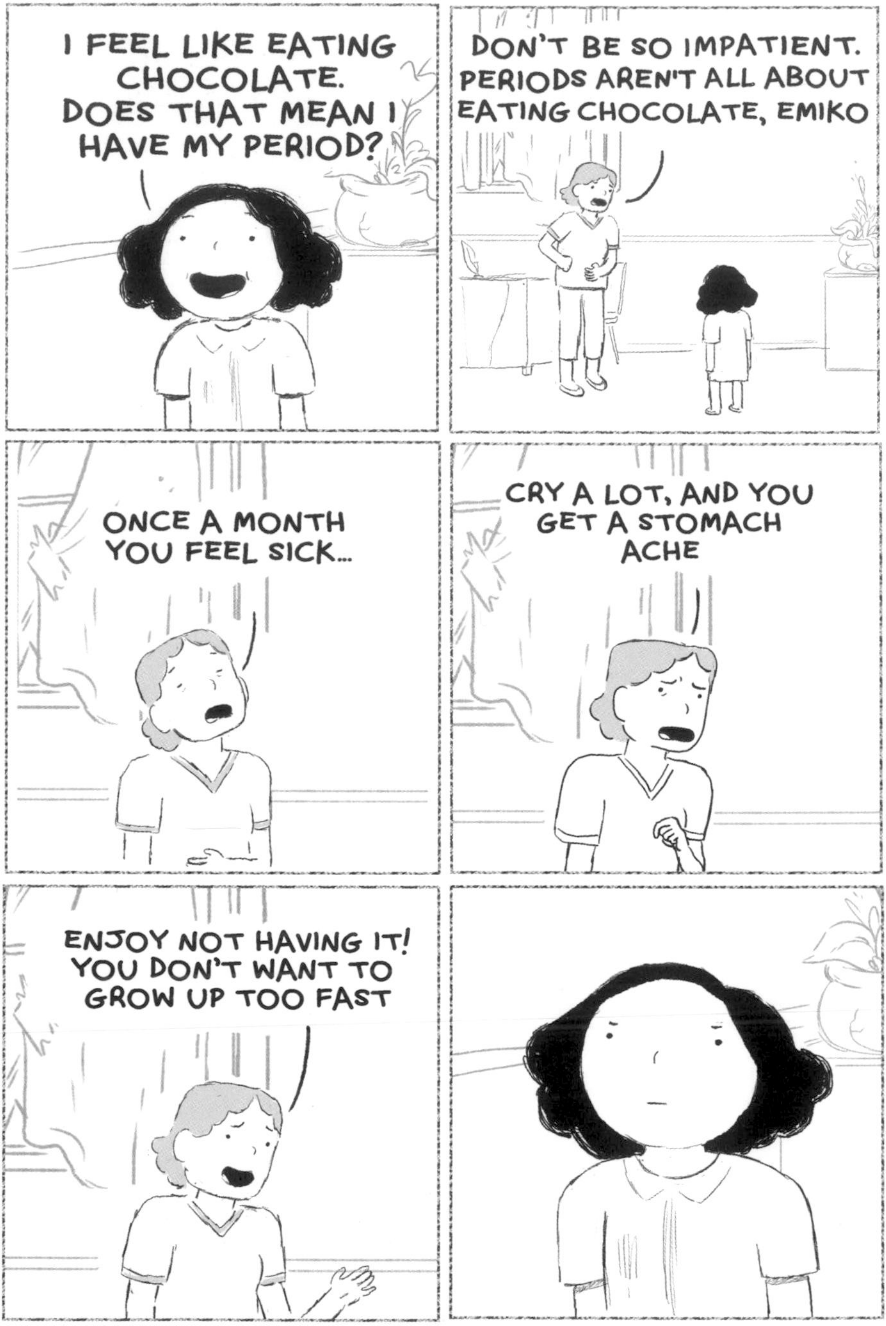
I FEEL LIKE EATING CHOCOLATE. DOES THAT MEAN I HAVE MY PERIOD?
DON'T BE SO IMPATIENT. PERIODS AREN'T ALL ABOUT EATING CHOCOLATE, EMIKO
ONCE A MONTH YOU FEEL SICK...
CRY A LOT, AND YOU GET A STOMACH ACHE
ENJOY NOT HAVING IT! YOU DON'T WANT TO GROW UP TOO FAST

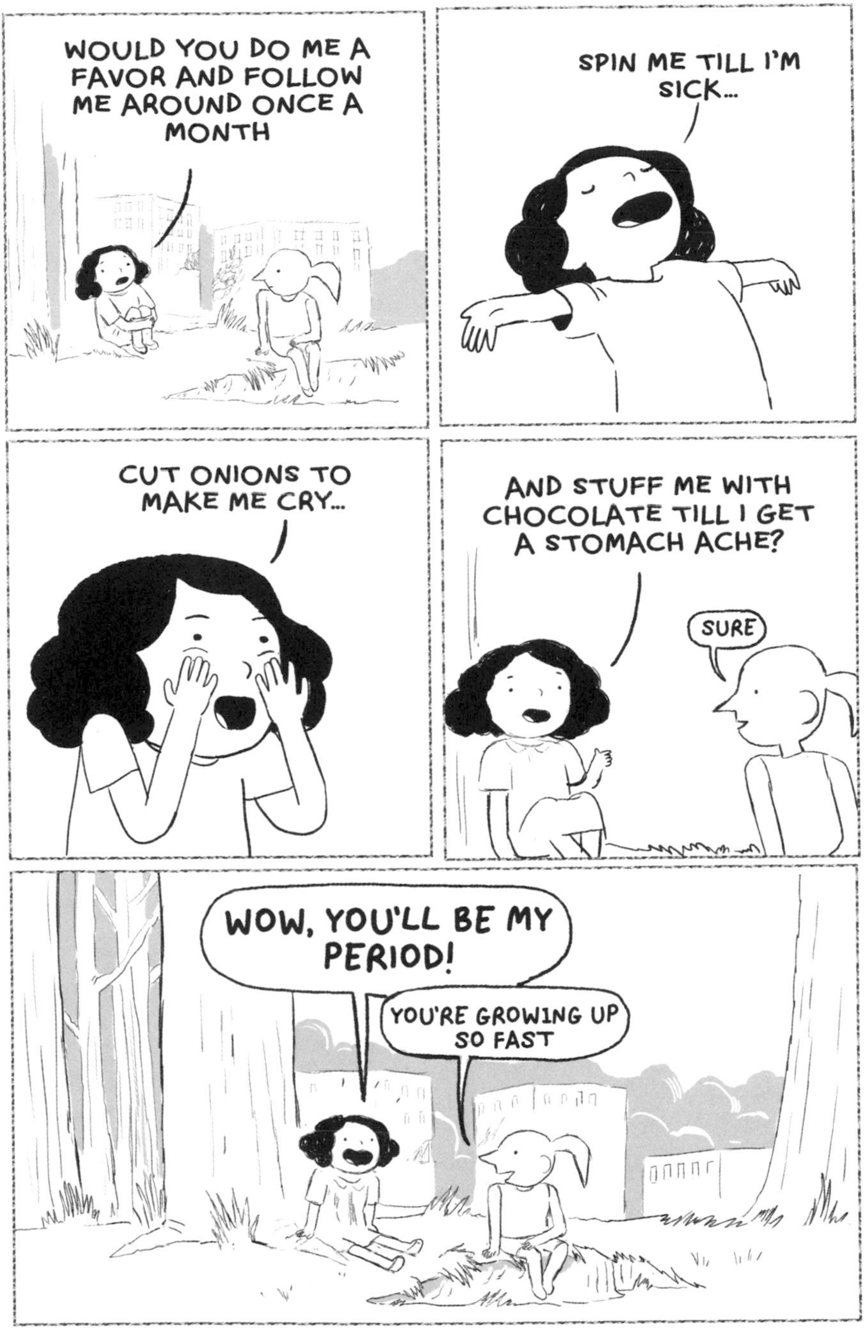
WOULD YOU DO ME A FAVOR AND FOLLOW ME AROUND ONCE A MONTH
SPIN ME TILL I'M SICK...
CUT ONIONS TO MAKE ME CRY...
AND STUFF ME WITH CHOCOLATE TILL I GET A STOMACH ACHE?
SURE
WOW, YOU'LL BE MY PERIOD!
YOU'RE GROWING UP SO FAST

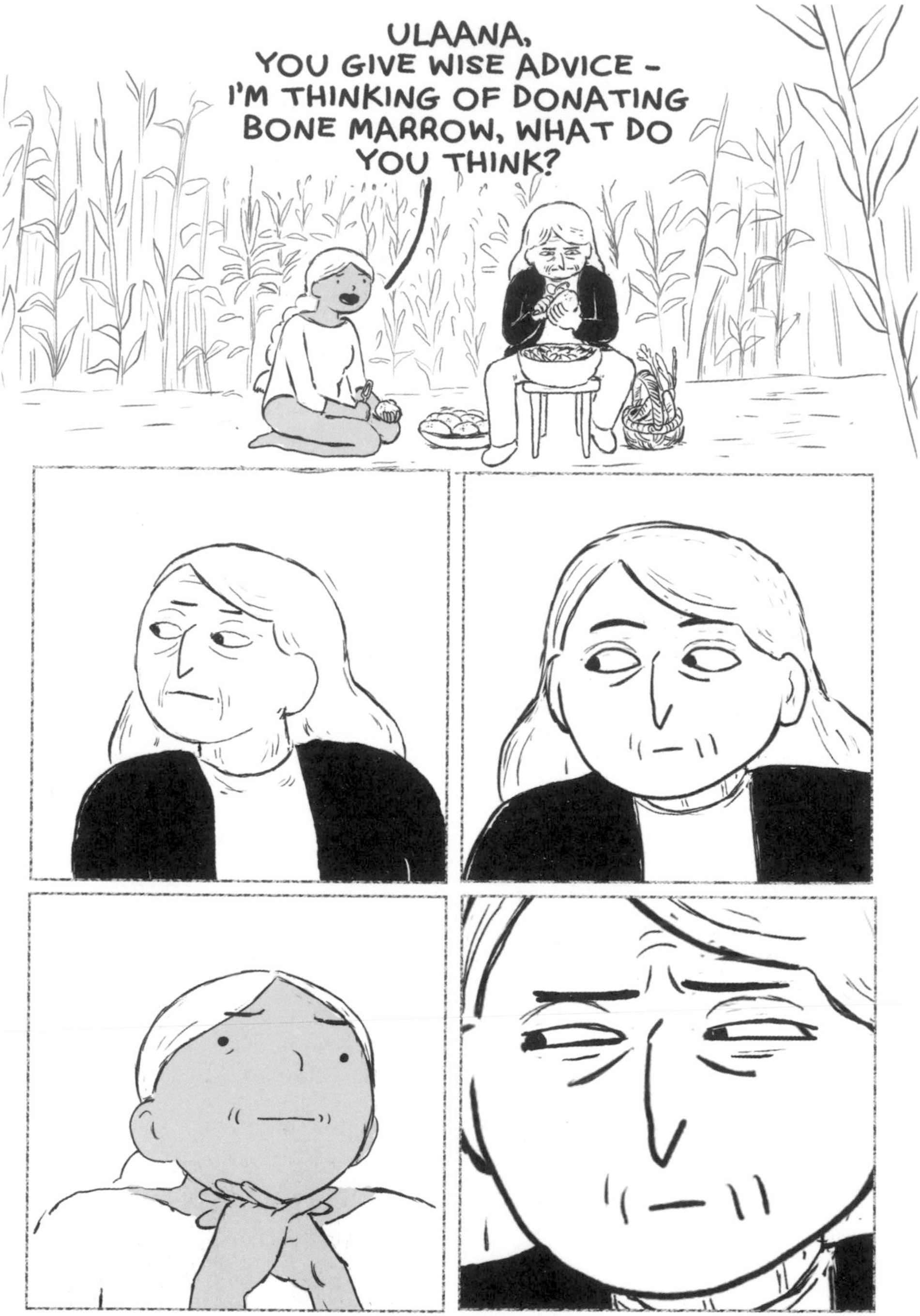
ULAANA,
YOU GIVE WISE ADVICE -
I'M THINKING OF DONATING
BONE MARROW, WHAT DO
YOU THINK?

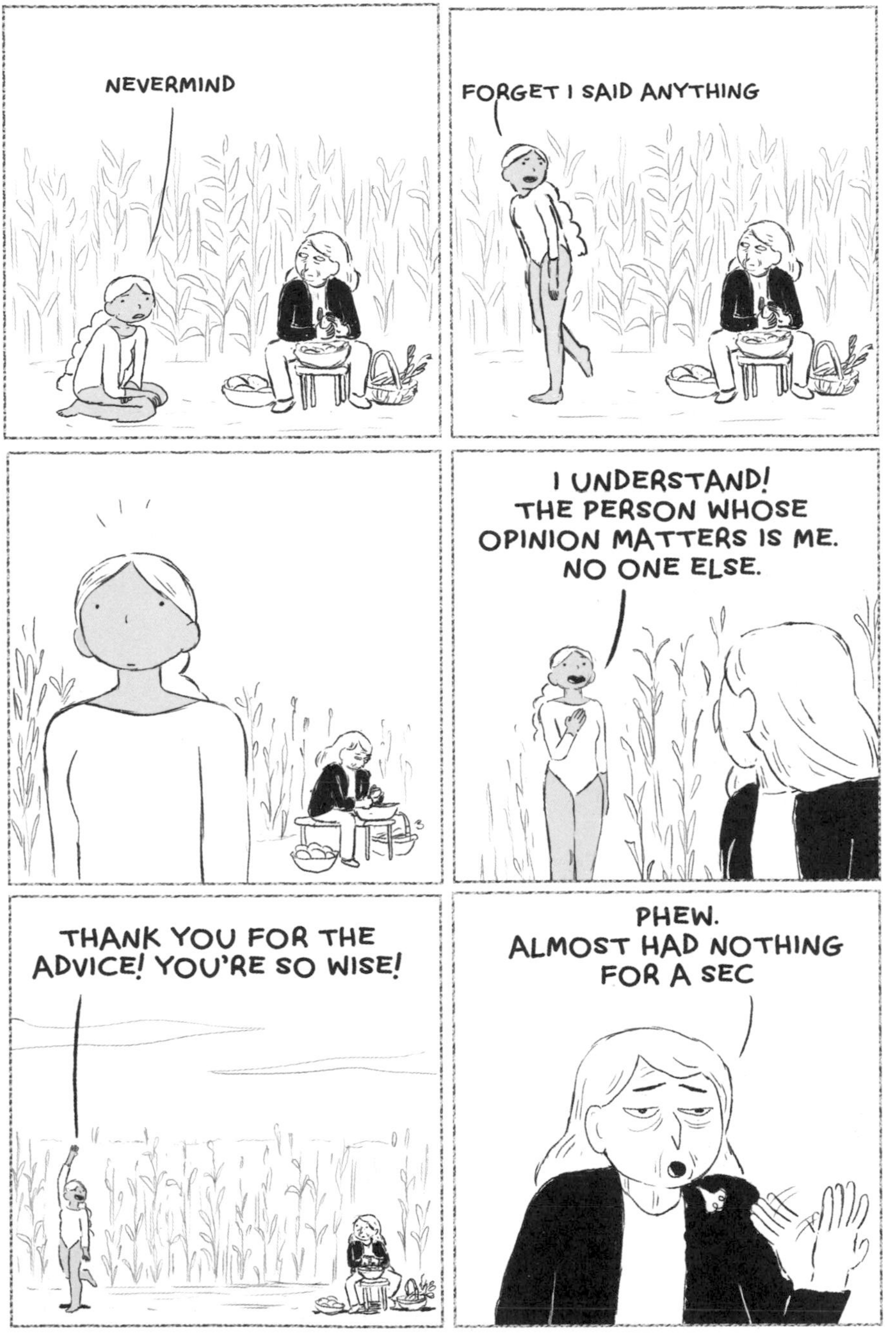
NEVERMIND
FORGET I SAID ANYTHING
I UNDERSTAND! THE PERSON WHOSE OPINION MATTERS IS ME. NO ONE ELSE.
THANK YOU FOR THE ADVICE! YOU'RE SO WISE!
PHEW. ALMOST HAD NOTHING FOR A SEC

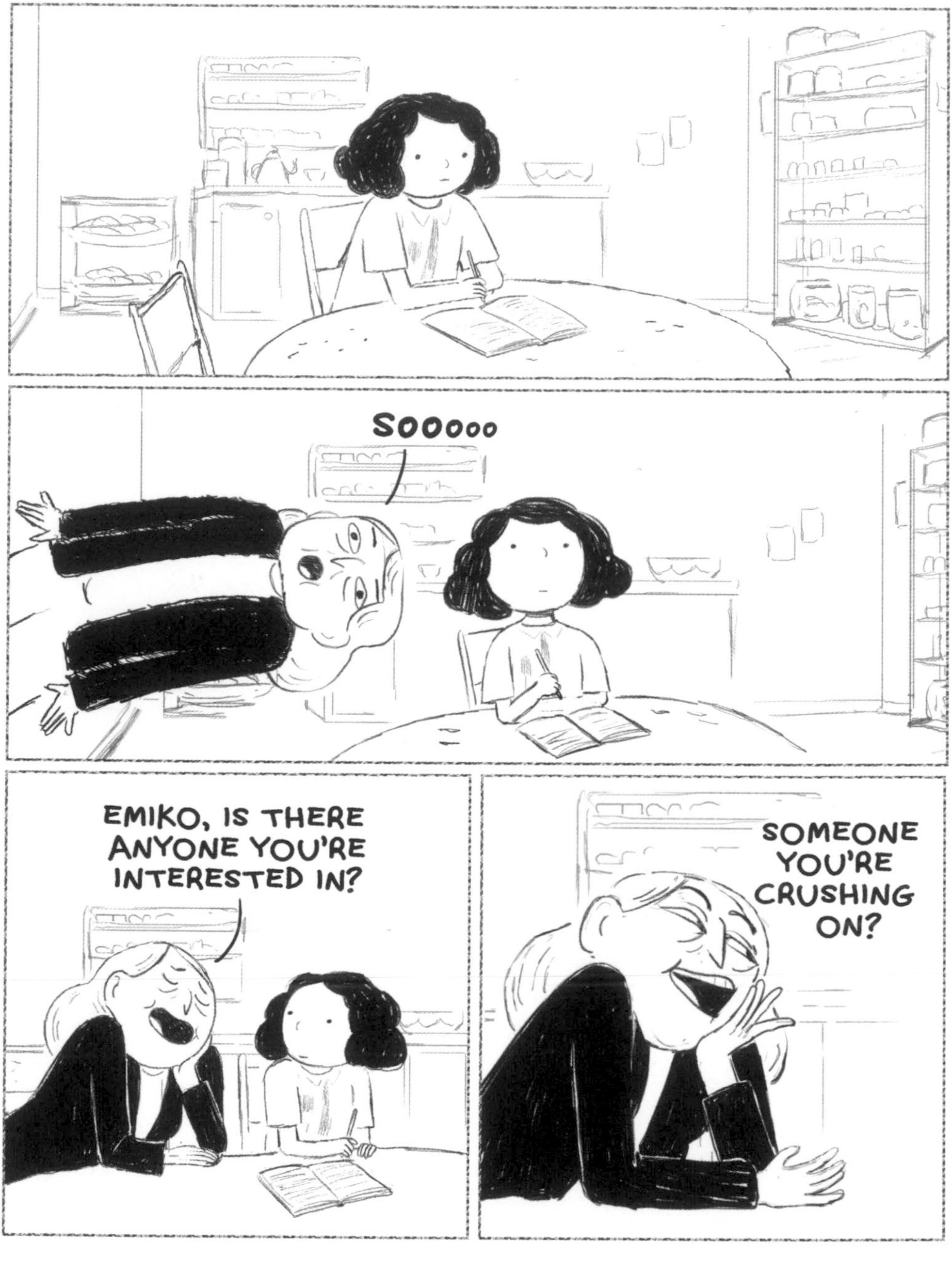
SOOooo
EMIKO, IS THERE ANYONE YOU'RE INTERESTED IN?
SOMEONE YOU'RE CRUSHING ON?

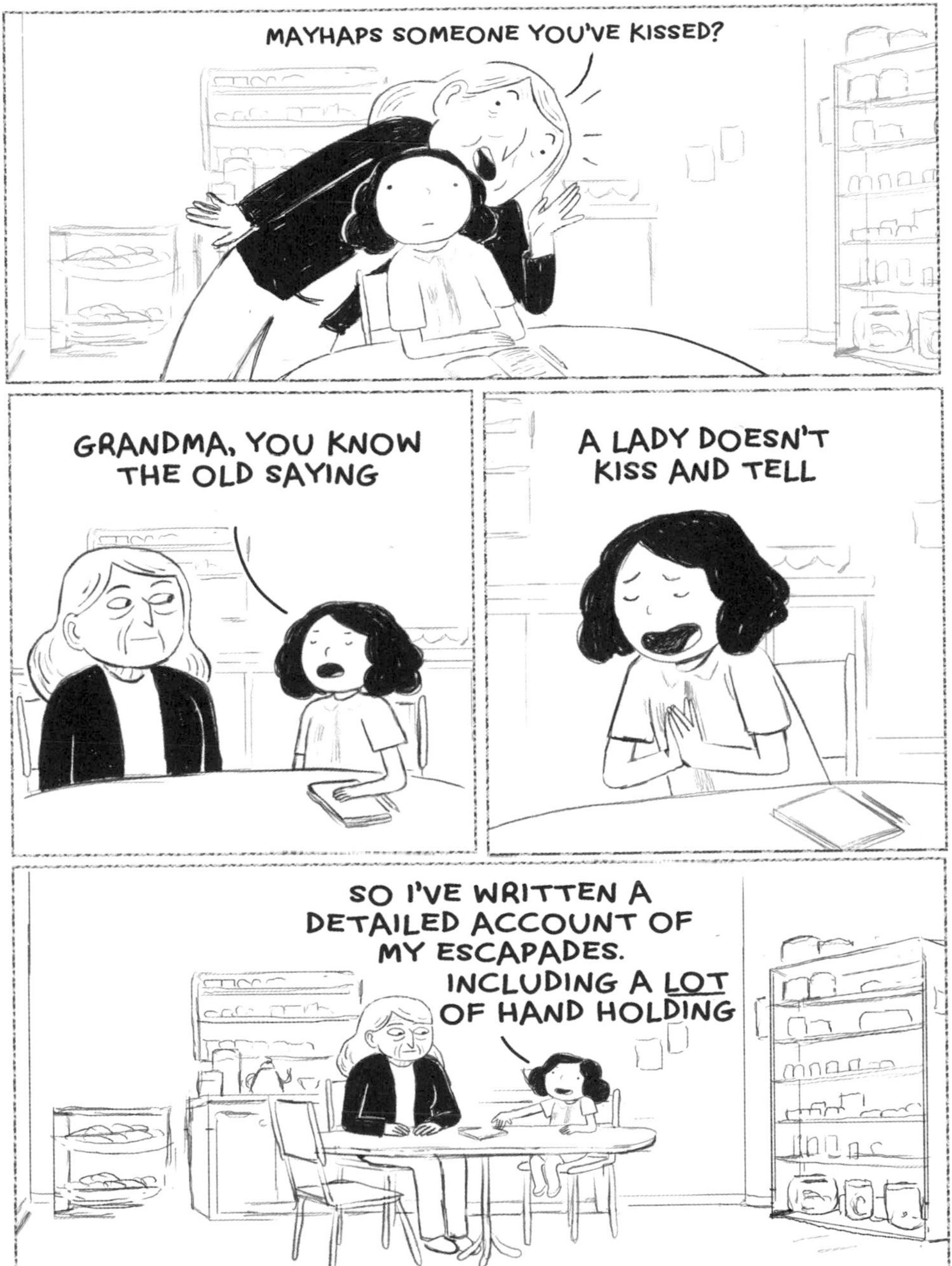
MAYHAPS SOMEONE YOU'VE KISSED?
GRANDMA, YOU KNOW THE OLD SAYING
A LADY DOESN'T KISS AND TELL
SO I'VE WRITTEN A DETAILED ACCOUNT OF MY ESCAPADES.
INCLUDING A LOT OF HAND HOLDING

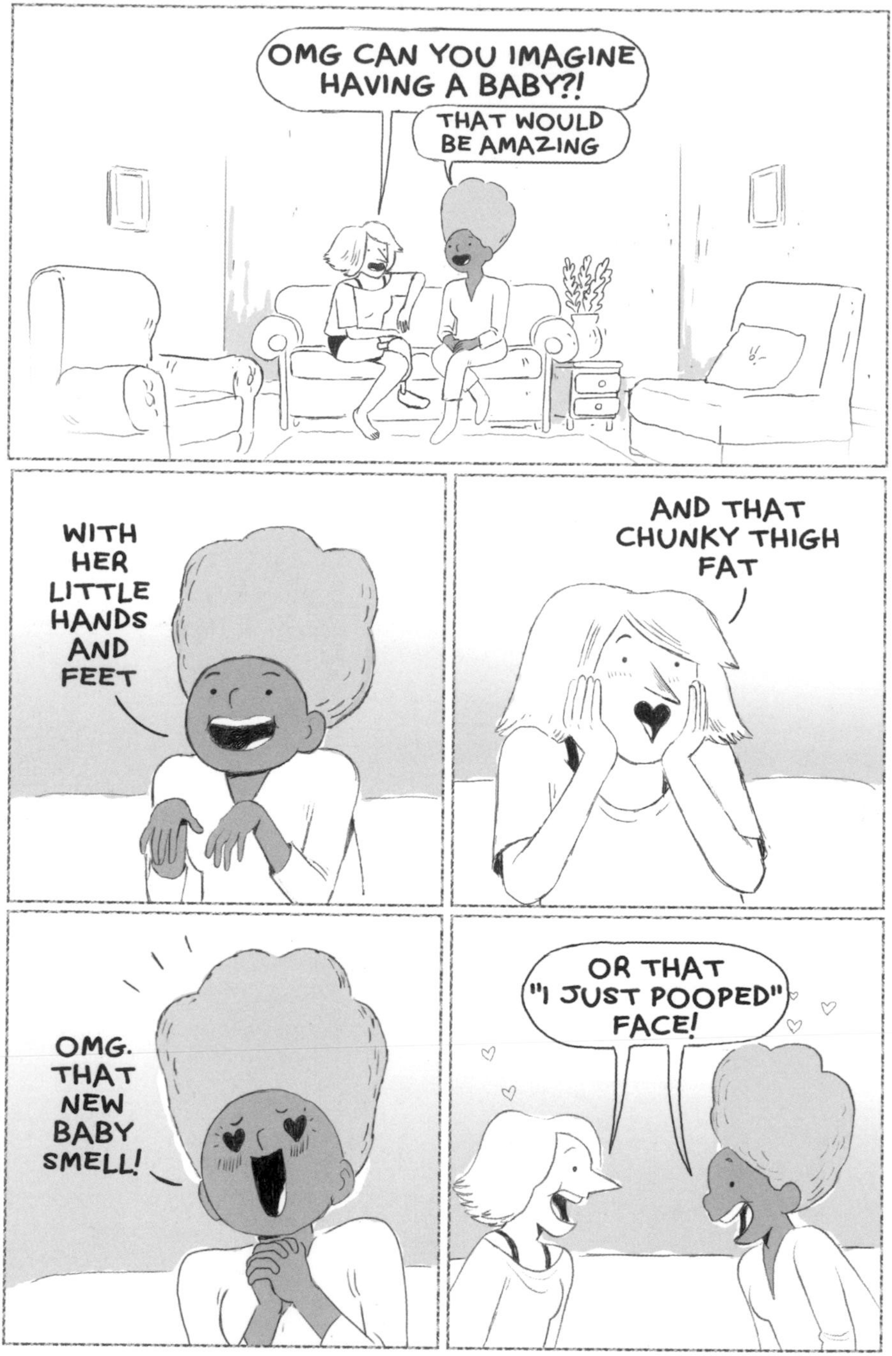
OMG CAN YOU IMAGINE HAVING A BABY?!
THAT WOULD BE AMAZING
WITH HER LITTLE HANDS AND FEET
AND THAT CHUNKY THIGH FAT
OMG. THAT NEW BABY SMELL!
OR THAT "I JUST POOPED" FACE!

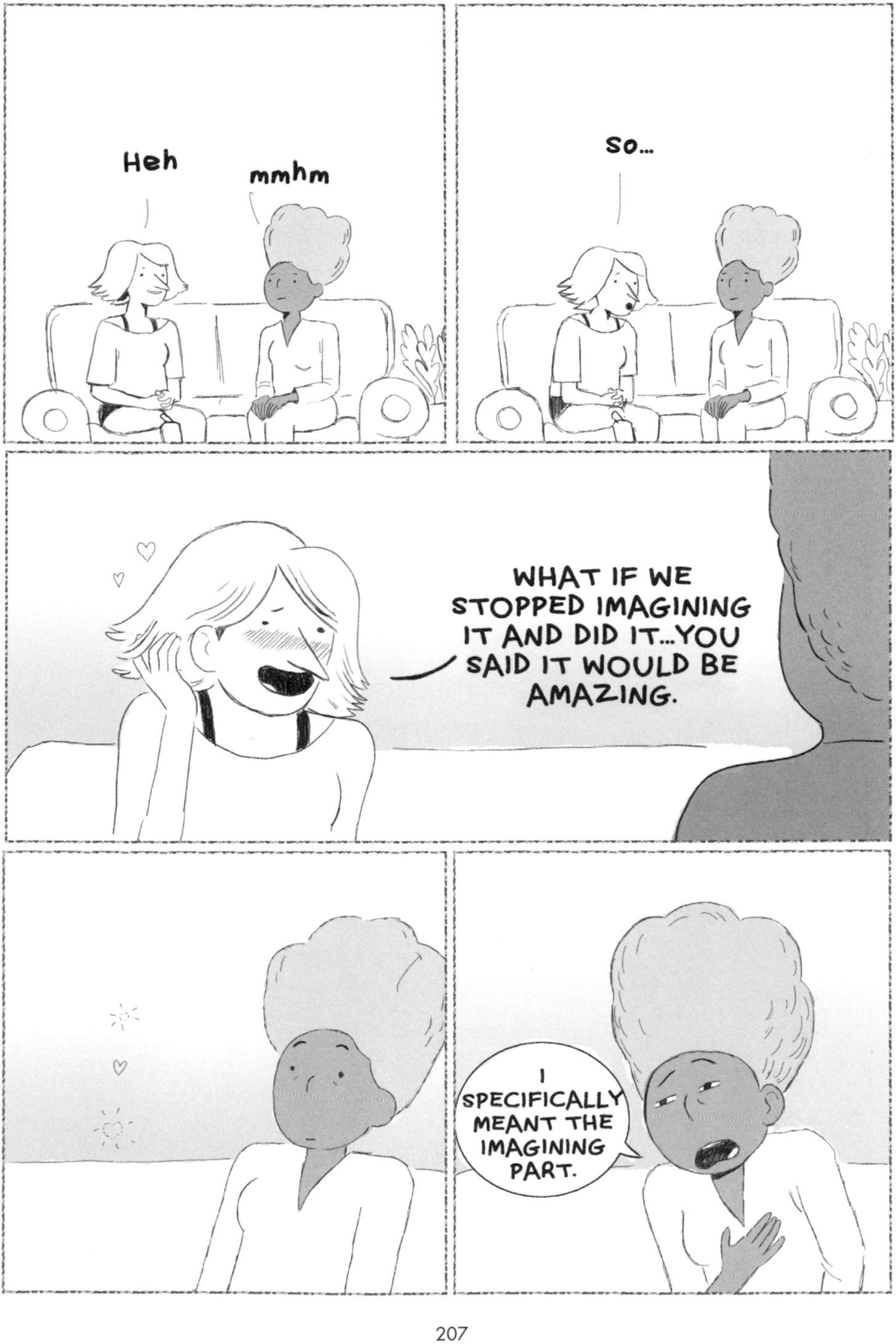
Heh
mmhm
SO...
WHAT IF WE STOPPED IMAGINING IT AND DID IT...YOU SAID IT WOULD BE AMAZING.
I SPECIFICALLY MEANT THE IMAGINING PART.

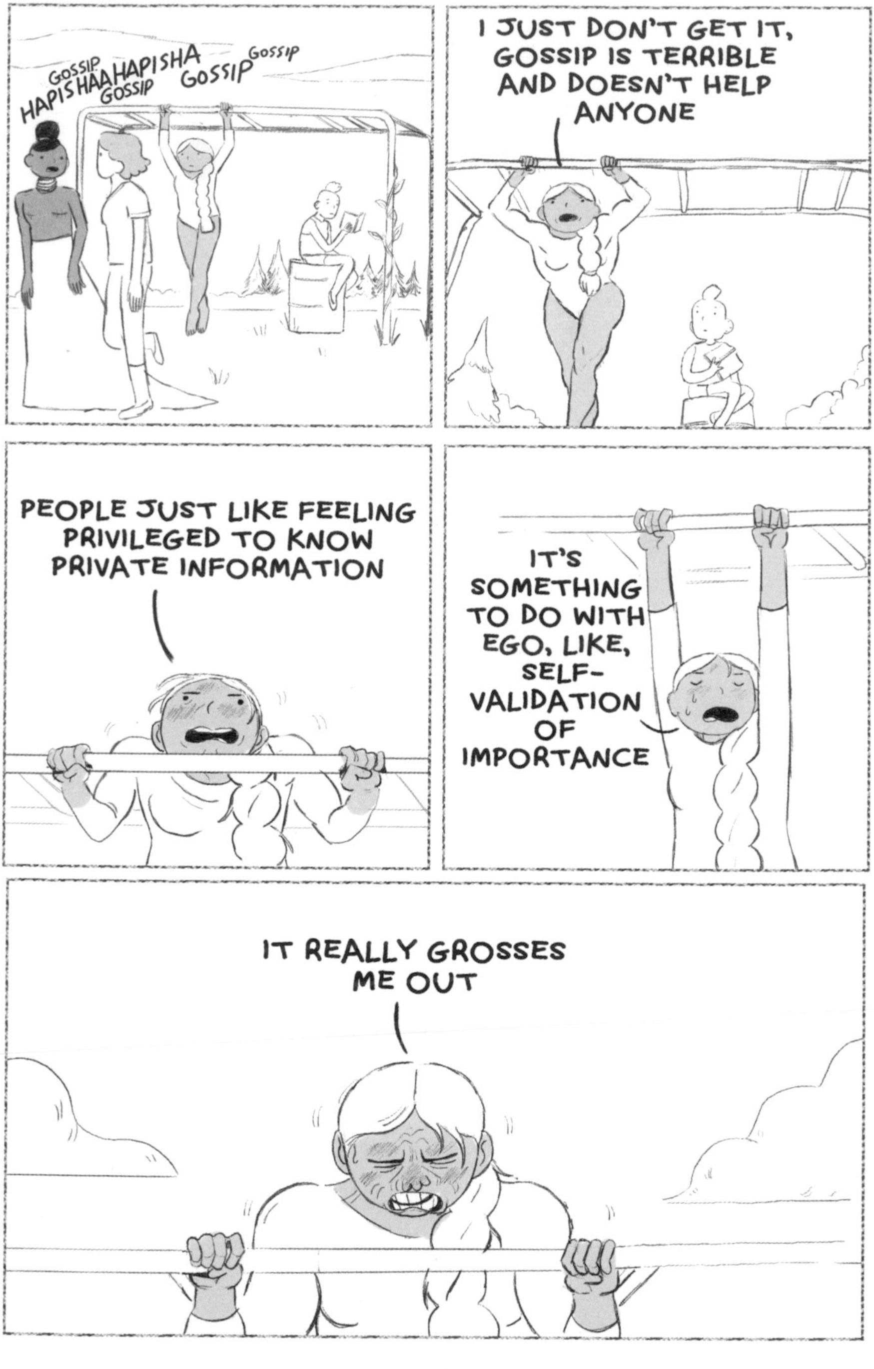
GOSSIP HAPISHAA HAPISHA GOSSIP GOSSIP GOSSIP
I JUST DON'T GET IT, GOSSIP IS TERRIBLE AND DOESN'T HELP ANYONE
PEOPLE JUST LIKE FEELING PRIVILEGED TO KNOW PRIVATE INFORMATION
IT'S SOMETHING TO DO WITH EGO, LIKE, SELF-VALIDATION OF IMPORTANCE
IT REALLY GROSSES ME OUT

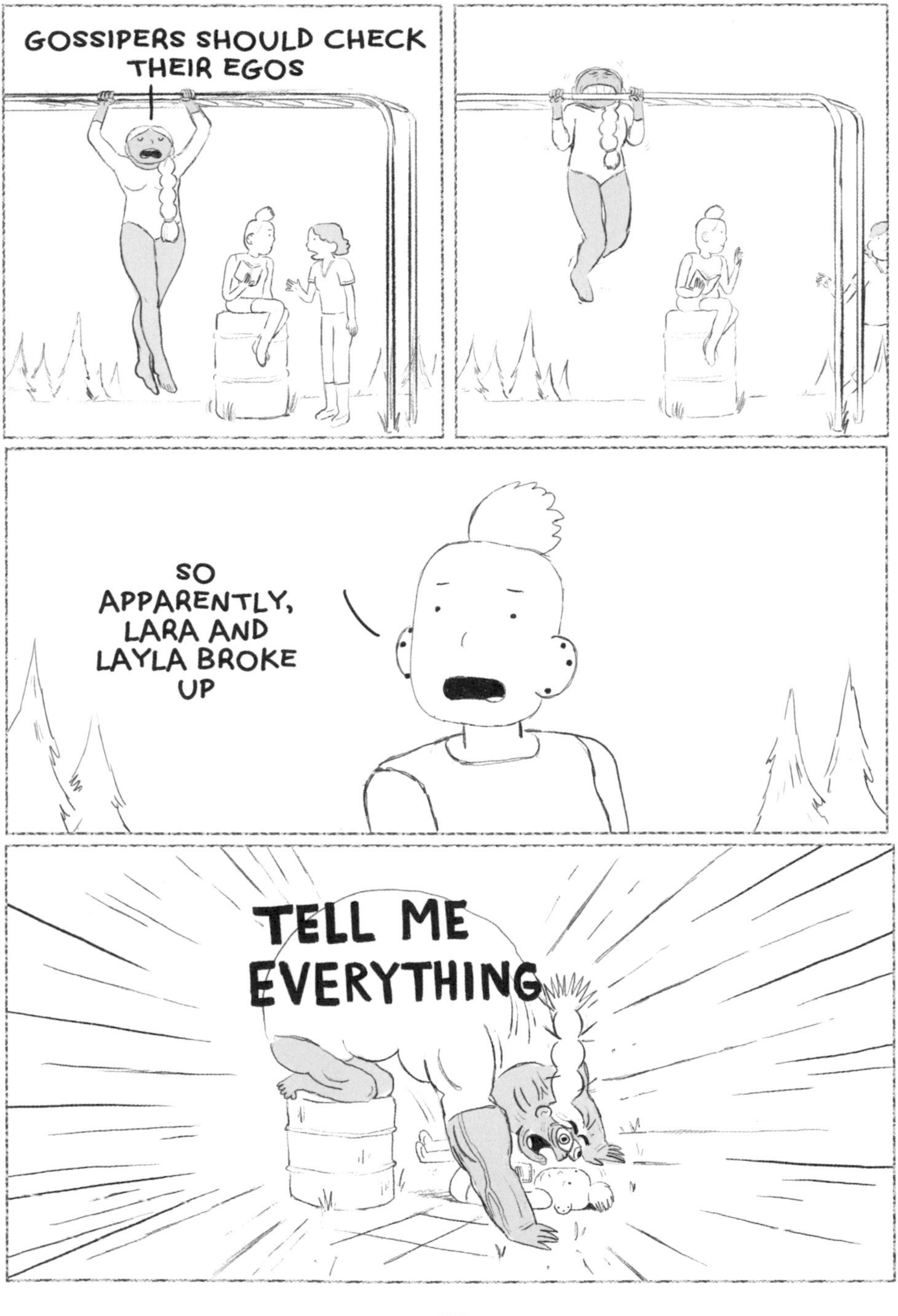
GOSSIPERS SHOULD CHECK THEIR EGOS
SO APPARENTLY, LARA AND LAYLA BROKE UP
TELL ME EVERYTHING

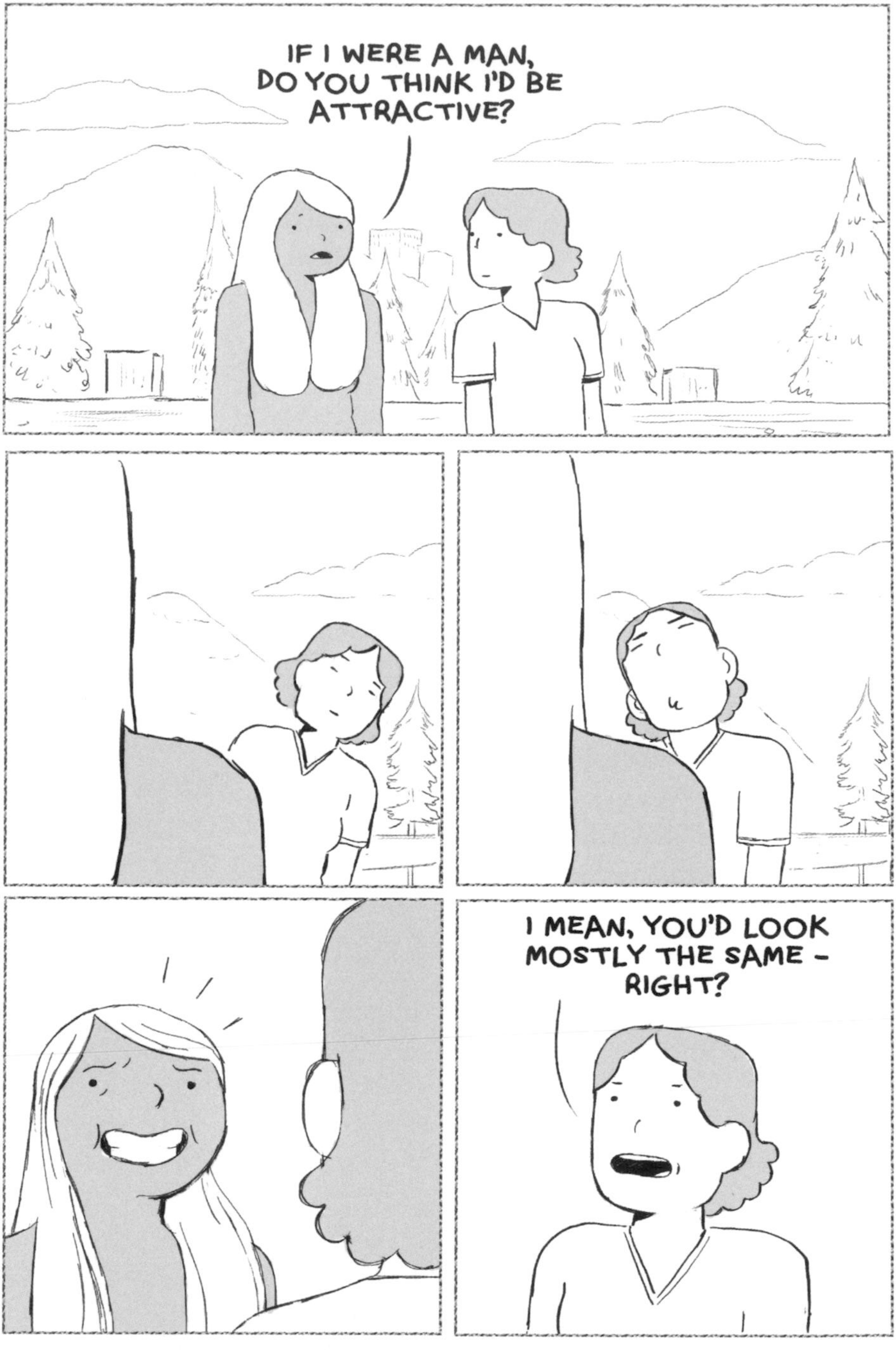
IF I WERE A MAN, DO YOU THINK I'D BE ATTRACTIVE?
I MEAN, YOU'D LOOK MOSTLY THE SAME - RIGHT?

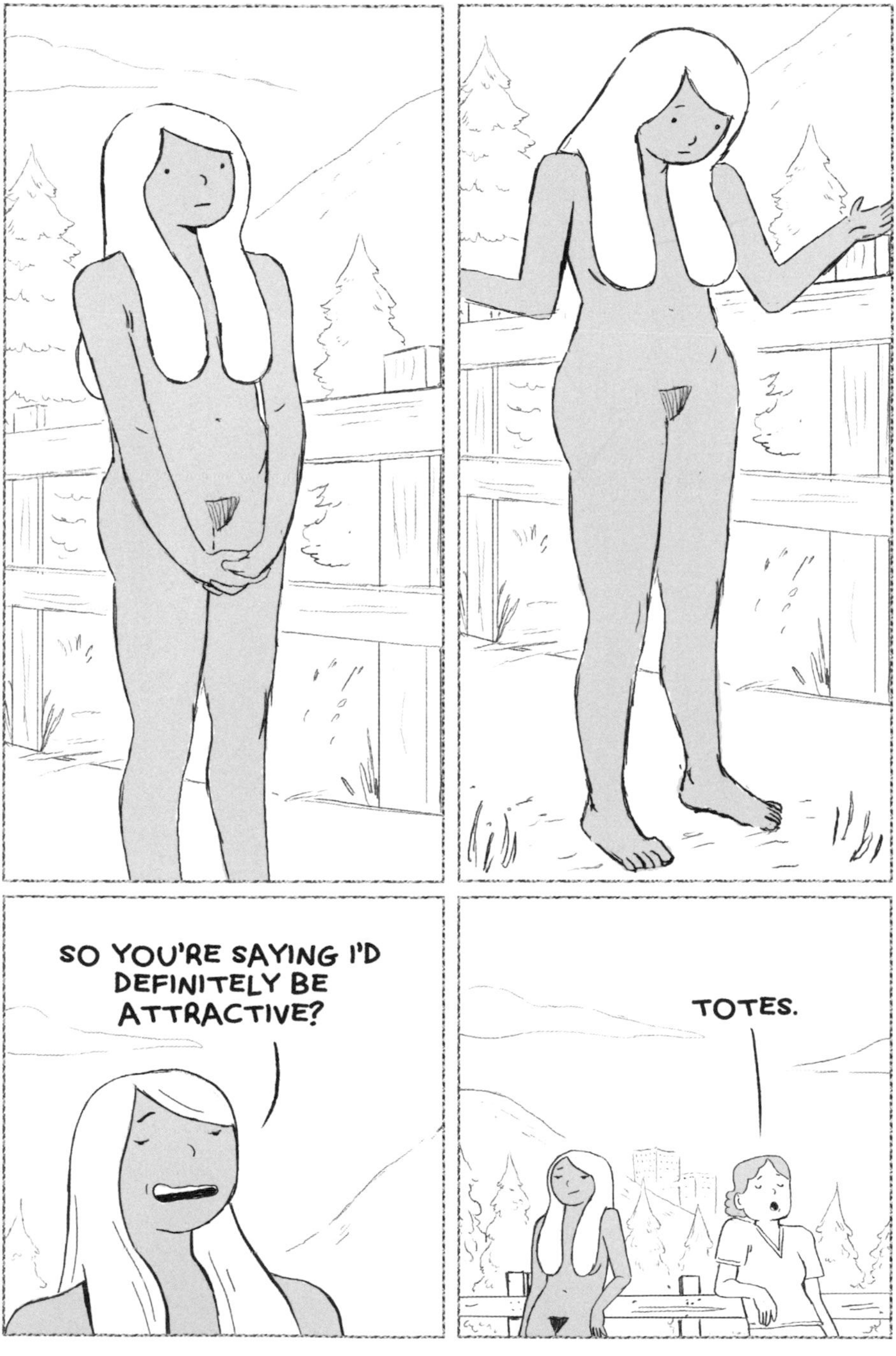
SO YOU'RE SAYING I'D DEFINITELY BE ATTRACTIVE?
TOTES.

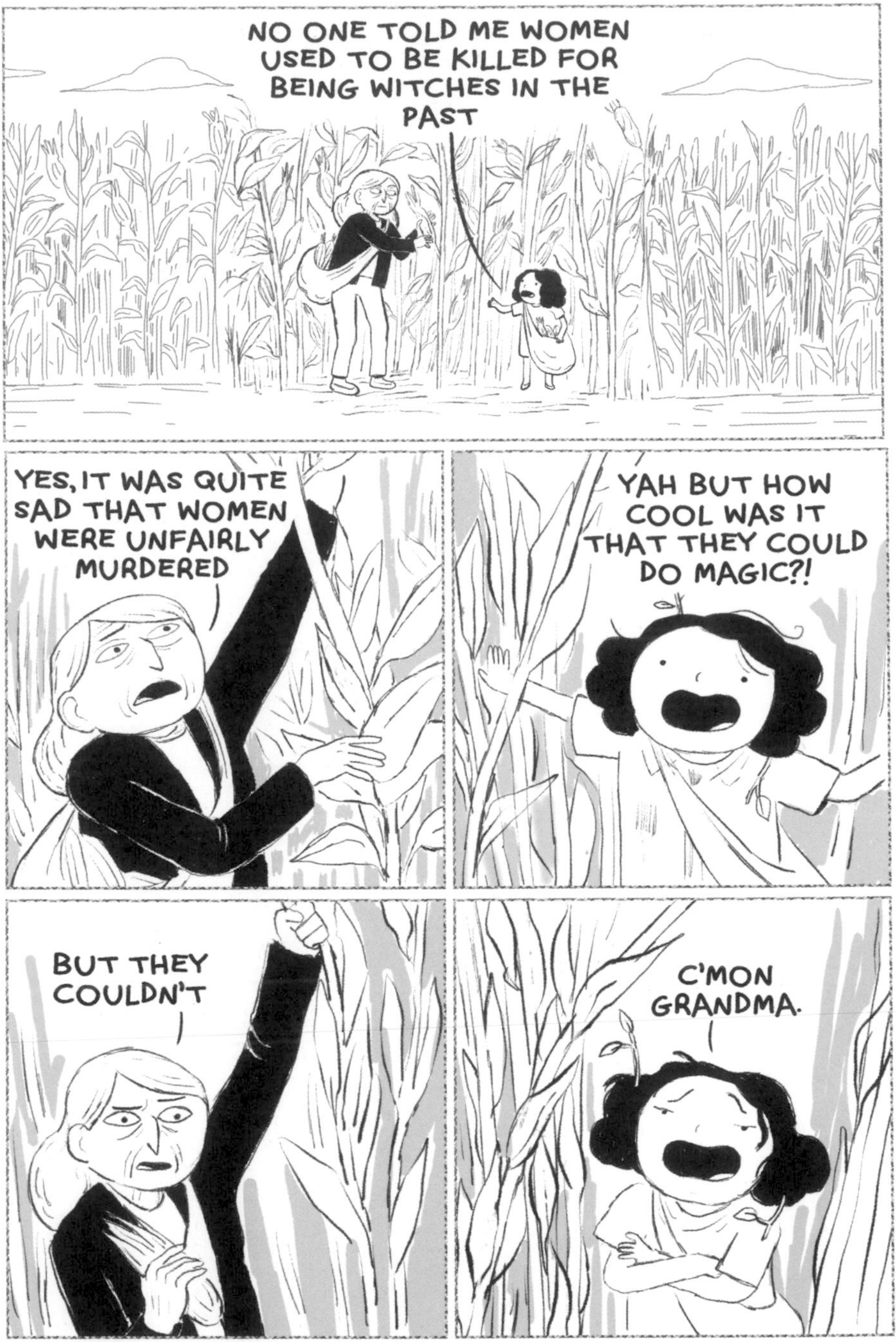
NO ONE TOLD ME WOMEN USED TO BE KILLED FOR BEING WITCHES IN THE PAST
YES, IT WAS QUITE SAD THAT WOMEN WERE UNFAIRLY MURDERED
YAH BUT HOW COOL WAS IT THAT THEY COULD DO MAGIC?!
BUT THEY COULDN'T
C'MON GRANDMA.

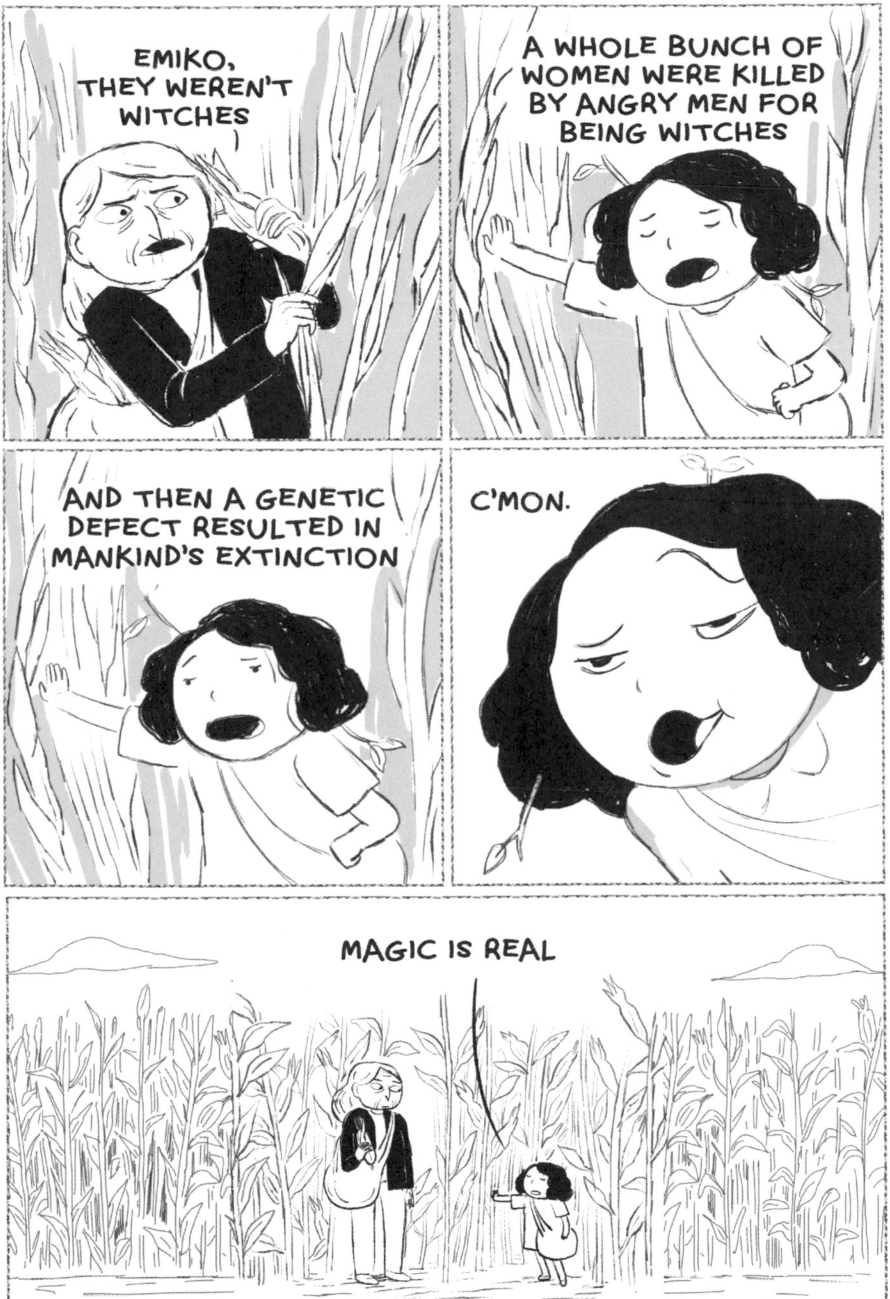
EMIKO, THEY WEREN'T WITCHES
A WHOLE BUNCH OF WOMEN WERE KILLED BY ANGRY MEN FOR BEING WITCHES
AND THEN A GENETIC DEFECT RESULTED IN MANKIND'S EXTINCTION
C'MON.
MAGIC IS REAL

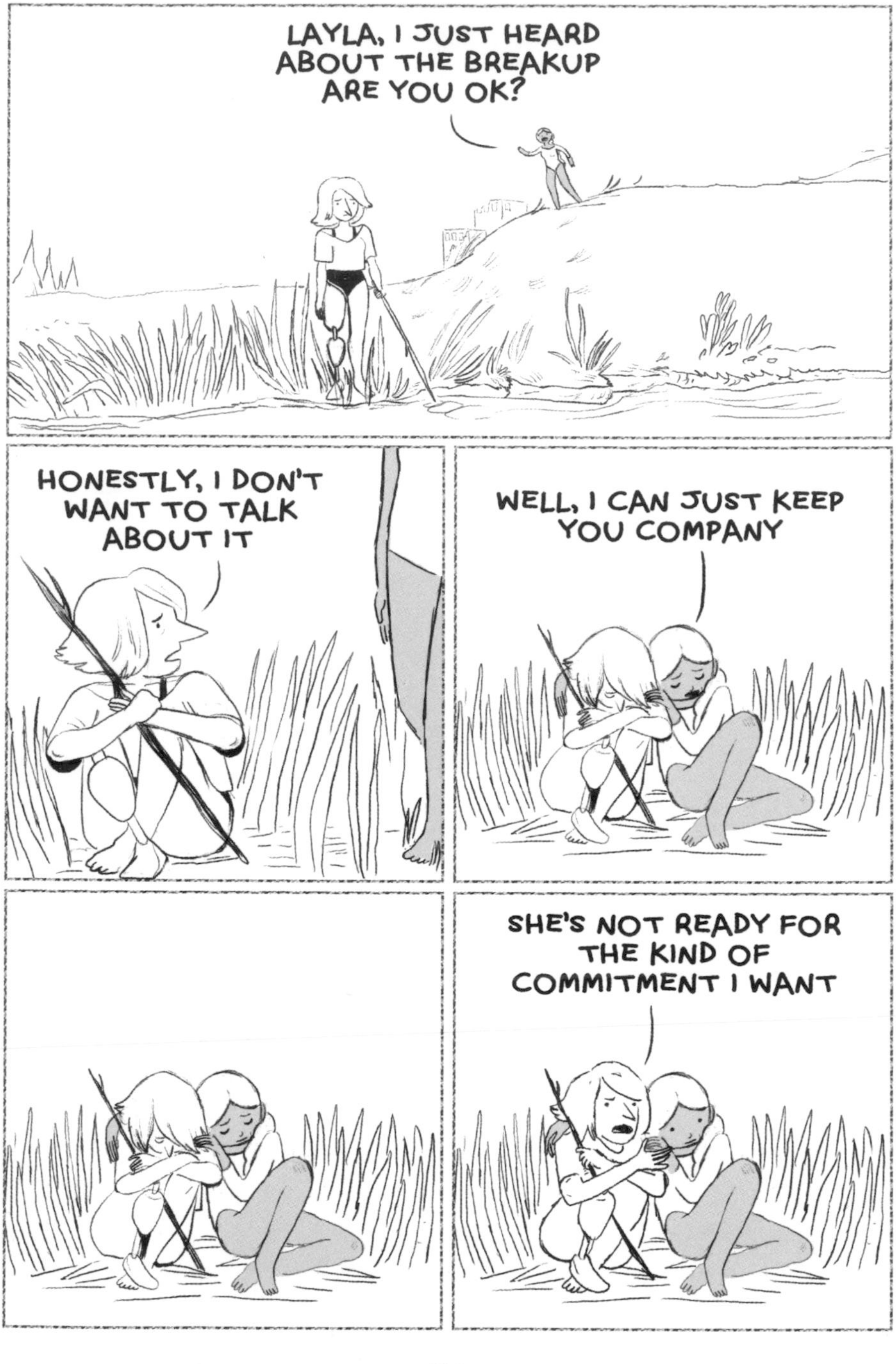
LAYLA, I JUST HEARD ABOUT THE BREAKUP ARE YOU OK?
HONESTLY, I DON'T WANT TO TALK ABOUT IT
WELL, I CAN JUST KEEP YOU COMPANY
SHE'S NOT READY FOR THE KIND OF COMMITMENT I WANT

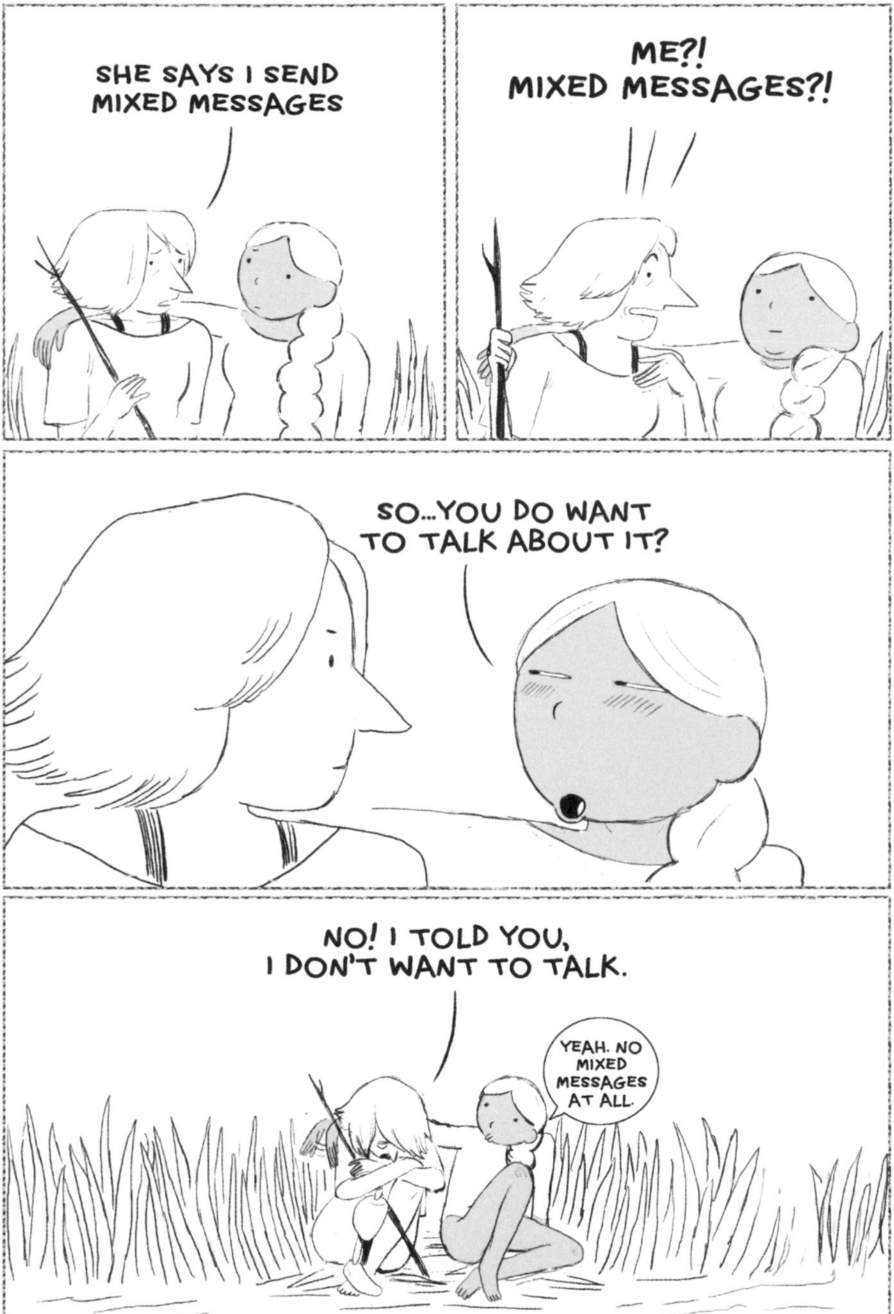
SHE SAYS I SEND MIXED MESSAGES
ME?! MIXED MESSAGES?!
SO...YOU DO WANT TO TALK ABOUT IT?
NO! I TOLD YOU, I DON'T WANT TO TALK.
YEAH. NO MIXED MESSAGES AT ALL.

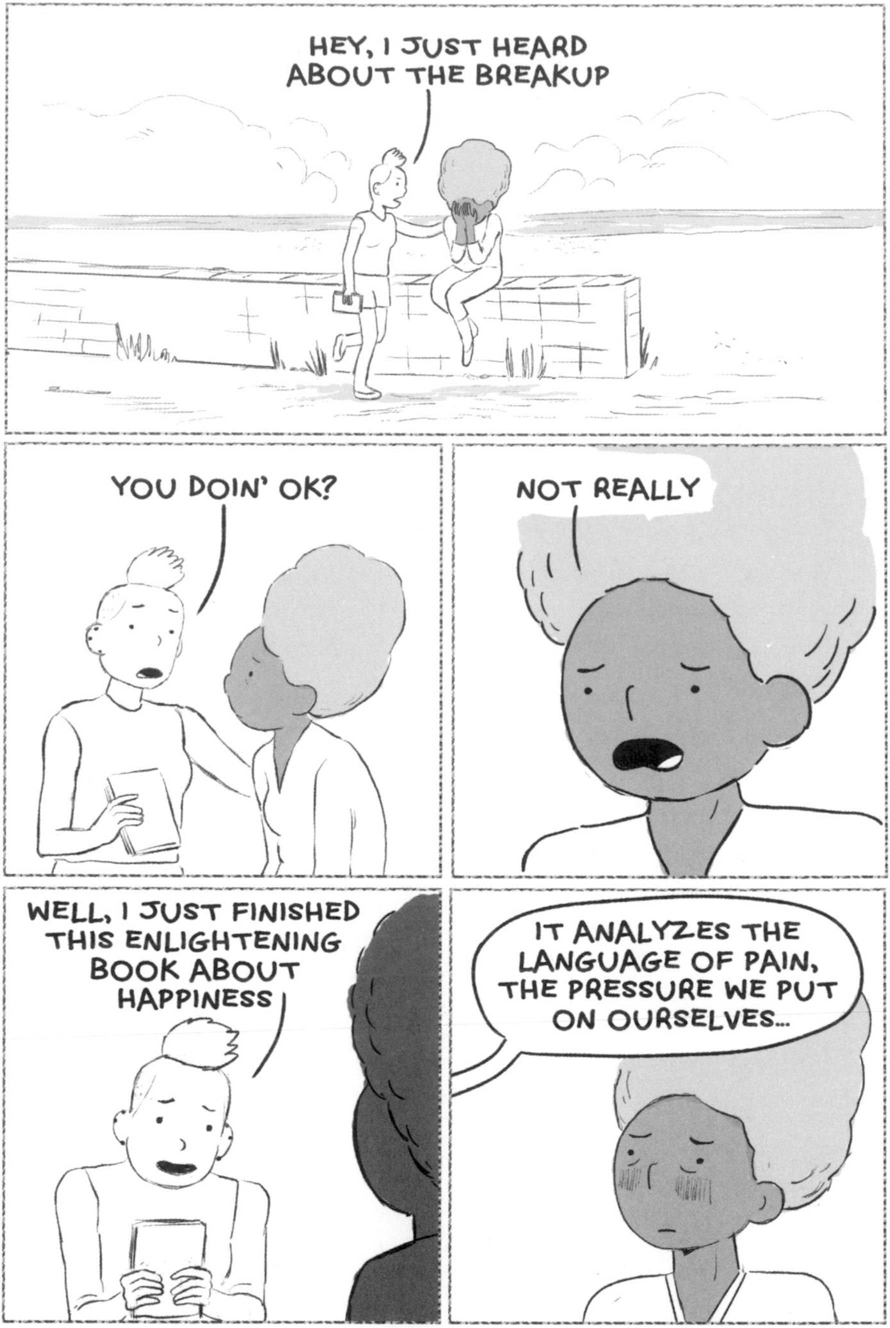
HEY, I JUST HEARD ABOUT THE BREAKUP
YOU DOIN' OK?
NOT REALLY
WELL, I JUST FINISHED THIS ENLIGHTENING BOOK ABOUT HAPPINESS
IT ANALYZES THE LANGUAGE OF PAIN, THE PRESSURE WE PUT ON OURSELVES...

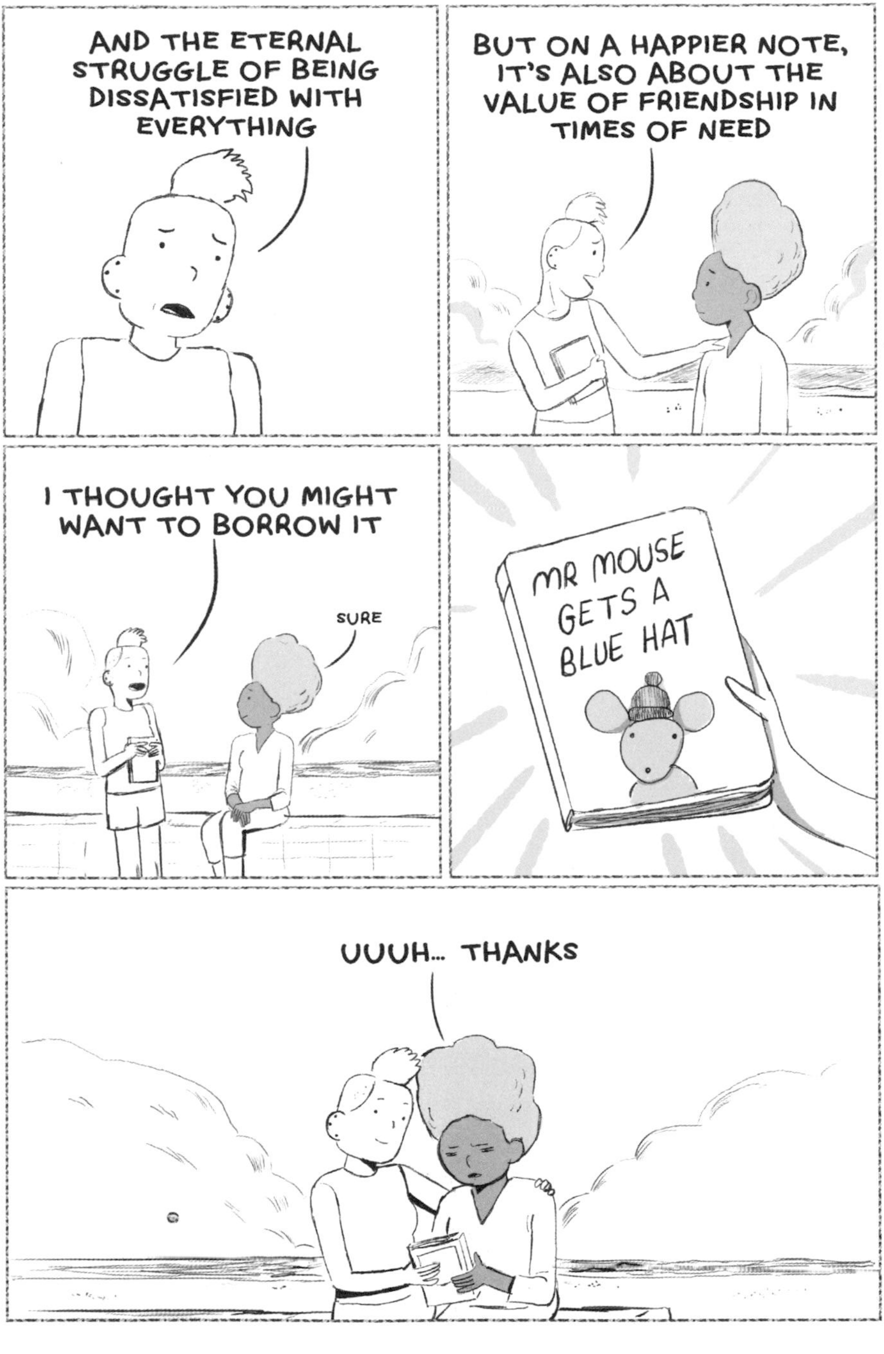
AND THE ETERNAL STRUGGLE OF BEING DISSATISFIED WITH EVERYTHING
BUT ON A HAPPIER NOTE, IT'S ALSO ABOUT THE VALUE OF FRIENDSHIP IN TIMES OF NEED
I THOUGHT YOU MIGHT WANT TO BORROW IT
SURE
MR MOUSE GETS A BLUE HAT
UUUH... THANKS

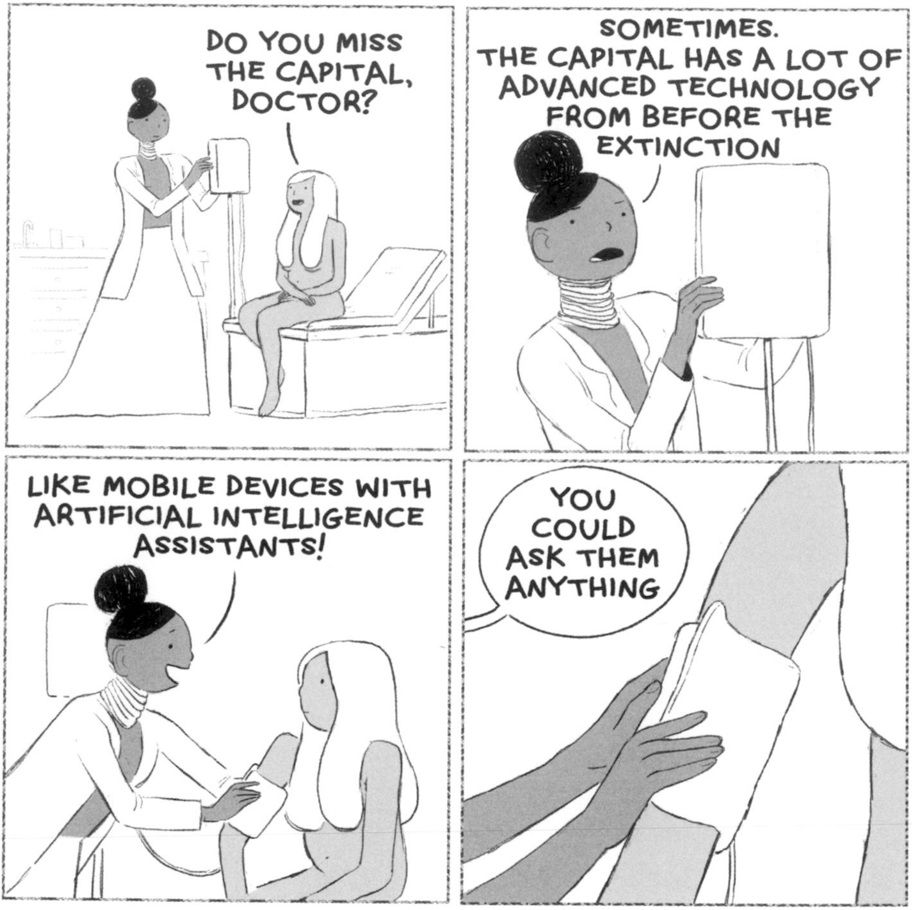
DO YOU MISS THE CAPITAL, DOCTOR?
SOMETIMES. THE CAPITAL HAS A LOT OF ADVANCED TECHNOLOGY FROM BEFORE THE EXTINCTION
LIKE MOBILE DEVICES WITH ARTIFICIAL INTELLIGENCE ASSISTANTS!
YOU COULD ASK THEM ANYTHING

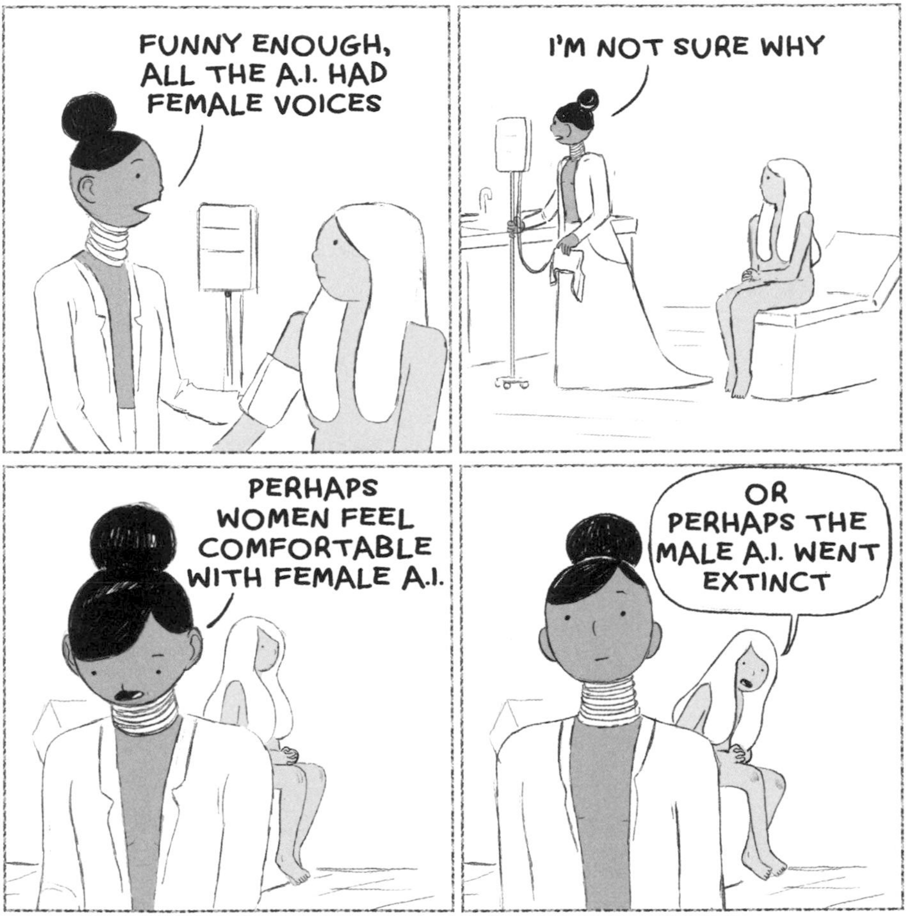
FUNNY ENOUGH, ALL THE A.I. HAD FEMALE VOICES
I'M NOT SURE WHY
PERHAPS WOMEN FEEL COMFORTABLE WITH FEMALE A.I.
OR PERHAPS THE MALE A.I. WENT EXTINCT

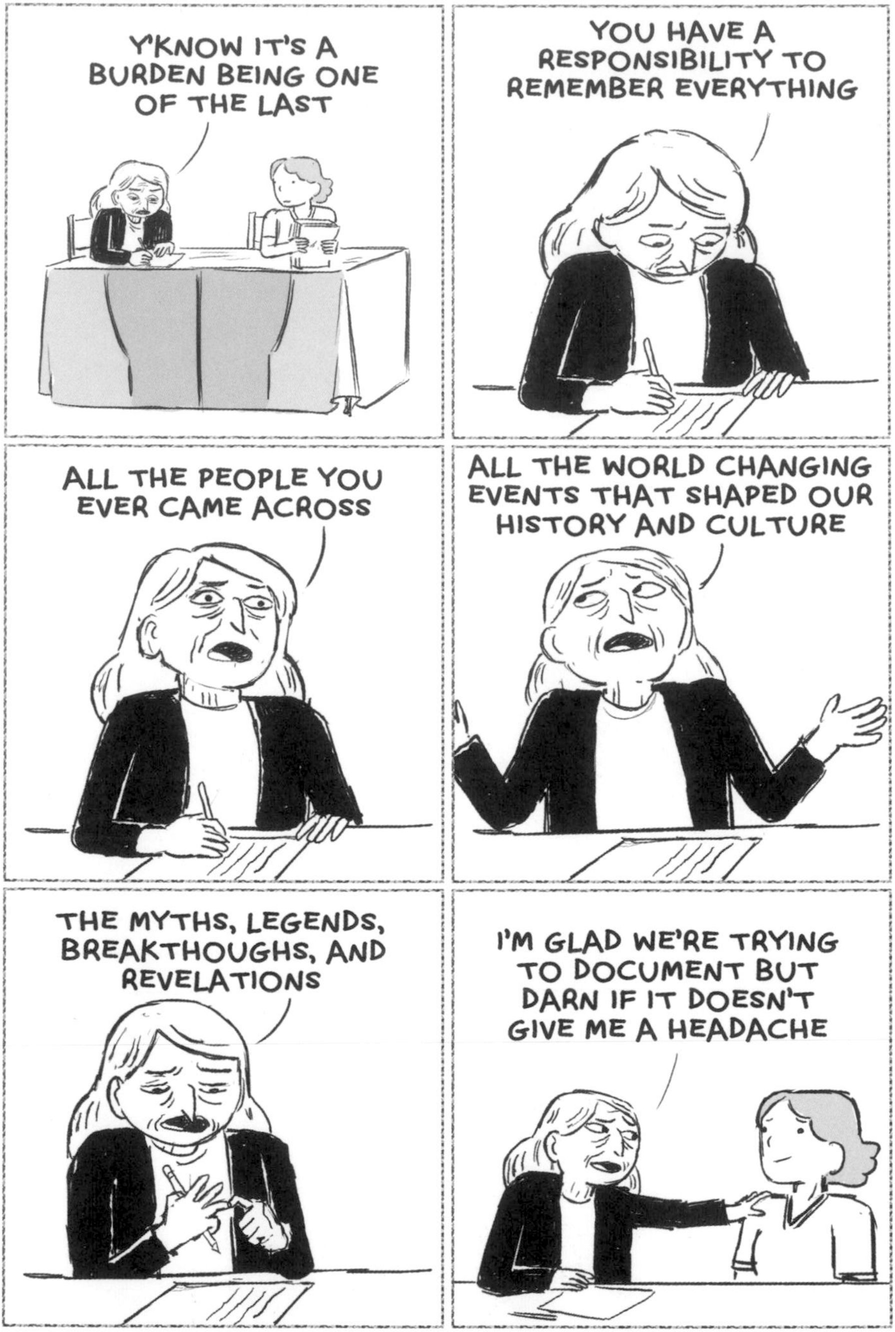
Y'KNOW IT'S A BURDEN BEING ONE OF THE LAST
YOU HAVE A RESPONSIBILITY TO REMEMBER EVERYTHING
ALL THE PEOPLE YOU EVER CAME ACROSS
ALL THE WORLD CHANGING EVENTS THAT SHAPED OUR HISTORY AND CULTURE
THE MYTHS, LEGENDS, BREAKTHOUGHS, AND REVELATIONS
I'M GLAD WE'RE TRYING TO DOCUMENT BUT DARN IF IT DOESN'T GIVE ME A HEADACHE

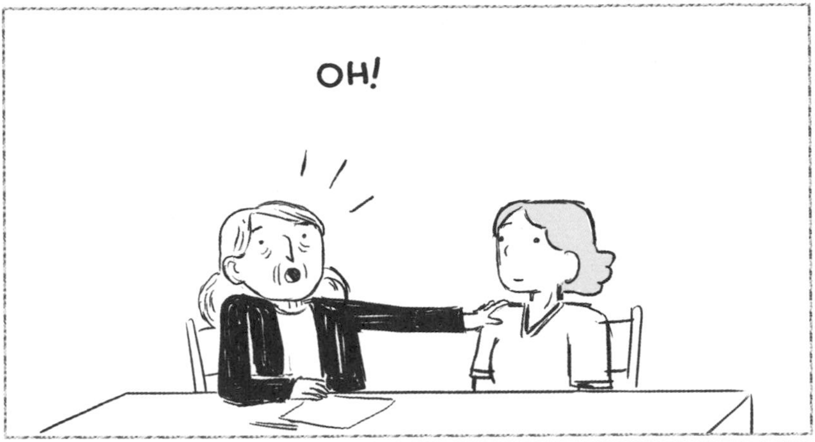
OH!

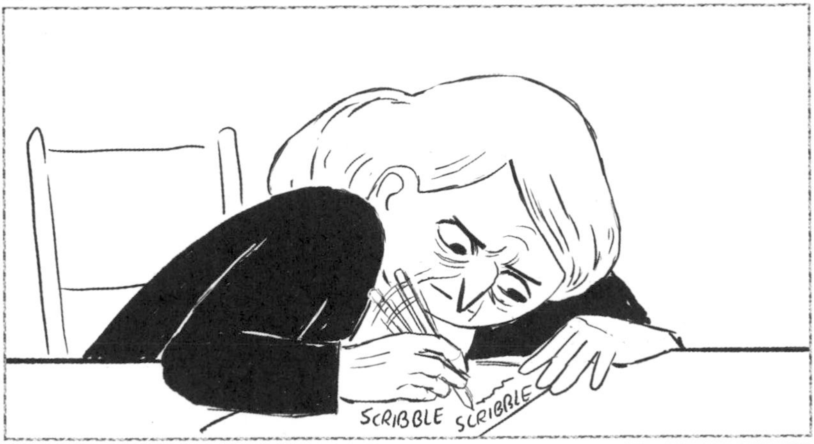
SCRIBBLE SCRIBBLE

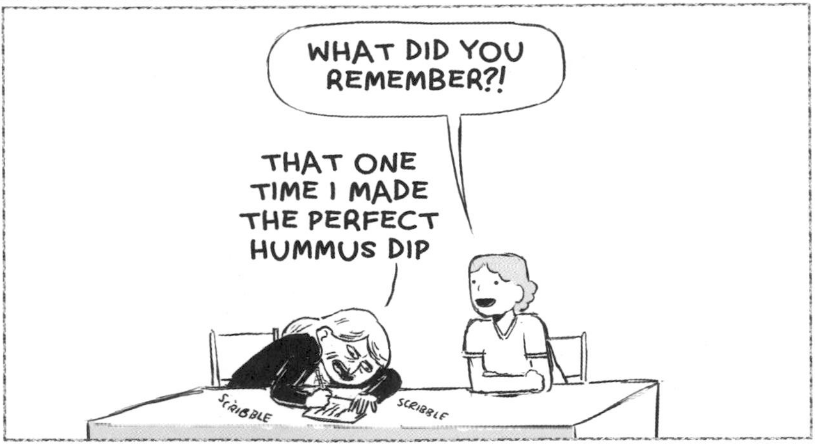
WHAT DID YOU REMEMBER?!
THAT ONE TIME I MADE THE PERFECT HUMMUS DIP
SCRIBBLE
SCRIBBLE

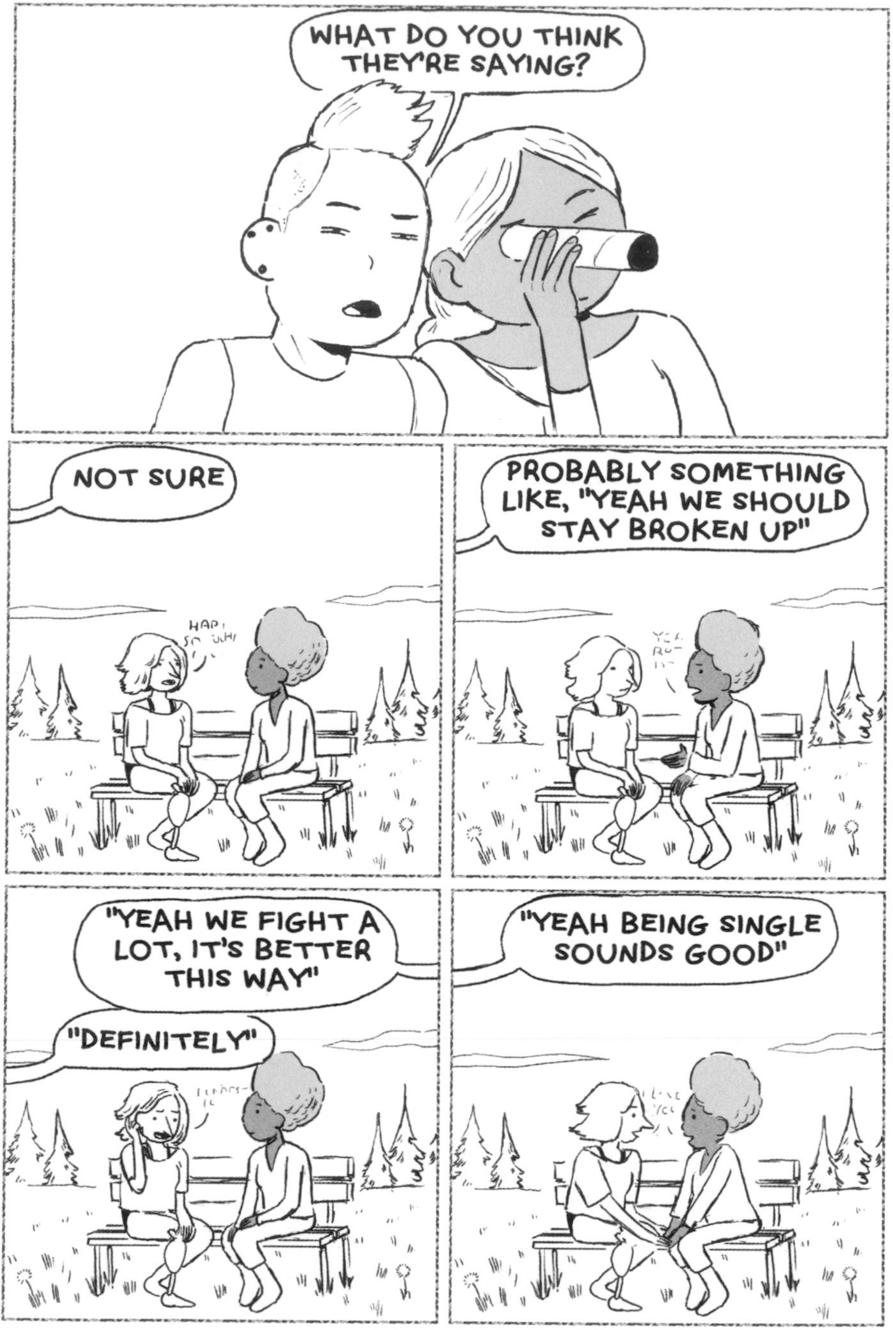
WHAT DO YOU THINK THEY'RE SAYING?
NOT SURE
PROBABLY SOMETHING LIKE, "YEAH WE SHOULD STAY BROKEN UP"
"YEAH WE FIGHT A LOT, IT'S BETTER THIS WAY"
"DEFINITELY"
"YEAH BEING SINGLE SOUNDS GOOD"

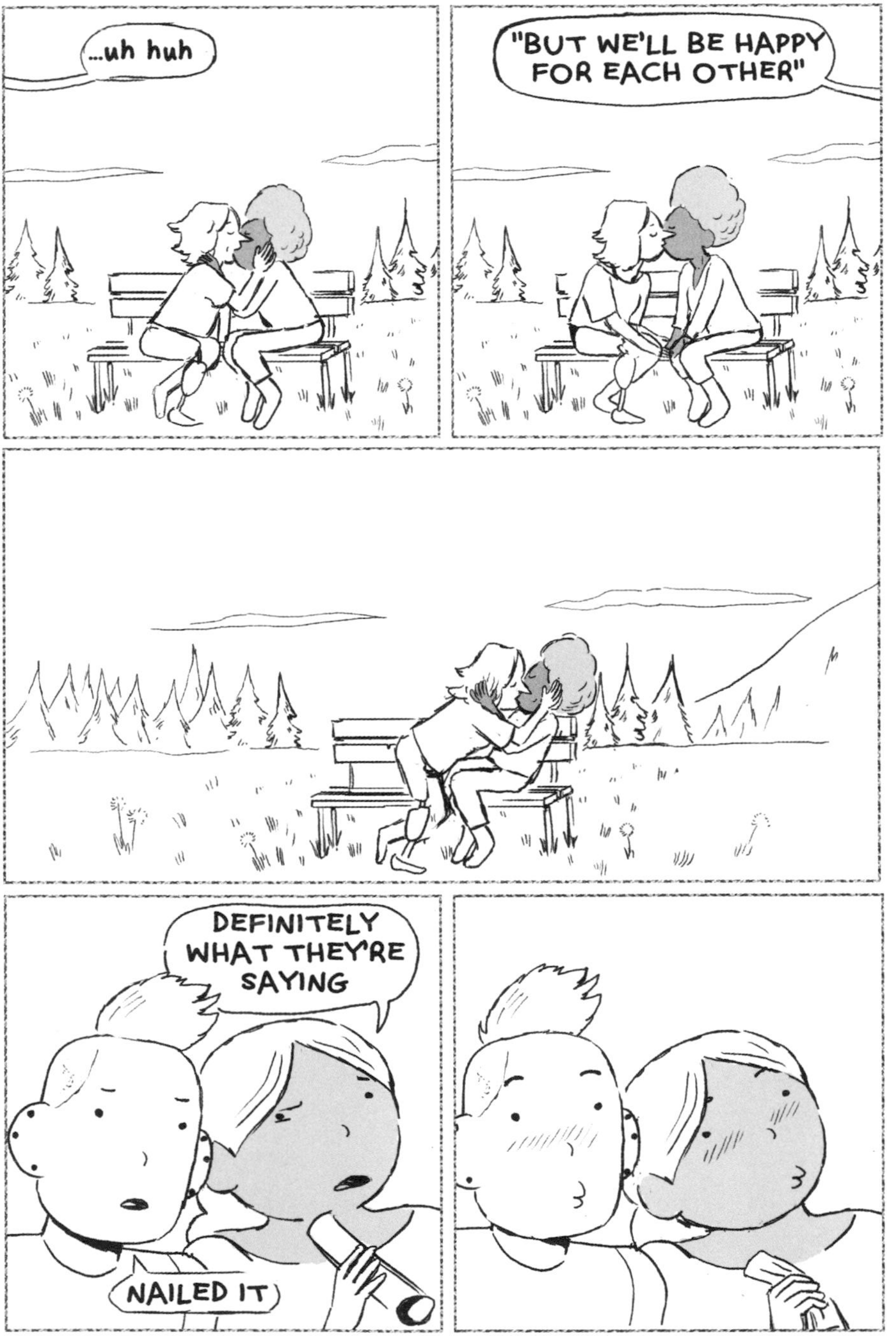
...uh huh
"BUT WE'LL BE HAPPY FOR EACH OTHER"
DEFINITELY WHAT THEY'RE SAYING
NAILED IT

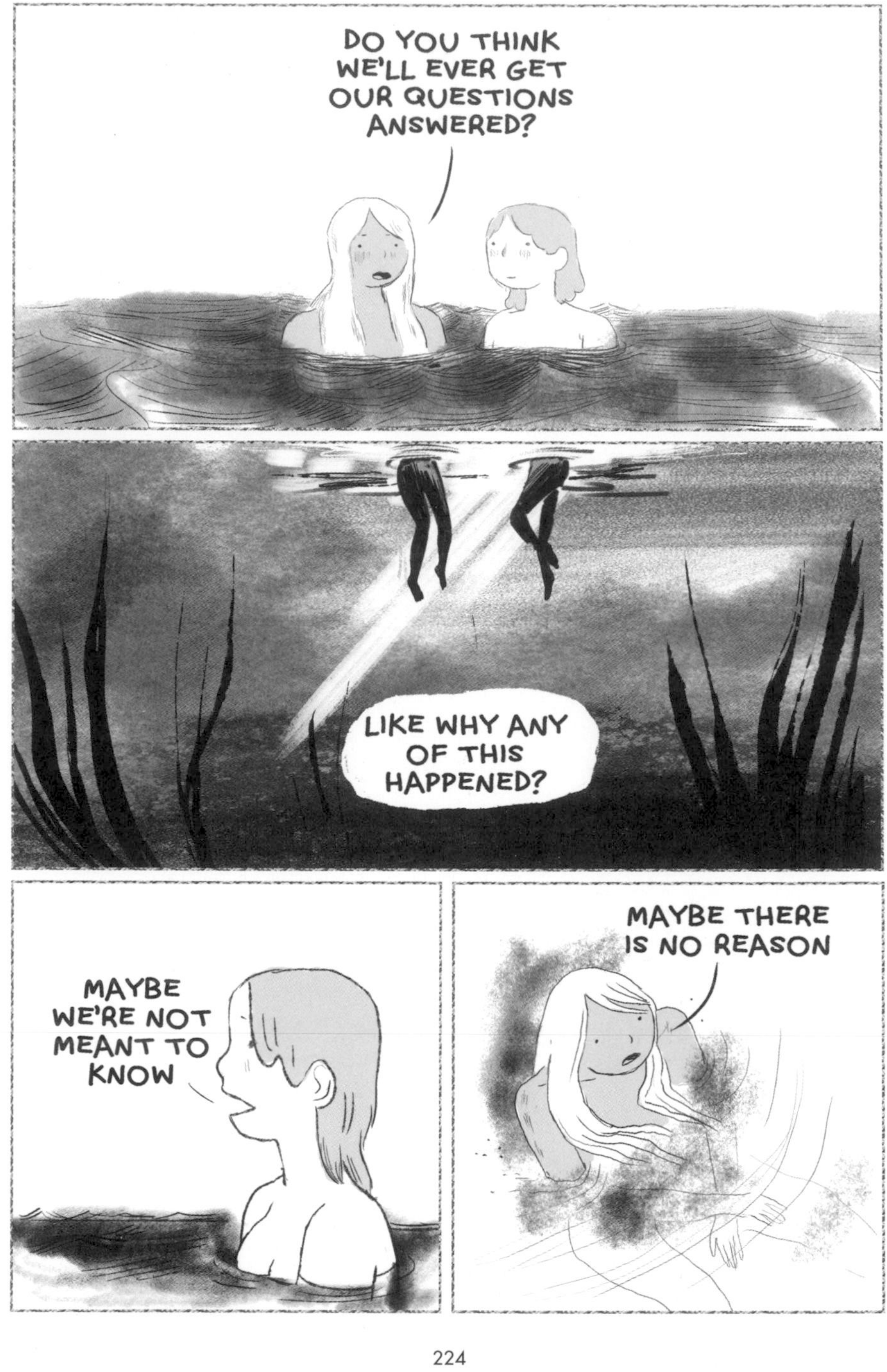
DO YOU THINK WE'LL EVER GET OUR QUESTIONS ANSWERED?
LIKE WHY ANY OF THIS HAPPENED?
MAYBE WE'RE NOT MEANT TO KNOW
MAYBE THERE IS NO REASON

MAYBE THE REASON IS BEYOND OUR UNDERSTANDING

I LIKE THAT. IT'S BEYOND US.

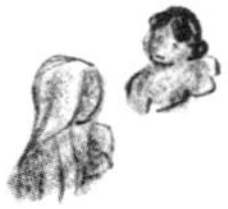

OR MAYBE HUMANKIND HAS A HABIT OF IDOLIZING THE UNKNOWN RATHER THAN ATTEMPTING TO UNDERSTAND IT.

EVERYTHING WAS MORE ETHEREAL WHEN WE WERE SWIMMING. I MISS IT

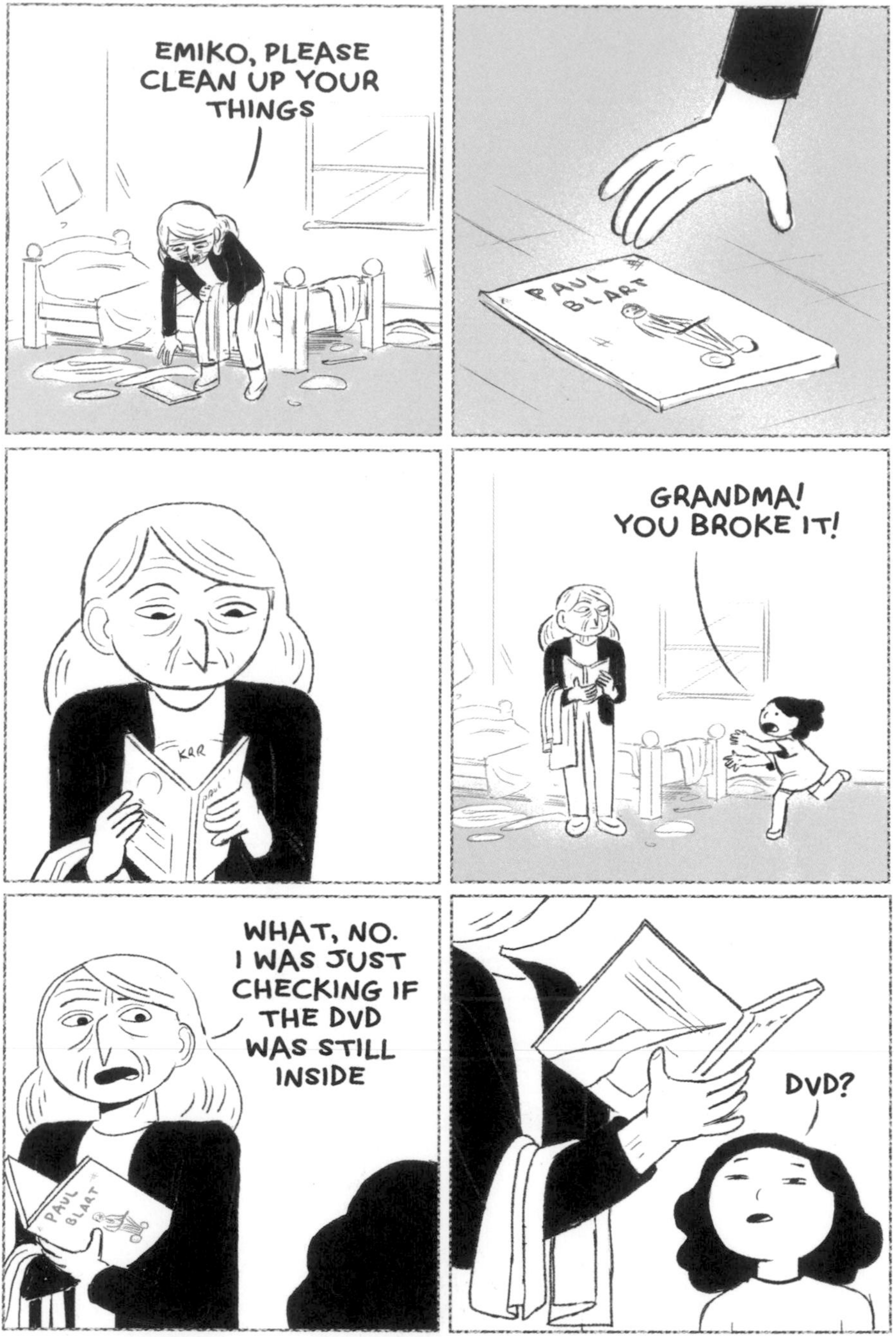
EMIKO, PLEASE CLEAN UP YOUR THINGS
PAUL BLART
KRR
GRANDMA! YOU BROKE IT!
WHAT, NO. I WAS JUST CHECKING IF THE DVD WAS STILL INSIDE
PAUL BLART
DVD?

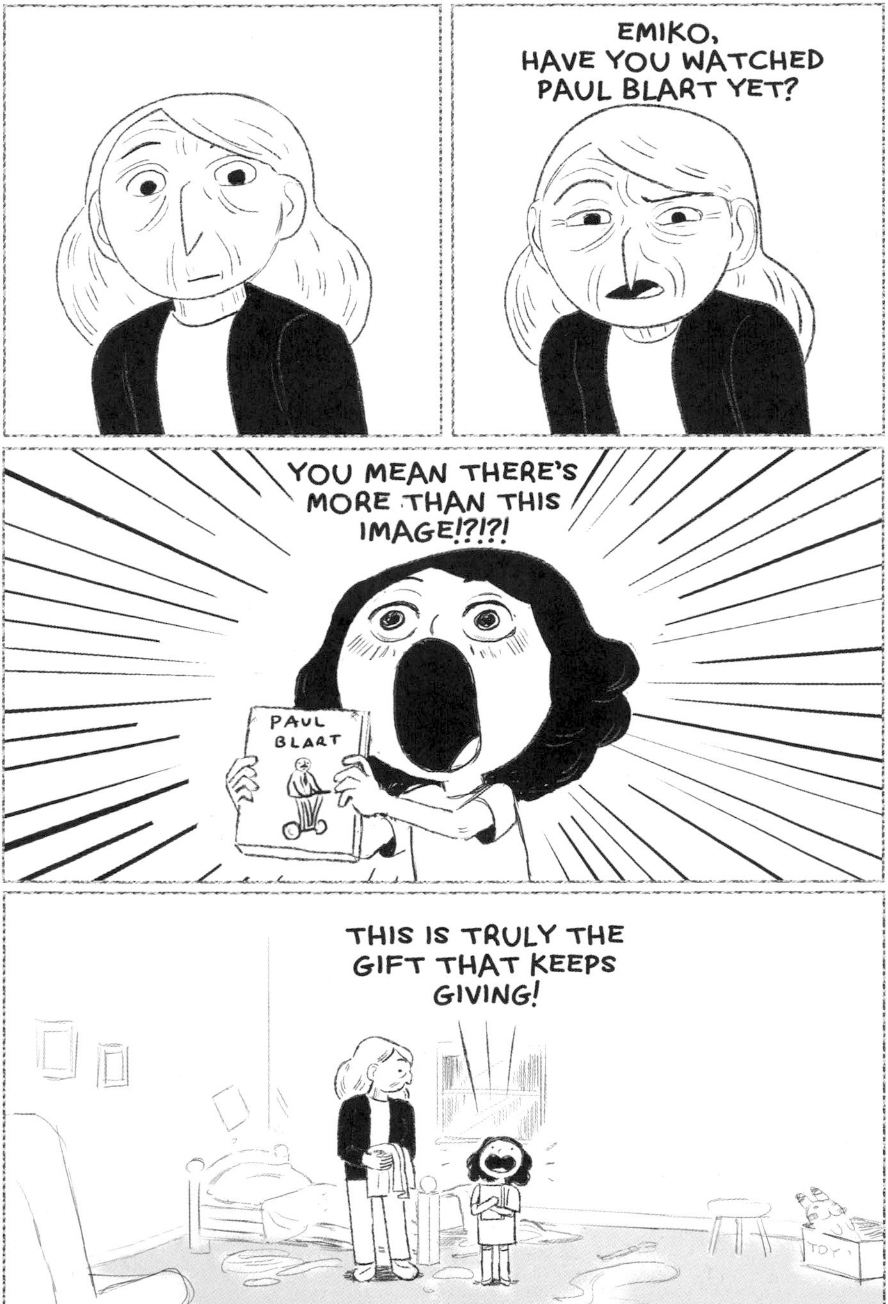
EMIKO, HAVE YOU WATCHED PAUL BLART YET?
YOU MEAN THERE'S MORE THAN THIS IMAGE!?!?!
PAUL BLART
THIS IS TRULY THE GIFT THAT KEEPS GIVING!
TOY

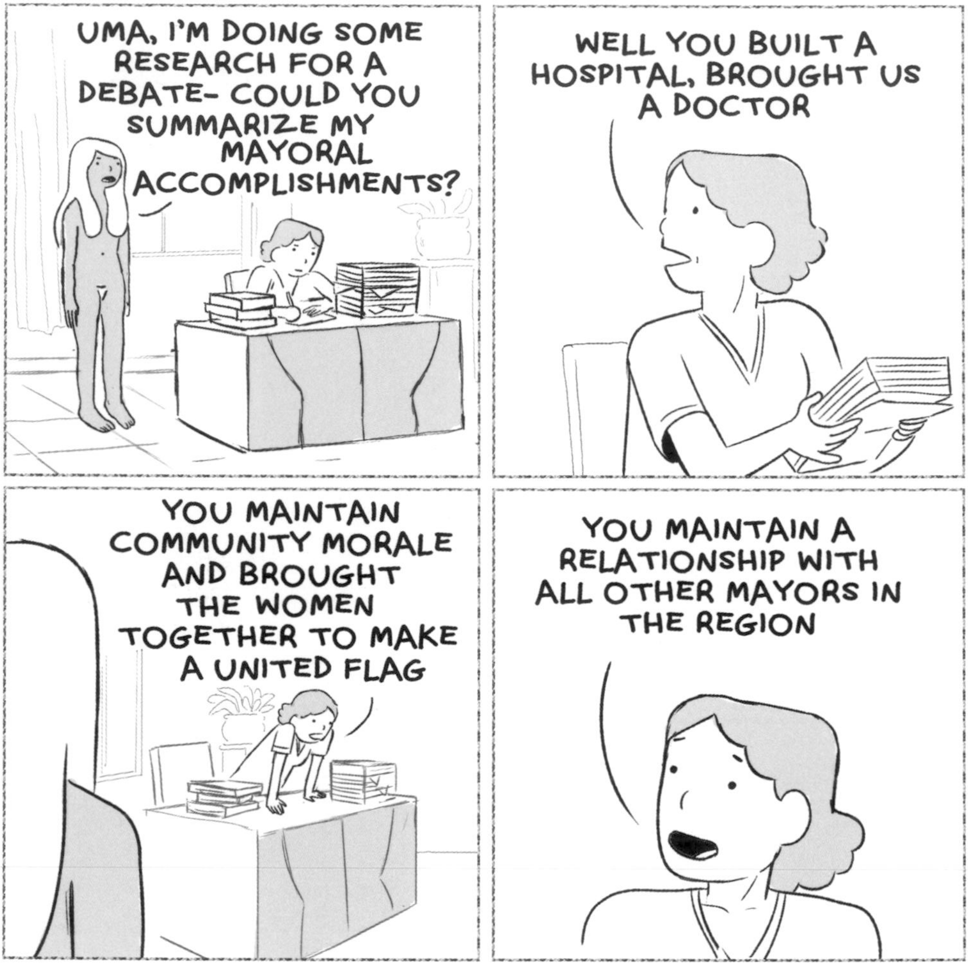
UMA, I'M DOING SOME RESEARCH FOR A DEBATE- COULD YOU SUMMARIZE MY MAYORAL ACCOMPLISHMENTS?
WELL YOU BUILT A HOSPITAL, BROUGHT US A DOCTOR
YOU MAINTAIN COMMUNITY MORALE AND BROUGHT THE WOMEN TOGETHER TO MAKE A UNITED FLAG
YOU MAINTAIN A RELATIONSHIP WITH ALL OTHER MAYORS IN THE REGION

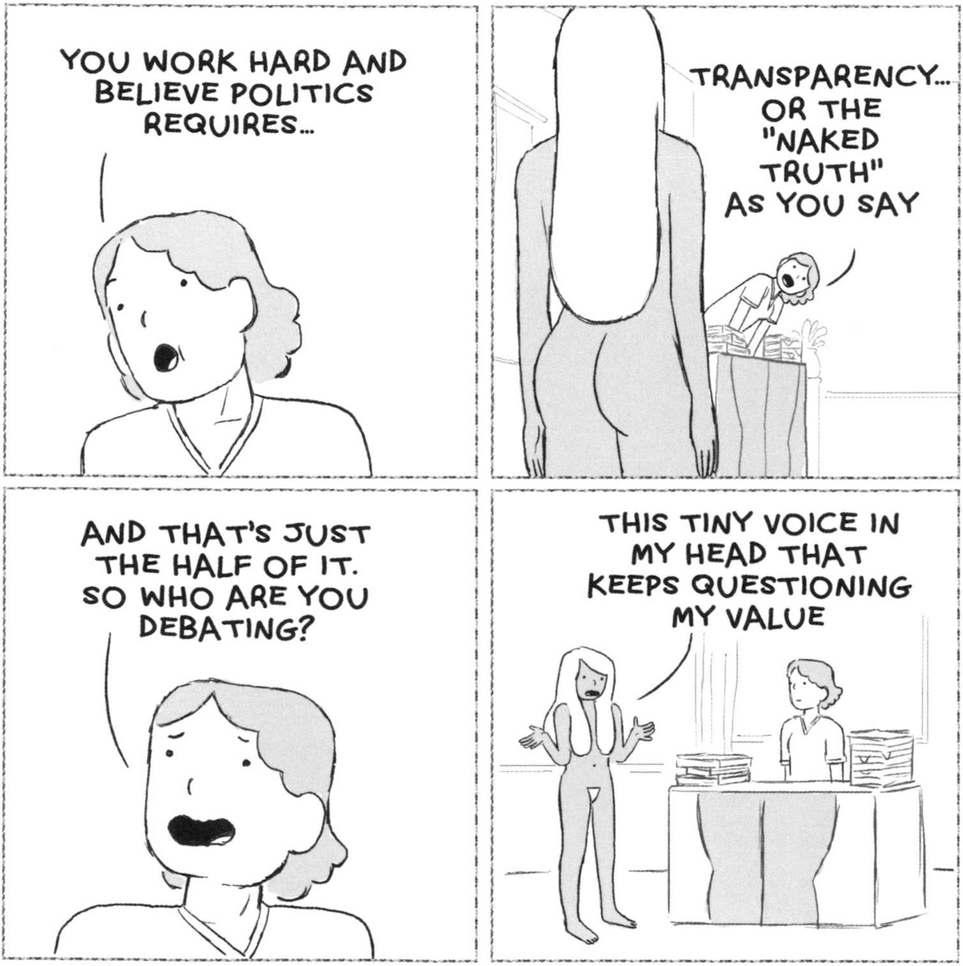
YOU WORK HARD AND BELIEVE POLITICS REQUIRES...
TRANSPARENCY... OR THE "NAKED TRUTH" AS YOU SAY
AND THAT'S JUST THE HALF OF IT. SO WHO ARE YOU DEBATING?
THIS TINY VOICE IN MY HEAD THAT KEEPS QUESTIONING MY VALUE

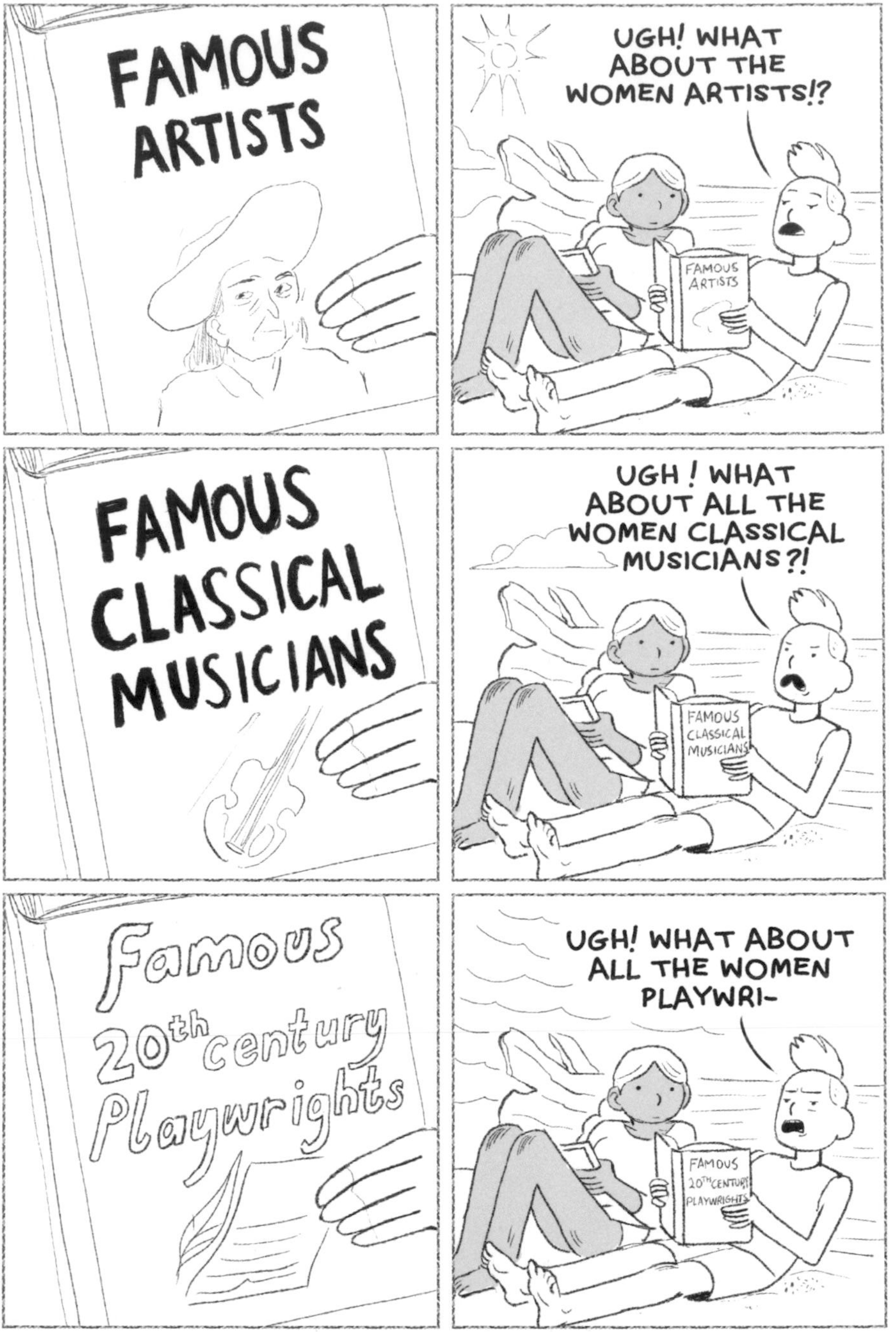
FAMOUS ARTISTS
UGH! WHAT ABOUT THE WOMEN ARTISTS!?
FAMOUS ARTISTS
FAMOUS CLASSICAL MUSICIANS
UGH ! WHAT ABOUT ALL THE WOMEN CLASSICAL MUSICIANS ?!
FAMOUS CLASSICAL MUSICIANS
Famous 20th century Playwrights
UGH! WHAT ABOUT ALL THE WOMEN PLAYWRI-
FAMOUS 20TH CENTURY PLAYWRIGHTS

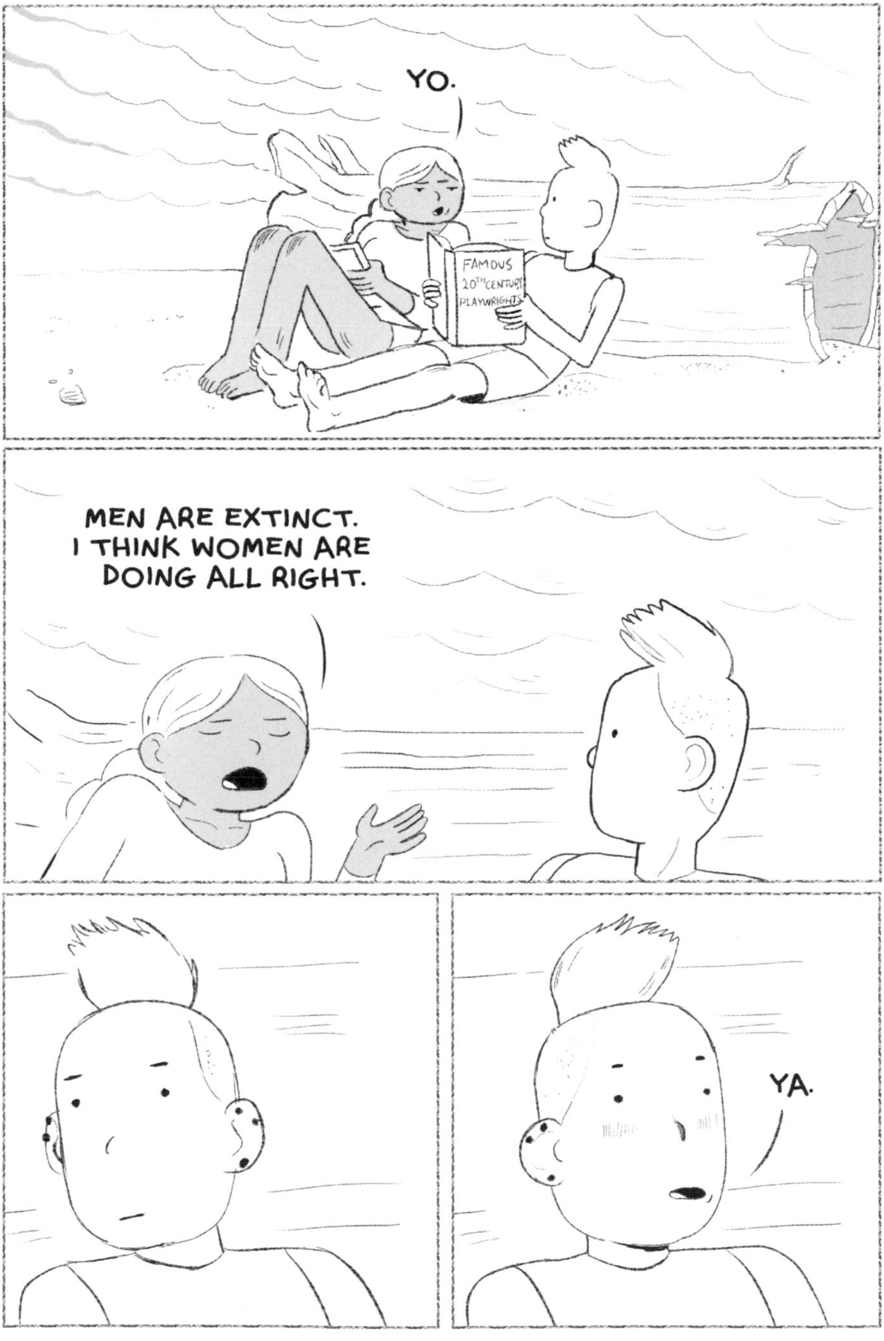
YO.
FAMOUS 20TH CENTURY PLAYWRIGHTS
MEN ARE EXTINCT. I THINK WOMEN ARE DOING ALL RIGHT.
YA.

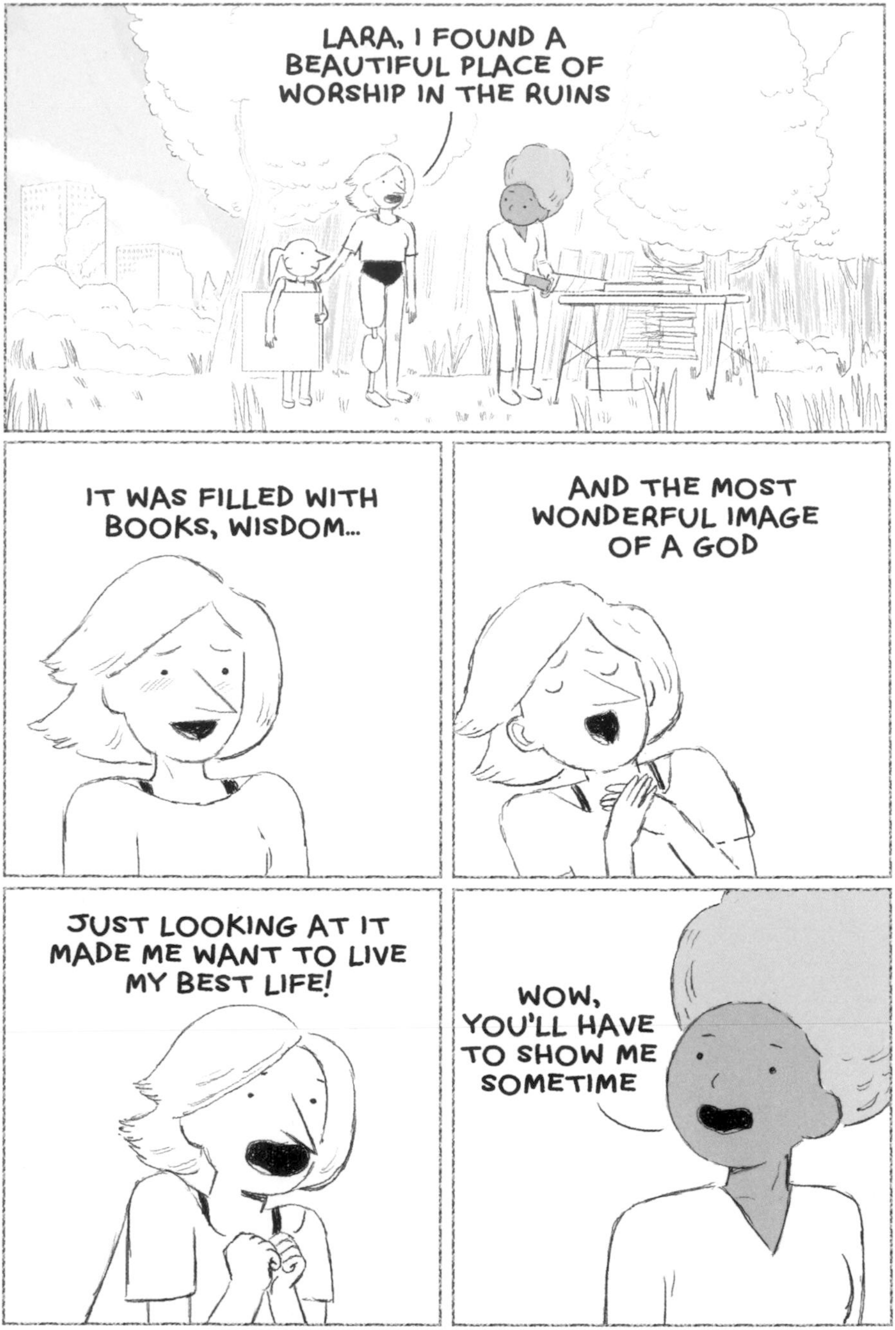
LARA, I FOUND A BEAUTIFUL PLACE OF WORSHIP IN THE RUINS
IT WAS FILLED WITH BOOKS, WISDOM...
AND THE MOST WONDERFUL IMAGE OF A GOD
JUST LOOKING AT IT MADE ME WANT TO LIVE MY BEST LIFE!
WOW, YOU'LL HAVE TO SHOW ME SOMETIME

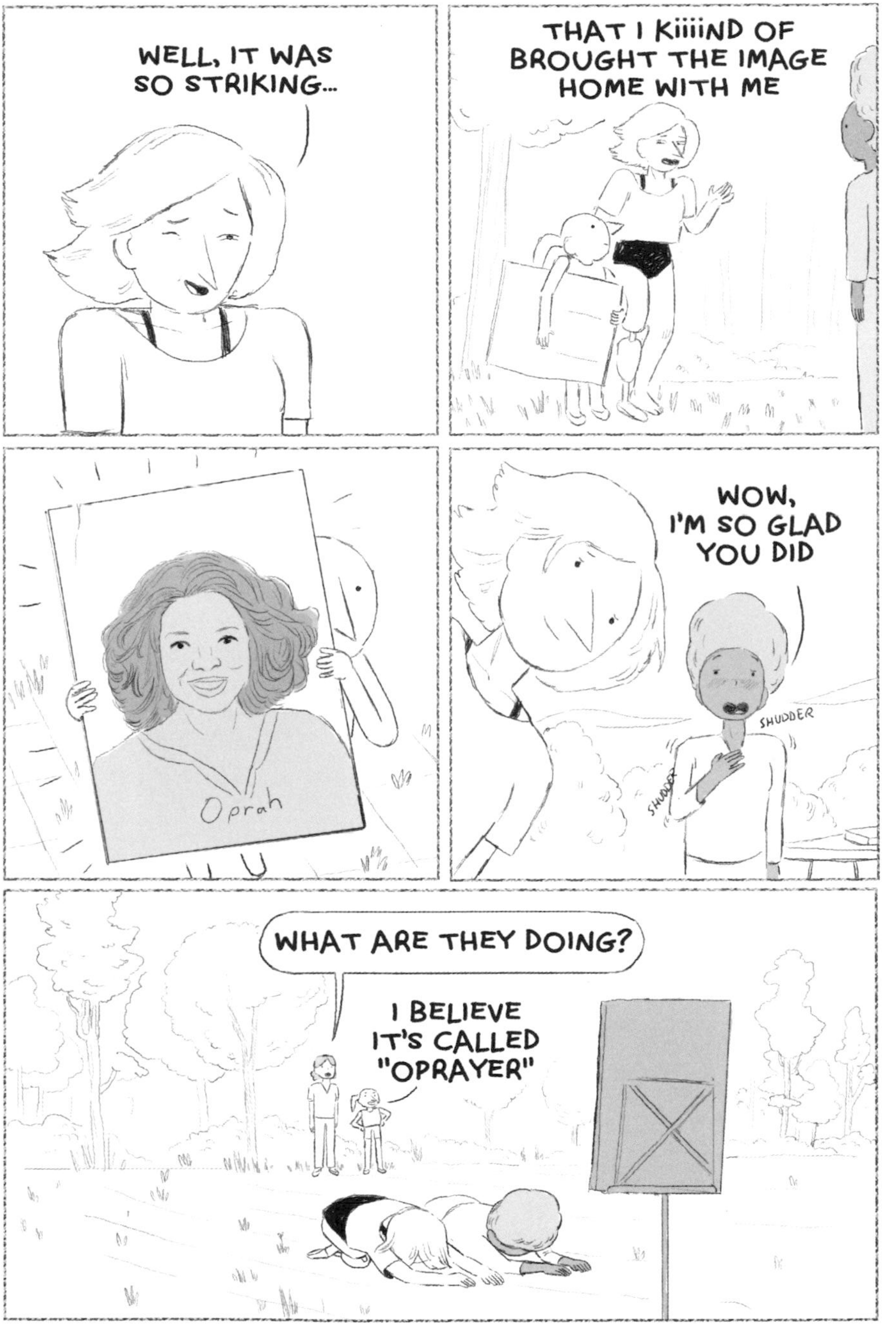
WELL, IT WAS SO STRIKING...
THAT I KIiiiND OF BROUGHT THE IMAGE HOME WITH ME
Oprah
WOW, I'M SO GLAD YOU DID
SHUDDER
SHUDDER
WHAT ARE THEY DOING?
I BELIEVE IT'S CALLED "OPRAYER"

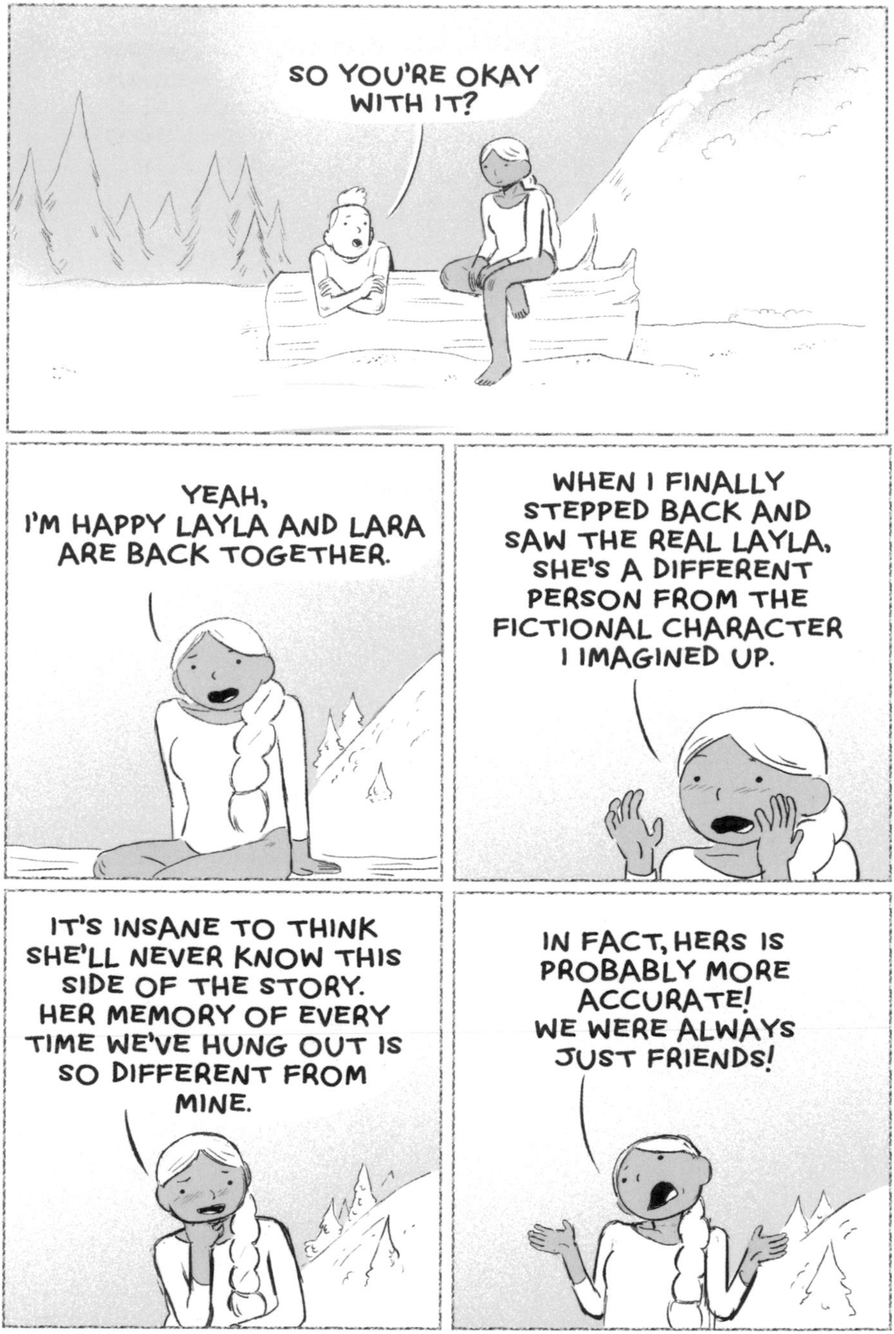
SO YOU'RE OKAY WITH IT?
YEAH, I'M HAPPY LAYLA AND LARA ARE BACK TOGETHER.
WHEN I FINALLY STEPPED BACK AND SAW THE REAL LAYLA, SHE'S A DIFFERENT PERSON FROM THE FICTIONAL CHARACTER I IMAGINED UP.
IT'S INSANE TO THINK SHE'LL NEVER KNOW THIS SIDE OF THE STORY. HER MEMORY OF EVERY TIME WE'VE HUNG OUT IS SO DIFFERENT FROM MINE.
IN FACT, HERS IS PROBABLY MORE ACCURATE! WE WERE ALWAYS JUST FRIENDS!

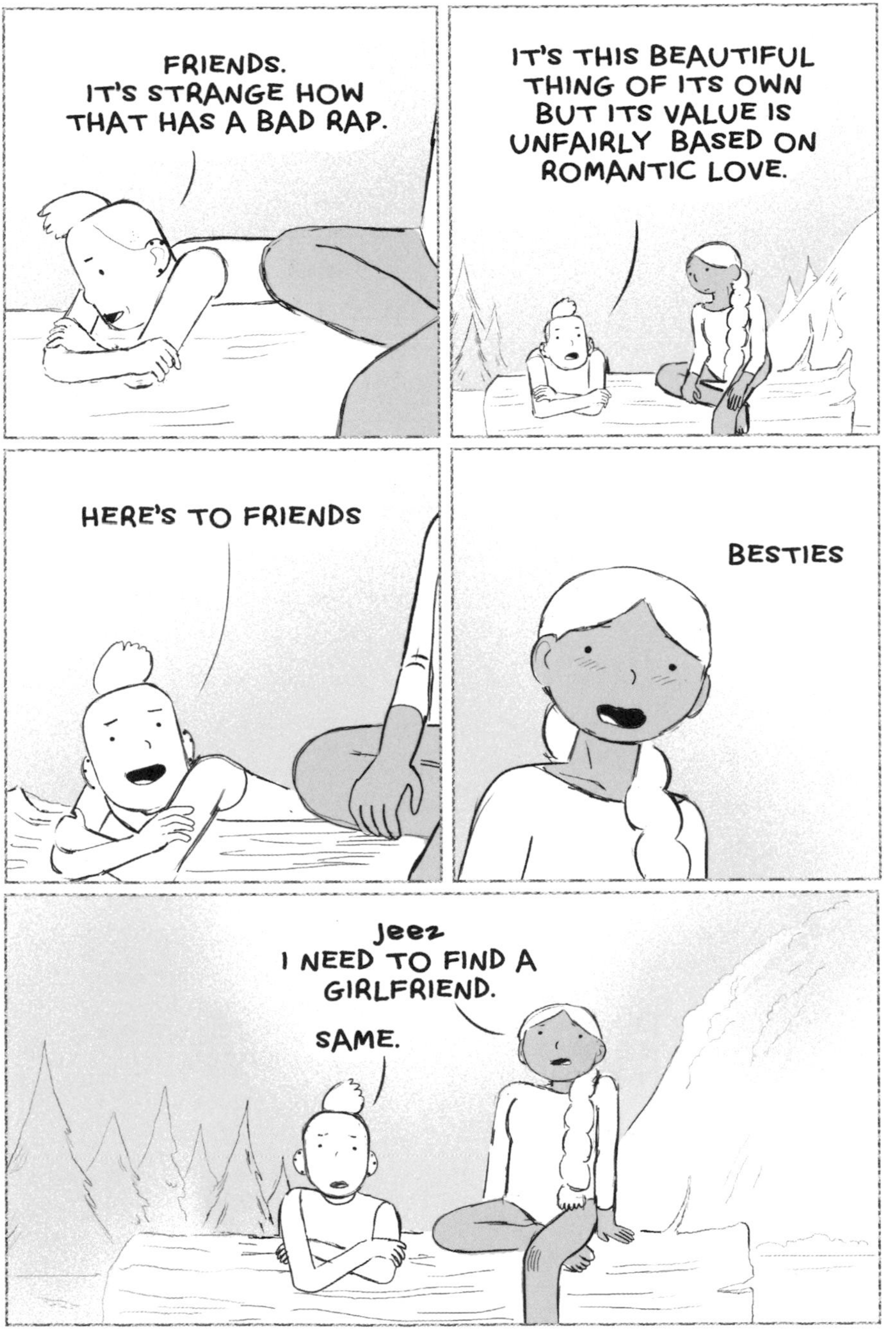
FRIENDS.
IT'S STRANGE HOW THAT HAS A BAD RAP.
IT'S THIS BEAUTIFUL THING OF ITS OWN BUT ITS VALUE IS UNFAIRLY BASED ON ROMANTIC LOVE.
HERE'S TO FRIENDS
BESTIES
Jeez
I NEED TO FIND A GIRLFRIEND.
SAME.

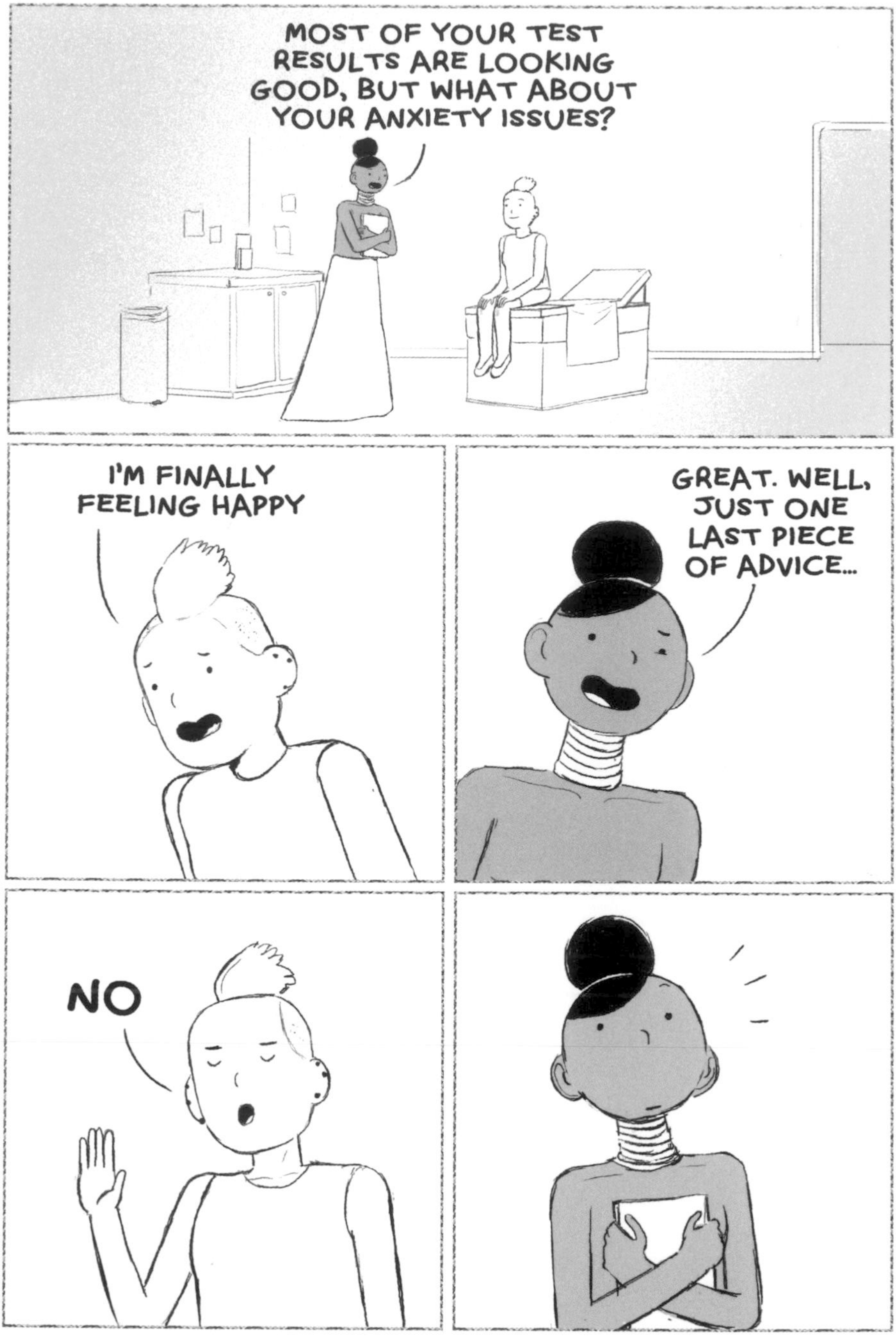
MOST OF YOUR TEST RESULTS ARE LOOKING GOOD, BUT WHAT ABOUT YOUR ANXIETY ISSUES?
I'M FINALLY FEELING HAPPY
GREAT. WELL, JUST ONE LAST PIECE OF ADVICE...
NO

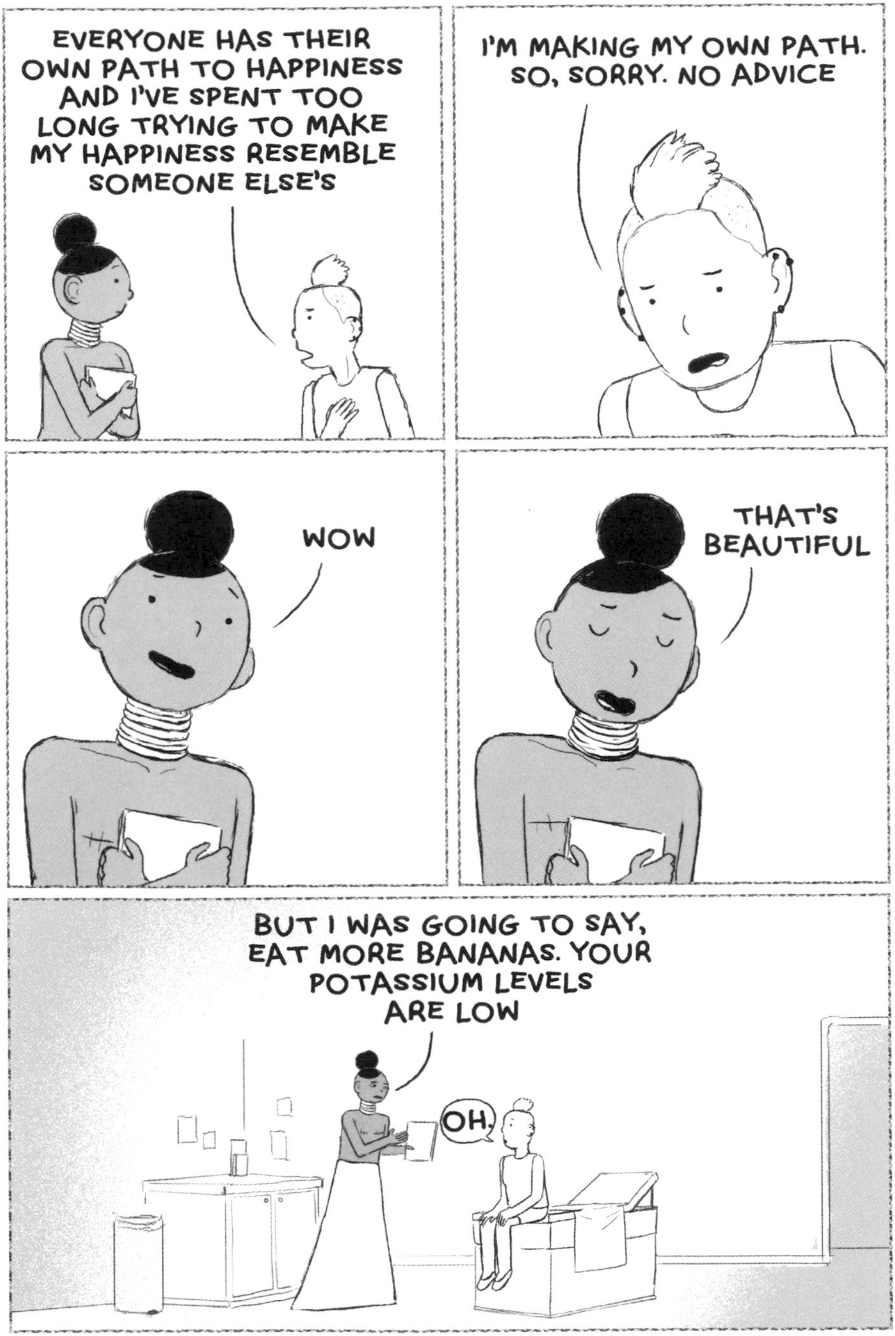
EVERYONE HAS THEIR OWN PATH TO HAPPINESS AND I'VE SPENT TOO LONG TRYING TO MAKE MY HAPPINESS RESEMBLE SOMEONE ELSE'S
I'M MAKING MY OWN PATH. SO, SORRY. NO ADVICE
WOW
THAT'S BEAUTIFUL
BUT I WAS GOING TO SAY, EAT MORE BANANAS. YOUR POTASSIUM LEVELS ARE LOW
OH.

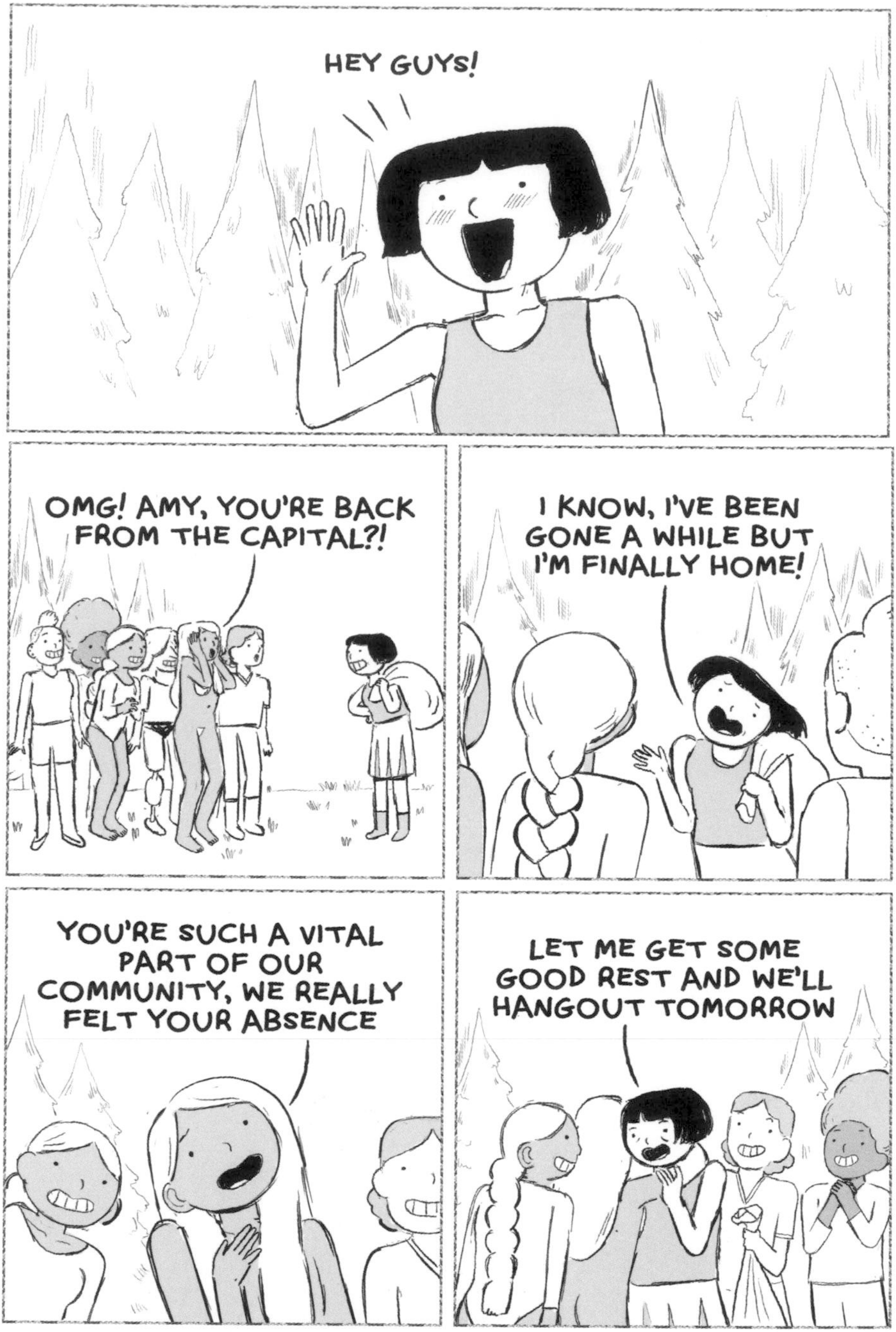
HEY GUYS!
OMG! AMY, YOU'RE BACK FROM THE CAPITAL?!
I KNOW, I'VE BEEN GONE A WHILE BUT I'M FINALLY HOME!
YOU'RE SUCH A VITAL PART OF OUR COMMUNITY, WE REALLY FELT YOUR ABSENCE
LET ME GET SOME GOOD REST AND WE'LL HANGOUT TOMORROW

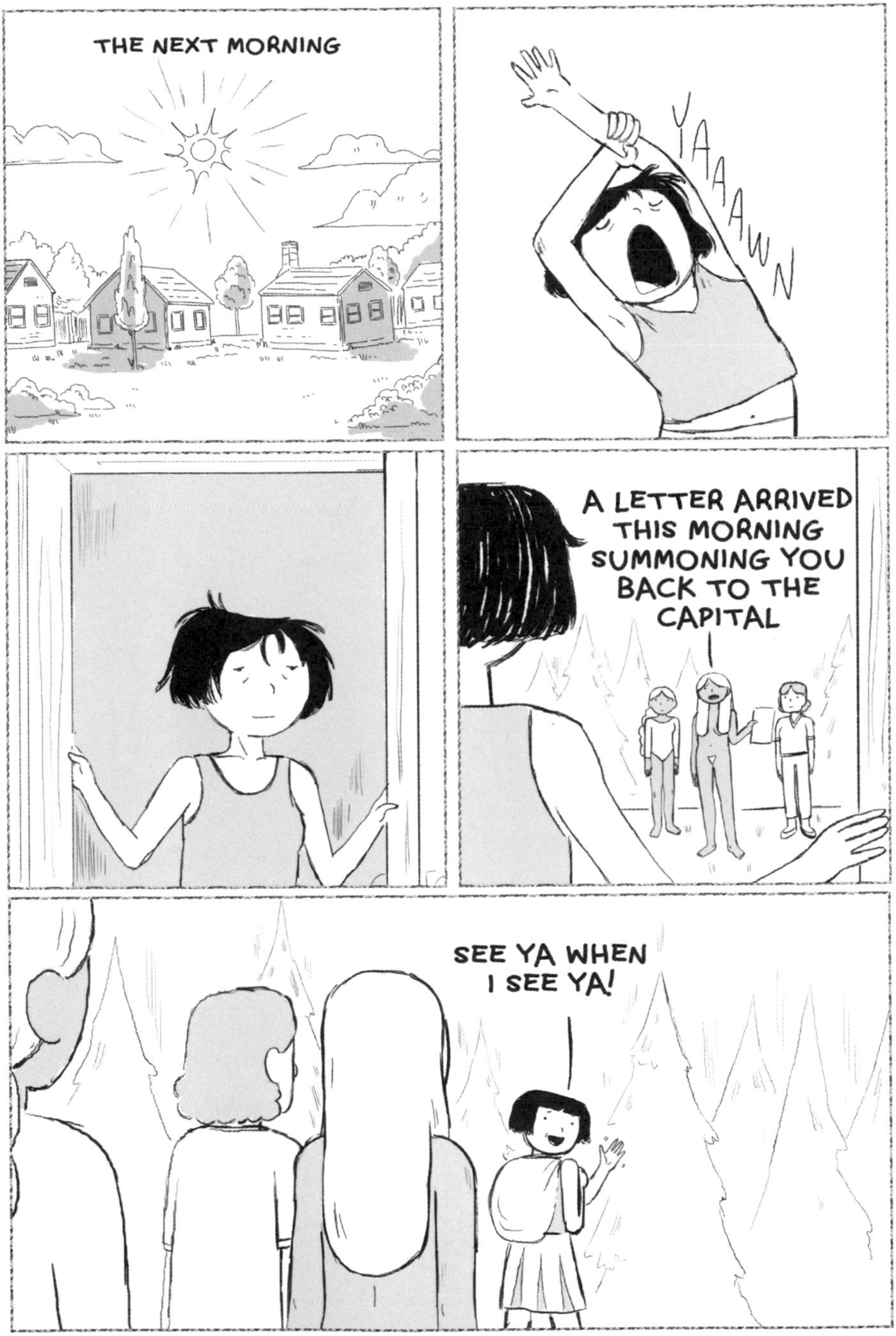
THE NEXT MORNING
YAAAAWN
A LETTER ARRIVED THIS MORNING SUMMONING YOU BACK TO THE CAPITAL
SEE YA WHEN I SEE YA!

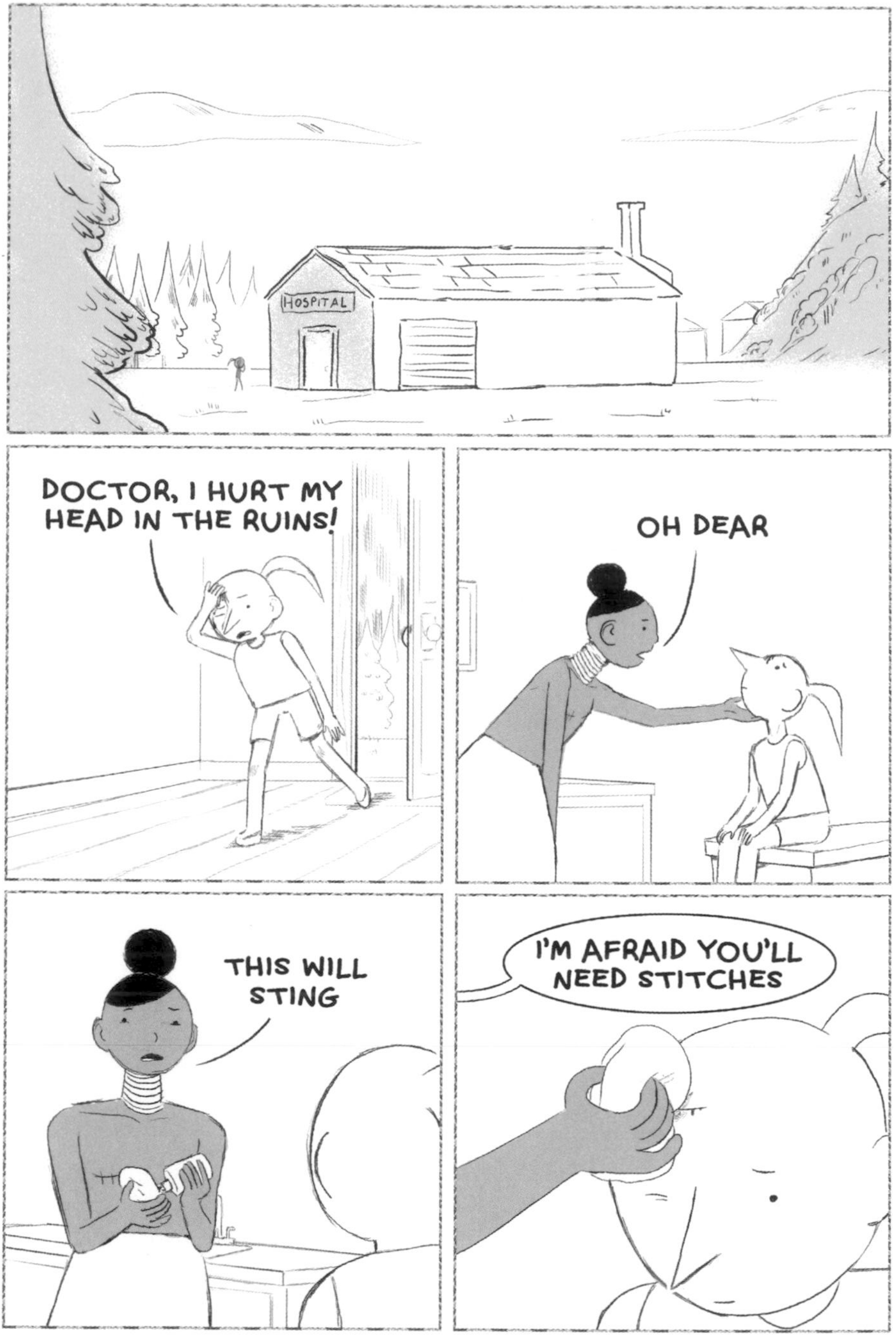
HOSPITAL
DOCTOR, I HURT MY HEAD IN THE RUINS!
OH DEAR
THIS WILL STING
I'M AFRAID YOU'LL NEED STITCHES

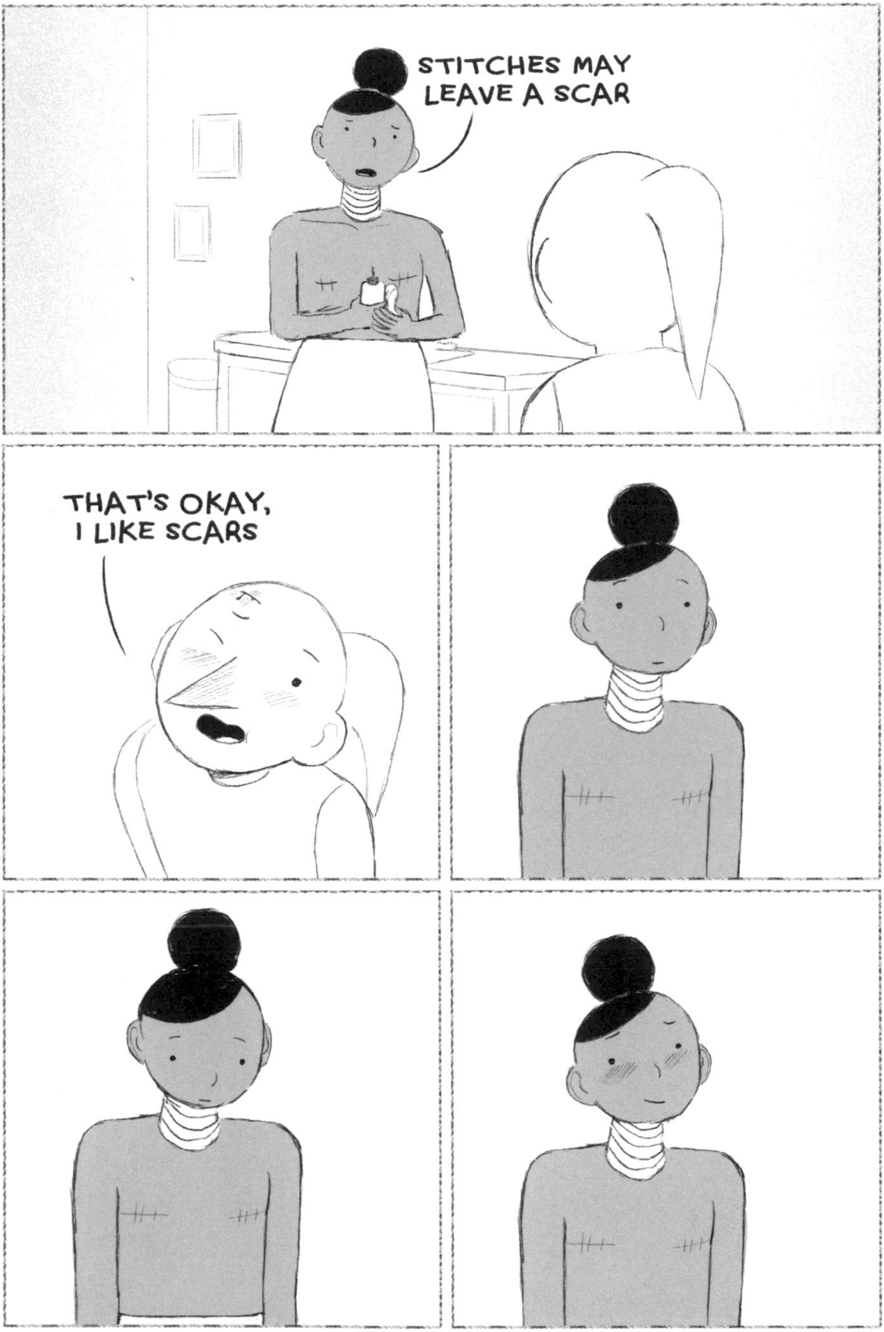
STITCHES MAY LEAVE A SCAR
THAT'S OKAY, I LIKE SCARS

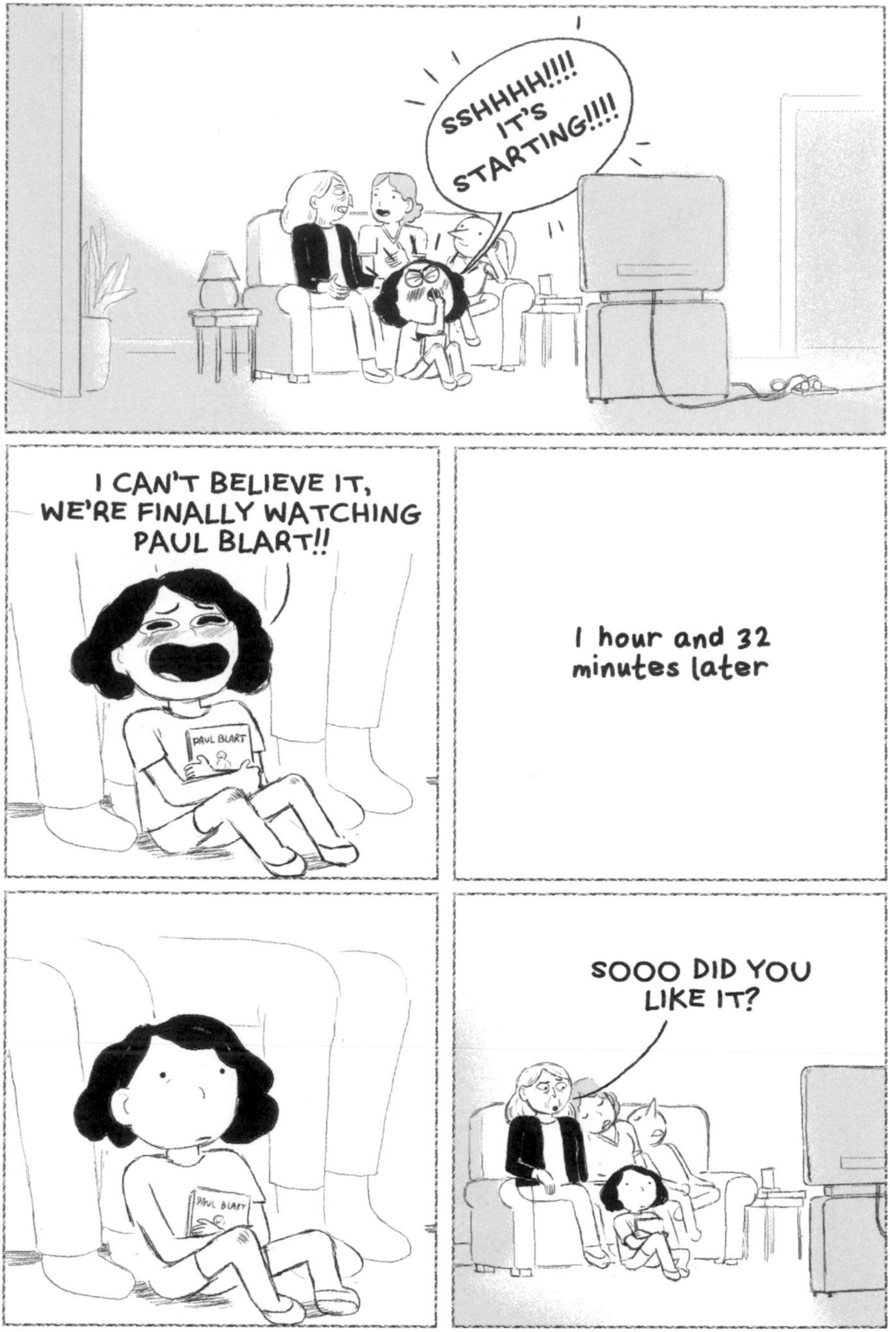
SSHHHH!!!! IT'S STARTING!!!!
I CAN'T BELIEVE IT, WE'RE FINALLY WATCHING PAUL BLART!!
PAUL BLART
1 hour and 32 minutes later
PAUL BLART
SOOO DID YOU LIKE IT?

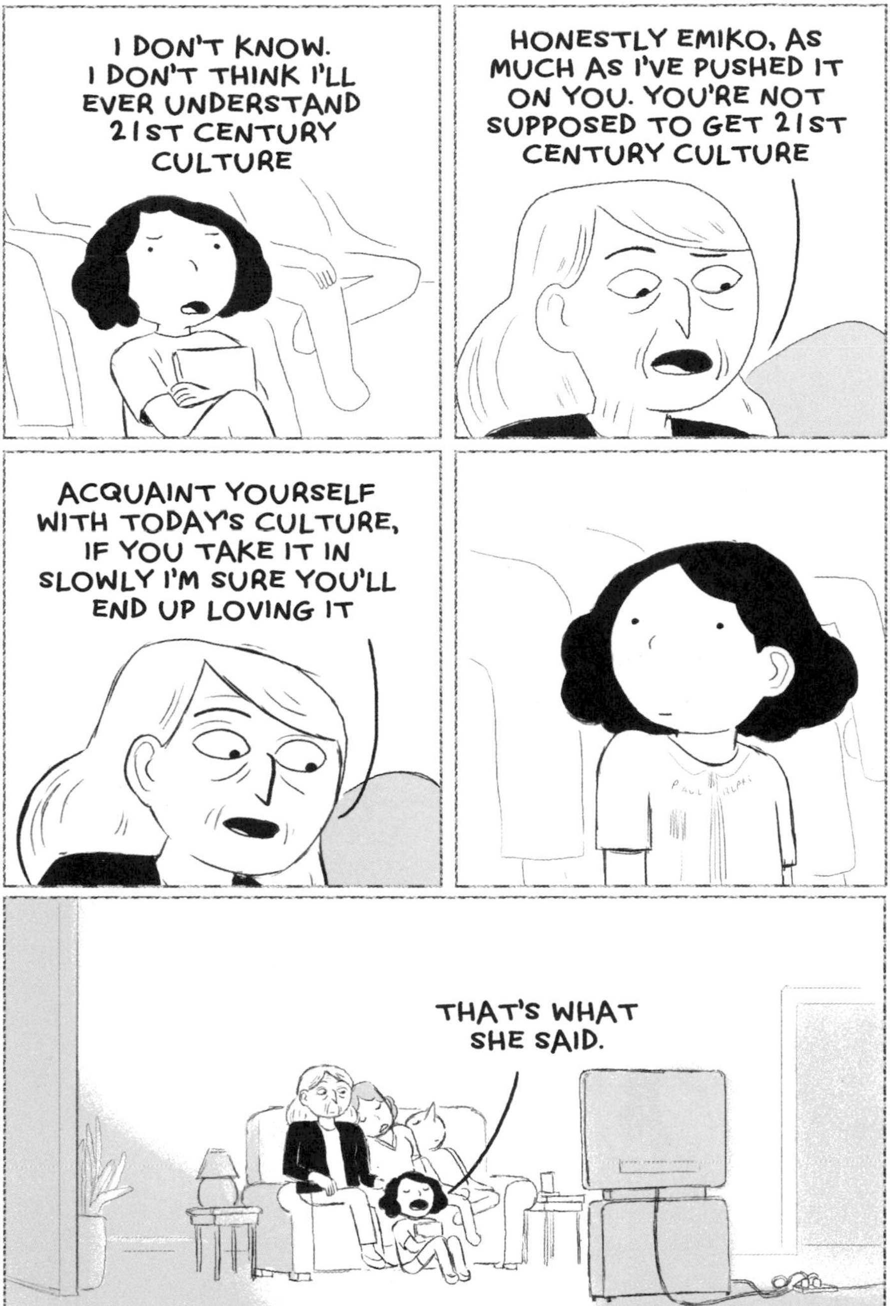
I DON'T KNOW. I DON'T THINK I'LL EVER UNDERSTAND 21ST CENTURY CULTURE
HONESTLY EMIKO, AS MUCH AS I'VE PUSHED IT ON YOU. YOU'RE NOT SUPPOSED TO GET 21ST CENTURY CULTURE
ACQUAINT YOURSELF WITH TODAY'S CULTURE, IF YOU TAKE IT IN SLOWLY I'M SURE YOU'LL END UP LOVING IT
THAT'S WHAT SHE SAID.

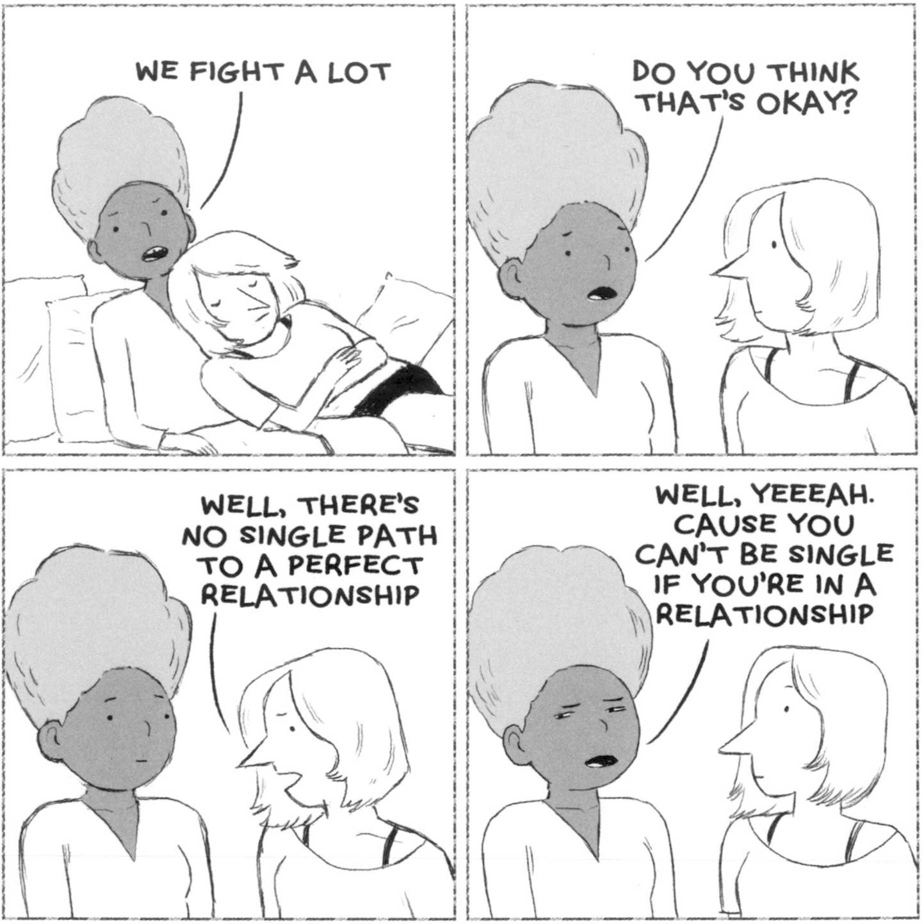
WE FIGHT A LOT
DO YOU THINK THAT'S OKAY?
WELL, THERE'S NO SINGLE PATH TO A PERFECT RELATIONSHIP
WELL, YEEEAH. CAUSE YOU CAN'T BE SINGLE IF YOU'RE IN A RELATIONSHIP

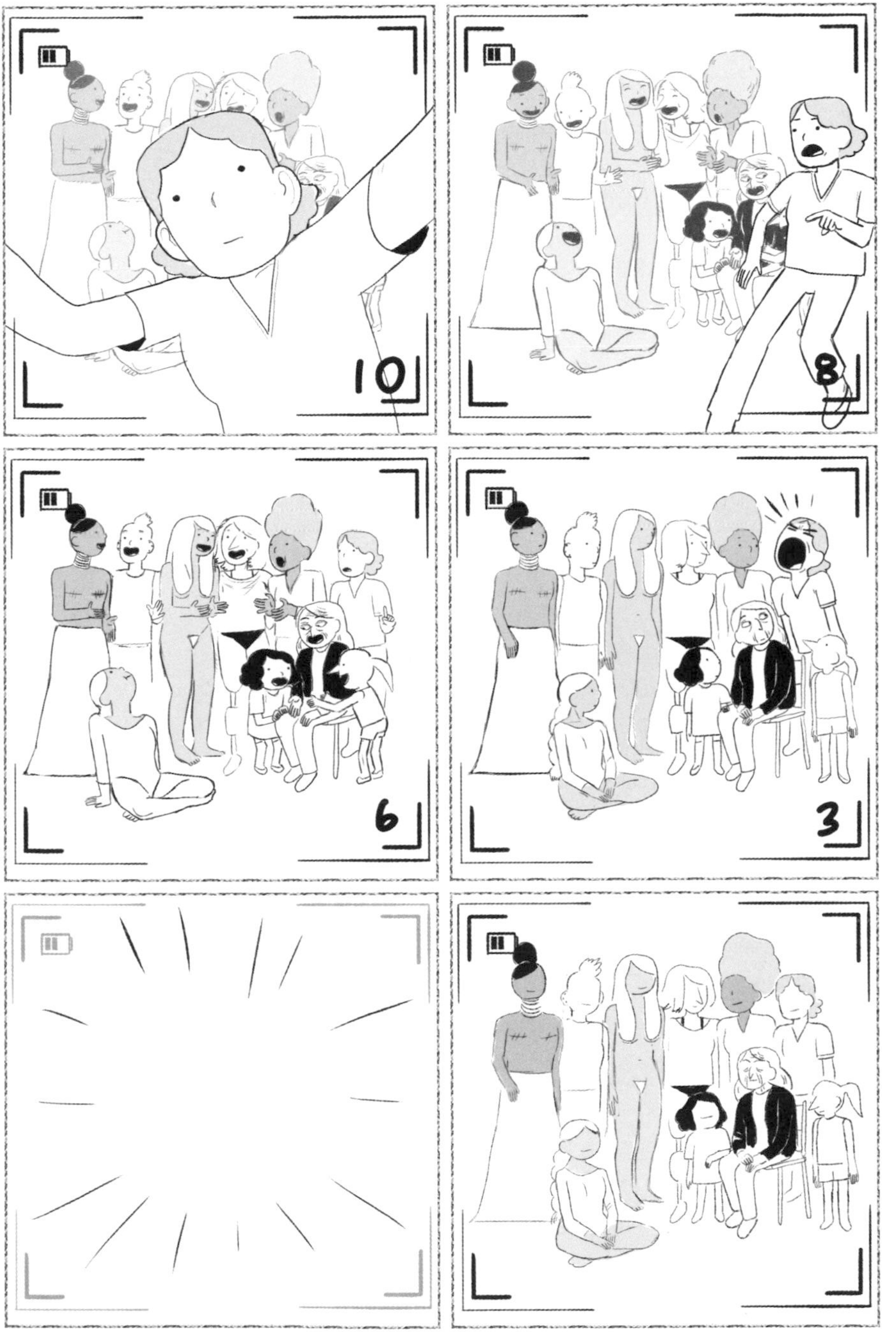
10
8
6
3

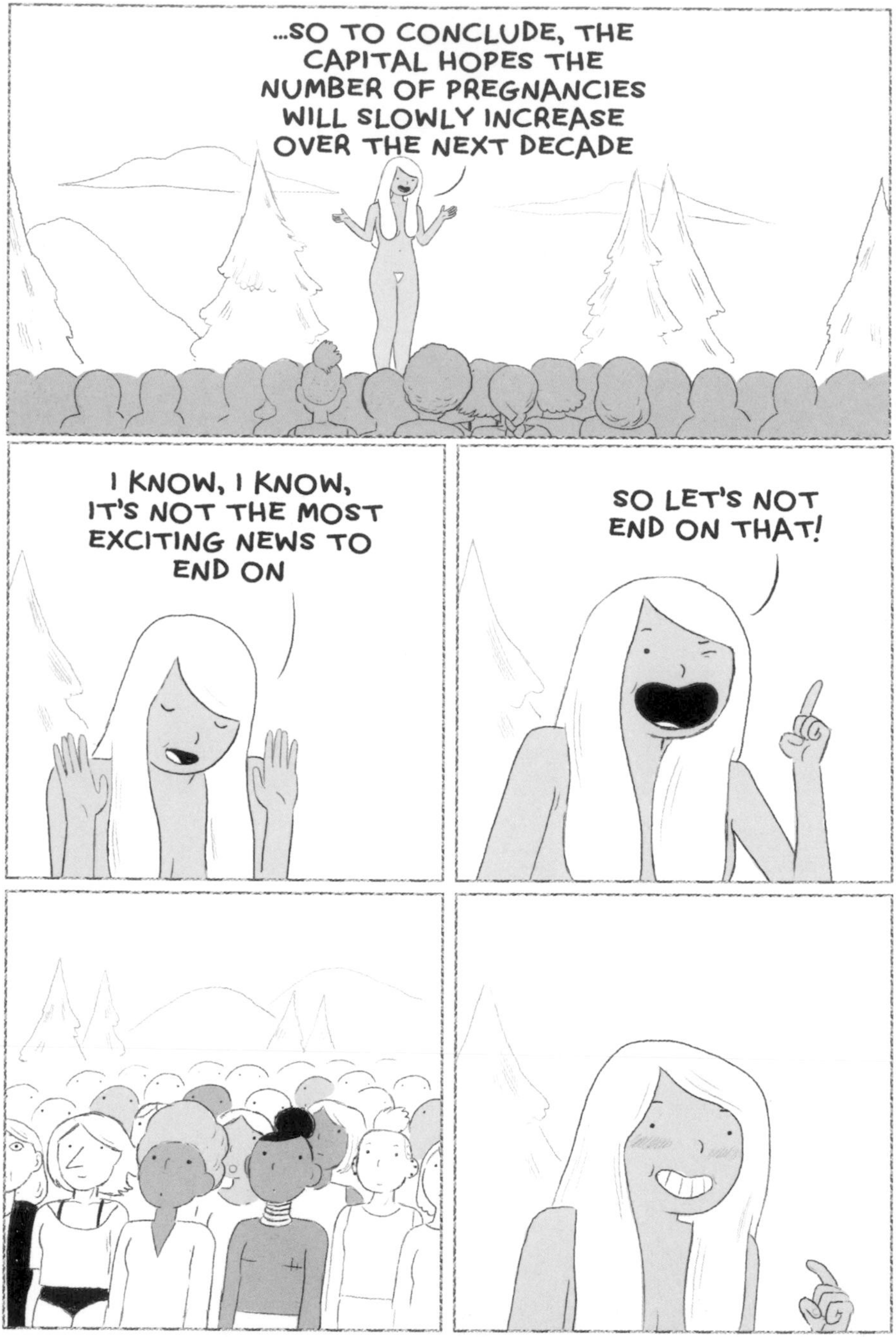
...SO TO CONCLUDE, THE CAPITAL HOPES THE NUMBER OF PREGNANCIES WILL SLOWLY INCREASE OVER THE NEXT DECADE
I KNOW, I KNOW, IT'S NOT THE MOST EXCITING NEWS TO END ON
SO LET'S NOT END ON THAT!

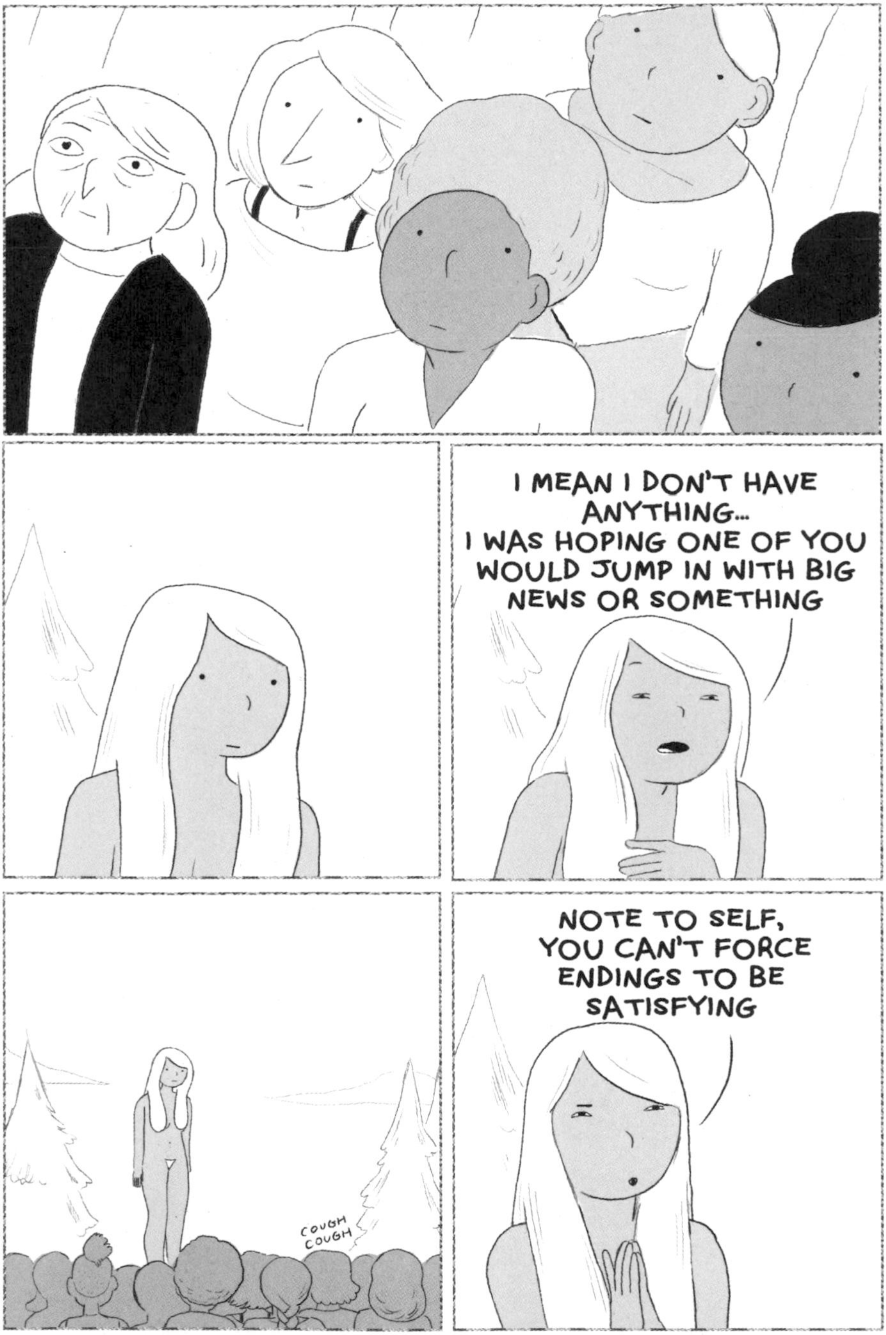
I MEAN I DON'T HAVE ANYTHING... I WAS HOPING ONE OF YOU WOULD JUMP IN WITH BIG NEWS OR SOMETHING
COUGH COUGH
NOTE TO SELF, YOU CAN'T FORCE ENDINGS TO BE SATISFYING

Dr. sharma would never know it,
but humankind was okay
afterall.

The women spent their days...

appreciating loved ones

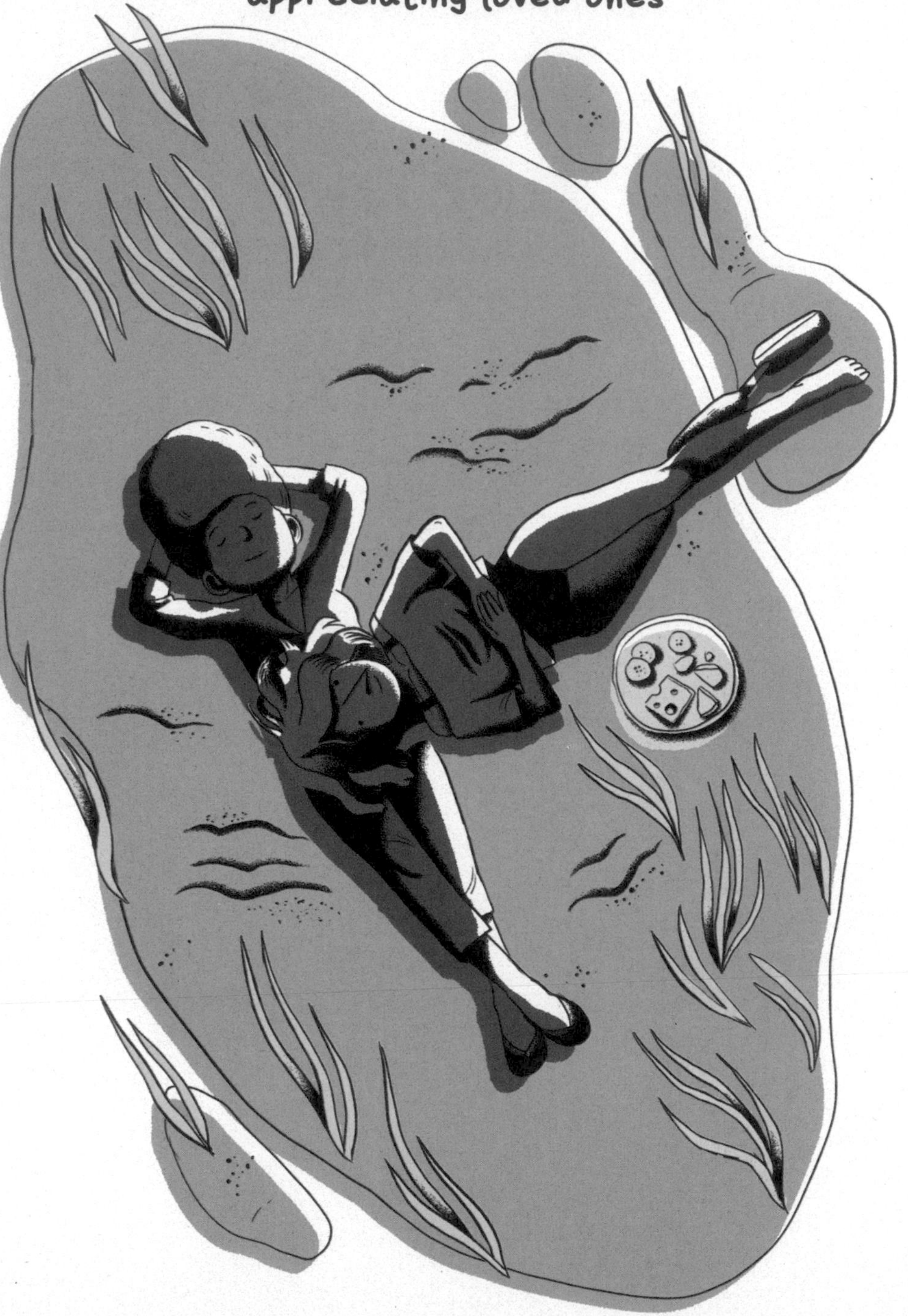

strengthening the community

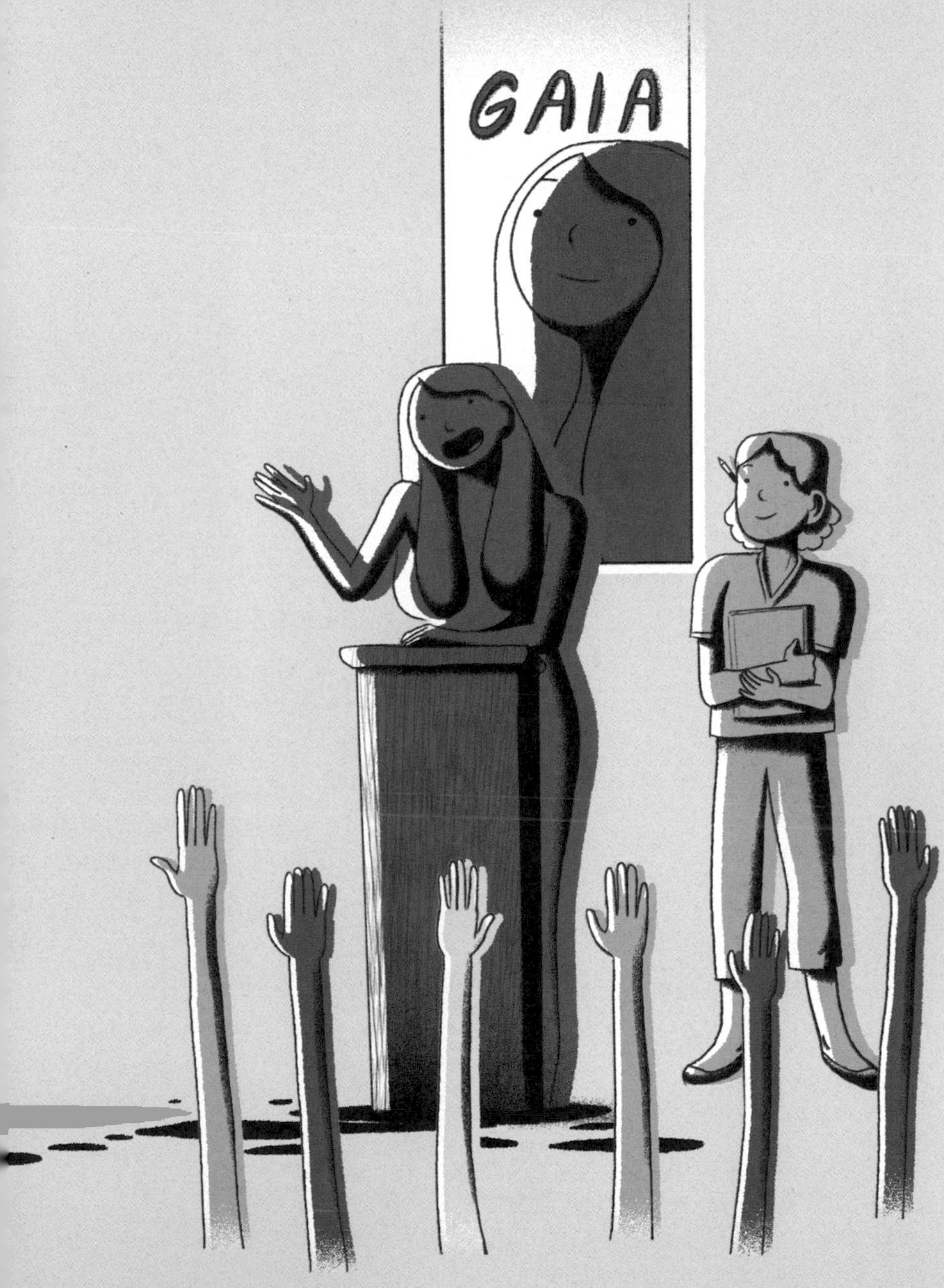
GAIA

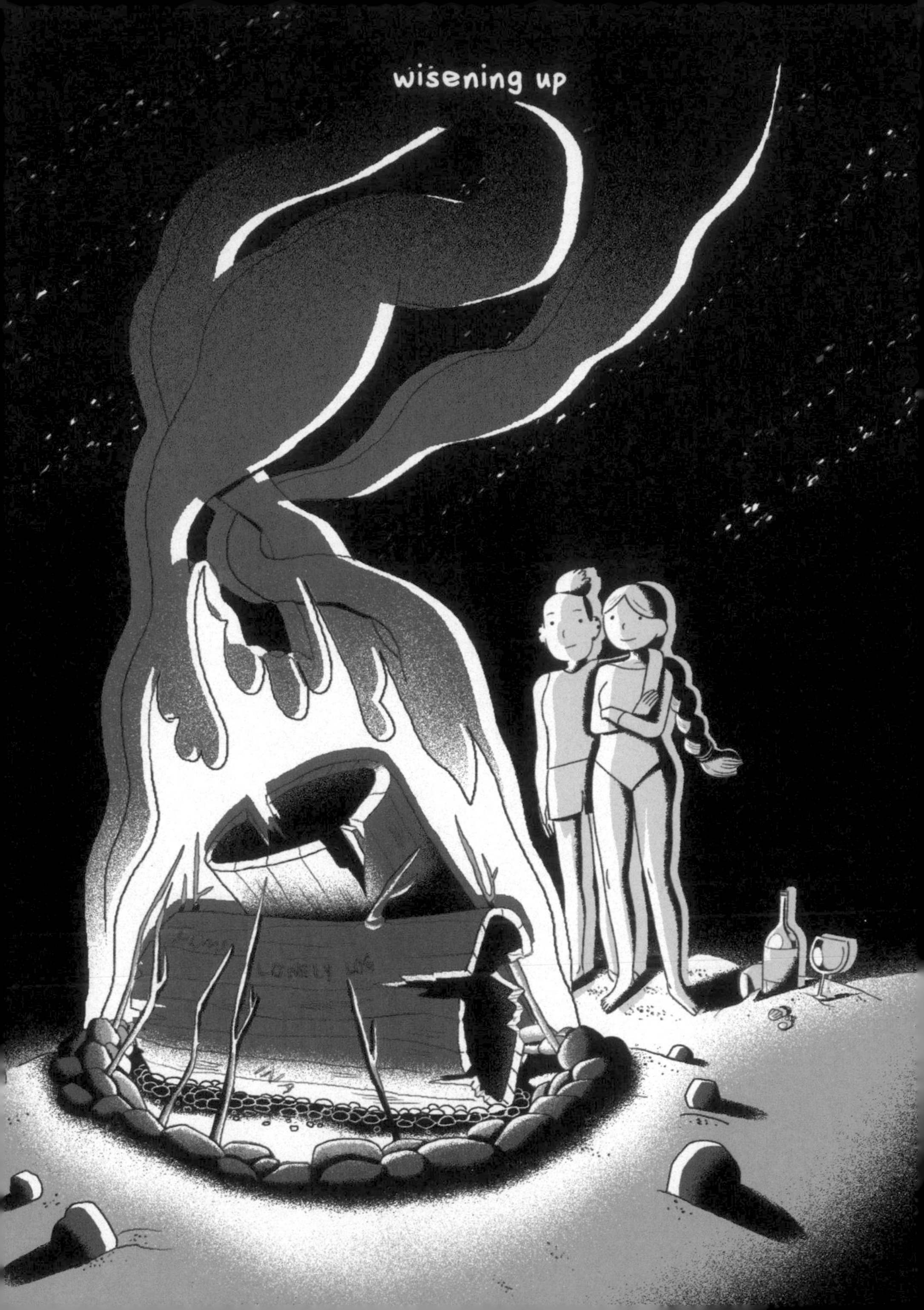
wisening up

growing older

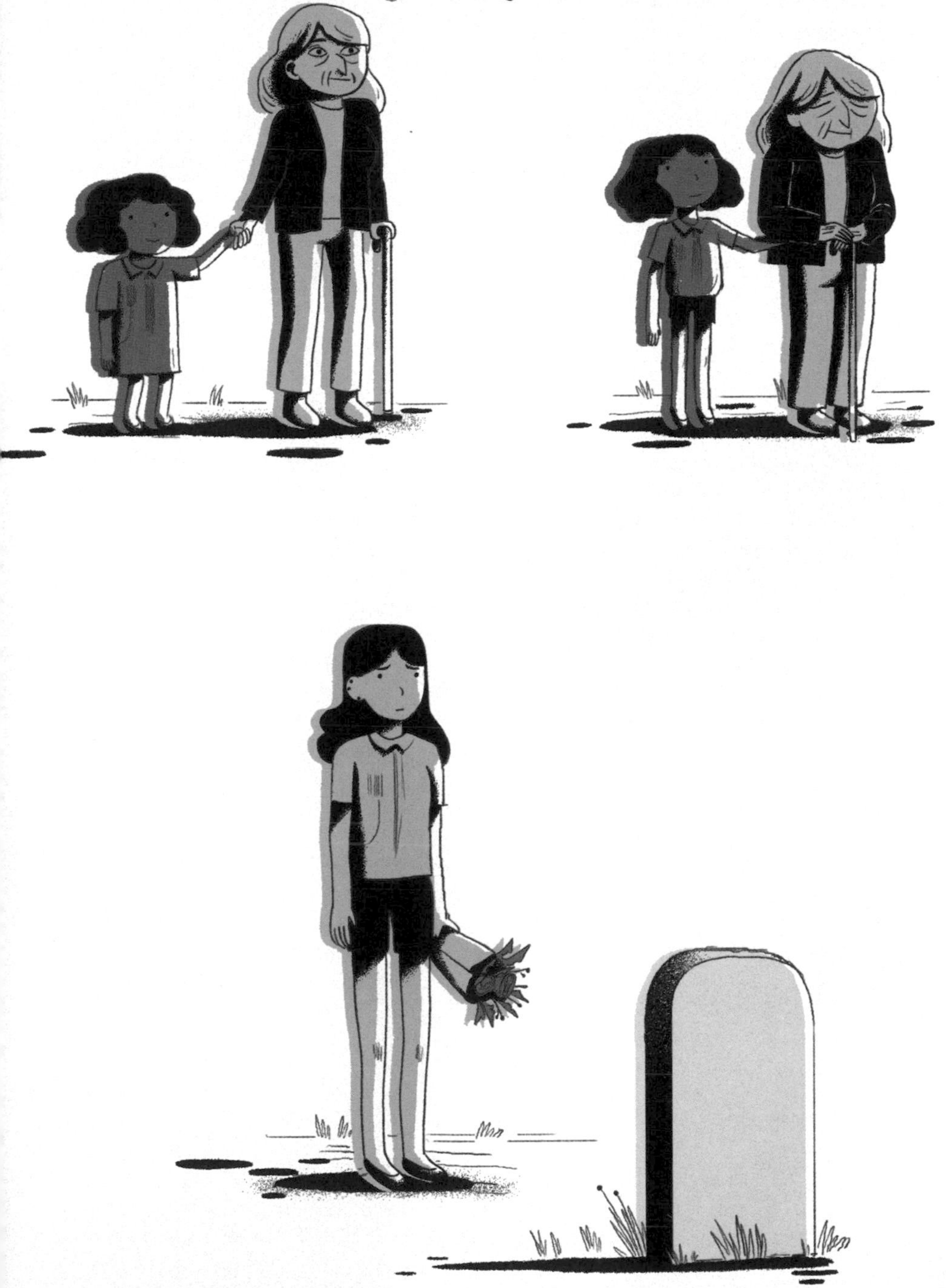

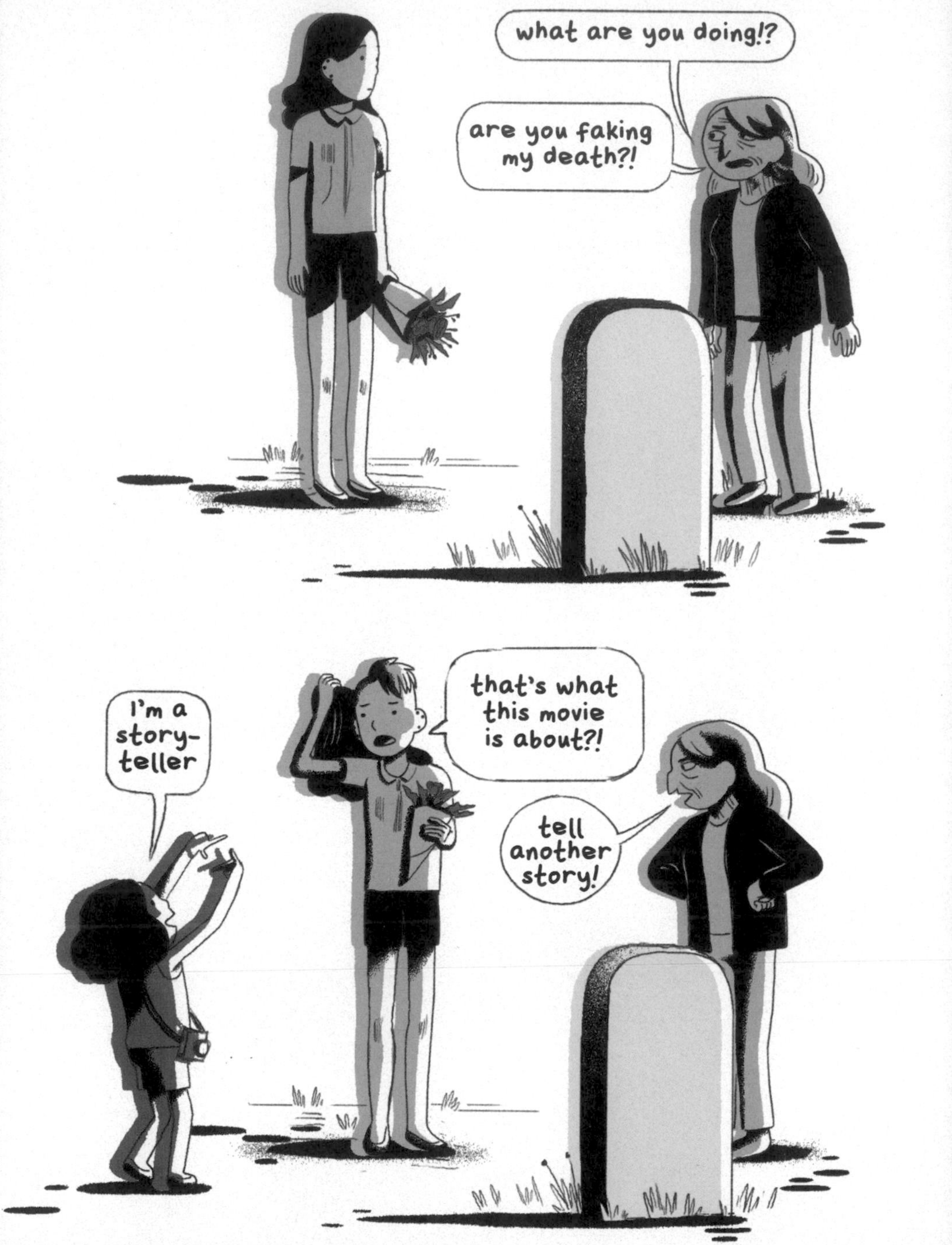
what are you doing!?
are you faking my death?!
I'm a story-teller
that's what this movie is about?!
tell another story!

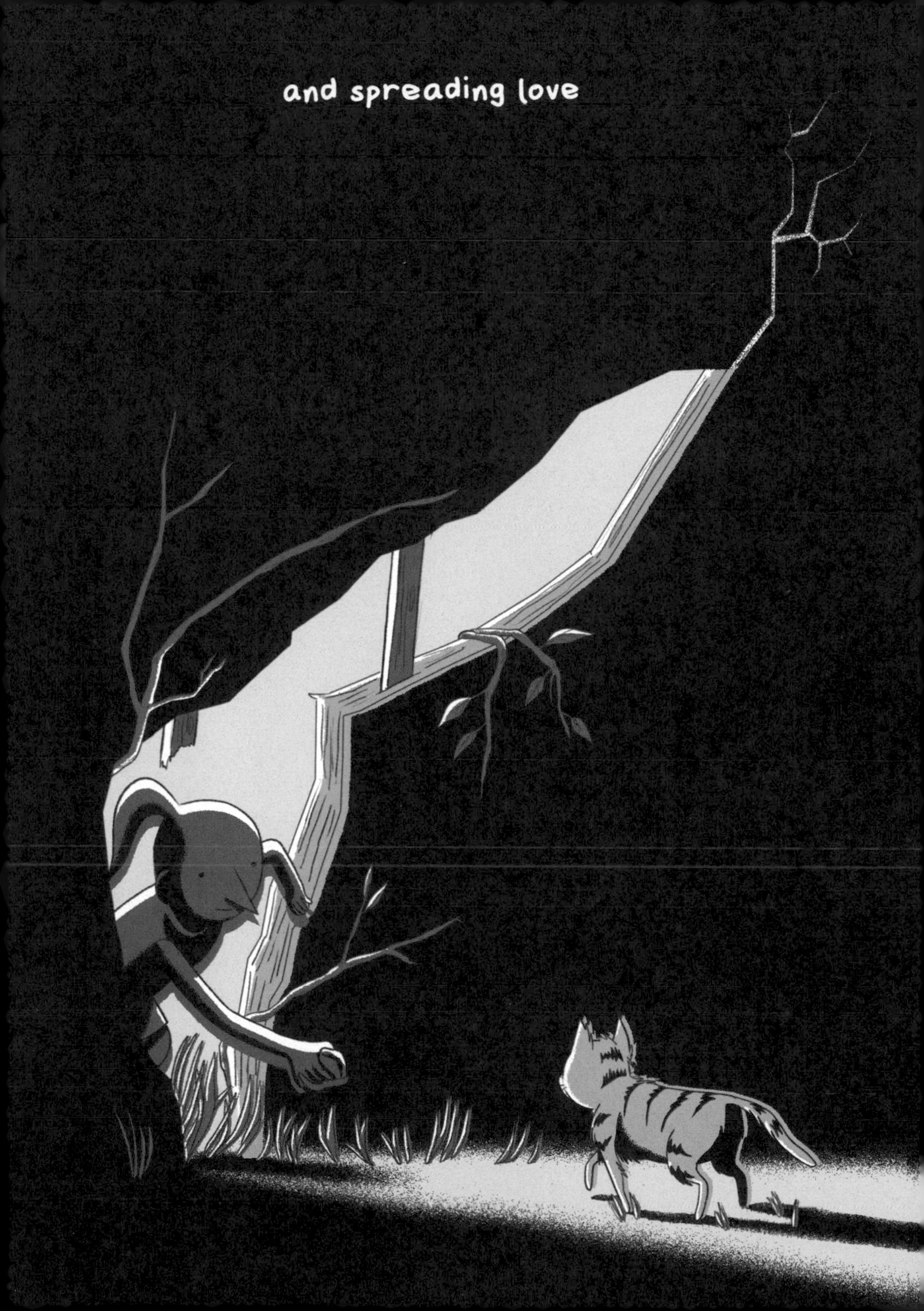
and spreading love

And what came after that?
Babies were born, segways were found,
and arachnid overlords defeated.
(that was a weird year)